John Lydgate, Josef Schick

Lydgate's Temple of glas

John Lydgate, Josef Schick
Lydgate's Temple of glas
ISBN/EAN: 9783337815288
Printed in Europe, USA, Canada, Australia, Japan
Cover: Foto ©ninafisch / pixelio.de

More available books at **www.hansebooks.com**

Lydgate's
Temple of Glas.

EDITED

WITH INTRODUCTION AND NOTES

BY

J. SCHICK, Ph.D.

LONDON:
PUBLISHED FOR THE EARLY ENGLISH TEXT SOCIETY
BY KEGAN PAUL, TRENCH, TRÜBNER & CO.,
57 AND 59, LUDGATE HILL, E.C.
1891.

DEDICATED

TO

PROFESSOR JULIUS ZUPITZA.

TABLE OF CONTENTS.

PREFACE ... ... pp. vii—ix

INTRODUCTION.

PART I.

CHAPTER I.	PRELIMINARY REMARKS... ...	pp. xi—xvi
„ II.	DESCRIPTION OF THE MSS. AND PRINTS	pp. xvi—xxx
„ III.	GENEALOGY OF THE TEXTS ...	pp. xxx—xlix
„ IV.	CRITICISM OF THE TEXTS ...	pp. xlix—liv

PART II.

CHAPTER V.	LYDGATE'S METRE	pp. liv—lxiii
„ VI.	LYDGATE'S LANGUAGE	pp. lxiii—lxxv
„ VII.	THE AUTHORSHIP OF THE T. OF GLAS	pp. lxxv—lxxxv
„ VIII.	CHRONOLOGY	pp. lxxxv—cxv
„ IX.	THE SOURCES OF THE T. OF GLAS	pp. cxv—cxxxiii
„ X.	STYLE OF THE T. OF GLAS ...	pp. cxxxiv—cxli
„ XI.	CONCLUDING REMARKS	pp. cxlii—clvii
„ XII.	THE APPENDICES	pp. clvii—clx

TEXT OF THE *T. OF GLAS*	pp. 1—57
APPENDIX I. THE COMPLEYNT	pp. 59—67
„ II. DUODECIM ABUSIONES ...	p. 68
NOTES	pp. 69—126
GLOSSARY	pp. 127—132
LIST OF PROPER NAMES	p. 133
ADDENDA	pp. 135, 136

PREFACE.

The arrangement of the Introduction will, I hope, allow me to dispense with much explanation by way of preface. It will be seen at once that, with the exception of some preliminary remarks in Chapter I, the first half of the Introduction, as far as Chapter IV, is devoted to a description of the various MSS. and Prints of the *Temple of Glas*, and the critical discussion of the text. The second half contains investigations with respect to the metre, the language, the authorship, the date, the sources, and the style of the poem. Chapter XI gives a synopsis of Lydgate's principal works, and attempts to draw up a programme for further investigations of the monk's productions; Chapter XII says a few words about the Appendices.

But with respect to one or two points an explanation may be due. It may perhaps be thought that some questions might have been more fully entered into, others less. I might have given a complete grammar of the *Temple of Glas*, and, in particular, a full and detailed synopsis of the whole sound-system; I might also have added, in the Chapter on metrics, a full analysis of all the minor metrical phenomena of the poem. But I have refrained from doing so, principally because I thought the instances in which Lydgate differs from his great master Chaucer in points of language and metre, had better be collected systematically in special treatises, which would deal exhaustively with the monk's peculiarities on these points. Thus I have contented myself with setting forth the principal characteristics of Lydgate's metrical system, and entering carefully into certain vexed questions of language, the elucidation of which was necessary for the construction of the text.

On the other hand I must perhaps apologize for having gone somewhat beyond my immediate task in the working out of the later chapters of the Introduction. So many inadequate or erroneous ideas having gained ground with respect to Lydgate, I was tempted to overstep the boundaries of my immediate province, and to endeavour to elucidate certain questions which have an indirect bearing only on our subject. This I have been led to do particularly in the eighth Chapter, on Chronology, and in the survey of Lydgate's works, in Chapter XI. If, in the assignment of some of the dates, there has of necessity been a certain amount of guesswork, yet I hope on the other hand to have given some reliable data which will enable us to gain a better insight into the sequence, and to gauge more accurately the extent of the monk's productions. Special researches into certain of Lydgate's works may prove more than one of my conjectural dates to be wrong; but no one will be more glad than myself if some of the dates can be made out *for certain*, even were they to prove my conjectures in those cases to be erroneous.

The notes are meant to answer a double purpose: first, to illustrate the usage of words and idioms in the poem by comparison with contemporary writings, whilst showing to what extent Lydgate was influenced by ideas current at the time. Secondly, I have collected in them a great many stock-phrases of Lydgate's with numerous quotations, which, with the monk's peculiarities of metre and language, will, I hope, do good service in the discussion of the genuineness of doubtful works. Of critical notes there are but few, as this side of the question has been dealt with at great length in Chapters II—IV.

If Chapter III, and in particular some of the lists of mistakes in the MSS., seem of undue length, it must not be forgotten that we have to do with Chaucer-MSS.; and thus it seemed to me desirable to derive as much information from our present text as it could afford us, towards establishing the respective value of some of these MSS. with more certainty. From this point of view, a list, for instance, like that in Chapter III, § 2, of the numerous mistakes in MS. G, will tell its own story without further comment.

In conclusion, the agreeable task devolves upon me of expressing my sincere thanks for much kind help which I have received in my work. In the first place, I have gratefully to acknowledge my deep indebtedness to the Duke of Devonshire and the Marquis of Bath, for their courtesy in placing two valuable copies of the poem at my disposal. In the same way I would also tender my hearty thanks to the Principal Librarian and the Trustees of the Advocates' Library at Edinburgh, for the most kindly accorded loan of the print in their Library. Canon Jackson I must thank for having so courteously

Preface.

enlightened me on several points connected with the Longleat MS. Further, I am indebted to Mr. Peskett, of Magdalene College, Cambridge, for giving me access to the Pepys-MS. For the use of the other old copies of the text I must thank the authorities of the British Museum, the Bodleian and the Cambridge University Library; for personal help of various kinds I have especially to thank Dr. Bullen, Mr. Graves, Mr. Bickley, and Dr. Macray. To Mr. Jenkinson and Mr. Gordon Duff I am much indebted for information with respect to Caxton's and Wynken de Worde's prints, as also to Prof. Tietjen, of the Berlin University, for some astronomical calculations. To Professor Skeat I would acknowledge my indebtedness, not only for the help derived from his many valuable works connected with this period of English literature, but also for much personal kindness in the matter. It goes without saying that I am greatly indebted to Dr. Furnivall's publications; but I beg also to express my acknowledgment of many a valuable hint which I have received from him in the course of my work. Last, but not least, I have to thank the scholar of whose teaching and influence this edition is a direct outcome—Professor Julius Zupitza.

J. SCHICK.

Berlin, January 1891.

INTRODUCTION.

PART I.

CHAPTER I.

PRELIMINARY REMARKS.

OF all Chaucer's successors in the field of English Poetry, none has been more prolific than John Lydgate, Benedictine monk of the Abbey of Bury St. Edmunds. Nor has any one enjoyed a greater popularity in his day, a popularity which, even more than a century after his death, had not yet died out. 'Daun John' was certainly considered the greatest poet amongst his contemporaries.[1] None less than the Victor of Agincourt and Duke Humphrey of Gloucester have been his patrons, and in compliance with their commands, his two or three most lengthy works were produced. The Earl of Salisbury, King Henry VI., and the Earl of Warwick—father-in-law of the proud "setter-up and plucker-down of kings"—were also among those who commanded the monk's pen. The great number of MSS. still extant, some exquisitely illuminated, and many a ponderous folio and curious quarto from the press of the earliest English printers, still testify, in the most tangible manner, to his past popularity. Many of his less comprehensive poems were not unfrequently assigned a position of honour beside those of his admired and revered master Chaucer,[2] and the voice of his contemporaries proclaimed that Chaucer, Gower, and Lydgate formed the poetical triumvirate of the period.

Naturally, in the present day, our opinion of the poetical value of the monk's long-winded larger productions must differ widely from the verdict of the 15th and 16th centuries; but even in more recent times, poets and critics of such prominent position as Thomas

---

[1] This opinion is particularly strongly expressed by Bale: "omnium sui temporis in Anglia poetarum, absit inuidia dicto, facile primus floruit." *Catalogus* 1557, p. 586.

[2] And, vice versâ, two of Chaucer's poems—namely, *Truth* and *Fortune*—are contained amongst *The prouerbes of Lydgate*, printed by Wynken de Worde; see J. P. Collier, Bibliographical Account (1865), I. 501; Lowndes, ed. Bohn III. 1419 (inaccurate); *Bibliotheca Heberiana* IV. 178; Brunet III. 1249.

Gray, Warton, and ten Brink have passed an indulgent, nay even a friendly judgment upon his poetical efforts.

But whatever the æsthetic value of Lydgate's productions may be, they afford a rich hunting-ground to the Chaucer-scholar, the archæologist, and the student of language or early typography. His works constitute, by their number and extensiveness, important documents of the English language in the first half of the 15th century, with notable differences from the language of Chaucer, both as regards phonology and vocabulary. Furthermore, they form a vast storehouse of mediæval lore, many of the most popular sources of the knowledge of the Middle Ages being, in a greater or lesser degree, incorporated in them; and as they are mainly translations or compilations made evidently for the best-educated of his nation, they furnish ample illustration of what was then considered as the highest literary culture. It is from this standpoint that an active energy has of late years been displayed in the editing, or in the careful investigation of some of Lydgate's works. In some cases, indeed, it was but a felicitous chance which brought our monk to the fore; thus his *Guy of Warwick* was published by Prof. Zupitza, in the first instance, certainly, as presenting one of the various treatments of this story; and when Dr. Horstmann had some of his legends printed, it was merely because they were legends. C. E. Tame also, and Hill-Cust, in their Lydgate-publications, did not make the study of Lydgate their primary object, the first having evidently religious aims in view, the two latter endeavouring to trace the sources used by Bunyan for the *Pilgrim's Progress*. But with these exceptions, the publications in question all have a direct bearing on Lydgate alone. There is, to mention the editions first, the well-known one of his *Minor Poems*, by Halliwell, for the Percy Society —of somewhat older date;—then, an edition of his *Æsop* has been brought out by Sauerstein in *Anglia IX.* (the Prolegomena forming a Leipzig Inaugural Dissertation), and several minor pieces, some of doubtful authenticity, are to be found in various books or periodicals. But, before all, it is Dr. Erdmann's forthcoming edition of the *Story of Thebes*, for the E. E. T. S., to which all students of this period of English literature must look forward with interest. For this poem is one of the triad of works usually associated with Lydgate's name, and a critical edition of it from the MSS. would settle many points of language and of versification, which latter has been especially censured in this poem.

Chapter I.—Preliminary Remarks.

The greatest merit, however, in furthering the study of Lydgate seems to me to be due to Prof. Zupitza. Not only has he himself edited *Guy of Warwick*, published an important notice concerning Lydgate's life, and is now bringing out the interesting story *de duobus mercatoribus;* but it was he also who first drew Dr. Koeppel's attention to the then "*brach liegende Lydgate-Forschung.*" Through Zupitza's suggestions, strengthened by those of Prof. Breymann, Koeppel was instigated to write his two admirable treatises on the sources of the *Story of Thebes* and the *Falls of Princes*, two most valuable and thorough contributions to the Lydgate-literature, reflecting—the latter especially—great credit on the extensive and varied learning of their author. It is, similarly, through Zupitza's influence that Dr. Borsdorf is preparing for us an edition of the *Court of Sapience*, not one of Lydgate's least interesting works; and if the present edition of his *Temple of Glas* should be found to contribute, in a slight degree, to a better knowledge of Lydgate, the merit, again, would be due to Prof. Zupitza.

This poem suggested itself as being particularly suitable for a republication. For the *Temple of Glas* was, without doubt, one of Lydgate's most popular works,[1] a fact amply certified by the numerous MSS. in which it always occurs with and amongst poems of Chaucer, and the successive prints by Caxton, Wynken de Worde, Pynson, and Berthelet, the second of whom printed it not less than three times in the course of a few years. In modern times, especial attention has been drawn to it by Warton, and high praise bestowed upon it. "The pathos of this poem, which is indeed exquisite, chiefly consists in invention of incidents, and the contrivance of the story, which cannot conveniently be developed in this place: and it will be impossible to give any idea of it's essential excellence by exhibiting detached parts." So the passage stands in Warton, in the first edition, page 418, a passage which would render superfluous any excessive praise to which I might be led away through the proverbial zeal of an editor for his own ware. In consequence of this high commendation by Warton, the poem has not unfrequently been noticed, and its intrinsic value dwelt upon—in most cases, I am afraid, upon the authority of Warton alone, as the poem was not easily accessible. Such a decided popularity for more than a century might be quite

[1] In spite of an assertion to the contrary by Blades (Caxton II. 59), who seems to have had difficulty in finding copies of it other than the prints by Caxton and Wynken de Worde, and MS. Add. 16165 in the British Museum.

sufficient to induce the analyst of literary currents to look with some interest upon a re-edition of the poem, even if the verdict passed upon its poetical value, when measured by an absolute standard, should be: "Very small, almost nil." For if nothing else, we must at least find a good illustration of the taste prevalent for more than a century, in a poem which found eager readers in the days of Henry Bolingbroke, and the time when Agincourt was fought, as well as through all the turmoil of the Wars of the Roses; which was among the first deemed worthy by Caxton of being printed, and which was still highly applauded immediately before the dawn of a new era. If, then, the interest in the "*bryght temple of glasse,*" as Stephen Hawes, in 1506, called the poem, faded away before productions of another stamp, it will only the better help to set off the glory of the morning that was destined to follow the dullest period of English literature.

But, even apart from these considerations, there were several questions which would invitingly challenge solution from the editor. First, the point of authorship presented itself. For, although Warton's criticism did great honour to the poem, this honour was not reflected upon the true author, as Warton had curiously assigned it to Stephen Hawes. This error had, by many, been copied for a whole century, and had, combined with typographical disputes, given rise to some entangled discussions. These difficulties will, I hope, once and for all be done away with by the investigations in chapter VII.

The point of authorship once settled, other questions confront us which demand a solution. Up to a quite recent date the opinion has prevailed amongst scholars that Lydgate's metre is exceedingly irregular, jerky, and halting. The question of his treatment of the final *e*—a question closely interwoven with the preceding—has also been a vexed one, and was difficult to decide from the materials available. Fortunately, not less than thirteen texts of the *Temple of Glas* have been found, thus forming sufficient material for a critical construction of the text, which cannot now, I think, differ much from the original. This preliminary criticism of the text furnishes us, on the one hand, with a firm basis on which to stand while grappling with the above questions; on the other hand, I hope, it will further our knowledge of a number of Chaucer-MSS., both with respect to their individual value, and the relations they bear one to another.

To conclude, a glance at its contents and the progress of its story, will show that our poem is, in its general framework, its *motifs*, and

Chapter I.—Preliminary Remarks.

the whole range of its ideas, in no small degree dependent upon the Chaucerian Muse, and thus bears a not uninteresting testimony to the wide influence of Chaucer upon the literature of his country. If I add that, in several respects, the *Temple of Glas* bears a decided family-likeness to the *Kingis Quair*, and that King James was probably not uninfluenced by Lydgate's poem, the latter may perhaps appear to deserve greater interest than one might be inclined to bestow on a poem of Lydgate's, when bearing in mind certain criticisms on him.

I have above alluded to the circumstance that our poem was, in deference to Warton's judgment, more praised than actually read. The best-known account of it is probably the one in Hazlitt's re-edition of *Warton*, which is especially calculated to give an inadequate conception of it. For on p. 61 of the third volume of this work, the introduction to the poem is alone taken notice of, and, in fact, the whole passage would rather impress the reader with the idea that the introduction constitutes the entire poem. It will not, therefore, be amiss, if, in a few words, we sketch its contents, the less as this will at once indicate the position of the poem with respect to other works of the same school. The story may thus be briefly told :

Heavy-hearted and oppressed by sorrow, the author lies down to sleep one December night and finds himself, according to the favourite *dream-motif* of that day, before a temple of glass, which stands in a wilderness, on a craggy rock, frozen like ice (1—20). Dazzled by the brilliancy of the sun-light reflected from the temple, he is unable to distinguish his surroundings, until clouds gather before the sun, and he discovers, after long search, a "wicket" affording access into the building (20—39). He enters, and there finds depicted on the interior walls of the circular temple, the figures of many celebrated lovers, taken from classic antiquity and mediæval saga, portrayed in various attitudes with "billes" in their hands, petitioning Venus to mitigate their woes (39—54). Next follows an enumeration of the various lovers (55—142), with a list of their complaints (143—246). Last of all the dreamer perceives a lady, the very pattern of all beauty and excellence, an angelic creature, who, in loveliness and virtues, surpasses all others of her sex, and "illumines" the whole temple by "her high presence" (247—314). She, too, like the rest, presents Venus with a "bille" of the sorrows of her love (315—320), which she then begins to pour forth (321—369). After hearing her complaint that she is separated from her lover, Venus consoles her, promising her union with her knight (370—453), for which the lady returns thanks (454—502). The goddess then throws down to her branches of hawthorn, admonishing her to keep them sacred, as a symbol of constant love (503—530).

Whilst dreaming thus, the poet finds himself, on a sudden, amongst a great multitude, who are bringing sacrifices to Venus in her temple (531—544). He leaves the crowd, and perceives a knight wandering alone, who, oppressed with the sorrows of love, holds a long soliloquy, and finally resolves to lay his trouble before the goddess (545—700). This being accomplished (701—847), Venus consoles him in like manner to the lady, and sends him forthwith to his beloved, to whom he is boldly to disburden his mind (848—931). With a heavy heart the knight goes on his way (932—969), and makes confession of his love to the lady (970—1039), who colours red "as the ruddy rose," and bashfully assents to his suit, in obedience to the will of Venus as her sovereign lady and mistress (1040—1102). The lovers now humbly present themselves before the goddess, who unites them with many admonitions (1103—1298), upon which all present praise Venus, and petition her to keep the lovers thus united by everlasting bonds (1298—1319). This prayer being granted (1320—1333), the whole temple resounds with a "Ballade" of praise to the goddess, sung by all true lovers present (1334—1361). These sounds awake the poet, who, saddened at finding the beauteous vision has faded, resolves to make a "litil tretise" in praise of women, until he finds leisure to "expound his fore-said vision" (1362—1392). The envoy, addressed to his lady, concludes the poem (1393—1403).

It may be well to note here that the two MSS. G and S, which differ from the rest in having various interpolations, have, at the end, from l. 1380 onward, a most tedious, drawled-out addition of above 600 lines, containing the *Compleynt* of a lover who is separated from his lady, added most likely by reason of the unclear purport of the last twenty-five lines of the poem. This is given as Appendix I in the present edition.

CHAPTER II.

TITLE OF THE POEM.—DESCRIPTION OF THE MSS. AND PRINTS.

BEFORE we proceed to give an account of the various MSS. and Prints, it may be well, at the very outset, to settle the title of the poem, with regard to which some doubts may remain after the perusal of the note in Warton-Hazlitt, III, 61. The matter is, in reality, very simple. All the texts of the poem give "The Temple of Glas" as the title, except MSS. F and B, where the poem in title, colophon and headlines, is called "The Temple of Bras."[1] Now chapter III, § 5, will show that F and B have many peculiarities in common which point to their being derived from one and the same original. We may therefore take it for granted that the error comes from their common source. I think we may even assign a reason for this error. It is not at all unlikely that the scribe of the MS. in question hit upon this wrong title because it seems to have been in use as another title for Chaucer's *Parlement of Foules*.[2] A comparison of line 231 of this poem furnishes the key to the occurrence of such a title for it;[3] for Lydgate's poem it is entirely unwarrantable, as in the decisive line 16 all texts, F and B not excepted, speak alike of a "temple of glas."

For the further title: *The dreeme of a Trewe lover*, etc., ir MS. S, see below, under 6, p. xxiii.

As we have said above, numerous texts of the *Temple of Glas* have come down to us. I have altogether come across seven MSS. and six Prints; one of the latter, however, is only a fragment. They are as follows:

A. THE MANUSCRIPTS.

1. T = Tanner 346.

Bodleian, Oxford. See **Skeat**, *Chaucer's Minor Poems*, p. xlii; *Legend of Good Women*, p. xli. On vellum; date 1400—1420. The poems contained in this MS. are in various handwritings, that of the *Temple of Glas* being one of the earliest; in fact, Dr. Macray tells me that it dates back, as nearly as possible, to the year 1400. Our poem begins on folio 76 a, and ends on 97 a. The title runs: *The tempil of Glas;* at the end stands: *Explicit*. Some of the capitals are ornamented, and illuminated in red and blue. The index at the

---

[1] In F, it is true, the word *Bras* has been, by a later hand, corrected to *Glas*, twice in the title (in one case Stowe's hand is discernible), and once in the colophon, also by Stowe.
[2] It occurs in the colophon of Caxton's Print in the University Library, Cambridge (A B. 8. 48. 6), and in the fragment of it in the British Museum (C. 40. 1. 1); cf. **Blades**, *Caxton*, II, 61; **Warton-Hazlitt**, III, 61, note 1; **Tanner**, *Bibliotheca Britannico-Hibernica*, p. 491; **Furnivall**, *Trial-Forewords*, p. 116; Catalogue of the Caxton Exhibition, No. 37.
[3] It is curious to notice that in this passage just F should read *glas* (as accordingly Morris has it).

TEMPLE OF GLAS.   b

beginning, in recent handwriting, has the item: *The Tempil of Glass, f[ecit] Steph. Hawes. v[ide] Pits.* This MS. is, with G, the oldest, and is altogether the best of them all. It has therefore been taken as the basis of the present edition, in which every deviation from it has been duly marked by brackets or asterisks.—For a description of the way in which T has been reproduced in this edition, see chapter IV.

Lines 96, 154, 216, 320 are omitted in T, as also in those MSS. which are most nearly related to it (F, B, P).

Some of its most conspicuous orthographical and phonetic peculiarities are the following:

The scribe often writes *w* alone for the usual *ew* in words like nwe, trwe, rwe, knwe, hwe; also in swe, 352 (but sue, 1180), eschwe 450 (but eschew 1181); always shew(e), 206, 305, 319, 916. This seems to indicate that the scribe of our MS. pronounced the vowel of the first group above also as a monophthong.—*ov* is often written instead of *ow;* so we find nov, hov, ʒov, morov, folov, sorov; lovli; sparovis 541; avove 771. A confusion of *w* and *v* appears further in woid (= vowed) 741 and 1128; nvfangilnes 1243; showe (= shove) 534. Between vowels *w* has sometimes been dropped, for instance in: waloing 12; sorois 967; foloiþ 416.—Letters not rarely stuck fast in the scribe's pen; for instance several times, the *i* or *y* in -li: goodl 1000; womanl 1020; mekel 1105.—Instead of *she* we find *sho* 72, 666; we have bein = ben 136, and sein = seen 935. In certain endings the scribe of T has a predilection for putting *i* instead of *e*; he writes for instance: Rauysshid 16, foundid 18, entrid 39, callid 219, wikkid 153; billis 50, hestis 59, oþis 59, tuʒgis 153, þingis 167; maʒis 402; rekin 91; werin 152; oþir 3, vndir 9, aftir 47, wondir 48, tendir 210; telliþ 110, beriþ 173; nedis 232; tempil 92, etc.—*i* in this MS. is often kept where other MSS. put *y* (for instance in the syllable -li); it presents, in this respect, a contrast especially to F, see **Skeat**, *M. P.*, p. xl; *Legend*, p. xli.

Although some of the above-mentioned peculiarities recall the northern dialect, yet they are perhaps not sufficient proof that the scribe was a Northcountryman.

2. F = *Fairfax* 16.

Bodleian, Oxford. See **Skeat**, *M. P.*, p. xl; *Legend*, p. xl; **Warton-Hazlitt** III, 61 Note. On vellum; date about 1440—1450 (on the first page is the date 1450). In the MS. missing lines have

Chapter II.—Description of the MSS. and Prints. xix

been filled in and other corrections supplied in various places in a small, neat handwriting. This is doubtless the hand of John Stowe,[1] the historian, as is shown by MSS. like Harl. 367, Tanner 464 (transcripts from Leland),[2] and Addit. 29729, a Lydgate-MS. copied by Stowe, according to his own words, from Shirley. *The Temple of Glas* extends in F from fol. 63 *a* to 82 *b* ; the title, however, is here given as *The temple of Bras*, but *Bras* has later been twice corrected to *Glas*, once, above, by Stowe and, below, by another hand. Colophon : *Explicit the temple of Bras ;* here *Bras* has only once, by Stowe, been corrected into *glas*. The running title is : *The temple of Bras* (see beginning of this chapter). In the table of contents at the beginning stands : *The Temple off Glasse*, by the side of which Stowe wrote *lidgate* (see chapter VII). At the commencement of this valuable Chaucer-MS. is written in Fairfax's hand: "Note y^t Joseph Holland[3] hath another of these Manuscripts," and at the end of *The Temple of Glas* in Stowe's hand: " Here lackethe .6.[4] leves that are in Josephe Hollands boke." As, however, the poem is complete in the MS., this remark must either refer to some poem which stood between *The Temple of Glas* and the following *Legend of Good Women* in Holland's MS., and which was not given in F ; or else the writer of this remark had before him, in " Hollands boke," a copy belonging to group **A**, with the *Compleynt* at the end, which appeared to him to be wanting in F. For ll. 96, 154, 216, 320, gaps were originally left in the MS. ; of these the one for l. 320 has been filled in by Stowe, the three remaining ones by another hand ; the line supplied for 96 being re-corrected by Stowe. Towards the end of the poem, ll. 1375 and 1385 are omitted. Further, there are found in the margin numerous crosses indicating mistakes, probably also put in by Stowe. The lines almost invariably begin with small letters.

---

[1] **Max Lange,** *Untersuchungen über Chaucer's Boke of the Duchesse,* p. 1, is wrong in supposing that ll. 31—96 of that poem have been filled in by Stowe, the writing in question being in a later Jacobean hand (Dr. Macray).
[2] This was pointed out to me by Dr. Macray.
[3] **Joseph Holland,** the Devonshire Antiquary ; several articles of his, dated 1598—1601, are to be found in **Thomas Hearne's** *Collection of Curious Discourses,* Oxford 1720, and in Sir John **Doddridge's** *Opinions of sundry learned Antiquaries touching the antiquity* . . . . *of the High-Court of Parliament in England,* London 1658. See **Wood,** *Ath. Ox.*, 2nd ed., London 1721, vol. 1, col. 521 (§ 605).
[4] According to this, *Warton-Hazlitt,* III, 61 Note, is to be corrected.

Chapter II.—Description of the MSS. and Prints.

3. B = Bodley 638.

Bodleian, Oxford. See **Skeat**, *M. P.*, p. xli; *Legend*, p. xli; **Warton-Hazlitt** III, 61. **Furnivall**, Odd Texts, p. 67 and 213. Paper with vellum quire-covers, 4°, about 1470—1480. *The Temple of Glas* begins on fol. 16 *b*, and ends on 38 *a*. The title is: *The Temple of Bras;* the running title the same; the colophon: *Explicit The Temple of Bras*. See under 2, and at the beginning of this chapter. The lines begin as a rule with capitals. Ll. 701—714 have been tampered with by another hand; hence they exhibit a number of arbitrary interlineations which again are now partly erased. B is very nearly allied to F, the two going back to a common source.

Ll. 96, 154, 216, 320, 1385 are omitted.—Two amusing notes have been written in the margin by a later reader. The speeches in the poem seem to have been too long for his taste—for which we could not blame him. At all events, he became impatient at not being able to make out who the speakers were; for, at the end of one speech (after l. 847), he put: "h^e vsq*ue* nescio quis"; and at the beginning of another (l. 970): " who in all godly pity maye be."

4. P = Pepys 2006.

Magdalene College, Cambridge. See **Skeat**, *M. P.*, p. lxvii; *Legend of Good Women*, xl; **Todd**, *Illustrations of Gower and Chaucer*, p. 116; **Furnivall**, Supplementary Parallel-Text Edition of Chaucer's *Minor Poems*, p. 27; *Odd Texts*, p. 265. Paper, about 1450. *The Temple of Glas* extends from page 17 to 52. The title has been supplied in a small, later hand as *Temple of glas;* the colophon is: *Explicit*. Our poem is written in two handwritings, the first including ll. 1—1098; the second beginning at the top of page 45, and extending to the end. The compiler of the Index seems to have thought that the poem was one of Chaucer's, like others contained in the MS.

The following lines are omitted: 154, 290, 346, 532, 552—555, 616, 818, 955—957, 1027.—Ll. 147, 148; 1330, 1331, and 207, 208 are transposed; in the last instance, the mistake has been indicated by two crosses in the margin. Ll. 124, 432; 96, 216, 320 differ entirely from those of the other texts; the three latter must have been omitted in the common original of T. P. F. B, and were most likely

Chapter II.—Description of the MSS. and Prints. xxi

supplied in their present form on the way from this original to P (see chapter III, § 10).

Many dialectal peculiarities occur in the part written by the first scribe :

ā for ō : behalden 34, knawe 261, knaw 430, owr(e) thrawe 608, 647, aweñ 938, knawe 1002.—u, ou, ow for o : suthe 43, goudly 56, lowke 230, rowte 307, sowne 392, shuke 524, gowd 684, 906, 977, 985, lulinesse 288, vnfoulde 360 [dulfull 52]; owr, owre (over) 608, 647.—Vice versâ, o for ou : flores 540.—

Orthography *quh* for *wh :* quhen 116, 119, 421 (qwhen 610), Quhame 314, quhat 567, swmquhyle 655.—*quh* for *h :* quhow 100, 117, etc., quho 599.—*wh* for *h :* who (= how) 17, 58, 63, 65, 67, etc. ; wher (= were) 46, 47, 92, 143.—*h* for *wh :* how (= who) 297, hoo 615.—*wh* for *w :* whete (= wite) 728 ; *w* for *wh :* wan 4.— *h* prefixed wrongly : hus 110, hws 1081.—*w* in the function of a vowel : lwfys 86, lwfith 157, lwfit 163, lwfe 212, 213 etc., Wpon 89, vertwe 297, 306, dwle 407, trwe 453, abwfe 466, swndry 609, etc., etc.—*w* for *v :* grewous 1, Rawishid 16, wisage 56, dissawyt 58, growe 109, Inwie 114, lowes 125, enwie 147, lower 149, etc., etc., (very numerous cases).—Vice versâ, *v* for *w :* vexit 69, vas 129, vitte 463, vaxeñ 508, vittes 831, vyttis 1029.—We find also *ey* for *e :* feyr 10, deyr 219, beyn 323, seyñ 506, apeyre 581, greyn 617 ; *ay* for *a :* naymly 229, laydy 468.—Vice versâ : twene 354, chene 355, presith 403, dispared 651, etc.—warde (= word) 360.—The MS. has also often -ir, -id (or -it), -is, in unaccentuated syllables.

These peculiarities leave no doubt that the first part was written by a northern scribe. There are moreover, besides the above-mentioned omission of fourteen whole lines, no end of careless mistakes in this portion of the MS., dittographies, omissions of words, syllables and letters, and other nondescript faults, in many cases presenting perfect nonsense. None of our MSS. have been so carelessly written as this particular part of P.

The latter portion of the poem, written by a second scribe, is not only almost entirely free from these northern forms, but it is altogether more correctly and carefully transcribed.

5. *G* = *Gg.* 4. 27.

University Library, Cambridge. See **Skeat**, *M. P.*, xliii (the passage quoted on p. xliv forms ll. 701—704 of *The Temple of Glas*, not a continuation of it) and *Legend of Good Women*, p.

xxii *Chapter II.—Description of the MSS. and Prints.*

xxxviii. On vellum; date about 1430? This MS. contains a well-known text of the *Canterbury Tales*, and is remarkable as having a different version of the Prologue of the *Legend of Good Women* (one of Bradshaw's favourite MSS., see **Prothero**, *A Memoir of Henry Bradshaw*, p. 357). With respect to the Temple of Glas also, it has a distinctive feature, in being, with S, the only MS. which contains the appendix named the "**Compleynt**." The "Temple of Glas" proper extends from fol. 458 a to 476 b (ending here with l. 1379); after that follows the *Compleynt*, which stops short at l. 563, at the bottom of fol. 482 b, the next leaf being cut out. Another leaf (= 513 according to the new pagination of the MS.) is wanting between fol. 479 and 480 (of the old pagination); thus, ll. 255—330 of the *Compleynt* are missing in G. The title stands already at the foot of fol. 457 b: *Here begynyth the temple of Glas*. Ll. 531—596 are wanting, not, however, in consequence of a missing leaf.

The Catalogue of the MSS. in the University Library wrongly splits up our poem into two parts (III, 173, 174):

    19. *The Temple of Glass* (fol. 458 a).
    20. *Supplicatio Amantis* (fol. 467).

But compare the Corrigenda (V, 598): "This copy differs from the printed editions, by having much more at the end. The last page is here wanting, but a complete copy of this recension, in the handwriting of John Shirley, is in the British Museum, Add. MS. 16165." The compiler of the Index of G apparently believed the poem to be Chaucer's, for he has, on fol. 488 b (the last leaf but one) at the foot, the remark: "The Temple of glasse and supplicatio Amantis not in the prynted booke."

MS. G is, with T, the oldest of our texts. It represents with S (and, in part of the poem, with F and B) another version of the text, exhibiting, in the body of the poem also, various interpolations, which will be discussed in chapters III and IV. Its peculiarities of spelling, etc., can be studied in the *Compleynt*, for which it has been taken as the basis.

    6. *S = Additional MS.* 16165.

British Museum. This is one of the MSS. of **John Shirley**, a gentleman who spent a considerable part of his time in copying poems of Chaucer and Lydgate. The MS. is on paper, folio; date about 1450. See **Skeat**, *M. P.*, xlv. Our poem extends from fol.

206 b to 241 b, and has been almost entirely copied by Shirley himself; but ll. 119—134 and 391—439 have been written by other hands. At the end of the *Regula sacerdotalis*, which precedes our poem, is written in the MS. : " Et ensy fine vn petit abstracte appellez regula sacerdotalis et comence vne soynge / moult plesaunt fait a la request dun amoreux par Lidegate · Le Moygne de Bury." The running title is : *The dreeme of a trewe lover ;* this, however, is not always uniformly the same, inasmuch as *trewe* is sometimes omitted, or *a* has been replaced by þe, or is altogether left out, etc. On folio 207 a stands in addition to this headline : "*made by daun John of þe tempull of glasse þat shall next folowe þe hous of fame*" (the words in italics supplied later); similarly, there is a later addition to the running title on fol. 212 a : *calde þe Temple of glasse by Lydegate*. See further chapter VII.—The colophon runs (on fol. 241 b) : "Here endiþe þe Dreme and þe compleynt of þe desyrous seruant in loue and filowyng begynneþe þe compleint of Anelyda," etc.

As has been intimated above, this is the only other MS., which, besides G, contains the *Compleynt*. Where, therefore, the first MS. is defective, the text of S is given in Appendix I, namely, in ll. 255 —330, and from 563 to end.

Folios 228—230 do not follow in correct sequence. It seems that fol. 228 b was, through an oversight, left blank; Shirley turned from fol. 228 a immediately to 230 a, and then to 230 b; on the blank side of 228 b he then wrote the continuation of 230 b. Folio 229 ought to stand before 228 (perhaps a mistake in binding?). The scribe himself draws attention to the right sequence of the pages.

Besides the many striking mistakes which S has in common with G, discussed in chapter III, S has omitted ll. 261—264 and 507 ; totally changed 594 and 618, and the latter halves of 1358, 1359, to make the rhyme suit l. 1356; in the interpolated stanza 3 b, line 4 is omitted, and a new one introduced; in place of ll. 741 and 742 one single line appears; two lines (the first = line 91) have been interpolated between ll. 28 and 29, and, before 736, line 727 has been, by mistake, repeated.

In the *Compleynt* ll. 157—176 are omitted in S; ll. 364, 378, 412, 474 are totally different from G, and lines 380 and 422 differ slightly. Compare also the lines 206, 207 in the two MSS.

Shirley's peculiarities of orthography are well known from Dr. Furnivall's publications[1] : his *e-* for *y-* (the prefix to the past parti-

[1] Compare particularly *Odd Texts*, p. 78.

ciple), as in: echaced 31, eblent 32, Eslawe 95, Ewownded 113, Eturned 116, Eentred 201, etc.; his -*eþe*, -*iþe* (3rd ps. sgl.): abydeþe, floureþe, bereþe, telliþe, sitteþe; his predilection for *ffs*: efft, alofft, sofft, wyff, stryff; his *eo* and *oe;* his invariable svarabhakti-vowel in *harome;* his *uw* in truwe, huwe, eschuwe, etc.; his pleonastic writing of *nexst*, etc.—He also often has the Scandinavian *þeyre.*— His reading *sounde of bras* (instead of *stede of bras*) in l. 142 does not reflect great credit upon his knowledge of Chaucer, nor does his reading *Physyphonœ* (for *Tisiphone*), in l. 958, say much for his classical scholarship. What with all the above-stated omissions and interpolations, and a whole legion of alterations which he introduced on his own hook, his MS. is one of our worst copies.[1]

7. *L* = *Longleat* 258.

In the possession of the Marquis of Bath. On paper and vellum; 4°.; date about 1460—1470. See **Furnivall**, Supplementary Parallel-Text Edition of Chaucer's *Minor Poems*, p. 143; Odd Texts, p. 251; Reports of the Commission for Historical MSS., third Report, Appendix, p. 188, at the bottom, and 189 at the top. Curiously enough, in the last-mentioned passage the *Temple of Glas* is not given in the contents of that MS. in which it really stands—namely, MS. No. 258, the Chaucer-MS. containing the *Parlement of Foules*, etc.—; but after the description of this MS. in the *Reports*, on p. 189, a further MS., *The Temple of Glasse*, on paper, of the 15th century, is mentioned. Canon Jackson, to whom I am much indebted for his information about this MS., tells me that this latter does not exist as a separate copy; he thinks that the *Temple of Glas*, which, in reality, stands first in MS. 258, has, in the table of its contents, as given in the *Reports*, been wrongly put at the end of the table as a separate "folio" of the 15th century. The *Temple of Glasse*, mentioned in the *Historical Commission Reports* on p. 188, in the middle of second column, is *Chaucer's Dreme*, or, as the poem has been better called, *The Isle of Ladies;* see **Thynne's** *Animadversions*, printed by Dr. Furnivall, p. 30; **Skeat**, *M. P.*, xxxii; **Koerting**, *Grundriss der Geschichte der Englischen Litte-*

---

[1] Shirley also wrote "poetry" himself. By an enormous jump, we come down from Chaucer to Lydgate; a little lower than Lydgate's poorest verses ranks the *Compleynt*, and with another decided step we descend from the *Compleynt* to Shirley's productions. See specimens of them in chapters VII. and VIII.

ratur, p. 157, note 1. This MS. is of the 16th century (about 1550), and has the number 256.

As we have just mentioned, *The Temple of Glas* stands, in L, at the beginning, from fol. 1 *a* to 32 *a*. The title is: *The Temple of Glas;* the colophon: *here endith the Temple of Glas.* On fol. 32 *a* were originally only the last two lines and the colophon; later on, Sir John Thynne wrote on the same page a poem by Rycharde Hattfeld; comp. Add. MS. 17492, fol. 18 *b*, where the same poem is to be found.[1] Ll. 211 and 212 are transposed; ll. 96, 609, 610, and 901 are omitted; the latter, however, has been filled in by a later hand, as well as the headings before 321 and 531, and the running title: *The temple of Glas;* various corrections also, as in ll. 426, 816, 818, 833, 844, have been supplied by the same hand.—In the table of contents our poem appears as " Templum vitreum."

The text of MS. L forms an interesting link between the recension of the Prints and of MSS. T. P. F. B; it must stand in close relation to the MS. which we may suppose Caxton to have used.—It has few peculiarities of spelling or phonetics; it writes *vade* for *fade* (508); *abought* for *about; grugging*, etc. (with *gg*), and invariably *dud* (= did, O.E. dyde). The Scandinavian forms *thair, them* (or *theim*) are of frequent occurrence.

Another MS., not now known, once in the possession of the Paston family, is spoken of in the *Paston Letters*, in one dated the 17th of February, 1471-72 (see chapter VII). *The Temple of Glas* seems also to have been contained in a MS. of Joseph Holland's; see above, under § 2 of this chapter. Moreover, the criticism of the known texts, in chapter III, points to the former existence of a considerable number of MSS. now lost sight of.

B. THE PRINTS.

8. *C = Caxton's Print.*

University Library, Cambridge, marked AB. 8. 48. 5. Unique.[2] 4°, without date, place, name of printer, signatures or catchwords. The type used (No. 2) shows that this is one of Caxton's oldest Prints, and belongs to about the year 1478. It contains thirty-four

[1] This I was able to ascertain through the kind help of Mr. Bickley, of the British Museum. The poem is about to be published, from the Addit. MS., in Dr. E. Flügel's *Lesebuch*.

[2] Of all the six prints known to me, I have, of each, seen but one copy. See, however, Lowndes, the copies mentioned by whom I could not always trace to their present possessors.

xxvi   *Chapter II.—Description of the MSS. and Prints.*

leaves, a—c⁸ d¹⁰; folio a₁, probably blank, is missing. The poem begins on a₂ recto, and ends on d₁₀ recto. The full page comprises twenty-three lines. The title is given at the top of a₂ recto : + The temple of glas + ; the colophon on d₁₀ recto : + Explicit the temple of glas +.

 See Conyers **Middleton**, *A Dissertation concerning the Origin of Printing in England*, 1735, p. 29 ; **John Lewis**, *Life of Caxton*, 1737, p. 104 ; **Ames**, *Typographical Antiquities*, 1749, p. 60 ; **Herbert** I, 79 ; **Dibdin** I, 306 ; **Panzer**, *Annales Typographici*, 1795, III, 561, No. 67 ; **Ritson**, *Bibliographia Poetica*, under No. 10 of the Lydgate-list ; **Robert Watt**, *Bibliotheca Britannica* I, 207 c ; Catalogue of the Caxton Exhibition, No. 34 ; and, particularly **Blades**, *Caxton*, 1863, vol. II, 59, No. 19.

The Cambridge copy seems once to have formed part of a volume of collections, belonging to Bishop John More of Ely (died 1714; see his portrait forming the frontispiece to vol. II of Dibdin), who procured it through John Bagford; see **Blades** II, 51; **Hazlitt**, *Remains of the Early Popular Poetry of England*, III, 24 ; *Bibliotheca Heberiana*, Part IV, 134 ; **Hartshorne**, *The Book Rarities in the University of Cambridge*, 1829, p. 135.—The various component parts of this volume have since been separated again. The other prints are all descended from Caxton's, as will be shown in chapter III.

 9. *W = Wynken de Worde's first Print.*

British Museum, King's Collection. It forms the third piece in a volume marked C. 13. a. 21, the two preceding it being the *Story of Thebes* and the *Assemble de dyeus*. See the description of the whole volume in **Hazlitt**, Hand-Book to the Popular, Poetical and Dramatic Literature of Great Britain, p. 358, No. 3 ; comp. also **Ward**, Catalogue of the Romances in the British Museum, I. 88.

The print is in 4°, containing a—c⁸ d⁴ = 28 leaves, with 28 lines on a full page. The Catalogue of the British Museum gives 1500 (?) as the probable date ; but Mr. Gordon Duff tells me that it must be somewhat earlier, perhaps 1498. This print has signatures, as have also the following ones ; in Pynson's print this is not visible, as the bottom of the pages has been cut off.—The print has no separate title-page ; the title is given at the top of a₁ recto : ¶ Here begynneth the Temple of glas ; immediately below the poem begins, and ends on fol. d₄ recto, in the middle, with the colophon : ¶ Explicit the Temple of glas. Underneath there are the : ¶ *Duodecim abusiones*, in Latin, followed on d₄ verso, by two English stanzas in rhyme royal (printed in Appendix II.). Below these is Wynken de Worde's device, No. 1 (= Caxton's small device, having his initials in black on a white

Chapter II.—Description of the MSS. and Prints. xxvii

ground, with black floral scrolls, *without* W. de Worde's name underneath); see **Herbert**, table between I. 116 and 117, left corner at the bottom; **Dibdin**, No. 1 of Wynken's devices.

This first print by Wynken de Worde was followed by two others (W2 and w, described in the two ensuing paragraphs) which have often been confused with each other and with Caxton's print,[1] so that many mistakes in connection with them are found in bibliographical and typographical works.

See **Ames** (1749), p. 86; **Herbert** I. 194, 195; **Dibdin** II. 303—305; **M. Denis**' *Supplement to Maittaire* (1789), No. 5992, vol. II. 673; **Panzer** III. 561, No. 67; **Ritson**, *Bibliographia Poetica*, p. 68; **Watt** I. 475c; **Lowndes** ed. *Bohn* III. 1419; **L. Hain**, *Repertorium Bibliographicum*, No. 15364, vol. II., pars II., 397; *Bibliotheca Westiana*, No. 1684; *Bibliotheca Heberiana*[2] (1831), part IV. p. 134. Our print W is probably also the one meant by Herbert, vol. I. p. 79 (bottom) and 80 (top); Mason-Heber's copy must have been very similar to the one in the Brit. Museum, if not of the very same impression.

The text of W is derived from C; see chapter III.

10. *W2 = Wynken de Worde's second Print.*

Advocates' Library, Edinburgh. 4°; a—d⁴ in eights = 28 leaves, with 28 lines on full page. No separate title-page; title at the top of a₁ recto : ¶ Here begynnyth yᵉ temple of Glas. Below it, the poem begins, and ends on d₄ recto; the colophon is: ¶ Explicit the Temple of glas. Immediately below follow the: ¶ *Duodecim abusiones*, in Latin and English; they end at the bottom of d₄ recto. On d₄ verso stands Wynken de Worde's device alone, No. 4 as given in Dibdin. The sign ¶ stands before every line throughout the whole poem. Folio b₇ and b₆ are bound in wrong order in the Edinburgh copy.

My attention was drawn to this print by Mr. Gordon Duff, who also told me that the date of it is about 1500.—This second print by Wynken de Worde is derived from his first one, as the evidence of the text shows.

See Catalogue of the Advocates' Library VI, 490, where this print is ascribed to Stephen Hawes.

11. *w = Wynken de Worde's third Print.*

In the possession of the Duke of Devonshire. This copy once belonged to the Duke of Roxburghe and, still earlier, to Dr. Farmer,

---

[1] The confusion of W with C arose from W having Caxton's device at the end. But Wynken at first used Caxton's own device, and the type furnishes decisive evidence that W was not printed by Caxton.

[2] For Heber and his bibliomania see Alliboue's *Dictionary;* also Breymann's edition of Marlowe's *Doctor Faustus*, p. x.

the well-known Shakspere-scholar and Librarian to the University of Cambridge. See Catalogue of the Library at **Chatsworth**, 1879, IV. 152 and IV. 340; *Bibliotheca Heberiana* IV. 134.—The print contains $a^6 b^8 c^6 d^4 = 26$ leaves in 4°, with 31 lines to the full page. This print has a separate title-page: on folio a_1 recto stands : ¶ Here begynneth the temple of Glas. Underneath is a woodcut formed of three blocks, representing in the middle a tree, to the right a lady, to the left a gentleman, as it would seem in a courting attitude. Two blank scrolls are respectively over their heads.

On folio a_1 verso the poem begins, and ends at the bottom of d_3 verso. On folio d_4 recto are the *Duodecim abusiones* in Latin, with the two stanzas in English. At the bottom of d_4 recto is the following colophon: ¶ Here endeth the temple of Glas Enprynted in London in Flete strete in the sygne of the sonne. by Wynkyn de Worde. On d_4 verso there is a large woodcut formed of four blocks; the two composing the border representing ornamental scrollwork of floral design, the upper enclosed block depicting the Virgin and Child standing in a cloister (or chapel?), the lower being Wynken de Worde's device No. 2 in Dibdin (Caxton's initials in white on black ground, with white floral ornamentation, and underneath the name of Wynkyn de Worde in smaller black letters on a white ground); see also **Herbert**, table between I. 116 and 117, right corner at the bottom.

Mr. Jenkinson, the Librarian to the University of Cambridge, tells me that the above-mentioned woodcut shows the date of our print to be not long after 1500. w is derived from W2, the second print by Wynken.

See **Brunet**, *Manuel du Libraire*, 1862, III. 1250; **Lowndes**, ed. *Bohn* III. 1419; *Bibliotheca Farmeriana*, p. 296, Lot 6451; **Dibdin** II. 304, Note †.

Herbert, p. 1778 (quoted by Dibdin II. 305), speaks of a print by Wynken de Worde with his device No. 5 as being in the Cambridge University Library, where, however, its existence could not be traced. Most likely Herbert meant the print described in this paragraph, as it was formerly in the possession of Dr. Farmer, once Librarian to the University.[1] The statements in Ames, Herbert, and Dibdin, with respect to Caxton's and Wynken's prints, are anything but clear or accurate.[2]

[1] The colophon of w and of the print referred to by Herbert are the same.
[2] I believe Ames (I, 86) and Herbert (I, 80 and 194) mean Wynken's first print W; later on, Herbert saw w also and took some notes from it which were

12. p = Pynson's Print.

Fragments in the Bodleian, Oxford. A print by Pynson is mentioned in **Ritson**, *Bibliographia Poetica*, p. 69 (top); but I should not have been able to trace it, had not Dr. E. Fluegel discovered four leaves of this print among the Douce-Fragments (No. 38) in the Bodleian. The leaves are in 4o, and are in a mutilated condition, owing principally to the bottom of the pages having been cut off. They have been put together in wrong sequence; leaf 1, recto, contains ll. 1327—1349, verso 1355—1379; leaf 2, recto, 1103—1126, verso 1131—1154; leaf 3, recto, 1159—1180, verso 1187—1208; leaf 4, recto, 1385—1403. Underneath is the colophon:

[Explicit][1] the Temple of glas.
[Emprynt] ed by . Rycharde Pynson.

On the last page stands Pynson's large device No. V in Dibdin. The *Duodecim abusiones* are not given in p. As the signatures have been cut off, we cannot say how many sheets or pages this print contained. As, however, the top-lines of the four leaves left of it coincide, by a curious chance, with those of b, we may, *perhaps*, infer that p had twenty-six leaves like b (and w).—The text of p is taken from W, the first print by Wynken. From this reason, we may perhaps conclude that p was printed sometime between 1498 and 1500.

---

made use of by Dibdin. Dibdin's account (II, 303)—unless, indeed, there is a fourth print by Wynken—is a shockingly confused medley of W and w. The title stands nowhere as Dibdin has it; by the alteration of the capital letters, as given by Dibdin, we might get W or w (not W2). The colophon annexed to this title is taken from w; its orthography is faulty, and it represents here the second part only of the full colophon in w. The beginning of the *Temple of Glas* is given from W, very faultily. The second colophon, introduced after these lines, is that of W or W2 (one capital wrong). The Latin part of the *Duodecim abusiones* is from W, with one slight mistake. Then Dibdin tells us that the two English stanzas stand on the last page; this applies only to W. But nevertheless, in the form in which they stand in Dibdin, these two stanzas are taken from w (Dibdin apparently following MS. notes of Herbert's); still many words are as in W (for instance, *yougth* in l. 18). Then follows the *beginning* of the colophon in w; then a controversy with respect to Dr. Farmer's copy (w) and that of Mason (W), etc.—every line only adding to the bewilderment of the reader.

Had the historians of Typography been accurate in trifles, matters would have been very simple; the accurate rendering of the title alone—or of the first two words of the poem alone—would have been enough to distinguish all the four prints C, W, W2, w.

[1] The brackets show what I have filled in myself, the paper here being torn away.

13. b = Berthelet's Print.

Bodleian, Oxford; marked S. Selden d. 45 (22). The print contains a^4 b^6 c^4 d^6 e^6 = twenty-six leaves in 4o, with thirty-one lines to the full page. Folio a_1 is devoted to the title and woodcuts, the title being on a_1 recto: ¶ This boke called the Temple of glasse / is in many places amended / and late diligently imprynted.—Underneath it stands a woodcut, representing Fortune on her wheel, blindfolded, bearing an unfurled sail in her hand, surrounded by kings and knights. On a_1 verso there is another woodcut, showing trees and flowers enclosed by a paling, in the midst of which stands a knight courting a lady.—The poem begins on a_2 recto, and ends on e_6 recto, in the middle; after it follow the: ¶ *Duodecim abusiones*, ending on e_6 verso; below them is the colophon: ¶ Thus endeth the temple of Glasse. Emprinted at London in Fletestrete / in the house of Thomas Berthelet / nere to the Cundite / at the sygne of Lucrece. Cum priuilegio.

The text of b is taken from w, Wynken de Worde's last print. It was from this print by Berthelet that Warton made his extracts (comprising ll. 14—41; 44—85; 137—142),[1] and these, again, served as basis for the German translation of ll. 55—66 and 75—81 in Alex. Buechner's *Geschichte der Englischen Poesie* I, 56.

See on this print **Warton-Hazlitt** III, 61; **Ritson**, *Bibliographia Poetica*, p. 69 (top); **Herbert** I, 463; **Dibdin** III, 348; *Bibliotheca Heberiana*, part IV, p. 134.

CHAPTER III.
GENEALOGY OF THE ORIGINAL TEXTS.
I. GROUP A.
§ 1. *Coincidences in MSS. G and S.*

It will be seen by a cursory glance that the two MSS. G and S exhibit common characteristics which point to a close relation between them. In both, the end of the poem, from line 1380—1403, is wanting, and, in its place, appears an exceedingly prosy appendix of over 600 lines, the "Compleynt," which was, I suppose, added in the two MSS. in consequence of the ambiguous expression of the last twenty-five lines of the poem, which seemed to leave

---

[1] Some of Warton's readings are taken from the MSS.; some are conjectural. I need hardly add that the latter are all wrong.

Chapter III.—Genealogy of the Texts.

scope for some such addition. Moreover, in both MSS. the five stanzas 3—7 (ll. 335—369) have been replaced by four others; line 510, and in connection with it, 513 and 514, have been altered, to bring in the name "Margarete" for the Lady (cf. also Compl. 395 etc.); similarly, in ll. 309 and 310 the motto of the lady has been changed (cf. also line 530); in l. 299, the colours of the lady's garment are given differently, most likely because our redactor did not consider the green colour, token of inconstancy, appropriate here. Another deliberate change has been made with the pronouns þou, þe, þin (altered to ȝe, ȝour, your in ll. 889, 1152; 883, 888; 854); and here the alteration can be easily detected as such, because in several instances the old pronoun has been either left (cf. ll. 852, 859 etc., 927 etc., 1151, 1156 etc.), or altogether omitted, or otherwise changed (cf. ll. 910, 926, 1172). The subjoined list gives the principal minor instances in which G and S agree in opposition to all other MSS.

Line 1. constreint] compleynt G. S. 9. Hadde hid *only in* G. S. 19. a] *om.* 51. compleint] compleyntes. 60. she was] was she. 66. pein] sorwe. 79. hade for Tristram al] for Trystram suffrede in. 81. him] hyre G. hir S. 89. walles depeint] wal depeinted. 93. lusti fresshe] fresshe lusty. 96. sawe I] I sawe S. I say G. 112. hov] of. 139. &] and ek. 161. ne] in. 200. in] In here G. in hir S. 215. oft] soore. 220. was to him] to hym was. 230. he doþ] men do. 244. for] thorowe. 251. which] the whiche. 269. so] or. 271. briȝter] is bryghtere. 321. of] to. 328. ful] cler. 331. her] *om.* 370. þo] as. 407. sorowis dul] sorwe dwelle. 418. ful] *om.* 457. plainli] only. 470. That] What. 511. þei do] it doth.[1] 632. hou] ȝow. 637. 2nd me] *om.* 697. ful] alle. 763. noþing can] can no thyng. 767. wot] wot that. 770. she] ye.—vnto] in to.—hir] youre. 778. euer was] was. 781. That was] Was. 785. To] And. 801. louli] lowe. 808. grace] your grace. 812. helth] helpe. 817. and] that. 818. 1st me] *om.* 819. not long] nowhile. 827. mater] preyer. 831. fine] myne fyve. 833. And] To. 835. O] *om.* 840. ȝe me whilom] whilhom ȝe me. 844. hi] wiþ. 854. þin] your.—I wil anon] anon I wyl. 873. For] But. 883. þe] ȝow. 888. þe] ȝow. 889. þou menyst] ȝe mene. 905. noþing] for no thyng. 910. þe] *om.* 921. if] *om.*— herte] crys. 922. wilte] lyst. 928. on þe] of the may. 939. he] hym. 958. I] And. 1007. lowli] low. 1010. shal so] so shal. 1028. deuyse] to devise. 1031. me of] of your. 1039. I] he. 1040. trwe] so trewe. 1056. vnto] to. 1081. Riȝt] Lych.—vs] bothe vs. 1082. þe] *om.* 1111. ȝe] they. 1152. þou] ye. 1164. And] But. 1170. and] *om.* 1172. neuer for] for no.—þe] neuer. 1180. biseli þou] besye the to. 1192. in] at. 1206. no] *om.* 1212. haue] *om.* 1239. On] In. 1270. shal þe knot] the knot shal. 1284. haue Venus] Venus haue. 1309. his] hesy. 1328. oure presence] here presyence G. hir heghe prescyence S. 1330. hir] fynal. 1331. prudence] prouidence. 1356. ȝe done appere] the sunne apperyth.

To these instances must be added all the common readings of F. B. G. S (see § 3), and the list of the coincidences of G and S might still be considerably augmented by adding all those of a more trifling character, and those which, though slightly differing, yet

---

[1] The long break here is accounted for by ll. 531—596 being omitted in G.

indicate a common source (see, for instance, ll. 21, 47, 151, 229, 515, 693, 826, 834, 938, 1076, 1141, 1143, 1337, 1368, 1377, and especially 870, 1305).

§ 2. *Differences between G and S.*

Notwithstanding the many cases in which MSS. G and S coincide, as set forth in § 1, they still cannot either of them have been derived from the other. For

α. G cannot be derived from S; since G is some twenty or thirty years older, and, moreover, S has a host of its own individual faults. But

β. neither is S derived from G; for ll. 531—596 are missing in G, whilst they are found in S; and the two MSS. further differ in the following passages, where S has, as a rule, the right reading:

63. falsed] Ifalsid.   65. hov] how that.   82. hou] of.   90. honged] hangyn.   95. I-slain] Slawe.   105. hurt] hit.—þurugh] for.   118. loue of þe] the love of.   133. lowli] only.   138. wiþ] that.   141. hou] *om.*   147. þei] there.   171. haþ] hadde.   183. lust of loues] lustis.   197. ful] wol.—soune] swoun.   201. Yentred] Irenderede.   206. of] in.   217. þat] *om.*   219. hir] hym.   241. &] or.   244. hindred] hemerede.   252. doþ hir] so thourgh.   254. clerenes] clennesse.   260. al] alle the.   263. þe] *om.*   265. Forto] ffor forto.   269. aungellike] agreable.   274. replenysshid] replevisshes.   287. bounte] beute.   290. or] *om.*   295. 3rd of] &.   299. and] & In.   325. Causer] Cause.   328. sterre] sterrys.—*persant*] passant.—*Stanza* 3 c, l. 6. þey] I.—   370. þe] that.   383. haþ] han.   395. storme] strem.   428. him] hem.   458. atones] attreynys.   484. to] *om.*   488. to ȝow hole I] hol I to ȝow.   505. þat] that it.   509. she haþ] I have.   515. kene] lene.   526. drede] degre.   529. from] for.   607. it] *om.*   608. possid] pressid.   615. for] but.   620. werre] werrys.   640. solein] sodeynly.—forto] to.   642. or] &.   644. And] *om.*   649. souerein] sodeyn.   669. wiþ hope I am] I am wiþ hope.   707. here] þe S.   *om.* G.   722. hoolli] only.   725. ones] only.   761. to] of.   762. if] *om.*   775. shal not] ne shal.   776. 1st ne] nor.   777. to] *om.* G.   788. þat] *om.*   798. nov on] vp on.   813. me hurte] myn herte.   818. socoure] sature.   829. life lust] lust lyf.   831. of] wiþ.   853. obey] tobeye.   872. of hir in no] in nomaner.   874. of] at.   892. biforne] to forn.   898. menyng] mevyng.   914. Fulli] ffullyche.   921. to] vnto.   926. þi] this.   935. covntenaunce] gouernaunce.   941. on] in.   956. as] *om.*   1052. noþing hir] hir nothyng myght.   1069. bi] at.   1077. 1st In] And in.   1078. on] of.   1093. list þis mater] this mater lest.   1125. Hou] How þat.   1135. nov] *om.* G (+ Prints).   1147. &] & at.   1150. hede] good hede.   1163. wheþer þei] wherso thow.   1174. euer] ay.   1177. myrþ] mercy.   1183. shal sone] sone shal.   1185. þe] *om.*   1190. vertue] beaute (+ B).   1200. may] ne may.   1225. so] *om.*   1229. be bonde of] ben bounde &.   1230. which] the wheche.   1231. goddis] knottys.   1246. giuen] gynnyn.   1248. assautes] assayis G.—or] nor.   1260. peyne wo] wo peyne.—&] *om.*   1273. bounte] beute.   1274. hert] hete.   1294. beþe boþe] boþe ben.   1311. ay dide] dede ay ek.   1317. hool of hem þe loue] ho the loue of hem.   1318. in] wyt.   1324. of] by.   1329. þurnȝ] in.   1338. in] wiþ.   1358. plesaunt] persaunt.

It is therefore evidently impossible that S should be derived from G. Hence we conclude that G and S go back to a common original, which we may denote by (GS).

Chapter III.—Genealogy of the Texts.

§ 3. *Group F B G S.*

For a certain portion of the poem, the readings of the MSS. F and B, which, as will be shown in § 5, go back to a common original (F B), are the same as those of G and S. First, between ll. 453 and 454, a new stanza is interpolated in all four MSS.; similarly between ll. 495 and 496 three more stanzas appear. Ll. 504—507 have evidently been tampered with by the scribe or redactor of the common original; the change of *grene* to *rede* in 504, which entailed a change of the corresponding rhymes in 506 and 507, reminds us of the scribe's dislike to the green colour in l. 299. Again, the motto of the Lady has been changed in l. 530 in all four MSS. (cf. l. 310). Moreover, there are not few cases of minor importance, in which the four MSS. F. B. G. S have the same reading, in opposition to all other MSS.; these are given in the subjoined list:

75. was] was also F. B. G. S.   429. maner] wyse.   483. loueþ me] I love (+ b).   488. wil] al.   504. braunchis] Roses.—grene] rede.   509. kepe] folowe.   529. in] to (+ b).   597. gif] gynne.—I wot] y wys.   609. a sondri] sturdy.   614. wil] shal.   635. within] with.—þou3t] owne þou3t.   636. ladi Venus] Venus lady.   649. nov] and now.   684. 1*st* so] to.   691. And] And me.   696. an] the.   703. contre] contrees.   706. In] Wiþin.   709. o ladi myn] lady and.   711. 2*nd* to] *om.*   7:3. sorow] sore.   733. grace] a grace.   749. saue] but.   752. wil be] ben.   762. And] So.   781. hem] hym F. G. him B. S.   877. dilacioun *only in* F. B. G. S.   934. in] as in.   955. þei] *om.* 988. ne] nor.   990. to] for to.—me to] vnto.   995. anone] in oone.   997. euer] *om.*   1008. ben] *om.*   1029. And] Ryght.—as my] my.—con] may (+ P).   1149. to] for to (+ S).   1258. bou3t] aboght (I bought P).

The following coincidences in three of the MSS. in question would seem also to be derived from the original (F B G S) common to all four:

582. stremes] percyng F. B. S; *and possibly* 577. in] which in F. B. wight in S (*ll.* 531—596 *missing in* G).   674. haue] had F. B. S (*corrected in* G ?).
Group F. G. S *appears in l.* 701. sorow] sorowful F. G. S; *and l.* 721. and shapeþ] to shape.
Group F. B. G (in which instances S would have altered the reading of the original; *appears in lines:* 610. ouerdrawe] to me dawe F. B. G. slake lawe S. 618. vnto] to F. B. G (S *having altered the whole line*).   668. paynis] harmes F. B. G.   700. *Heading* Supplicacio amantis F. B. G (S *translates this into English*).   725. ne] *om.* F. B. G.   954. Help] Helpynge F. B. G.   Helpen S. 973. shul] shuld F. B. G.   1009. began] gan F. B. G.

It is, however, easy to see that these coincidences, in all four MSS., cover only a certain part of the poem. Thus, the substitution of four new stanzas for the five stanzas 3—7 (ll. 335—369) is only found in MSS. G and S; the change of the motto is, in all four MSS., found only in line 530, not in line 310. And, a point of still greater weight, the end of the poem does not, in F and B, follow the version represented by G and S: lines 1380—1403 are found in their proper place, and the *Compleynt* does not appear in F and B.

A close examination of the above list will show that the minor coincidences occur in continuous sequence, only from l. 429—1029. The isolated coincidence in l. 75 must be a mere chance, as the above-mentioned interpolations, etc., between l. 75 and 429 are not to be found in F and B, and, I think, the same may fairly be supposed with regard to the coincidences in ll. 1149 and 1258, the former one, especially, being of a very trifling character: in fact, it can hardly be counted here, as it occurs also in MS. L.

From all this we conclude, that from l. 429 (or a little before) to l. 1029 (or a little after) the common original (F B) of F and B follows the version represented throughout the whole poem by G and S.

§ 4. *Differences between (F B) and (G S).*

It is now incumbent upon us to determine the exact kind of relation existing between these two groups of MSS. § 1 will have sufficiently shown that G and S, throughout the poem, form one group derived from an original (G S); § 5, as has already been anticipated, will show the same thing to be true of F and B with respect to an original (F B). Now the question arises whether either of these two groups could have been derived from the other. This question will be settled at once by a comparison of the two lists of coincidences, of G and S on the one hand, in § 1, and of F and B on the other, in § 5. There are, between ll. 429—1029, in both lists, such numerous and characteristic readings in each of the groups, that, at a glance, the supposition of one group being derived from the other must be given up. The only satisfactory solution, therefore, is that (F B) and (G S) come from an original (F B G S) = **A** common to all four.

We have thus proved the existence of a group **A** of manuscripts, represented, in general, by the MSS. G and S throughout the poem, and by MSS. F and B, in a certain part of it (ll. 429—1029). Whether this part was wanting in the original used by the scribe of (F B), so that he had to recur to another copy, or whether the MS. (F B), or one of its ancestors, was written by several scribes, one of whom had been given two or three quaternions of the second version as his copy—must remain a matter of conjecture.

II. MSS. T F B P.

§ 5. *Coincidences in F and B.*

THAT these two MSS. follow one another very closely is already well known from Chaucer's Minor Poems. For the *Book of the Duchesse* see Lange, *Untersuchungen über Chaucer's B. of the D.*, pp. 7—10; Koch, *Anglia* IV, *Anzeiger*, p. 95. Skeat, *M. P.*, pp. lviii and xli. For the *Parl. of Foules* see Furnivall, *Trial Forewords*, p. 53; Koch, *Anglia* IV, *Anzeiger*, p. 97; Skeat, p. lxi. For the *Hous of Fame* see Willert, *Ueber das Hous of Fame*, 1883. For the *Legend of Good Women*, see Skeat's edition, p. xli. See also Dr. Furnivall's reproductions of Chaucer-MSS., in several places.

The same holds good for the *Temple of Glas*. For the two MSS. F and B deviate in the following instances from the remaining texts: In both l. 1385 is wanting. Both have the same title: *The Temple of Bras;* the same colophon, the same headings before lines 321, 370, 461, 531, 701, 848, 932, 970, and the same rubrics after 847 and 931, and at the side of 696. Minor points of agreement are:

84. for-wrynkked] for wrynkeled F. for wrinkelid B. 193. These] The F. B. 221. so] sone. 242. 2nd he] *om.* 436. him] *om.* 437. him] *om.* 452. þingis] thinge.—*Stanza* 19 a, l. 1. so sore to yow] to yow so sore.— 470. hert] her.—*Stanza* 25 c, l. 7. layis Pyis] pyes layes.—506. even] evere F. euer B. 570. subieccioun] obieccion. 571. bicome] be bounde. 577. in] which in. 586. at] in. 606. now] new F. nyw B. 619. can] *om.* 627. dar] ne dar. 636. whom] to whom.—souȝt] thought. 650. Nou] *om.* 651. were] where. 653. not] *om.* 662. it] *om.* 666. noþing] noght. 684. 2nd so] to. 696. into] in. 715. henens] heuynessh F. heuenyssh B. 722. al] *om.* 738. Whiles] while. 746. eke] al. 751. Of] and. 758. A] *om.* 793. þe] thys. 882. Ne] He. 1152. þat] thys that. 1166. ay] eke.—*Cf. also* 568. nou am] am now F. I am now B.

To these coincidences in F and B are to be added all the common readings of the four MSS. F. B. G. S, s. § 3; of T. P. F. B, s. § 9; of T. F. B, s. § 10, and of T. P. F. B. L, s. § 13.

§ 6. *Differences between F and B.*

But there are also considerable differences between F and B, which show that neither of them can have been derived from the other. The individual mistakes of F, in which B has preserved the right reading, are the following:

Line 1375 is wanting in F; one rubric in B, at the side of l. 454, which may come from the original, is not found in F (on the other hand, five rubrics in F, one after l. 502, the other four at the side of 1040; 1104—1106; 1110 and 1271 respectively, are not to be found in B).—Minor points:

16. spirit] scripture F.   58. deceyued] descended.   103. prison] *om.*   209.
þere] they *altered to* them.   239. his] this his.   259. &] *om.*   282. hei3] *om.*
284. forto] to.   300. al] *om.*   337. And] a.   374. al] of (+ b).   412. And]
As.   442. he] ye.   476. vuto] and to.   486. to] in.   501. Me] and.   557.
1*st* Of] and.   560. -al] *om.*   572. come] kan.   605. were] was.   618. is] yt.
621. gete] grete.   688. siþ] such.   735. restreyne] refreyne (+ L. G.).   754.
ground] growed.   768. wil] wolde.   853. obey] weye.   922. þou] then.   957.
allas] but allas.   987. I-persid] y presed.   1109. desseuer] disserne.   1216.
his] thys.   1232. 1*st* &] of.   1280. toke] take.   1308. Orpheus] or Phebus.
1340. ri3t] *om.*   1347. forto] made to.   1390. þe] *om.*   1396. to] *om.*   1397.
And] I.   1402. þat] the.

The foregoing list proves, I think, conclusively that B cannot be derived from F; for it is impossible to believe that B in all the afore-mentioned cases could have, of itself, found the true reading again.

But, on the other hand, it is even more impossible that F should in any way be a direct descendant from B. For F is older, and, apart from this proof, a long list of individual mistakes in B might be drawn up, which do not appear in F. We hence conclude that F and B, throughout the whole poem, go back to a common original (F B).

§ 7. *Common Readings of MSS. T and P.*

Although very different as to age, and even more as to quality, MSS. T and P must stand in some close connection with each other. For they have, in common, a number of very characteristic mistakes, which could scarcely have been committed twice over by different scribes. They are the following:

323. hauteyn] ha doten T. hadoten P.   439. Wherso] Wheþir T. P (so also in W and the Prints dependent on it).   465. his hygh request] *om.* T. P.   478. Siþ ye] Wiþ þe.—appese] haue peas.   677. to be bold] bihold T. be holden P (+ be holde G. S.).   733. wold] wil T. wulle P.   872. Demen] Semen.   877. dilacioun] dillusioun.   935. seen] sein T. seyn P.   1000. er] *om.*   1044. ran] it ran T. P (+ W. W2. w. b.).   1346. Be] We.

I would especially point to the common readings of T and P in the above list, in ll. 323, 465, 478 (two instances), 677 (this mistake was also made by G and S, most likely independently from T and P), 872, 877, 1044, 1346. To this list must be added all the coincidences of the groups T. P. F. B (s. § 9), T. P. F. B. L (s. § 13), and T. P. L (s. § 14).

§ 8. *Relation of MS. P to T.*

The way which first occurs to one of accounting for these remarkable coincidences in T and P is doubtless the supposition that P is a direct descendant from T, a supposition suggesting itself the more readily from the circumstance that P is a MS. of considerably later date than T, exhibiting no end of omissions and mistakes characteristic of a continuous corruption of the text through several generations of MSS. But the following list of individual mistakes in T, not shared by P, will prove that this supposition cannot hold good.

133. lowli did] did lowli T. 192. So soote] To sute. 201. Yentred] Y-rendred T (+ L. G). 380. offence] defence. 456. had] haþ. 502. of] to. 563. by] in. 587. hir] him. 608. possid] passid. 664. myself] myschef. 673. þurgh] þouȝ. 705. oft] of. 706. Elicon] eleccion. 821. 2nd l] om. 939. þouȝ] þat T (+ S). 983. to] om. 1057. behest] hest. 1188. herte myne] hertes mynd. 1280. toke] eke. 1289. That] And.—and] þow. 1293. of] to. 1297. shal] om.

As therefore the hypothesis of one MS. being derived from the other must be given up, the above-mentioned singular coincidences in T and P seem to point to the following conclusion:

T and P are both derived from a common original (T P), s. diagram on page xli; but as P is some fifty years later than T and greatly corrupted, one or more connecting links have probably stood between P and (T P). This will be further corroborated by the arguments in §§ 9, 10, 13, 14.

§ 9. *Group T P F B.*

The readings of all these four MSS. agree, in opposition to the others, in the following instances:

154. om.—96, 216 and 320 seem also to have been originally omitted; in their stead, to make up the couplet, P, or, more likely, a scribe between P and (T P) supplied, in each case, another line out of his own head. 338. is] om. 412. þis] þus. 1082. list] om. 1098. relesen] plesen T. F. B. recouer P. The common original of the four MSS. seems to have read plesen, for which mistake P, or a scribe between (P T) and P, attempted a correction; but he did not hit on the true original reading relesen, but only its synonym recouer.— 1222. þere] here. 1333. Reading tyme for contune in the original of T P F B altered by B?

To this list are, of course, to be added all the common readings of the group T. P. F. B. L (s. § 13).

There is, in this list, a conspicuous gap in the coincidences of T. P. F. B, between ll. 412 and 1082. This agrees very well with, and is accounted for by, our statement above that, from ll. 429—1029 (about), the readings of (F B) follow group **A**.

Now, the groups (T P) and (F B) are evidently not derived from one another, as the list of the coincidences common to each particular group alone (in §§ 5 and 7) will show. We conclude, therefore, that the two groups (T P) and (F B) go back to a common original (T P F B).

xxxviii   Chapter III.—Genealogy of the Texts.

§ 10. MSS. T F B.

The characteristic coincidences of these three MSS. are the following:

119. a] *om.* T. F. B.   160. in] on.   408. her] *om.*   518. for] *om.*   857. be behynd] behind.   1045. femynyte T. F. B. pure femynite P.   1098. relesen] plesen.   1113. as hit is] at his.   1257. in] *om.*   1291. For] Forþe.

If our arrangement of the MSS. T. P. F. B., arrived at by the discussions in the preceding paragraphs, and shown in the diagram on page xli, be correct, it would naturally be expected that all the mistakes made by the common original of T. P. F. B would propagate themselves equally into the four MSS. Mistakes made by the scribe of (F B) we should expect to find in F and B, mistakes of (T P) in T and P alike. So the above list of mistakes common to (F B) and T only, without P, would seem, at first sight, to testify against the correctness of the above arrangement. But only at first sight; for I think it is not too bold to suppose that the original (T P F B) had all the above readings now only found in T. F. B.; that from there they crept into T. F. B., whilst on the way from (T P) to P a scribe supplied the respective corrections. For these mistakes, characteristic though they be of the close connection between F. B. T., were nevertheless easy to correct; in certain cases, as for instance, ll. 119, 408, 1113, 1257, they quite challenged a correction; the common readings of the three in l. 518 and 857 must be a mere chance, as in this part of the poem F and B follow group A; line 1098 has been discussed in § 9; the remaining coincidences in ll. 160, 1045, 1113, 1291 are of quite a trifling character.

Further proofs that between (T P) and P some more careful scribe had tried to correct certain conspicuous mistakes, are afforded by the readings of P in lines 18, 1189 (s. § 13, end); 463, 494 (s. § 14, end), and by the substitution of new lines, in P, for the missing ones, 96, 216, 320.[1] The gap in ll. 96 and 97 was characteristically filled in. The scribe of (T P F B) had, after copying the first *sawe I* in l. 96, evidently caught sight of the second *sawe I* in l. 97, and thus omitted two half-lines. This patched-up line was thus left standing in P, with the slight alteration of *þis* to *thus*, and a new line was added to make up the couplet.

If we thus consider the common readings of T. F. B., given in

---

[1] Stowe must have, in some way, got hold of two of the new lines in question, as his substitutions in the corresponding places in F coincide with those of P (in ll. 96 and 320).

this paragraph, adding all those of T. F. B. P in § 9, and of T. P. F. B. L in § 13, it becomes apparent that, on the one hand, there exists a near connection between T. F. B., a connection well known from the text-criticism of Chaucer's *Minor Poems*. But, on the other hand, the above discussion will, I hope, have sufficiently shown that our theory of a close relation of T to P, advanced in § 8 and established on the basis of very remarkable coincidences in T and P, is not upset by some readings common to (F B) and T only.

III. MS. L A LINK BETWEEN PRINTS AND MSS. T P F B.

§ 11. *Coincidences of L and the Prints.*

THE Prints of the *Temple of Glas* all go back to the first one, printed by Caxton about 1478. We shall attempt to show in this §, that MS. L stands in close relation to the MS. which, we may fairly be allowed to suppose, Caxton had as his copy. The subjoined list gives the readings common to MS. L and to the Prints.

2. 2*nd* for] *om.* L. Pr.   10. sore] colde.   16. in] into (+ S).   154. or] or any.   180. sore] so.   191. 2*nd* þat] *om.* (+ S).   233. efter p*er*auenture] perauuter after he.   276. so] *om.* (+ S).   284. of] of her (+ P).   310. and] of.   311. þis] was L.   was so Pr.   320. this] *om.*   331. woful] woful hertes.   345. witte &] out of.   362. þat closid] In the colder L.   the colder Pr.   377. þe] thy (+ P).   384. ȝe] ye ben.   397. awakiþ] waketh.   411. ende and fine] fyne and ende.   517. 2*nd* for] *om.*   576. whiles þ*a*t] while.   602. soris] sorowes (+ S).   614. ouershake] overslake (+ S).   618. is] hit is.   625. euen] euer.   658. would] wol L.   wil Pr.   666. pen] Whan.   678. For] And.   799. þan] than of.   843. bi] with.   877. dilacioun] dissolucion.   975. &] and of.   1019. þis] the.   1045. femyny[ni]te] verray femynyte.   1047. gan] began.   1096. it] *om.*   1120. maked] forged (+ G).   1128. haþe vowid] vowed hath.   1138. for] for his.   1164. champ*a*rtie] them party.   1233. ȝou dide] did you (+ P).   1248. Ne] Ner L.   Nor Pr.   1249. men may no] no man may.   1265. plein] playnly (+ S).   1272 ? off] *om.* (+ T !).   1290. myrþe] myrthes (+ G).   1363 ? Which] With (+ T !).   1367. so] *om.*

A common feature of MS. L and the Prints is also the frequent introduction of the Scandinavian forms *their, them (theim)* for the *her (hir)* and *hem* of the other texts.

§ 12. *Relation between L and the Original of the Prints.*

In spite of the coincidences enumerated in § 11, L cannot have been the original of the Prints, as it has a great number of individual mistakes which are not shared by the Prints. A complete list of the mistakes of L alone might be easily drawn up from the various readings given at the bottom of the pages in the text; as they are too many to be enumerated separately, it may be as well to point out a few conclusive instances. Lines 96, 609, and 610 are missed out.

Chapter III.—Genealogy of the Texts.

For line 901 a gap was left by the original writer of the MS., which was filled in by a later hand. Lines 211 and 212 are transposed. A few conspicuous mistakes of minor importance in L are the following:

14. oppresse] expresse L. 176. Tresour] tresouns. 198. bi] with gret. 238. forþ] sory. 271. sonnyssh] goodly. 426. douteþ] doughter. 515. dures] distresse. 539. þer were with blood] there that blede. 540. floures] om. 703. contre] Court. 747. Hir trouth hir faiþ] Hire faith hire trouthe. 900. viage] message. 1094. take] om. 1252. euer is] is neuer. 1364. oute] om.

Much less can we suppose that L can have been copied from one of the Prints; for, besides L being probably older than the oldest of them, the Prints represent quite a distinct group by themselves, with a host of deviations from all other texts. We must, therefore, conclude that L and the original of the Prints (the MS. used by Caxton), come from a common original (L. Pr.). Line 901 proves, perhaps, that another MS. must have stood between L and (L. Pr.).

§ 13. Group T P F B L.

To find the relation in which the original (L. Pr.) of L and the Prints must have stood to the other texts, we will begin with the coincidences of L with (T P F B). They are the following:

78. 2nd al only in T. P. F. B. L.   81. him.   96 (?) om.   175. of] in.   605. cauȝt] lcauȝt.   1004. distres.   1057. 2nd of.   1191. þenk] þenk þat.   1402. face] hir face.

We see again, that, with the exception of two instances, namely, ll. 605 and 1004, no coincidences of this group are to be found in the middle of the poem; for, as we have seen, from l. 429 to l. 1029 (F B) follows group A. We are, I think, fairly entitled to add the few coincidences in T. L. F. B to the above list:

18. liklynesse] liknesse T. F. B. L.   1189. ȝyue hir] hir ȝyue.   1230. is knytt] ȝe knytt T. F. B. L. om. P.

In the first two cases P seems to have corrections, introduced on the way from (T P) to P.

§ 14. Coincidences in T P L.

For that part of the poem in which F and B follow the first group A, the legitimate representative of group T. P. F. B. L would be T. P. L, with F. B missing. We find, accordingly, the following common readings in T. P. L:

495. 2nd to] om. T. P. L.   497. ful] hole.   534. croude] bronte.   638. am] I am.   655. bold] hold.   676. al] om.   703. al] om.   843. flaumed] bavmed.   872 (?) Demen] Semen T. P.   Seyen L.

Chapter III.—Genealogy of the Texts.

Near the beginning and end the two coincidences appear:

123. Almen] al men (*corrupted line*). 1283. þrifti] tristi T. tristy L. P.

The following common readings of T and L may also go back to their original (T P L)—P, again, would have corrected or attempted to correct:

463. beaute] *om.* T. L. vi'te P (*attempted correction*).   494. last now] lust T. L. life P. 976. I shal] shal l. 990. haþ bound me to] me haþ bound vnto.

The unimportant coincidence in l. 213. 2*nd* at] *om.* T. L (before l. 429) must be by chance.

§ 15. *Group* **B** *of Texts*.

We will now attempt to summarize the arguments contained in the preceding paragraphs, and, as the result of these investigations, to establish a theory as to the relation between all the MSS. other than G. S, which latter form, as we have shown before, a distinct group **A** by themselves.

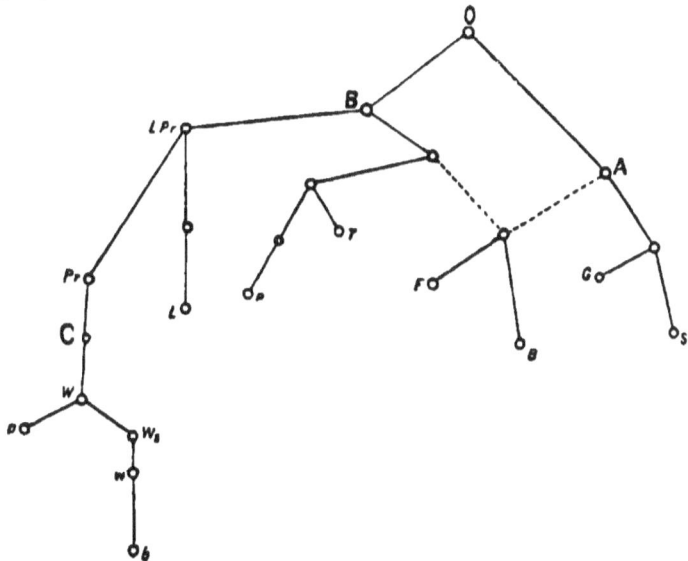

First then, we must be allowed to anticipate here the proof contained in section IV of this chapter, that all the Prints go back to the oldest one by Caxton. Moreover, we may be allowed to suppose that Caxton had a MS. as his copy, which we may denote by (Pr.), it being the original of the Prints. This MS. goes back, with L, to a still older original (L. Pr.), as we have shown in § 12; between L and (L. Pr.) a connecting MS. seems to have existed. Again, in § 9, we arrived at the conclusion that a MS. (T P F B) existed, from which the four MSS. T. P. F. B were drawn in two groups. Now, I think, the simplest way of accounting for all the coincidences and deviations, respectively, enumerated in the foregoing paragraphs, is to suppose that (L. Pr.) and (T P F B) go back to a common original **B**, as the source of the whole second group of texts. The two archetypes **A** and **B** of the two groups, would then in some way or other go back to the original **O**, that is, the poem as it was written by Lydgate himself.

The only objection of any weight to this pedigree of the MSS. in our group **B** seems to be that the Prints have the right reading in certain cases, in which L, in common with T. P. F. B or T. P, differs from them, as for instance in 1402. face] hir face T. P. F. B. L; or in 497. ful] hole T. P. L; see the full lists in §§ 13 and 14. For in such a case we must suppose that this reading appeared already in **B**, and has thence found its way into the individual MS. T. P. F. B. L. On the way to L it must have passed through (L. Pr.), and in the regular course of mechanical copying ought to have propagated itself into the Prints as well. If, therefore, such an error is not found in the Prints, we must suppose that Caxton (or, in some cases, perhaps his original) had found the right reading again. Nor need we be surprised at that. Throughout the Prints, and not least in Caxton's, we find a tendency to modernize the language and to make the poem altogether more palatable to the public of the day. If therefore Caxton, in his endeavour to produce a readable text from his corrupted copy, hit on the true reading in some dozen cases out of the very numerous instances of alteration, this would betray no incredible amount of sagacity on his part. The nature of the few cases in question seems certainly to warrant this supposition.

One point still remains to be accounted for. Lines 154, 216, 320 are missed out in T. P. F. B, which is easily explained by their being omitted in the original (T P F B). In the same way line 96 is left out, not only in T. P. F. B, but also in L. Now, if that line had been omitted by the original of group **B**, it would not appear how the Prints have got the line correctly. The simplest explanation that suggests itself, seems to be that L made the same mistake again, as (T P F B); here also the scribe's eye must inadvertently have wandered from the one *I sawe* to the other in the next line.

Chapter III.—Genealogy of the Texts. xliii

IV. THE PRINTS.

§ 16. *Caxton's Print.*

THE Prints of the *Temple of Glas* present to us an aspect of the text differing considerably from that of the MSS. The first, by Caxton, already exhibits the principal features common to them, the most important of which are enumerated in the subjoined list:—

Lines 156, 157 are omitted. The same headings are found before ll. 321 and 701.—þurgh has been changed to *by* in ll. 105, 443, 515, 867, 871, 1217, 1331, 1344, 1350, 1357.—Changes of the old imperative: 513, 721. Beþ] Be ye. 721. shapeþ] shape ye. 808. takeþ] take ye. 812. sufferiþ] suffre ye. 869. vndirstondeþ] vnderstande ye. 976. takeþ] take ye. 1272. Comeþ] Come ye.—For the introduction of the Scandinavian forms *their, them*, see § 11, end.—Other alterations are: 8. ihorned] horned and Pr. 21. me þouȝt] *om.* 31. Ichaced] chaced. 44. euere] a. 49. &] & som. 63. was falsed] falsed was. 67. hov] how that. 69. Ful ofte wex] Was. 76. hir] *om.* 77. a noþir] other. 81. him] sire, syr. 90. was honged] henge. 106. Of] On.—ȝunge] lusty yong. 113. in] *om.* 130. and] and al the. 132. god] the god. 136. to] there to. 138. goodli] the goodly. 144. of] *om.* 149. iput] put. 166. ful] right. 172. haþ] hath had. 175. eke] *om.* 177. al againes] agaynst al. 178. Wher] Where as. 197. *with* ful] *om.* 199. tender] *om.* 205. to curen al] for to coueren. 206. outward] *om.* 211. of] of fre. 218. And] And after. 250. Hov þat] *om.* 251. riȝt] *om.* 254. bi] *om.* 265. Forto] That for to. 291. &] or. 293. and] *om.* 298. benigne and] right. 299. al] *om.* 305. And] To. 311. þis] was so. 323. of] by. 333. ȝour grace may] may your grace. 338. al] *om.* 362. That hatter] The hotter that I. 376. so forþ lyue] so lyue forth. 378. þe] *om.* 386. Haue] And. 394. also] *om.* 408. hir] *om.* 428. cherissh nov] now cherisshe. 440. his hert I shal] I shal his herte. 463. eny] *om.* 488. to ȝow hole I] I hooly to you. 495. to your] *om.* 499. haue] *om.* 506. it] *om.* 531. and] *om.* 532. þat] *om.* 541. faire &] *om.* 543. 2nd with] *om.* 555. Nere þat he hade] Yf that he had not. 568. so] *om.* 573. riȝt] *om.* 576. loue and serue] serue and loue. 586. Iȝolde] so yolde. 595. no] ony. 597. gif a werre] renne awey. 600. &] and so. 602. forto sound] to founde. 605. she were late] late she was. 609. *with*] of.—a] *om.* 620. your] his. 636. þat] *om.* 644. drede agaynward] agaynward drede.—& saiþ] *om.* 647. Haue] Hath. 657. ful] ful the. 668. opon] on. 670. of þat] how. 672. þan doþ] doth me thenne. 677. 2nd to] and. 679. merci] pyte. 687. þe] *om.* 694. þat] *om.* 703. contre] mounte. 704. 2nd þi] *om.* 705. oft] *om.* 714. þe] yet the. 726. restreyne] constrayne. 733. me] *om.* 735. me not] not me. 736. haþe ȝeue me] me hath yeue. 748. his] her (+ P). 757. secre & wondre] wonder secrete and. 766. a] *om.* 775. uot] neuer. 788. shottes] shott. 800. not] no thing. 804. clepe] I clepe. 811. Nou] *om.* 814. helpe] helth.—hir me] me her. 818. nou] *om.* 820. nov] you. 834. ȝov] now. 859. The] This. 863. alway] althing. 871. þurngh euil] by ony. 882. þat] but. 899. merci] pyte. 910. þe here] to her. 919. but] *om.* 939. a] *om.* 956. directe as nov] as now directe. 959. sustren forto helpe me] suster to calle help vpon. 968. him] *om.* 990. hath me bound vnto. 1002. þe soþe] my peynes. 1015. ȝe shuld as nov] as now ye shold. 1039. graue] begraue. 1046. so] *om.* 1070. bound] drowned. 1095. oure hertes boþe at] bothe our hertes in. 1122. for] of. 1147. at] *om.* 1165. *With*] Ayenst. 1173. denoid] voyd. 1191. in fire hou] hou in fyre. 1206. shalt] *om.* 1207. Reioise] Shal reioyse. 1209. flour] the flour. 1215. þe] these. 1219. also I wil] I wil also. 1225. depured] pured. 1230. which] that. 1232. 1st &] *om.* 1235. doþe] doth. 1239. founde] found of. 1254. may] ther may. 1257. As] And. 1259. þat] *om.* 1263. he] it. 1268. nov do] do now. 1291. life] lyf to telle. 1302. vnto] to. 1305. song] songes. 1318. plite] wyse. 1320. so] *om.* 1322.

haþ made a ful] made a.   1327. ouer] euermore.   1380. 2nd a] om.   1383.
fulle] om.   1391. So] om.   1397. þat] om.

This long list, in which some trifling coincidences are nevertheless omitted, shows, without further comment, how widely the Prints differ in character from the other texts, although adhering distinctly in the main to group **B**. These readings, first appearing in C, have all crept into the succeeding Prints, whose mutual relations it will be the object of the following paragraphs to point out.

§ 17. *Wynken de Worde's first Print, W.*

In the prints later than Caxton's we can, as a rule, clearly distinguish two leading features: namely, first, they correct the obvious mistakes of their predecessor and thus gain certain readings (fewer or more as the case may be), superior to those of their original. Secondly, they all add a great many more mistakes to those already inherited from Caxton's print. The corrections of some of Caxton's mistakes, found in W, are:

13. began C.] gan W.   23. cam] gan.   119. he] her.   258. Surmounted] Surmounteh (*h* by mistake for *th*).   322. in] all.—the] in.   345. For] Fro.— for] fer.   381. han they] han.   426. This] This is.   439. you] ye.   522. fyne] fayne.   587 and 588, *transposed in* C, *are, in* W, *in right order*.   700. this] thus.   779. lasteth] lasted.   910. lowe the] lowly.   942. to] for to. 950. I with my silf] with my selfe I.   963. not to peynt] to peynt not.   1055. is] his.   1143. world] wold.   1177. approched] approcheth.   1178. axid] axeth.   1215. syn] fyn.   1234. onermore] euermore.— bewreke] be wreke. 1358. twinkyng] twynklyng.   1361. Fortune] Fortuned.

Both Prints have wrong readings, differing from one another, in ll.:

41. &] om. C. and now W.   117. gan to chaunge] chaunged C. began to chaunge W.   180. pleined] pleyneth C. playnen W.   612. when] whan that C. what that W.   1140. lateþ] late ye C. late your W.   1236. ferse] fair C. fyry W.   1336. gonne] begun C. goon W.

The new mistakes, introduced by W, are the following:

eke changed to *also* in ll. 155, 241, 243, 246, 252, 273, 293, 294, 855, 1117; the archaic form *eke* having been left standing in ll. 77, 97, 398, 746, 1173, 1209, 1210 and many more.—159, 163. oþir eke] also other.—182, 187. elde] olde.
95. vnwarli] unwardly W.   178. force noon] noo force.   239. graue] in his graue.   247. alderlast] at the last.   249. statne] statute.   309. was] om. 323. ben] om.   394. dropping] drepynge.   416. foloiþ] folowed.   437. so] om.   439. Wherso] Whether.   449. baspectes] by aspecte.   450. teschwe] teshewe.   551. semed] semeth.   618. kouþe] knowen.   651. were] werre. 656. ginneþ] begynneth.   667. my] the.   674. þen] that.   683. seith] sayd. 689. dovmb] doun.   722. case] care.   726. hire] om.   727. at þo lest] atte laste.   841. euenlich] lyke wyse.   871. compassing] rehercyng.   890. she] he.   905. maist þou] may you.   946. wo as] wooes.   980. in] om.   1028. ʒou] ye.   1044. ran] it ran.   1053. hir] om.   1092. be heled] beheled.   1125. most] oft.   1142. pace] space.   1182. renue] renewe.   1257. deinte] deute.

1284. haue] had.   1305 changed considerably.   1368. Me þou3t 1] My thought.
1379. to] om.

As W, therefore, has all the characteristic readings of C, and differs from C only in certain corrections, and new mistakes of its own, we may conclude that Wynken, in his first edition of the poem, copied from Caxton's print. We may suppose that the corrections all came from Wynken himself; even the two or three more remarkable ones in ll. 322, 587 and 588. 950, 963 hardly warrant the supposition that Wynken had recourse to another source than Caxton's print.

§ 18. *Pynson's Print.*

Although this is but a fragment, there is nevertheless no difficulty in assigning to it its proper place in the pedigree of the Prints. It must have been derived from W, Wynken de Worde's first print. For, first, it follows the readings of W very closely, and wherever W differs from C, p gives the reading of W. This is the case in the following lines:

1117, 1125, 1140, 1142, 1177, 1178, 1215, 1336, 1368, 1379 (for the specification of which see § 17).

Add hereto the coincidence of such an extraordinary spelling as l. 1160. wm̄yen (= women) in both prints W and p.

Therefore p cannot have been derived from C. But neither can it have been derived from a print later than W, as is shown by the following coincidences in p and W, where these prints have preserved the old reading in opposition to the second print W2 by Wynken, whose mistakes have, for the most part, crept into the still younger prints w and b:

1104. tweiu] sweyne W2. w.   1121. he] ye W2. w. b.   1130. Ay] As W2. w. b.   1337. In] An W2. w.   1370. gret] frete W2. w. (b).

Some new mistakes occur also in p:

1149. do] om.   1182. renewe] om.   1197. þi] the.   1201. dai] om.   1332. hem] hym.   1341. 3oure] oour.   1377. that] om.   1378. as] om.   1379. wryte] wyrte.

I think the above arguments can leave no doubt that p had W as its original.

§ 19. *Wynken de Worde's second print, W2.*

This print has all the characteristic readings of W, reproducing W's corrections of C as well as its own numerous new mistakes. It hardly supplies any corrections beyond mere printer's mistakes, whilst it exhibits a great many new errors:

1. thou3t] through W2. 16. a] om. 26. gan] om. 37. In] I. 38. gone]
om. 62. next] nex. 73. trouth] through. 85. When] What. 105. vnwarli]
vnwardly. 139. leydons] leydous. 145. In] Is. 200. ofte] oft a. 204. for
to] or to. 205. hir] they (for *theyr?*). 231. þuru3] om. 248. cristal] orystall.
252. donne] om. 254. In] I. 273. of] yf. 318. wil] stylle. 347. yonde]
yonder. 391. þis with*in*] thir within. 401. mate] wate. 450. teschwe]
teshewe W. to shewe W2. w. b. 472. while I line] lyue whyle. 480. to
t*ur*ne] to forne. 512. is] om. 514. mai] many. 533. pres] preces. 535. in
his] iu. 582. wiþ] within. 616. til] ryl. 617. vnwarli] wardly. 638. so]
loo. 660. þat] om. 664. encrese] lencrece. 718. influence] infulgence. 720.
þis] his. 796. menyng] menyng. 839. Hir] om. 845. of] om. 890. she]
om. 926. adoun] and a doun. 944. felt] lete. 968. at] om.—his] is. 985.
god] good. 1001. rwe] knewe. 1013. offend] offence. 1079. to obei] to beyc.
1092. men] man. 1104. twein] sweyne. 1121. he] ye. 1130. Ay] As. 1253.
doubilnes] om. 1263. it] it it. 1269. 3o*ur*] you. 1312. queme] quene.
1337. In] An. 1370. gret] frete.

There remains no doubt that W2 was derived from W.

§ 20. *Wynken de Worde's third print, w.*

This print must have followed W2 as its original, for it has all
the readings of W2, with a few corrections and many new mistakes
of its own. In some cases tangible errors of W2 have been very
thoughtlessly reproduced, for instance, in ll. 37, 73, 145, 200, 204,
248, 254, 273, 616, 664, 1104, 1337.

w supplies corrections in the following ll.: 205, 514, 551, 727,
926, 1001, 1269, 1372.

Unsuccessful attempts at correction appear in ll.:

318. stylle W2] skylle w. 391. thir within] therwithin. 617. wardly] inwardly. 944. lete] ledde. 1125. it] om. 1253. For the omitted *doubilnes* w
supplies *falsnes*. 1312. and quene] the quene.

New mistakes are introduced:

Ll. 366, 367, and 390 are omitted in w.—219, 464, 816, 840, whilom] somtyme. 1. For through] Throughe w. 2. pensif hede] pensyfnes. 18. as] all.
25. persing] passynge. 31. haue] than. 62. next] nex W2. next her w. h.
86. lones] loued. 106. faire] the fayre. 188. Ay] Alwaye. 192. be to] to be.
207. wepen] where. 292. &] om. 356. feruence] feruente. 357. mot] may.
381. han] than. 385. chaunge] chaunce. 399. somme] om. 406. to] the.
422. ioi] no Ioye. 426. douteþ] dowte it. 478. nov] om. 492. to]
om. 527. þis] the. 530. de mieulx en mieulx magre] better & better after
my gre. 537. Descriuen] Dysceyne. 542. offerin] om. 547. þe] om. 608.
possid] tossed. 620. many] om.—him] dare hym. 686. to] lo. 765. axen]
axely. 815. ey3en] euen. 842. het] hit C. W. W2. it w. 862. oure] her.
886. wiþ] and. 890. as] om. 898. menyng] menne. 903. fortune] forne.
933. I gan] gan I. 951. want] lacke. 977. first] om. 991. That] My.
1055. menyng] meuyng. 1135. 3oure] om. 1162. cuermore] euer. 1183.
ouergon] be gone. 1210. eke] ete. 1232. Ione] Inno. 1299. aboute] aboue.
1307. 2*nd* her] om. 1312. and quene] the quene. 1345. Venus ladi] lady
Venus. 1357. si3t] light.

Moreover, in a considerable number of cases, where the older
Prints C. W. W2 had left the pure English forms *her, hem,* w has

introduced the Scandinavian forms *their, them;* *it* also occurs for *hit.*

§ 21. *Berthelet's Print.*

Into such a corrupted state had the text of the *Temple of Glas* sunk, when Berthelet, on account, doubtless, of its still enduring popularity, set about issuing another edition. As many passages had become entirely unintelligible, he attempted an out-and-out revision of the text, which thus differs from its immediate predecessor at least as much as Caxton's print differs from its nearest relations, the MSS. of Group **B**. Berthelet's principles were very simple: where he met with obsolete words or inflexions, he modernized; where there were evidently corrupted or unintelligible readings, he got rid of them, as a rule, by some radical cure, more or less appropriate; the three lines omitted in w he supplied out of his own head, nor did he feel pangs of conscience in changing, without any apparent reason, a great many other things which it would have been better to have left untouched. The question as to which of the preceding prints he took for his copy, is easily solved: as his print gives not only the few corrections, or attempts at correction, introduced by w, but also the greater part of the mistakes which first appear in w, there can be no doubt that this last print of Wynken de Worde's served as his original.

To do justice to Berthelet, we first subjoin a list of his successful corrections, in which he found the old true reading again, a list which puts the corrections in Caxton's print, or those in MS. P, quite in the shade, as regards their number, sometimes their sagacity, and always their appropriateness to his purpose.

9. Had] Hydde b. 15. that *restored in* b. 16. a *restored.* 93. the *restored.* 194. to] for to. 200. it *restored.* 204. or to W 2. w] for to. 231. thurgh *restored.* 309. was *restored.* 310. of] and. 377. thy] the. 378. Thy] The. 381. haue *restored.* 400. also reioyce *in the right order.* 406. the] to. 416. folowed] foloweth. 422. no] *om.* 436. hym sette *in the right order.* 437. so *restored.* 472. lyue whyle] while I liue. 480. toforne] to turne. 517. of] for. 533. preces] preace.—with *restored.* 537. Dysceyue] Discrynen. 542. offre *restored.* 547. the *restored.* 574. her] his. 616. ryll] tyll. 626. that *restored.* 661. one] a. 718. infulgence] influence. 749. sauyng] sane. 765. axely] axen. 796. meuynge] meanyng. 845. of *restored.* 850. that] thouga. 916. to *restored.* 935. 2nd the *restored.* 960. 2nd of *restored.* 1013. offence] offende. 1052. vndenysed] vnaduysed. 1053. her *restored.* 1055. meuyng] menyng. 1061. so moche] as much as. 1092. man behelde] men be healed. 1104. sweyne] tweyne. 1113. Ful] Fully. 1125. oft] most. 1138. thenne] trouthe. 1210. ete] eke. 1257. dente W. W2. w] dente b. 1279. lady *restored.* 1284. had] haue. 1299. aboue] aboute. 1314. lusty] lykely. 1337. An] In. 1340. this] thus. 1368. My thought] Me thought I.

Some of the well-intentioned, but unsuccessful, corrections in b are:

For lines 366, 367, and 390, missing in w, b has substituted some of his
own.—26. gan] *om*. W2. w. dyde b.   86. loues] loued w. loue the b.   150.
haue] hath.   192. to be] with the.   207. Thus] There.—where] *om*.   252. and
also the storme] in brightnesse echone.   256. the] in.   356. feruent
and] feruent.   391. therwithin] therfore within.   415. by] to.   443. hym
selfe] he wolde.   492. be at] in to.   839. Hir] *om*. W2. w. Myn b.   842. be
hit] be it w.   by it b.   903. fortune] forne w. forther b.   933. so] as.—I
gan *in the right order*.   934. so] sore.   1030. preue] me preue.   1054. of
roupe] of whiche C. W. W2. w. so moche b.   1125. is] *om*. w. hath ben b.
1363. With] *om*.

Thus far we have enumerated Berthelet's corrections. We now
proceed to give other more or less systematic changes in b:

The demonstrative pronoun *tho*, answering to O.E. þâ, is replaced by *those*
in ll. 1165, 1337, 1351. Similarly, the adverb of time *tho* (also = O.E. þâ)
is replaced by *than* in ll. 370, 525, 1366, 1369. *Tofore* has been changed into
before in some 17 cases; *thou* into *you* 852; *thou sorowest* into *ye sorowe* 860;
the into *you* 859, 874; *thin* into *your* 854, 861.

These changes, the first of which are owing to Berthelet's tendency
to modernize his text, are at least excusable, and certainly they
answered to the requirements, or taste, of his readers. But, unfortunately, Berthelet also thought that the readings of his copy were
corrupted in many places where, in reality, they were right. Such
is the case in the following lines:

23. gan] cam.   180. pipyng] wepyng.   225. they] he.   233. That] Yet.
275. ennewed] endewed.   320. was] foloweth.   407. gan] became.   483.
loueth me] I loue.   539. blood] blood.   572. god] the god.   651. man] a
man.   695. haue] haue made.   724. ne dare alas] alas ne dare.   860. That]
And.   1060. of] for.   1061. That] And.   1090. is founden] fyndeth.   1093.
to] *om*.   1266. that] if.   1348. Willy] Worthy.   1366. for] sore.

The number of these cases might be augmented; but, in some of
them, it is obviously difficult to say whether Berthelet believed he
was restoring the original reading, or simply wished, by fair means or
foul, to improve upon the copy before him. Further, what is still
worse, he made a great many apparently quite unwarrantable and
uncalled-for alterations, in which his individual caprice seems to
have been his sole standard: thus he interpolated four lines between
314 and 315, and completely changed whole lines, as 314, 315, 319,
545—548, 882, 950, 951, or half-lines, as in 318, 374, 1190.[1] To
point out his countless smaller alterations would avail nothing, the
more as they are one and all contained in the *apparatus criticus*.

If, to sum up, we consider the above lists, we must, I think, in
fairness give Berthelet credit for his many real corrections in the
first list; as to those which follow next, we must at least pass a

---

[1] Or had he a copy of w before him, in which some of these lines were
obliterated?

Chapter IV.—Criticism of the Texts.

verdict of "tamen est laudanda voluntas,"[1] all the more readily as there are comparatively few mistakes arising from his own inadvertency. We must certainly allow that the "in many places amended and late diligently imprynted," put with an evident sense of satisfaction on his title-page, is not altogether unjustified.

But, on the other hand, we are in justice bound to say that Berthelet's text is, by a long way, the one furthest removed from the original, as it came from Lydgate's hand. This, of course, is in some measure not so much Berthelet's own fault, but is rather accounted for by the fact of his Print being the last offshoot of a long generation of MSS. and Prints. It is, nevertheless, instructive to note how Berthelet, with all his emendations and critical sagacity, only managed to produce the worst text of all, and how he was wrong even in such a case as the one pointed out in the footnote below, which, in his eyes, must have appeared a masterpiece of conjectural emendation. These considerations are apt to dim in no small degree the lustre of the nimbus, surrounded by which, some people tell us, the "Conjectural-Kritiker" walks in unapproachable majesty.

CHAPTER IV.

PRINCIPLES FOR THE CONSTRUCTION OF THE TEXT.

§ 1. *Group* **A** *corrupted.*

In the foregoing paragraphs it has been shown that the existing texts of the poem form two groups **A** and **B**, the first represented by MSS. G and S, and, for part of the poem, also by F and B; the second by the rest of the MSS., and the Prints. As there are some radical differences between the two groups, we have now first to discuss which of the two is the most likely representative of the older and purer text.

From what we have intimated in Chapter III, § 1, it will already have been gathered that we do not consider group **A** as representing the original version. G and S alone give the *Compleynt* at the end, and no one is likely to be of opinion that this wretched production can possibly have formed an original continuation of the *Temple of Glas*. For although the poetic value of the *Temple of Glas* may not rank high,

---

[1] This certainly applies in the case of such an alteration as that in l. 724. For as he found the word *case* in l. 722 corrupted in his original into *care*, he again made good the lost rhyme in l. 724 by transposing the *ne dare alas* of his original to *alas ne dare.*

TEMPLE OF GLAS.   *d*

yet this bungling piece of patchwork is much inferior to it. Throughout the *Temple of Glas* it is obvious that the author endeavours to present to us the action of his poem in clearly-defined outlines; but these 600 lines, which are entirely foreign to the general tenour of the *Temple of Glas*, and which have been tacked on to it in such an ill-judged manner, spoil the composition as a whole most cruelly. Granted that the action in the *Temple of Glas* is poor and overweighted by long, tiresome speeches, yet the narrative clearly ends and is complete at line 1380, and we expect the close of the poem somewhere near there. The *Envoy* which follows (ll. 1393—1403), and which is thus not given by G and S, is quite characteristic of Lydgate. Here, too, he has not forgotten the request to "correct" his poem, if any word be missaid in it; a close which is as sure to come in at the end of a work of Lydgate's as the famous white horse in a picture of Wouwerman's. We have mentioned above that the *Compleynt* was most likely added here in consequence of the ambiguous and unclear purport of the last 25 lines, where the author (ll. 1380 and 1381) promises a "litil tretise," "in pris of women," "Hem to comende, as it is skil & riʒt." But where is anything of this programme carried out in this miserably stupid concoction?

To conclude, not the shadow of a doubt can remain that the *Compleynt* has nothing whatever to do with the *Temple of Glas*.[1]

Some of the minor interpolations also may readily be discerned as such. Thus the three stanzas interpolated in group **A** after stanza 25, are certainly far from being in harmony with the general tenour of the poem, and it seems more appropriate that the lady's thanks to Venus should end with laud and reverence to her name and excellence, rather than with jays, pies, lapwings, and owls. Very much the same holds good of the four stanzas put, in G and S, instead of stanzas 3—7. The expression "fryed in his owene gres" (Stanza 3 *c*, l. 1) may be quite appropriate in the mouth of the Wife of Bath, but certainly it is not so from the lips of our gentle Lady. We readily allow that the lady's complaint to Venus (ll. 335—369) is somewhat vague in expression, and can in no sense be called a masterpiece; but the substitute (stanzas 3 *a*—3 *d*) must surely be pronounced even less successful.

The above considerations are calculated to make us mistrustful of

---

[1] I wonder very much whether it is by a mere chance that MS. G, not only in the *Temple of Glas*, but also in the Prologue to the *Legend of Good Women*, follows quite a different version.

Chapter IV.—Criticism of the Texts. li

the more extensive deviations of group **A** from **B**. Thus the single stanza interpolated between ll. 453 and 454, also arouses our suspicion, although innocent enough in itself; so does, similarly, the change of the motto of the Lady in ll. 310 and 530, and the alteration of the colours in ll. 299 and 504 (green being considered by the redactor the symbol of inconstancy; see Skeat, *M. P.*, p. 387). What must make us question still more the correctness of the common readings of G and S, is that we find distinct changes in these two MSS. alone, even in that part of the poem where F and B follow the same group and yet differ from G and S. So, for instance, in l. 510 G and S alone attempt to give a name to the Lady, namely, "Margarete,"[1] and change lines 513 and 514 accordingly, whilst F and B do not deviate from the readings of the other texts. This shows that some of the deliberate and important changes in G and S may come from (G S) rather than the archetype of group **A**, even when not controlled by the readings of F and B.

Another alteration in G and S, not warranted by the readings of F and B, is the change of the pronouns þou, þe, þin to ȝe, ȝour, *your* in certain lines. Venus is addressed in the poem, both by the knight and lady, as *ye;* she, in her turn, addresses the lady as *ye*, and the knight as þou. But, in fact, the author himself sometimes seems to have been shaky in his principle, and, in ll. 857 and 865—868, Venus addresses the knight also as *ye*. G and S, however, make Venus address the knight as *ye* in several other instances; as in 854, 883, 888, 889; 1152; in the first four cases certainly wrongly; in the last it cannot be controlled by F and B. Decidedly wrong also is the alteration in l. 1356; for the reading of G and S destroys the rhyme in ll. 1358 and 1359. Shirley, indeed, attempted to restore the rhyme, and the "poetry" introduced by him for that purpose is quite worthy of him.

But, on the other hand, there are, without doubt, certain minor passages in the poem in which group **A** has preserved the right reading. Thus F. B. G. S are correct in reading *dilacioun*, l. 877; *dillusioun* in T. P, and *dissolucion* in L. Pr., are evidently wrong, as both sense and metre show; compare, for the meaning of *dilacioun*,[2] ll. 1089—1092, 1193, 1206. Further, in l. 635, *omne* (as given in

---

[1] This name was perhaps introduced here in connection with *Compleynt* 395, etc. Were this certain, we might be led to suppose that the *Compleynt* appeared first in (G S), rather than in **A**.

[2] This word happily illustrates the way in which the texts of type **B** group themselves into three sub-divisions, namely (L. Pr.), (T P), and (F B).

d 2

F. B. G. S) is wanted to make up the full line; so is *also* in l. 75 (here *also* seems, in F and B, to be a later correction); on the other hand, *ben* makes a syllable too much for the metre in l. 1008. It cannot be decided with certainty which of the two groups is right in ll. 990, 997, 1029. G and S alone seem to have preserved the right reading in 1328, 1331; in 75, and perhaps in l. 9.

But they are certainly incorrect when, between ll. 429 and 1029, F and B do not go with them; as in 778, 781, 808, 870, 910. In the case of the first three lines, this consideration did not present itself so clearly to me, when I introduced the reading of group **A** into the text; I believe now that the text-criticism absolutely obliges us to let the singular accentuation Ántonyús, the monosyllabic, and even the trisyllabic foot at the beginning of lines 808 and 781 pass unchallenged. See chapter V on Metre. The readings of G. S seem to me to be doubtful or wrong in ll. 1, 19, 31, 79, 81, 112, 407, 470, 632, 770, 1111, 1170, 1172, 1212, 1270, 1284. Group **A**, and in particular G. S, has a decided tendency to improve upon the metre, and, especially, to do away with the monosyllabic first measures.— In many other instances the readings of Group **A** and **B** are equally good; in such cases I have left the reading of T in the text.

All the foregoing discussions prove that in a critical edition of the text, group **A** must not be taken as the basis; at the most, we may introduce a few of its readings where they seem to be old and good.

§ 2. *MS. T taken as the basis.*

After thus discarding group **A**, little doubt remains as to which text in **B** we have to turn to. We must, from the first, reject group (L. Pr.); for neither representative of it, L or Caxton, is old or good. The prints after Caxton's, being all derived from his, are of course of no value whatever for the construction of the text; for even when a deviation from their respective original restores the true reading, any such successful correction has only the value of a conjectural emendation.

In the two remaining sub-divisions (T P) and (F B), we cannot think of taking the younger representatives P and B. So only T and F are left. Their text does not differ much; but the scale will be turned at once in favour of T, if we consider that it is older, and that, for part of the poem, F follows the version of group **A**.

I have therefore chosen MS. T as the basis of the present text.

Chapter IV.—Criticism of the Texts. liii

The obvious mistakes made by T alone have been, of course, corrected; but I have marked, in the text, every deviation from T. I have used brackets to supply omissions, be it of words or syllables or letters; if the nature of the deviation from T could not be indicated thus, I have marked the altered word, or the first of a group of altered words, by an asterisk. The reading of T is, even in the slightest instance of correction, always given in the list of various readings at the bottom of the pages, whenever it cannot be gathered at once from the nature of the sign introduced in the text. Thus [hid], in l. 9, means that I have supplied the whole word; long[e] in l. 12, that the e is not to be found in the MS. In a case like the latter the reading *long* of the MS. has not been expressly given, as there can be no doubt about it. The asterisk before *in*, in l. 160, shows that *in* does not occur in the MS., and a glance at the various readings will show that T has *on* instead. Similarly, in l. 133, we gather that T reads *did lowli*, not *lowli did*.

Changes introduced without a particular notice are the following. The whole punctuation is mine. The MS. has only in some cases marks for the cæsural pause; they are quite superfluous, teach us nothing, and would only interfere with the other punctuation.—ff at the beginning of a line has been changed to F.—Capital letters have been put more regularly in proper names; for in many cases it was impossible to say whether the letter standing in the MS. was a capital, or small. The scribe has frequently joined on the indefinite article, or certain adverbs, such as *so*, and the negation, etc., to the word following it; these I have separated.

The contractions, which are rather numerous in our MS., have been expanded in the usual way. Several instances in this MS. seem to show that *r* with a curl to it, was meant by the scribe for *re ;* so in re[r]pent 1076; decembre 6; often in euere (= every), l. 26, 41, 450, 476, 1257 (*euere* in full occurs, for instance, in ll. 44 and 139), and in some other cases of less conclusiveness. I do not say at all that the scribe, therefore, purposely put *r* with a curl for *re* in every case where it occurs; even in the above-mentioned lines it *might* be only a pleonastic writing, the well-known abbreviation for *re* (or *er*) being attached to the *r*. This would then be similar to cases where ou^{ur} stands for o^{ur}, which former I transcribe by our. I have, however, for the sake of consistency and in accordance with the principles of the E. E. T. S., in every case printed re for *r* with the curl.

The readings of the various texts are all given in full at the bottom of the pages, when they represent variations of meaning; mere orthographical variations, or phonetic ones of no consequence, have not been reproduced. The reader has thus in every case the full available material before him by which he may judge for himself in questions concerning the metrics and language of Lydgate.

Conservatism—perhaps pushed too far—in reproducing the MS. has prevented me from putting in the final *e*'s, whenever the metre did not manifestly show that they were *absolutely* indispensable, especially at the end of the line, or the first half-line. To quote a case to the point, I believe that Lydgate read line 1042 just as Chaucer read line 442 of the *Parlement of Foules;* I have, however, not added an *e* to *fressh*, as T does not give it, and the line is, as it stands, a regular Lydgate-line. I readily grant that this method may be too cautious; but then we avoid the necessity of introducing further questionable alterations on this already slippery ground.

PART II.

'Επειδή καὶ τὸν οἶνον ἠξίους
πίνειν, ξυνεκποτέ' ἐστί σοι καὶ τὴν τρύγα.

CHAPTER V.

LYDGATE'S METRE.

§ 1. *Lydgate's metrical forms in general.*

A CONSIDERABLE portion of the discussions in the following Chapters will consist in setting forth Lydgate in the light of an epigone of a more resplendent epoch, from which but a few stray rays found their way into the dull, dark period of the 15th century. Not least do we perceive this epigonic aspect of the monk's poetry when we examine its outward garb. Lydgate is entirely dependent on Chaucer in the choice of all his principal metres. He found the beautiful and wonderfully harmonious versification of Chaucer ready made to hand, and he thought it best to adopt it without more ado. Thus Chaucer's principal metric forms are represented in the monk's works, transformed, it is true, by many a license, into the peculiar Lydgatian structure of verse, which anything but improves upon that employed by Chaucer. The metrical forms mostly used by Lydgate are the following:—

A. The 7-line stanza ("rhyme royal," five-beat lines, with the sequence of rhymes ababbcc). This stanza is employed in the *Falls of Princes*, *Life of Our Lady*, *Court of Sapience*, *Edmund and Fremund*, *Albon and Amphabel*, *Assembly of Gods*, *Black Knight*, *Chorl and Bird*, *Æsop*, *De duobus Mercatoribus*, *Flour of Curtesie*, *Secreta Secretorum*, and in part of the *Temple of Glas*, not to mention the minor poems.

B. The metre ranking second in importance is the heroic couplet, where two five-beat iambic lines rhyming with each other form the unit of the metrical system. This is the metre of the most important of the *Canterbury Tales*, the *Legend of Good Women*, etc.; the epic metre of Chaucer by way of eminence. In imitation of his master, Lydgate employed it in his two most prominent epic works, the *Troy-Book* and the *Story of Thebes*. Part of the *Temple of Glas* is also in this metre.

C. The third metrical form of importance is the four-beat couplet, the metre of Gower's *Confessio Amantis*, the *Hous of Fame*, the *Romaunt of the Rose*, etc. Lydgate has employed it in *Reason and Sensuality*, and in the verse-translation of Deguileville's first *Pilgrimage*.

These afore-mentioned metres are also employed in many minor poems, where, of course, numerous other metrical forms also appear, especially the 8-line stanza. Of Lydgate's prose-writing[1] only one certain specimen seems to be extant, namely, the *Serpent of Division*; whether the prose-translation of Deguileville's second *Pilgrimage* was done by Lydgate, seems to me extremely doubtful.

As I have already intimated, the *Temple of Glas* is written in two of the above metres used alternately, namely, the heroic couplet and the 7-line stanza. The former of these is, speaking generally, employed in the epic parts of the poem, whilst the stanzas are used for the lyrical parts. But it is true that this distinction is not maintained strictly throughout the poem; occasionally narrative appears in the stanzas, whilst on the other hand, the long soliloquy of the Knight is written in couplets (ll. 567—693). Toward the end of the poem, we have a "Ballade" (ll. 1341—1361), *i. e.* three 7-line stanzas with a refrain, the last lines of the stanzas being substantially the same (see ten Brink, *Chaucer's Sprache und Verskunst*, p. 213). The three rhymes a, b, c, required to make up a stanza, are, moreover, in this form of the "ballade," identical in all three

---

[1] "Carmina quoque latina composuit, & in soluta oratione nonnulla," says the not altogether dependable Bale, *Summarium*, 1548, fol. 203 a.

stanzas; in our present one they end in *-ist, -ere, -inne*. We have a ballad of similar structure and function in the Prologue to the *Legend of Good Women* (ll. 249—269); also at the end of the *Flour of Curtesie*, frequently in the Envoys of the *Falls of Princes;* again in the *Isle of Ladies*, ll. 2213—2233, and at the end of the *Court of Sapience;* in the last two poems, however, the burden alone recurs, with slight variations; the rhymes *a* and *b* are different in the three stanzas. Our present ballad, which can only boast of identical rhymes in three consecutive stanzas, is but one of Lydgate's less brilliant feats in the art of rhyming; he has elsewhere envoys consisting of a considerable number of stanzas—in one case (*Falls of Princes*, fol. 66 *d*, etc.) amounting to nineteen—in which the three rhymes *a, b, c* of the first recur in all the following ones.

§ 2. *The Structure of the Verse.*

Lydgate himself was not very proud of his metre. He explains his system to us in the following lines from the *Troy-Book* (fol. E, *b*), which, if they do not reflect great credit upon his metrical art, are at least delightfully candid :

> "And trouthe of metre I sette also a-syde ;
> For of that art I hadde as tho no guyde
> Me to reduce, whan I went a-wronge :
> I toke none hede nouther of shorte nor longe."

Accordingly, poor Daun John's metre has been very severely criticized ; Ritson says that there are scarcely three lines together of pure and accurate metre, and Professor Skeat has even as late as 1884 the following sentence in his Preface to the *Kingis Quair* (p. xxxii) : "The net result is that the lines of James I., like the lines of Chaucer, are *beautifully musical*, and quite different from the halting lines of Lydgate." Nor need we wonder that a juster estimate of Lydgate's metre was not sooner arrived at. There is hardly a good critical text of Lydgate's writings existing, and the metre in the corrupt MSS. and Prints deserves indeed the severest strictures that have been laid upon it. There are, in the later MSS., and particularly in some of the prints, hundreds and thousands of such halting lines as

> "In Wiltshire | of Englond | two priestes | there were,"

which seem to have simply no metre at all ; in the present instance the line can only be scanned, so far as I can see, by one means, namely, by the assumption that Lydgate intended to introduce Firdausî's line into English poetry. The greatest wonder to me is how the public of the time of Caxton and his immediate followers could read these things as verses; their ears must surely have been singularly impenetrable to anything like rhythmical harmony. If, however, we go back to Lydgate himself, the case is after all not so bad. The monk thinks it great fun to make himself out worse than he really is—a peculiarity of which we shall have to say more in Chapter X—and we know that even his great master Chaucer alludes humorously to possible defects in his metre.

The most successful attempt to set forth Lydgate's metrical peculiarities, is, so far as I know and am able to judge, Professor Schipper's account in his *Englische Metrik*, I, § 196. My own observations, based on a critical text, tend to confirm the results arrived at by the Professor, and I think there can remain no doubt as to the correctness of Schipper's views in general, although in many particulars I cannot agree with his scanning of Lydgate's lines. We may say, roughly speaking, that Lydgate has five types of the five-beat line— even if we make no distinction between lines with strong (monosyllabic) and weak (dissyllabic) rhymes.

A. The regular type, presenting five iambics, to which, as to the other types, at the end an extra-syllable may be added. There is usually a well-defined cæsura after the second foot, but not always. Examples:

Line 1: For thóu3t, constréint, || and gréuous héuines[se].

B. Lines with the trochaic cæsura, built like the preceding, but with an extra-syllable before the cæsura. Examples:

L. 77: There wás eke Ísaude — || & méni anóþir mó.
L. 91: And máni a stóri, || mo þéu I rékin cán.
L. 120: List óf his gódhode || his fóurme tó transmwe.
L. 1093: Wherfóre, as Vénus || list þís matér to guíe.

This redundant syllable before the cæsura is often found in Chaucer, and, again, in the Elizabethan dramatists, and greatly contributes towards giving variety to this metre, which, in less skilful hands, easily becomes monotonous. This "epic" cæsura is also well-known in Romance poems (see Tobler, *Vom französischen Versbau*, p. 69, etc.), particularly in Italian, French, and Provençal. In our poem this type is very common; the following lines either must be read, or are best read according to it: 39, 102, 105, 164, 198, 227, 244, 276, 298, 329, 367, 401, 406, 409, 429, 444, 463, 484, 541, 543, 553, 609, 678, 679, 690, 698, 722, 750, 759, 770, 792, 797, 801, 835, 853, 859, 864, 898, 953, 960, 1000, 1017, 1034, 1038, 1053, 1073, 1078, 1089, 1100, 1126, 1164, 1176, 1188, 1206, 1237, 1302.

Chapter V.—Lydgate's Metre.

I believe there are many more lines which we may suppose Lydgate to have read in this way; and, again, there are a great many others about which it is impossible to decide.

C. The peculiarly Lydgatian type, in which the thesis is wanting in the cæsura, so that two accented syllables clash together. Examples:

L. 905 : For spécheles ǁ nóþing máist þou spéde.
L. 309 : Enbróuded wás ǁ ás men mýȝte sé.
L. 1200 : Siþ nóon but shé ǁ máy þi sóres sóund.
L. 1368 : Me þóuȝt I wás ǁ cást as íu a tráunce.
L. 1398 : If ény wórd ǁ ín þe bé myssáide,
L. 579 : Hou éuer gód ǁ fórto réken áll.
L. 580 : Myȝt máke a þíng ǁ só celéstiál.

This line is peculiar to Lydgate, or, at least, is more developed in his works than anywhere else. The second half of the line is here treated, as the whole line is in type D, the first syllable, so to say, being cut off. The development of this type may, to a certain degree, also be due to the increasing tendency to drop the final *e*. This type is very common in all Lydgate's works, and our *Temple of Glas* exhibits many lines of this peculiar metrical structure, the most important of which I enumerate in the following list: Ll. 18, 63, 127, 159, 245, 246, 255, 412, 434, 485, 491, 503, 536, 567, 578, 592, 681, 689, 767, 794, 836, 845, 848, 849, 858, 911, 913, 942, 1005, 1028, 1030, 1049, 1084, 1106, 1141, 1145, 1150, 1261, 1270, 1328, 1373, 1395.

D. The acephalous or headless line, in which the first syllable has been cut off, thus leaving a monosyllabic first measure. Example:

L. 1396 : Unto hír ǁ & tó hir éxcellénce ;
L. 1311 : Óf musíke, ǁ ay díde his bísynés ;
L. 1158 (?) : Róte þin hért, ǁ and vóide dóublenés.

Most likely we must add l. 489 ; Lydgate, I should think, read *Thánking*; Gower would read *Thankènde*. There is hardly another *certain* example of this type in the *Temple of Glas*. For although the text of this poem can, in general, be reconstructed with sufficient certainty, yet there are, just with respect to this particular question, certain discrepancies between the two groups **A** and **B**, which allow of an ambiguous interpretation : namely, either G and S exhibit the true old reading, which represented a more regular type ; or, G and S show a tendency to tamper with the metre, considered deficient by them, and especially to do away with these monosyllabic first measures.

Chapter V.—Lydgate's Metre.

I am inclined to think that the second interpretation holds good in the majority of cases (cf. Chapter IV, § 1). Thus, I think, we must consider lines 808 and 870 as acephalous; so also l. 265 (G and Prints alone exhibiting an alteration), perhaps also 79. Lines 9 and 954 may be doubtful.

E. Lines with trisyllabic first measure. The occurrence of such lines in our poem is uncertain; but two lines may belong to this class, if we read them in the following way:

L. 781 : Thắt wăs féiþful fóund, til hém depártid dépe;

L. 1029 : Ănd ăs férforþe ás my wíttes cón concéyue.

Lines 496 and 1037 do not belong to this class; *this is* is to be read *this'*, as a monosyllable; see, for instance, Chaucer's *Parlement of Foules*, 411 and 650.

In many cases it is, however, impossible to classify a line as belonging incontestably to any particular one of the above-named types. It not unfrequently happens with Lydgate, as with all doggerel-poets who have not a sensitive ear for rhythm, that his verses can be read in two or three different ways. Type A and C particularly may often seem to have equal claims to a line, according as we read or drop the final *e* before the cæsura. For instance, l. 3 belongs to type C, if we read *went*, as the MS. has it; but it belongs to type A, if we read *wentë*, sounding the final *e*. In our present case it is impossible to decide: Lydgate usually sounds the *e* of the weak preterit, but he has also unquestionably *went* in l. 546. The same holds good of types A and B; for instance, l. 395; *clerep* may be a monosyllable or a dissyllable. Again, type C and D might lay claim to one and the same line; for instance, l. 63, which may be read:

Hou þát she wás ‖ fálsed óf Iasón ; *or:*

Hoú þat shé ‖ was fálsed óf Iasón.

In cases like the last I am inclined to assign the line to type C, as there are so many more indisputable instances of it than of type D.

I must add here that Lydgate seems sometimes to have a double thesis; but the instances are rare and uncertain in our poem. This may be the case in ll. 1082, 1170, 1172; 910, 1212, all of which, however, are uncertain,[1] inasmuch as they either present doubtful

---

[1] So are almost all the examples, adduced by Schipper, p. 495, in support of the double thesis: we have most likely to scan: For thĕ sixte Hérry; *wedyr*, in line 2, is treated as a monosyllable, to be pronounced somewhat in the same way as modern French *quat'* for *quatre* (words in *re* or *le* are very commonly so treated by Lydgate; cp. the line quoted by Schipper on p. 497); in line 3 I

readings, or may be scanned smoothly by slurring. Further, Lydgate
very often makes the arsis fall on unaccentuated syllables; for instance: Hertès, 1097, 1211; Demèn, 872; vndìr, 809, 1111, 1213;
Whilòm, 816; Fairèst, 1341; Opìr, 1038; Makìng, 939; Singỳng,
1340; Ledìn, 239; Gladèst, 703; Passèþ, 252, etc.

Again, alliteration, particularly in the form of alliterating formulæ,
is very common in Lydgate. Many words, like *servise, fortune, beaute*,
etc., have a double accent, perhaps to a greater extent than in Chaucer.
Elisions, slurrings, hiatus, synizesis, etc., occur very much in the same
manner as in Chaucer. I think I had better leave a careful and
detailed synopsis of these phenomena to some special treatise on Lydgate's metre; the question of the final *e*, which it was absolutely
necessary to investigate closely for the construction of the text, will
be fully discussed in the following Chapter.

§ 3. *The Rhyme.*

The rhyme is, in general, pure and skilfully handled. The
principles followed by Lydgate are much the same as those of
Chaucer, for which reason I will only draw attention to certain
points which are of special interest or which are peculiar to Lydgate.

As to the quality of the rhyme-vowel, Lydgate makes no difference
between open and close sounds; open and close *o* or *e* being treated
exactly alike. For instance: wo : do 1370, so : do 637, also : do 902
(compare, however, with regard to these examples, ten Brink, § 31,
72); stoode (O.E. stôd) : abode (O.E. âbâd), *Falls of Princes*, fol. 9 c
and 21 a; wode (O.E. wôd) : abrode, *F. of Pr.* 22 b. *Drede* rhymes
with *rede* (O.E. rêd) 641, 1367; with *lede* (O.E. lêdan) 1198; with
hede (O.E. hêafod) 526; with *womanhede* 764; with *mede* (O.E. mêd)
352, 413, and *spede* (O.E. spêd) 681. *Speche*'(O.E. sprêc) rhymes
with *leche* (O.E. lêce) 917, and with *seche* (O.E. sêcan) 1166; *clene*
(O.E. clêne) with *grene* (O.E. grêne) and *to sene* (O.E. tô sêonne)
504, &c. (cp. again ten Brink, § 25). Similarly, no difference is made
between *ei* and *ai*, for instance: maide (O.E. mægden) : leide (O.E.
legdon) 207; peine : complaine 145, 723, 942; disdein : vain 155,
etc. In three cases we find an assonance[1] in place of the rhyme:

---

should scan : of cólour fúll cov'náble ; in the 5th and 6th line *for* and *the* are
probably to be omitted ; read further in the 6th line *at thentring*, and in the 9th
The childre of Seth; in ll. 7, 8 and 4 we have probably to accentuate súpport, ré-
port, dévise, if, indeed, we have not, in the last case, to substitute *wise* for *devise.*

[1] Assonances in the *Black Knight* have been pointed out by Skeat, in the
Academy, Aug. 10, 1878, p. 144, col. 1: forjnged : excused, 274; ywreke :
clepe, 284.

ll. 125, 126 ascape : take ; ll. 856, 858, 859 : perfourme : refourme : mourne; and ll. 1017, 1018 : accepte : correcte. We need not blame the monk too much for this oversight ; for sometimes, assonances are put unawares by poets who are particularly conspicuous for the purity of their rhymes, such as Chaucer (see *ten Brink*, § 329), and *Robert of Gloucester* (see Pabst, *Die Sprache der me. Reimchronik des R. von Gloucester*, § 4).

Of course there are plenty of cheap rhymes in Lydgate ; suffixes, such as -(*n*)*esse*, *-ful*, *-hede*, rhyme frequently with each other ; we have further in the *Temple of Glas*, binde : unbinde, 1269 ; liȝt : liȝt, 1341 ; herte : smerte, etc.; in one case (ll. 1013, 1016) Lydgate repeats the same word *wise* to rhyme with itself. Lydgate, as well as Chaucer, uses double forms of the same word for rhyming purposes; thus *deye* rhymes with *obeye* in ll. 587 and 772, with *suie*, 983 ; but it rhymes also, in the form *dye*, with *fantasie* and *specifie*, l. 514 ; with *crie*, 998. We have, moreover, *swete* rhyming with *hete* 510 ; but *soote* rhyming with *rote* and *bote*, 458. *eye* is made to rhyme with lie, 73, Emelie 106, regalie 262, deye 232, and was evidently pronounced ȳe. The rhymes prove that Lydgate often used the Kentish *e* for O.E. *y* ; in our poem we have thus *lest* (: *best* : *rest*), 483 ; the Tanner-MS., however, writes in all cases where the word occurs, *list* or *lust*. We find, further, *mynde*, l. 732, rhyming with *ende* and *sende;* and, again, l. 1241, mynd : ende. Compare, on the other hand, the rhymes mynde : finde, ll. 741 and 830 ; kynd : mynde : behind, 343.[1] Romance words in *-oun* are very common ; the rhymes prove that Lydgate sounded the vowel as a long *u* (as in Modern-English *ruth*) : soun : lamentacioun, 197 ; toun : Palamoun, 101 ; doun : lamentacioun, 566 ; prisoun : adoune, 647 ; compassioun : renoun : adoun, 926. But we have also rhymes like Iason : anon : gone, *F. of Princes*, fol. 11 *d*, &c. (cp. ten Brink, § 71).

A peculiarity of Lydgate's is that he frequently rhymes words ending in *-ire* with those in *-ere*. This has several times been pointed out ; as by Sauerstein, in *Lydgate's Æsopübersetzung*, p. 17 (bottom) ; Prof. Zupitza, in the *Deutsche Litteraturzeitung*, 1886, col. 850 ; Koeppel, *Mitteilungen zur Anglia*, 1890, p. 92. We have the following rhymes in the *Temple of Glas:* chere : desire, 315, 563, 729 ; praiere : desire, 543 ; daunger : desire, 776 ; pantere : desire,

---

[1] See, on the promiscuous use of *i* and Kentish *e* in the Suffolk-dialect, Horstmann, *Introduction to Bokenam*, p. xi ; Hoofe, in *Englische Studien*, VIII, 239.

603; wire : spere, 271; зеrе : desire, 1201; daunger : fire, 631; зеrе : fire, 473. The regular form for the words: *continue, discover, recover,* is in Lydgate contune (ll. 1333 ; 390); discure (ll. 629 ; 916, 161); recure (l. 1226). Impure rhymes seem to be : yonder : wonder, 577,[1] and socoure : endure, 818; *socoure* elsewhere rhymes with words in *-oure,* not in *-ure.*[2]

I have now to say a few words on the number of the syllables that form the rhyme. There can be no doubt that we have the strong, monosyllabic rhyme in lines like 11, 12 ; 15, 16 ; 77, 78, etc.; the weak or dissyllabic rhyme in lines like 5, 6 ; 99, 100 ; 107, 108, etc. In cases like 23, 24 (*place* : *face*); 103, 104 (*smert* : *hert*) the rhyme would be certainly dissyllabic in Chaucer. The question is whether this also holds good for Lydgate's language. Now we cannot deny that some strong arguments might be brought forward in support of the theory that the final *e* in such cases is mute in Lydgate. In the present poem Lydgate has the rhymes grace : trespas, l. 1031 ; assaie (*infin.*) : nay, 643 ; assaie : say (I saw, O.E. seah), 693 ; peine : agein, 1138 ; peine : wellbesein, 1169 ; chaine : tweyn (but *tweyne* is perhaps dissyllabic, as in Chaucer), 354, 1106 ; repente (*infin.*) : entent : sent, 497 ; repente (*infin.*) : entent : jugement, 1076 (*entent* is usually a dissyllable in Lydgate, see ll. 304, 384, 1335); Iocound : founde (*pp.*) : abounde (*infin.*), 1174 ; despit : wite (O.E. wīte), 165—*wite* is also a monosyllable in l. 208—; in l. 1049, we have, I suppose, to read *pastë* (p. t.), to rhyme with *castë* (infin.). Sometimes we also meet with the rhyme *ý* : ie in Lydgate's works, although not in the *Temple of Glas;* for instance, more than once in the *Black Knight.* All this shows that there is in Lydgate a considerable advance beyond Chaucer in the dropping of the final *e* in Romance words, or rather, to express it more exactly, Lydgate does not always refrain from doing at the end of a verse what Chaucer does not hesitate to do in the middle. Chaucer would read vílainý only in the middle of a line, Lydgate would do the same also at the end in the rhyme. With Teutonic words the monk seems to be far more careful; I can find only one example of such rhymes in our poem which would be inadmissible in Chaucer's system,

---

[1] This rhyme, however, occurs also in Chaucer, *Man of Law's Tale*, l. 920 ; in *Havelok* 922 we have the spelling *yunder.* We find this rhyme elsewhere in Lydgate, for instance *Falls of Princes*, fol. 20 *b.*
[2] We have the rhyme *ye socour : youre cure* also in the *Romaunt of the Rose*, l. 3539. The language of this poem often reminds one of Lydgate, both in its rhymes and in its vocabulary.

Chapter V.—Lydgate's Metre. lxiii

namely (ll. 392, etc.), sone (O.E. sôna) : mone (O.E. môna) : don (O.E. ge-dôn). The same rhyme-system occurs in the *Falls of Princes*, fol. 174 c. We may, however, note that *sone* in Chaucer is always a monosyllable in the middle of the line; see *ten Brink*, § 327.

As, however, the following chapter will show that the final *e* is sounded by Lydgate nearly in all cases in which Chaucer sounds it, I believe that Lydgate thought it proper to read the words in question as dissyllables, although his Suffolk-dialect may sometimes lead him astray. As the matter is not *absolutely* certain, I have refrained from any interference with the Tanner-MS. in such cases, in so far that I did not add any final *e*'s at the end of the line or immediately before the cæsura, even where I believe Lydgate would have sounded them. The MS., with its very numerous sins of omission and commission in this respect, thus shows us all the more clearly how matters stood in general with regard to the final *e* shortly after 1400.

I believe that according to the types set forth above, nearly all Lydgate's lines, perhaps even the very unruly ones of the *Story of Thebes*, can be made to scan tolerably. Still, the above-given exposition of Lydgate's metrical system will seem little calculated to bear out the statement by Berkenhout, *Biographia Literaria*, p. 317 (copied in A. D. Burrowes's *Modern Encyclopædia*, VII, 201), according to which Lydgate's versification is "much more harmonious" (*sic*) than that of Chaucer. But, on the other hand, we must at least grant that, if the metre of Lydgate is "halting," there is, as a rule, method in this halting.

CHAPTER VI.

LYDGATE'S LANGUAGE.

§ 1. *General Characteristics.*

THE first thing that strikes us in comparing Lydgate's and Chaucer's language is that the first is a great deal more modern than the latter. This has already been frequently noticed, and is in the main correct. The modern stamp, however, of Lydgate's language seems to result principally from the choice of words, rather than from phonology and inflexions. Chaucer, as compared with Lydgate, uses many more concrete words, which are mostly of Old-English origin, and, to a great extent, are now obsolete or have completely died out; Lydgate, especially in his more pretentious works, uses many abstract words of French or Latin origin, which in most cases are still in use or are at least intelligible. As he has, however, an extensive vocabulary at his disposal, many interesting words rarely met with in English literature are found in his writings, so that his name must be of frequent occurrence in historical dictionaries of the English language.

In accordance with his propensity to expatiate on his own qualities, Lydgate has also bequeathed to us his opinion on his own language, which is, of course, again expressed in that same self-deprecatory, apologetic style which characterizes his other utterances concerning his own abilities and performances. Among the many passages in which he reviles the "rudeness" of his own language, the most interesting is the one in the prologue to the *Court of Sapience*,[1] which runs thus:

> "I knowe my selfe moost naked in all artes,
> My comyn vulgare eke moost interupte;
> And I conuersaunte & borne in the partes
> Where my natyfe langage is moost corrupte,
> And with moost sondry tonges myxte & rupte.
> O lady myn, wherfore I the beseche (*Clio*)
> My muse amende, dresse, forge, mynysshe & eche."

That Lydgate occasionally uses dialectal forms varying from those of Chaucer, is certain. The principal phonetic peculiarities, so far as they are apparent in the rhymes, have been noted in § 3 of the last chapter. If it is true that Chaucer was Lydgate's "master" in more than a figurative sense, and that he "corrected" some of the early poems of his young admirer, he would doubtless have pointed out, as things to be avoided, these dialectal peculiarities, the dropping of the final e in certain instances, and type C of Lydgate's metre.

It would be useless here to give a full analysis of the sound-system of the *Temple of Glas*, as it would be almost entirely a repetition of ten Brink's book on Chaucer's language. Again, there is little difference in the inflexional system of Chaucer and Lydgate; but as there has been some doubt about this point, especially with regard to the sounding of the unaccented syllables, I must deal with Lydgate's inflexions in greater detail. I shall therefore point out the instances in the *Temple of Glas* which tend most to throw light upon this question, hoping that the ground on which we stand will have been made firm by the metrical investigations of the preceding chapter, and by the text-criticism contained in Chapter III. A few

---

[1] I must, however, note here that the genuineness of this prologue has been called into question; see Warton-Hazlitt III, 60, note 4; Blades, Caxton II, 115; Ames, *Typographical Antiquities* (1749), p. 67.

further illustrations of certain points, gathered here and there from Lydgate's other works, may not, I hope, be unwelcome.

§ 2. *The Inflexions of the Temple of Glas. Declension.*
I. *Substantives.—Strong Masculines and Neuters.*

Nom. and Accus. without ending; inorganic e in weyë,[1] acc. of *wey* (l. 897, 639 ?[2]) See ten Brink, *Chaucer's Sprache und Verskunst,* § 199 note; Sachse, *Das unorganische e im Orrmulum,* p. 7.

Genitive in ës: liuës 1196; daiësye 74. Dissyllables: heuens 715. *Dative in ë*: kyndë 224; goldë (: biholdë)? 112.

Plural in ës (often written *is*[3] in MS. T): opis 59; stremës 252, 1101, 1342; stonës 301, 310; harmës 314, 618, 686; stormës 515; bemys 718; weiës 1168, etc.—In the *Secreta Secretorum* (MS. Ashmole 46, fol. 102 *b*) occurs the rhyme: desirs (*read* deseris): cler is; in the *Falls of Princes,* 111 *b,* we have *thestates* rhyming with the Latin genitive "*lese magestates*" (*sic*); *ib.* 127 *d*: warres: far is; *Edmund* III, 634, ground is: woundis; in the *Pilgrimage* 172 *a*: Instrumentys: entent ys. But we have also rhymes like succours: deuinours: shoures, *Falls of Princes,* 19 *b.* The neuters also usually end in -ës; þingis 167; yeris 202; wordys 320, etc.; kneis 459; soris 602, 1200; shottes 788; wittes 1029. The old Plural without an ending occurs in *folk* 193, 400.

ja-stems. witę l. 208 (O.E. wíte). But ë in *Pilgrimage,* fol. 216 *b*:
"Ther-whyles the chesë fyl a-doun."

I am not aware of a good example, in the *Temple of Glas,* of the ë in *i-* or *u-*stems; but compare for the latter, *Pilgrimage,* 98 *a*:
"How goddys sonë, man to saue"...
ib., 252 *b*: "My wodë shal on euery syde"...

The octosyllables of the *Pilgrimage of man* and of *Reason and Sensuality* lend themselves much better to a grammatical analysis of Lydgate's inflexions than his five-beat line.

---

[1] ë means that the *e* is sounded, ę, that it is mute.
[2] The frequent notes of interrogation mean that the metre does not absolutely warrant the sounding of the final *e*; in most instances, however, I am inclined to read it as a full syllable. In some doubtful cases I have refrained from putting dots to the *e*. I may remark here that, on account of the ambiguity of Lydgate's metre, *conclusive* examples on this point are rarer than might be supposed at first sight. In some few cases it will be found that I have here decided with more absolute certainty in favour of sounding the final *e* than when I first constructed my text.
[3] The Suffolk-dialect shows a predilection for *i, y* in the endings; in O. Bokenam's *Legends* we have rhymes like knelyn: mawdelyn (8, 1098); see Horstmann's *Introduction,* p. xi. Cp. also, with respect to Chaucer, *ten Brink,* § 62.

lxvi   Chapter VI.—Lydgate's Language.

Strong Feminines.

Nom. ends usually in ë : lovë 1317 ; dedë 341 ; helthë 812 ; rouþë 873. In the case of *love*, the ë is due to O.E. u ; in the other instances it crept into the nominative by analogy of the oblique cases. See *Sachse*, §§ 7 and 8 ; *ten Brink*, § 207.
But we have also love 1143, 1256, 1265 ; drede 672 ; tale 903.
Genitive in ës : lovës 86, 125, 183, 573, 633.   worldis 1208.
Accus. and Dative end a.) in ë : ʒouþë 448 ; trouþë 455, 1081 ? 1102, 1235, 1249 ; whilë 549 ; specchë (?) 760 ; talë 910 ; salvë 922 ; helpë 952 ; myrþë 1177 ; lovë 1337.
b.) *in e :* ʒouþe 199 (*rhymes with* couþ ; the same rhyme occurs *Falls of Princes*, 211 *d* and 214 *a*) ; while 217, 626 ; love 327, 1351 ; worlde 729 ; rouþe 1054 ; trouþe 1277.
Plural in ës : woundis 816 ; sorowis 967 ; talës 1182 (?).
Old Dative Plural : whilom 568, 816.

n-stems.

a.) *Masculines.* Nomin. ending in ë : hopë 643, 676 (?) ; timë 1204 (?).
Nom. in e : time 1194, 1377.   mone *rhymes with* don 394 ; plei 183 (*plei* is a monosyllable also in Chaucer, see *ten Brink* § 211).
Oblique cases in ë : hopë 657, 892.
Plural in ës : sterrës (?) 252, 1341 ; dovuës 541 ; lippës 1049.
b.) *Feminines.* Nom. in ë : sunnë 396 ; hertë 337, 829 (?)—Nom. in e : herte 775.—lady (O.E. hlǽfdige) remains the same in all cases : Nom. 250 etc. ; Gen. 1160 ; Dat. 158, 966, etc. ; Acc. 134, etc.
Genitive in ës or ë : hertës 340, 502, 915, 1212 ; sunnë bemes, *Falls of Princes*, 31 *d* ; hertë roote, *Pilgrimage*, 224 *b*.
Dative and Accus. in ë : erþë 581 ; sunnë 21 (?) ; hertë 80, 312, 363, 726, 756, 825, 839, 888 (?), 920, 945, 986, 1044, 1182, 1188, 1205 ; wekë 1201.
Plural in ës : hertës 323, 529, 619, 1088, 1095, etc. ; *genitive,* hertis 1083.
c.) *Neuters :* (e)yʒë (?) 105, 231, 262, 850 ; Plural (e)yʒën 40, 582, 1047, 1103.

Romance Nouns.

These also usually keep their *e*. We have formë 120 ; forcë 178, 1247 ; gracë 333, 733 ; sperë (sphere) 396 ; entailë 37 ; peinë 798, 1260 (but compare the rhymes in 1140, 1169) ; festë 473 ; joyë 1129 (but joye 880?) ; inkë 961 ; rosë 1042 ; Troië 95 ; Romë 101.

Chapter VI.—Lydgate's Language.   lxvii

But we have also cause 953; Cupide 855; and when the accent is thrown back: Fórtune 519; bálaunce 641; bállade 1338; sérvise 155, 719.—In the *Secreta Secretorum*, fol. 110 a, we have "som" (= French *somme*) rhyming with the Latin genitives "principum" and "virtutum."

Plural in ës: billës 50; peynës 479, 668, 805, 951, 1001, 1286; vicës 1181.

Polysyllabic words form their plural in es: sérvauntes 1126.

II. *Adjectives.*

The *ja-stems* keep their e: sootë 192; newë 681, 657 (?), 606 (?), 7 (weak); trwë (weak) 71. We have also mychë (= O.E. mycel), l. 941.

Plural. It is difficult to find good examples of Nom. and Acc. Plural in the *Temple of Glas*. It seems we must read somë in l. 147, although Chaucer has somë only in the rhyme (for instance, *Troil*. IV. 967); see *ten Brink*, § 255 and 327. In the *Ormmulum* we have sume, see *Sachse*, § 77; in Gower somë is very common; in *Reason and Sensuality*, fol. 287 a, we have the line:

"Sommë square and sommë rounde;"

similarly, in the *Pilgrimage*, fol. 52 b: "Sommë swyfft & sommë soffte;"
    ib., fol. 190 b: "With dedly synne as sommë do;"
    ib., fol. 76 b: "Sommë pressen to the table;"
ib., Cott. Tib. A. VII, fol. 58 b: "Sommë hyh and som[ë] lowe;"
Story of Thebes, fol. 371 b: "And bé Iasón ‖ sómë bókes tell."

But it is true, that in all other cases in the *Temple of Glas* we have some: 49, 50, 51, 151, 162, 169, 179, 244, 539. Most likely we have to read briʒtë in 705, but this would be the weak form here. We have also the Scandinavian boþë (the ë representing an older ending) 1294, 345, 790, 510 (?); also in 1108, 1224. Boþe occurs in l. 1084.

In the oblique cases we have ë: widë 204; goodë 462; allë (?) 807, 973, 1165; but alle, 752, 1351.

We have, of course, the distinction between the strong and weak adjective. The latter has an ë also in the Singular, being the continuation of fuller endings in Old-English. The weak adjective stands:

1. *After the definite article:* longë 12; fresshë 70, 93, 1042 (?); fairë 786; gretë 87, 787 (?), 984; holë 97; ʒungë 106; saddë 377; þe samë 841; þilkë 81; þe whiche 514; hardë 957; selfë 846; blakë (?) 330; riʒtë 975.—*ja-stems:* nwë 7; trwë 71.—Compare

e 2

also þo soþë 1002, and Skeat's Note to Group G, l. 662 of the *Canterbury Tales*.

For cases like *The bestë tau3t* (l. 292; cp. also l. 558, *the mostë*?), see *ten Brink*, § 246, end of note.

2. *After a demonstrative pronoun:* Thcse yongë 193; þis fairë 454.

3. *After a possessive pronoun:* hir gretë 265; my fullë 489, 830, 1383; his hiddë, 967; Oure hiddë 1087; myn hiddë 988; ȝoure gladë 1344; his ownë 535, 938; myn ownë 635; ȝoure oldë 1222. —But we have also: Hir sad 750; your hole 857; his long 1122.

4. *Before proper names:* fresshë May 184; ooldë Januari 185; ȝungë Piramus 780; óld Satúrne, or óldë Sáturne? 389 (*Sáturne olde* occurs in *Story of Thebes*, Prol., l. 3).—Cp. bright[ë] Phebus, *Story of Thebes*, Prol., l. 1.

These cases certainly confirm Zupitza's opinion on this treatment of the adjective; see *Deutsche Litteraturzeitung*, 1885, col. 610. I do not think that Freudenberger's attempts to explain away the respective cases in Chaucer quite hit the mark (*Ueber das Fehlen des Auftakts in Chaucers heroischem Verse*, p. 36, etc.).

5. *Before a Vocative:* clerë 715.

But we have no different form for the weak adjective of more than one syllable: The feiþful 378; The inward 1290; þis woful 936; ȝour dredful 717; my forseid 1389, etc.

Romance Adjectives.

*palë 4 (the asterisk means weak form); benygnë (?) *449, 1110 (?); *clerë 715; *justë 1331; *fersë 1236; *rudë 1393; and, of course, doublë 167, and humblë 472, 697, 925; but sóverain *415, 649.

III. *Numerals.*

twoo 348, 1255, 1314, and tweyn 354, 1081, 1104 (read tweynë?), 1298, 1322; fivë 831.

IV. *Pronouns.*

The same as in Chaucer. With regard to the final *e* I note: yourës (?) : showres 1215; doubtful yourcs 1076, 1130, 1134; similarly hires 593; þe whichë (?) 514; attë = at þe 405, etc.; hire 766, 783; but compare *Pilgrimage*, 229 *b*:

"Ded to hyrë the presente."
Ib., Cott. Tib. A. VII, fol. 96 *a* : "Towchynge hir[ë], the mercer."

It has been said that Lydgate uses the Scandinavian forms þeir, etc., throughout. This is not borne out by the MSS.; only the late

Prints gradually introduce these forms. Lydgate has always, like Chaucer, þey in the nominative, hir in the genitive, and hem in the dative and accusative.

V. Adverbs.

Formed from adjectives by adding ë. No decisive example in the *Temple of Glas*, but elsewhere in Lydgate; for instance, *Life of St. Edmund*, III, 1041 :

"Sweyn affraied loudë gan to crye."

Story of Thebes, fol. 358 a : "On whiche thing the kyng gan sorë muse."
Pilgrimage, fol. 231 b : "Thogh the bowe be strongë bent."

In the *Temple of Glas* we have longë (or long?) 38; derë (*ja-stem*) 1258, but see the various readings; sore̥ or sorë ? l. 180 (type A or B?); 1202 iliche̥ or lichë ? Other examples of adverbs in e are: þan 672, 799 (but þannë, which is particularly frequent in Gower, in l. 596?); oftë 69, 169, 193, 200, 231, 669; sone̥ 1185, and also in the rhyme, l. 392.—outë (?) 662 (cp. outëward 340, but outward 563); aboutë 28, 933 (used as a preposition); withoutë 154, 211, 308, 365, 379, 385, etc., etc.; atwixën 348; besidë 248.—aboue̥ 466.

Adverbs in -es: agaïnës 177, 181; nedës 232, 1063; atonës 458; onès (?) 725; hennës 481, 1025; towardis 1048; þennes (?) 1316; ellës 917 (elle̥s 1032; in 819, 1131 most likely ellës); always while̥s 172, 576, 738, 790, 1011, 1109, 1324. We have, of course, also the suffix -ly to form adverbs; further, forms like "of nwe," l. 615, "of hard" 1319, etc.

For an explanation of "The bestë tauȝt," in l. 292, I refer the reader to *ten Brink*, § 246, end of note: the sign ë of the weak adjective, properly belonging to *tauȝt*, is shifted to the adverb *best*.

VI. Composition.

The composition of words in Lydgate is effected on the same principles which we find in Chaucer, and, indeed, as early as in the *Orrmulum*; the e in particular, which stands between the two parts of the compound—be it organic or inorganic—being sounded by Lydgate as by Chaucer and Orrm. Thus we have : lodëster 612; spechëles 905; causëles 150; kyndënes 747; rekëles 918; hawë-thorn (O.E. hagaþorn) 505; of course, secrënes 900; secrëli 365; privëli 635, 1014; bisëly 1180; further, richëli 302; always humbëlly, humbëli (as if for humblëli) 491, 773, 852, 1047; benignëte 1296; benignëly 711, 849; jugëment 1079; duëte 800 (for the adjective duë, see *ten Brink*, § 239); surëte 1259; goodëly 851.

But we have nearly always mekẹli: 324, 371, 469, 482, 589, 868, 915, 994, 1084, 1105; mekëli occurs in 1281. Further, namẹli 229; softly 371; truli 431 (elsewhere trewëly); derknes 401, 1211, 1357; swetnes 403; meknes 76, 621; goodnes 745.

§ 3. *Conjugation.*

I need not dwell on the formation of the tenses of strong and weak verbs, as this is the same in Lydgate as in Chaucer. More important for our purpose are the endings of the verb, with regard to which I wish particularly to elucidate how far they were sounded as distinct syllables or not. I proceed at once to give the endings.

Infinitive in ën, ë: takë 13; biholdë 34; walkë 42; reportë 43; puttë 52; askë 164; wynnën 177; shapë 195; curën 205; makën 236; ledin 239; findë 242, etc. etc. (some sixty or seventy conclusive instances).

But sometimes we have also apocope of the ending: shewẹ 206; voidẹ 253; vufoldẹ (?) *rhyming with* bold 360; repentẹ 500; clerẹ 611; tel 663, 964; comẹ 924; farẹ 1063; berẹ 1234, and always havẹ 54, 165, 229, 375, 418, 425, etc. Dissyllables end in ẹ: guerdonẹ 1031; disseuer (: euer) 1314; rekin 91, 579. *n* kept in the rhyme : gon : one 26; gon : allone 548, but se : Penalope 68; se : tre 89; se : Canace 137. So also 233, 269, 302, 309, 612.

Gerund: We have to seinë : compleyne 1325; but also to seinẹ : again 157. Indecisive is l. 506 : to sene, *rhyming with* grene. We have further, to do : so 637; to do : wo 1371.

Indicative Present, first person, ends in ë (?) *and* ẹ : stondë 689 (infinitive?); takë (?) 769; axë (?) 800; want or wantë 951? menë or menẹ 1402? (see note). We certainly have þankẹ 1060, hauẹ 349, 366; and in polysyllables : mérvailẹ 585; tréspacẹ 1018.

Second person, in ëst: Enclynyst 324; Gladest 703; soroist 860; menyst 889. Also ẹst; MS. T even writes tast for takẹst 602. In rare cases we have the ending *-es*: thow tellys : bellys, *Pilgrimage* 102 *b*; thow pursues : stewes, *ib.*, fol. 141 *a*; thow tell[ys] : ellys, *ib.*, 275 *b*.

Third person in ëþ (no Umlaut in the stem-syllable) : abidëþ 222; fallẹþ 231; passëþ 252; surmountëþ 258; louëþ 1292, etc. Also ẹþ in comẹþ 656; contraction in saith 644, 653, etc.; sleiþ (: deþ) 782; fleith 603; liþ 722, 865; seþ 862 (the vowel comes from the infinitive); the þ of the ending is absorbed in the dental consonant at the end of the stem in forms like : siṯ 184 (but sittëþ 894, 1118); bitt

Chapter VI.—Lydgate's Language.

676; list 297, 314, etc.; stunt 890, 1259 (standëþ? 1186); bint 1096; fint 1263.

Besides the usual form in -eþ, Lydgate has also the northern form in -es (for singular and plural), not very frequently, but more so than Chaucer. So we have in the *Troy-Book* telles : welles $G_5 c$; dawes : wawes $M_4 d$; fyghtes : knyghtes $O_2 a$; endytes : rytes $Aa_3 a$; bytes : rytes $Aa_3 a$; *Falls of Princes* ledes : dedes, fol. 184 c; telles : shelles; 192 b; disdaynes : mountaines 194 a; *Secreta Secretorum* 125 a : techys : lechys; *Reason and Sensuality* 207 a : obeyes : ydeyes (ideas); tellys : wellys, 214 b; *Story of Thebes* leres : baneres, fol. 363 c; *Pilgrimage* ordeynys : chaumberleyn[y]s, 35 a; espyes : skyes 170 a; gouernys : posternys, 181 b; thynkes : drynkes 195 a; espyes : delycacyes 196 a; shynes : wynes 229 a; espyes : lyes 265 a; shewes : thewes, 275 b; pulles : bulles 296 a.

Plural in ën, ë: putten 166; lovë 167; passen 393; rejoicë 400; greven 663; knowë 723; witen? 797; causen 1343; bië 1351. Lydgate has also e in the rhyme, as the following passage from the *Court of Sapience*, $e_8 b$, proves, where the monk says of the dialecticians:

"With sophyms straunge maters they discusse,
And fast they crye oft : 'tu es Asinus'!"

list seems always to be a monosyllable, also when in the plural and in personal construction : 478, 482, 868, 983, 1000.

A remnant of the old ending seems to remain in haþ 171. We find this ending occasionally also in the rhyme; so in the *Troy-Book* $L_1 a$: they gothe : wrothe (so also *Pilgrimage*, fol. 52 b); they seyth : ffeyth, *Pilgrimage*, fol. 101 a. As has already been said, Lydgate uses also the northern form -es in the Plural : telles : elles *Troy-Book* $K_5 a$ and $Cc_4 c$; specifies : fantasies *Story of Thebes*, 363 b; duellys : ellys *Reason and Sensuality* 272 a; discriues : striues (noun), *Falls of Princes* fol. 145 b; shewes : thewes, *Pilgrimage* 180 b; men peyntes : seyntes 271 b; they lookys : bookys, 272 a; telles : elles, 303 a; ye tellys : ellys, ib. 152 a.

Subjunctive, Singular in ë, Plural in ën: þou felë 1178; most likely also þou aracë 894; þou fynë 910; perhaps þou herë 1184; but certainly þou hauę 896. *Plural :* ȝe takën 1124.

Imperative, Singular, second Person, no ending: Lat 1198, 1205; come 1214; takę 1174. Weak verbs : wissę (O.E. wissa) 637; lokę (O.E. lôca) 894; put 891, 1403; rotę (?) 1158. Romance words generally seem to have ë : voidë 1158; of course, suffrë 1161; auauntę 1172; sue 1180; remue 1182; but Tempest 1157.

Chapter VI.—Lydgate's Language.

Plural, second person, in ëþ: þinkiþ 391; Remembrëþ 398; trustëþ 412; doutëþ 426; Folowiþ 511; shapëþ 721; takëþ 808, 976; sufferiþ 812; grauntëþ 1034; latëþ 1140; settëþ 1240. *Ending eþ:* Comeþ 1272; Haueþ (= Haþ) 714. Moreover, we have *let* 878, 961, 1094, 1177, 1179, 1247, which may be a contraction (see Morris, *Prologue*, p. xxxvii, note *a*); latëþ occurs in l. 1140. Dissyllables : guérdoṇe 1139.

Participle Present, in -ing: persing 25; passing 226; Thanking 489 (have we to read Thankingë?), 498; sleping and dremyng 531; Sayyng 700, 1110; Making 939; Singyng 1340; Glading 1356; Prayeng 1384. We have certainly to read -ingë in the following lines from the *Pilgrimage*, fol. 166 *b* :

"Travayllyngë [*plural*] nyht & day."
Ib., fol. 170 *a* : " Remewyngë fro that place."

also in *R. & S.*, fol. 274 *a* : " Nor the ravysshingë sowns" (*weak form*).

The form in *-ende* (Gower's form) occurs in the rhyme, in *Falls of Princes* 173 *a:* shinend[e] : attende : Legende.[1]

Verbal noun, ending also in -ing: casting 105, 231 ; peping 180; bidding 509; cherisshing 869; compassing 871; in *-ingë* (?) : variynge (: wringë, *inf.*) 216.

Strong Preterit, with Ablaut as in Chaucer; I mention, sey (I saw), rhyming with lay 532, and with assai 694 (cp. *Troil.* II, 1265 : say : day). *Plural :* founḍe 216; Gunṇe 1305; always werẹ 47, 181, 199, 210, etc. We read, however, also *gunnë*, in the *Pilgrimage*, fol. 156 *a* :

"And as we wente & gon[në] talke ;"
similarly, *ib.*, fol. 284 *b* :

"The dropys gonnë for to glyde ;"
and even in the Singular, 2nd person, we have *comë:*

" Off thylke hous thow komë fro," *Pilgrimage*, fol. 16 *a* ;
" Off swych fylthe thow komë nouht," *ib.*, fol. 147 *b*.

But, again, we have *thow spak* (O.E. þû sprǣce), rhyming with *lak*, *Pilgrimage*, 177 *a*, and *thow gan* (O.E. gunne), rhyming with *man*, *ib.*, 264 *b*.

Subjunctive: werẹ 161, 605, 660, 679, 1131, 1291; nerẹ 555. But also in *ë* :

"Woldë god yt stoodë so," *Pilgrimage*, 172 *b*.

Weak Preterit. See *ten Brink*, § 194. *Ends a. in -ëd:* lastëd

---

[1] We have *-ende* also twice in O. Bokenam's *Legends:* lyuende 9, 377 ; diedende 12, 252. See Horstmann's *Introduction*, p. xii.

Chapter VI.—Lydgate's Language.

779 ; departid 781. *Plural:* pleynëd 151 ; louëd 157, 163 ; compleynëd 175.

b. in të, dë, t(e), d(c) *:* þouȝtë 15, 532, 694 ; nystë 17 ; myȝtë 68, 286, 595, 1021 ; mostë 61, 341 ; rouȝtë 939 ; mentë 1288 ; didë 80, 116, 945, 1055, 1233 ; woldë 591, 847, 893, 1143 ; sholdë 191, 372 ; hurtë 813 ; hadë 316, 578 ; pastë (?) 1049 ; castë (?) 1103. *Plural:* brentë 840 ; woldë (?) 658, 1017, 1027 ; criden 193 ; wenten 505 ; mighten 280 ; myȝtë 89, 137, 309 ; pastë (?) 1105. But we have e̩ in shulde̩ 668 ; wolde̩ 214 ; coude̩ 409 ; þouȝte̩ 21, 527 ; moste̩ 232 ; wente̩ 546 ; felte̩ 788 ; nyste̩ 1371 ; made̩ 994 ; hade̩ 202, 1372 ; calle̩d(e) 219 ; knele̩d(e) 697 ; wolde̩st 922.

Past Participle. Strong; ends *in* ën, ë: holpën 141, 376 ; foundën 1090, 1239 ; chosën 433 ;—*in* e̩: bounde̩ 990 ; ȝcue̩ 736. Note also sein (O.E. gesegen) 1377 ; further *done* : mone : sone 395, but *do* : also 903.

Weak, ends in ëd: Ioynëd 5 ; foundid 18 ; falsëd 63 ; Iturnëd 99, 116 ; Endurid 171 ; closid 362 ; wapëd 401, etc. etc. We have makëd 1120, but mad 1091, 1322, 1354.

Polysyllables, with the accent thrown back, end in -e̩d: Ráuysshe̩d 16 ; enlúmynd 283 ; cómpast 1053.

Contractions: knyt 338 ; put 397 ; I-hid 793 ; het (O.E. gehǽted) 842 ; hurt 615, etc. The prefix I- is very common, in Teutonic and Romance words : I-went 31 ; I-blent 32 ; I-slain 95 ; I-sett 47 ;—I-chaced 31 ; I-entred 201 ; I-stellified 136, etc. etc.

I hope the above examples have made it clear that Lydgate still pronounced the final *e*, or the *e* in unaccented inflexional syllables, in the main as Chaucer, and indeed even Orrm, pronounced it. Thus Lydgate decidedly stands in point of language, as in everything else, on the mediæval side of the great gulf that intervenes between Chaucer and the new school of poetry which arose in the 16th century. It is somewhat difficult to ascertain precisely to what extent the dropping of the final *e* gradually made itself felt in the metrical system of that age. Ellis (*On Early English Pronunciation*, I, 405) was inclined to make the time of Caxton the great turning-point as regards pronunciation in general ; so far as the dropping of the final *e* in poetry is concerned, my own observations tend to confirm his opinion.[1] Evidently the *e* first gave way in Romance words, and later on in those of Teutonic origin. This gradually led

---

[1] We have, however, as yet no minute analysis of the versification of Hawes, which might somewhat modify the above-expounded view.

to a phase in the language in which double forms—with mute or sounded *e*—were allowed and used to a great extent in poetry. This is already the case with Chaucer, and even more so with Lydgate and his followers. As we have pointed out above, this state of the language may even, with Lydgate (and Occleve), have led to a new metrical type, namely, our type C. After the middle of the 15th century, a time of great confusion in language and metre seems to have followed. The transcripts of the older poets made at that time, and the prints of their works by Caxton and his immediate successors, show palpably that the public of that day had lost all feeling for anything like regular metre. After this period of total decay and anarchy, we see not only how poetry itself, but also the language rises, as if new-born, out of this chaos; in Surrey, for instance, final syllables would be rarely sounded, which are silént in Modern English.

This question of sounding or dropping an *e* at the end of a word may at first sight seem a very insignificant thing; but, in reality, it entails a great change in the whole poetical phraseology. It means that nearly all inflexions lose their syllabic value, that ever so many dissyllabic words become thus monosyllables, and ever so many time-honoured formulæ, inherited by one poet from another, become no longer practicable. Lydgate could unhesitatingly take from his master Chaucer any such forms as *the shenë sunnë, the grenë levës, smalë foulës, this yongë lordës namë, oldë stories tellën us;* but the new school of poetry, in the 16th century, could not easily adopt such archaic stock-phrases without their jarring on the ear of contemporary readers. Instead of Chaucer's *my grénë yéares*, Surrey has to say *my frésh green yéars;* instead of Chaucer's *sóotë flóurës*, Sackville says *sóot fresh flówers;* and for the dropt two syllables in Chaucer's *smálë fóulës,* he makes again up by an addition: *smáll fówls flócking.*

Still these examples will show that the difficulty in point of language was in no way so great that it might not be easily overcome by a real genius, who had sufficient originality to strike out a new path for himself. Our Lydgate would not, of course, have been the man to do this, had it been necessary; but, according to our analysis of it, the state of his language did not even call upon him to do so. For, as we have seen, in his language the system of certain allowable double forms still prevailed in the main, and such a system, although it was very detrimental to the smooth flow of Lydgate's verse, would by no means be a hindrance to a true poet and master of form; on the contrary, instead of hampering him, it would only give him greater freedom.

Chaucer uses such double forms, as *force* and *fors*, *cométh* and *comth*, without any injury to the flow and melodiousness of his metre. For a further illustration of this usage of Chaucer and Lydgate, scholars have rightly pointed to the similar state of things in modern German. Thus Goethe would use *Liebe* and *Lieb'*, *flehet* and *fleht*, as the metre might require; he even, without hesitation, puts double forms side by side, as in the two beautiful lines from *Faust*:

"Es *regt* sich die Menschenliebe,
Die Liebe Gottes *regt* sich nun."

Nevertheless, no one would think of taking exception to these lines steeped in perfect melody.

Whilst we must, therefore, make due allowance for the increasing difficulty of creating a new metrical canon, it would nevertheless be wrong to infer that the dreariness of this period in English literature is due only to this state of the language. It is even less possible for us to save our monk's reputation upon the strength of the oft-repeated assertion that this decay was due to the unsettled state of public affairs after Chaucer's death. For the Wars of the Roses did not begin till half a century after Chaucer was laid in his grave, and even between 1400—1450, there is no work of any decided poetical value—except perhaps Lydgate's *Reason and Sensuality*. The wars in France would not have disturbed an English poet much: the Weimar-poets wrote in the midst of the wars against Napoleon, and, indeed, the earlier part of the Anglo-French war, with the Battle of Agincourt, ought certainly to have called forth rather than stifled the poet's voice.

The true explanation of the barrenness of this period in English literature, as in corresponding periods in world-literature in general, is simply that an ebb in the tide of poetical talent had set in. Nature had to rest before she could give birth to the *diva proles* of the Elizabethans. And if a period of almost two hundred years of barrenness may appear of undue length, let us not forget the uniqueness of the race that was to come: it took three full nights to create Heracles.

CHAPTER VII.
THE AUTHORSHIP OF THE POEM.

I. *Stephen Hawes's supposed Authorship.*

IT has been mentioned in the preliminary remarks that the *Temple of Glas* was still a very popular work at the beginning of the 16th century. Whilst on the one hand Wynken de Worde's, Pynson's and Berthelet's presses issued new editions of it, Lydgate found, at the same time, a most enthusiastic admirer in the person of Stephen Hawes, the author of the *Pastime of Pleasure*, so highly praised— far too highly, I think—by Warton as a forerunner to Spenser. As to Hawes's admiration of Lydgate, we have the recorded evidence of Wood in the *Athenæ Oxonienses*, edit. of 1721, vol. I, col. 6[1]: (Stephen Hawes was) "highly esteemed by him (*King Henry VII.*) for his facetious Discourse, and prodigious[2] Memory; which last did evidently appear in this, that he could repeat by Heart most of our *English* Poets; especially *Jo. Lydgate* a Monk of *Bury*, whom he made equal in some Respects with *Geff. Chaucer.*" But even without this express testimony of Wood, Hawes's own works would speak even more eloquently for his excessive reverence for Lydgate; for there is no opportunity let slip—be the work small or large, be it at the beginning, in the middle, or at the end—to inform us of Lydgate's transcendent accomplishments in poetry and rhetoric. When he thus, in chapter XIV of the *Pastime*, comes to enumerate those who distinguished themselves in poetry, he starts off in an animated panegyric extolling Lydgate above all others as his master κατ' ἐξοχήν. But, in this passage, he gives us also something more valuable than his opinion of Lydgate, namely, a list of some of his works, at the end of which he says of the monk:

> "and the tyme to passe,
> Of love he made the bryght temple of glasse."
> (Edition for the Percy Society, p. 54.)

Even if we had no further external evidence, we should, I think, still be justified in considering the passage quoted from Hawes as a fairly reliable witness to Lydgate's authorship of the *Temple of Glas*. At all events it starts us in the right direction for settling this question.

But curiously enough, on the other hand a tradition has sprung up which would make the author of the *Temple of Glas* this very Stephen Hawes, who, as clearly and expressly as possible, tells us that the poem was written by Lydgate. We first meet with it in the *Scriptorum illustrium maioris Brytanniæ Catalogus*, by John Bale,

---

[1] Almost literally repeated in Lewis, *Life of Caxton*, 1737, p. 103, note t; see also *Warton-Hazlitt* III, 170.

[2] This is, I think, a most appropriate epithet for a memory that can retain Lydgate, especially those long-winded productions where he says the same thing a hundred times over. But what an idea, to learn Lydgate by heart!

Chapter VII.—The Authorship of the Poem. lxxvii

the well-known theologian, historian of literature, and dramatic writer. In the edition of 1557—1559, printed at Basle, on page 632, under "Centuria octava," No. LVIII, a "Templum crystallinum" in one book is ascribed to Hawes. The same error is, later on, also found in John Pits, *Relationum historicarum de Rebus Anglicis Tomus primus*, Parisiis 1619, cap. 903 (under the year 1500). Hence, in both Bale and Pits, the *Temple of Glas* is wanting in their long catalogue of Lydgate's writings (Bale, p. 586 and 587; Pits, cap. 820), and the same omission naturally occurs in other works which derive their information from these sources. So Ghilini, in his *Teatro d'Huomini Letterati*, Venice 1647, vol. II, 130, rests his evidence on Pits, and, in his turn, at least in his list of works, serves as an authority to Papadopoli *Historia gymnasii Patavini*, Venetiis 1726 (vol. II, 165): both these also omit the *Temple of Glas* in their lists of Lydgate's works. In the same manner, our poem is passed over in silence by the Bishop Josephus Pamphilus, in his *Chronica ordinis Fratrum Eremitarum sancti Augustini*, Romae 1581, p. 88[1]; by Winstanley, *The Lives of the most famous English Poets*, 1687, pp. 33—37; in Zedler's *Universal-Lexicon* (1738), XVII, 944; in J. A. Fabricius, *Bibliotheca Latina mediæ et infimæ Ætatis* (1754), IV, 95, and in Joecher's *Gelehrten-Lexicon*, 1750 (all dependent on Bale or Pits).

To return to positive evidence, we again find Hawes expressly stated to be the author in Wood's *Athenæ Oxonienses*. In the edition of 1721, vol. I, col. 6, a work with the title *The Crystalline Temple*, is ascribed to Hawes, a title which betrays at once that it was taken from Bale's or Pits's Latin. Somewhat later, however, than the testimonies of Bale, Pits, and Wood, an entry in Ames, *Typographical Antiquities*, first edition, 1749, gave a fresh start to this

---

[1] Pamphilus makes Lydgate an Augustine monk (an error repeated in Edward Phillips, *Theatrum poetarum*, 1675, p. 113 of the Modern Division—another of Phillips's "flagrant inaccuracies" spoken of by Dyce); he, moreover, gives 1482 as the year of Lydgate's death, for which he is duly censured by Pits. This, I conjecture, may have originated in a confusion of the Benedictine John Lydgate, Monk of Bury, with the Augustine John of Bury (born at Bury), who, according to Bale (centuria octava, No. XX, p. 595), flourished about 1460. The Augustine is also mentioned in Fuller's *Worthies of England*, 1662, under Suffolk, p. 69. Leland, in his *Commentarii de Scriptoribus Britannicis*, Oxonii 1709, p. 448, treats in Cap. DXLV of a "Joannes à fano Eadmundi, Carmelita Gippovicanus," a commentator of St. Luke's gospel, who seems to be identical with Bale's Ioannes Bury. A book by Philip Elsius, with the title *Encomiasticon Augustinianum*, Brussels 1654, quoted by Zedler and Fabricius as an authority on Lydgate, and criticized by Labbé, *Bibliotheca Bibliothecarum*, Paris 1664, p. 142, has not been available to me.

lxxviii Chapter VII.—*The Authorship of the Poem.*

erroneous theory of Hawes's authorship. In that work, on p. 86, the following print is mentioned as having been brought out by Wynken de Worde:

1500. Here bygenneth the temple of Glas, *wrote by Stephen Hawes grome of the chamber to king Henry VII. It contains 27 leaves in Octavo.*

This passage in the first edition of Ames is surrounded by a whole labyrinth of misunderstandings in the various editions of Warton, Ames, and Wood. For Warton (*Hist. of English Poetry*, 1778, vol. II, p. 211, note h) believed that the words printed in italics, in the above quotation from Ames, were included in the title of Wynken de Worde's edition, which, of course, is not the case. The words in italics merely express Ames's individual opinion with respect to the authorship; his authority might have been Bale, Pits, or perhaps Wood, unless, indeed, Herbert (I, 195) is right, according to whom Ames may easily have derived the statement in question from a written notice in a copy of one of Wynken de Worde's prints, then in the possession of James West (afterwards of Mason and Heber), to whose library Ames had access.

Ames gives the date of the print in question as 1500, so that the book would have come out in Hawes's life-time. Now it seemed unlikely to Warton—labouring as he was under the afore-mentioned delusion and having, moreover, Bale's testimony before him—that a poem, not from Hawes's pen, should have been published, by a contemporary printer, with his name prefixed to it. This argument would not seem, in itself, very strong, and it is all the more curious that Warton should have decided for Hawes's authorship, as he was confronted by the above-quoted passage, in which the latter himself attributes it to Lydgate.[1] As Warton's opinion that Hawes's name was put on a title-page of the *Temple of Glas*, is not borne out by an examination of the three existing prints by Wynken de Worde—one of them, most likely W, we may fairly assume to have been of the same impression as West's copy used by Ames—not a vestige of rational support from this quarter is left for Hawes's authorship.

Unfortunately, the discussion of these arguments spread from Warton to the later editions of Ames by Herbert and Dibdin—controversies about the various prints by Caxton and Wynken de Worde making matters still worse—and thence the theory of Hawes's author-

[1] And also by Speght's authority (going back to Stowe?), see section II of this chapter.

ship found its way into innumerable other works. To disentangle the details of this confusion, and to assign to each of the combatants his exact share of right and wrong in this maze of arguments and refutations, would be a task of some length and difficulty, and would certainly avail nothing for our purpose, as the matter is, without all this, so conspicuously clear. With respect to the typographical part, the best course to pursue appeared to me to give a clear and full description of the prints known to me, and with respect to the authorship, the following pages will establish Lydgate's claim beyond any doubt.

Some of the handbooks, encyclopædias, etc., which give Hawes as the author, are enumerated in the following list. They are, of course, of no authority whatever, being all more or less mechanically copied from Warton or others of the authorities mentioned.

S. **Paterson**, *Bibliotheca Westiana*, No. 1684 ; **Edward Phillips**, *Theatrum Poetarum Anglicanorum*, 1800 (dependent on Warton) ; **G. Ellis**, *Specimens of the early English Poets*, 1811, I, 416 ; **Chalmers**, *Biographical Dictionary*, 1814 ; **R. Watt**, *Bibliotheca Britannica*, 1824, I, 475 e ; **J. Gorton**, *General Biographical Dictionary*, 1851 ; **Alex. Buechner**, *Geschichte der englischen Poesie*, 1855, I, 56, and *Abriss der engl. Litteratur-geschichte*, 1856, p. 10 (dependent on Warton) ; **H. J. Rose**, *Biographical Dictionary*, 1857 ; *Biographie Universelle* (Michaud) 1857 ; *Nouvelle Biographie Générale*, 1858 ; **Allibone**, *Dictionary of English Literature*, 1859 ; **Larousse**, *Dictionnaire du 19ᵉ siècle*, 1873 ; **Maunder-Cates**, *The Biographical Treasury*, 1873 ; **Th. Cooper**, *Biographical Dictionary*, 1873.

Also in the Catalogue of the Tanner-MSS. in the Bodleian, by **Hackman**, 1860, under No. 346, Hawes is given as the author, probably from the notice in the index of the Tanner-MS. 346, where Pits is quoted as the source (see Chapter II, § 1). Other writers have wisely preferred silence on the subject, considering its uncertainty ; thus the *Temple of Glas* is not mentioned in the articles on Lydgate and Hawes in the *Encyclopædia Britannica*. W. D. Adams's *Dictionary of English Literature* valiantly attempts to be impartial, assigning it severally to either, neither or both ; see articles Hawes, Lydgate, Temple of Glas.[1] The most distorted account of our poem, however, is given in **Ersch** and **Gruber's** *Encyclopädie* (1828), under article Hawes, where it is stated that Hawes's *Temple of Glas* is meant as a parody of Chaucer's *Temple of Fame!* Crabbs (sic) *Dictionary* is given as the source, where, however, the last monstrosity is not to be found.[2]

We must, however, not omit to repeat here that the *Temple of Glas* was hitherto not easily accessible, a circumstance which makes the repetition of such a glaring error made over and over again, for a

[1] Hazlitt also, in his Handbook (1867), seems to have been uncertain about the authorship ; as he gives an account of our print W under *Lydgate*, I at first overlooked the fact that he had already noticed our prints C, p, w, b under Hawes.
[2] There are several dictionaries by George Crabb ; a *Universal Technological Dictionary*, 1823 ; a *Universal Historical Dictionary*, 1825 ; and *A Dictionary of General Knowledge*, 1830 (and later). As the article in Ersch and Gruber came out in 1828, the second must be meant.

whole century and more, at least excusable. For even those who were willing enough to get their information first-hand, must often have found no other text available, except the extracts in Warton. These, as has been mentioned, were taken from the last and worst print, that by Berthelet; their language in its modernized form much resembled Hawes's, and the metre seemed to be very much the same as that of the *Pastime of Pleasure,* namely, to all appearance, there was often none at all.

II. *The Supporters of Lydgate's claim.*

But, on the other hand, there have always been scholars who rightly assigned the *Temple of Glas* to Lydgate. Such is the case in Speght's edition of *Chaucer*, 1598, fol. 394 b, col. 2, 1. 16 (ed. of 1602, fol. 376 b, col. 2, l. 13), where we find *The temple of Glasse* in the "Catalogue of translations and Poeticall deuises . . . by Iohn Lidgate . . . whereof some are extant in Print, the residue in the custodie of him that first caused this *Siege of Thebes* to be added to these works of *G. Chaucer*" [*i. e.* Stowe]. Speght's testimony is thus all the more valuable as evidently going back to Stowe.

Further, John Lewis, in his *Life of Caxton*, 1737, p. 104, calls Lydgate the author;[1] also Th. Tanner, in his *Bibliotheca Britannico-Hibernica*, 1748, p. 491, ascribes a *Temple of glasse* to Lydgate in the long list of his works, and so does, on his authority (?), Berkenhout, in the *Biographia Literaria*, 1777, p. 318. Even the very same Ames, who wrought such havoc by the above-quoted passage (*Typ. Ant.*, p. 86), calls in the self-same work, on p. 61, Lydgate the author; so does also Ritson in his *Bibliographia poetica*, 1802, p. 68 (No. 10 of Lydgate's works); see *ib.* p. 59. A fact which spoke strongly against Hawes's authorship, seems to have first been pointed out by George Mason, in an entry in his copy of a print by Wynken, quoted by Dibdin II, 305, note at the bottom, and Warton-Hazlitt III, 61, end of note; after Mason, Hallam spoke of it again in his *Introduction to the Literature of Europe*, 4th ed. 1854, I, 311. The fact was this, that the *Temple of Glas* is mentioned in the *Paston Letters*, as early as February 17th, 1471-72, when Hawes was pro-

[1] A still earlier writer on typography, C. Middleton, does not give, in his meagre account of the Cambridge Collection, any author's name for the *Temple of Glas;* he most likely knew little concerning the authors of the pieces in question. See his *Dissertation concerning the Origin of Printing in England*, 1735, p. 29.

Chapter VII.—The Authorship of the Poem.

bably not yet born.[1] The passage in question occurs in a letter from John Paston, Knight, to Johan Paston, Esquier, where it runs (John Fenn's edition, vol. II, p. 90, Gairdner's edition, III, 37): "Brother, I comaunde me to yow, and praye yow to loke uppe my temple off Glasse and send it me by the berer herof."

In the footnote to the above quotation Fenn also hesitates between Lydgate and Hawes as author; Gairdner gives Lydgate alone. Cf. also Gairdner III, 300 (Fenn II, 300), where, in the *Inventory off John Paston's Books*, mention is made of "a blak Boke," which contained, amongst other pieces, the *Temple of Glasse*. The argument against Hawes's authorship, contained in this passage from the *Paston Letters*, will, indeed, be rendered superfluous by older evidence adduced in section III of this chapter; nevertheless, the passage is valuable as giving further proof that, some seventy years after its composition, the *Temple of Glas* was still read, a fact still more strongly testified to by Caxton printing it seven or eight years later.

In more recent times there has hardly been a scholar of note who, deluded by Warton or Ames, has stuck to the impossible theory of Hawes's authorship. Thus Lydgate has been restored to his rights in the re-edition of *Warton* by Hazlitt (III, 61), and besides this, I may be allowed to point to a few other works, in all of which Lydgate is held to be the author:

> **Hallam**, *Introduction to the Literature of Europe*, I, 311; **Collier**, *Bibliographical Account* I, 367; David Laing, Hawes's *Conversyon of Swerers*, etc., Preface, p. IV; J. F. **Waller's** *Imperial Dictionary*, which expressly contradicts Warton; **Klein**, *Geschichte des Dramas* XII, 691; **Lowndes**, ed. Bohn III, 1419; H. **Morley**, *English Writers* II, 433 note; Mrs. **Browning**, *Book of the Poets*, 1863, p. 123; H. M. **Fitzgibbon**, *Early English Poetry*, p. xxxii, and xxxvii; **Skeat**, *Chaucer's Minor Poems*, in several places; J. **Churton Collins**, in T. H. Ward's *English Poets* I, 175; **Chambers's** *Encyclopædia*, 1890, article Lydgate; *Dictionary of National Biography*, 1891, article Hawes.

III. Lydgate's Authorship established.

There still remains external evidence of a yet more decisive character for Lydgate's authorship. For we are not disappointed, if we look for evidence of the oldest and most authentic kind in that quarter where we should most naturally expect to find it. I mean the Manuscripts. There are, indeed, only two of all the seven MSS. which give the name of an author, namely, Fairfax 16, and Shirley's Add. MS. 16,165; but in both cases we have the good fortune to

[1] The poem is also mentioned in a list of the contents of a MS. of the Marquis of Bath, ab. 1460 A.D.—F.

know the hand that assigns the poem to our monk. In MS. F the author's name does not occur in the handwriting of the copyist of the poem itself; but the name "lidgate" is added to the respective item, in the table of contents, by the same hand that supplied the missing ll. 96 and 320 and some other corrections in F, namely, that of John Stowe (about 1560).

Further, in the second MS., we have Lydgate's name given several times in a handwriting which is even some hundred years older, namely in Shirley's. In his Add. MS. 16,165, the name of the author stands in the title (see Chapter II, § 6) as "Lidegate. Le Moygne de Bury"; in the headlines: on fol. 207 a as "daun John," on fol. 231 a as "þe Munke of Bury," on fol. 232 a as "Lidegate"; lastly on fol. 212 a the name is added to the headline, so that this latter runs as follows: "þe dreme of A lover *calde þe Temple of glasse by Lydegate*" (the part in italics added later). The handwriting in the two additions on fol. 207 a and 212 a differs[1] somewhat from that of the text itself; in the other passages it is undoubtedly Shirley's own. But there is yet another passage in this MS., unquestionably written by Shirley himself, which may afford still further proof for Lydgate's authorship of our poem. It is the identical passage which Skeat, Chaucer's *M. P.*, pp. xlv and xxxiii, note 3, takes as a proof that the monk was author of the *Black Knight*. Shirley has added to this MS. a prologue of 104 lines in verse, written upon two leaves of parchment at the beginning, which describe the contents of the volume. The order of the pieces in the MS. is: 1. Chaucer's translation of Boethius; 2. The gospel of Nicodemus (translated by John Trevysa); 3. þe desporte of huntyng (or "maistre of the game"), by Edward, Duke of York; 4. A Complaynte of an Amorous Knight [= *Black Knight*]; 5. Regula sacerdotalis; 6. The Dreme of a trewe lover [= *Temple of Glas*]; 7. Compleint of Anelida; lastly, a number of smaller poems. These Shirley, in the above-mentioned versified prologue to his MS., enumerates in the following order: Boethius (ll. 25—34); Gospel of Nicodemus (ll. 35—44); Maistre of the game (ll. 45—61); then the Regula sacerdotalis (ll. 61—71), thus omitting No. 4 (the "black Knight"); after this he has (fol. 3 a):

"Þanne and ye wol þe wryting suwe,   72
Shul ye fynde wryten of a knyght,
Þat serued his soueraine lady bright,

---

[1] Also noted by Dr. Furnivall, *Suppl. Par.-Texts of Ch. M. P.*, p. 46.

Chapter VII.—The Authorship of the Poem.

> As done þees louers Amerous,
> Whos lyff is offt seen parillous, 76
> Askeþe of hem, þat haue hit vsed—
> A dieux Ioenesse, I am refused—
> Whos complaynt is al in balade,
> Þat Daun Iohan of Bury made, 80
> Lydegate, þe Munk cloþed in blacke—
> In his makyng þer is no lacke—
> And thankeþe Daun Iohan for his peyne,
> Þat to plese gentyles is right feyue, 84
> Boþe with his laboure, and his goode :
> God wolde, of nobles he hade ful his hoode."[1]

The order of sequence points decidedly to the *Temple of Glas* (comp. l. 72 above); moreover, considering the length of the poem as given in Shirley's text (some 2000 lines, against 681 of the *Black Knight*), it is little likely that our poem should have been passed over. Lastly, to this "poetical" table of contents is added, at the top of the first page, a short summary, in which No. 4 is called *þe dreme for lovers* (Black Knight), No. 5 *þe Ruyle of preestis*, No. 6 *þe compleynt of a lover* (Temple of Glas), which latter expression is quite in accordance with l. 79 above. I do not mean, however, to deny altogether the possibility that the *Black Knight* may have been in Shirley's mind when he wrote the passage in question; the expression *al in balade* [*i. e.* in seven-line stanzas], in l. 79, would especially hold good for that poem, and the above lines certainly give but an inadequate idea of the *Temple of Glas*. Be this as it may, we have at all events Shirley's sure testimony for Lydgate's authorship, not only of the *Temple of Glas*, as specified above, but also for the *Black Knight*. For Lydgate's name has, in the latter poem also, twice (on fol. 192 *a* and 193 *a*) been added to the headline; it stands in the title, on fol. 190 *a* (bottom), and on fol. 200 *b* we have as running title : *Lenvoye of daun Iohn.*

To sum up : 1. *Hawes cannot be the author.* One is seldom able to refute an error more completely than this theory of Hawes's authorship. For first, it has been shown that Warton's advancement of this hypothesis was based on a misunderstanding of Ames. Secondly, if, in favour of Hawes, Bale's or Pits's authority be brought forward,

---

[1] May we conclude, from ll. 83—86, that Lydgate was still living, when Shirley wrote this? Shirley died on Oct. 21, 1456, aged 90, see Stowe's *Survey of London*, ed. Thoms, 1876, p. 140. "John Sherley wrat in ẏ tyme of John Lydgate in his lyffe tyme," says Stowe in Add. MS. 29,729, fol. 179 *a*. Stopford Brooke, in his excellent little Primer, p. 55, gives 1449 (which seems to be wrong) as the date of the death of Shirley, whom he has honoured far too highly in mentioning him twice, whilst, for instance, some of the pre-Shaksperian dramatists are barely named.

our answer is that there is a MS. of the *Temple of Glas*, Tanner 346, which is a hundred years older than Hawes's principal work. Thirdly, if doubts should be raised respecting the age of the MS., we have the express statement of Hawes himself, who ascribes the poem to his admired master. 2. *Lydgate must be the author.* For, by way of external evidence, we have the witness of three reliable authorities who all call him so, namely Shirley, about 1440 or 1450, Hawes, about 1506, and Stowe, about 1560. The internal evidence is equally convincing. First, the testimony of language and metre. There are unfortunately as yet no special treatises on Lydgate's language and metre, and, indeed, to undertake such a thing would be premature, before we have some more critical editions of his works. But, after the preliminary researches in Chapters V and VI, we may say as much as that the language of our poem is quite in accordance with the more prominent peculiarities of Lydgate's. Thus there is a slight advance in the disregard of the final *e* beyond Chaucer: we have in our poem specimens of the confusion of *-as* and *-ace* rhymes (not however of *-y* and *-ie* rhymes, as in the *Black Knight*, to give an instance of one of his earlier poems); also the Teutonic words *sone*, *mone*, and *don* (p. p.), rhyme with each other.— The treatment of the final *e* in general, is altogether the same as in other recognized works of Lydgate, so far as I have been able to investigate the subject. We have also another outspoken peculiarity of Lydgate's in our poem, namely, that he rhymes words in *-ere* with those in *-ire*, as has been noted by others in more than one place. See, on this matter, Chapters V and VI.

The best account of Lydgate's metre, and the most successful in its results, seems to me to be contained in Prof. Schipper's *Englische Metrik*. The unmistakable characteristics of the verses of our monk exhibit themselves throughout the *Temple of Glas*.[1] See Chapter V.

Lydgate's style is justly denounced as being intolerably drawled-out, incompact, and full of anacolutha; and although the greater part of the *Temple of Glas* may, on the whole, be superior to his lengthy works, yet the Lydgatian "drivelling"[2] long-windedness is not to be mistaken in the speeches of our poem.

Ample examples have been given in the notes illustrating some

[1] I would here note that I had myself, in every respect, arrived at the same conclusions before consulting Schipper's book. I merely make note of this in order to corroborate the distinguished scholar's statements.

[2] For this expression, which so exactly hits the right nail upon the head, I am indebted to Ritson, with whom, however, I have a bone to pick by and by.

of Lydgate's favourite expressions and ideas; thus his pen quakes, when he has to "endite of wo," l. 947; thus he invokes the Furies, instead of the Muses, when he has to relate something dreadful (l. 958); the lady with hair "like gold-wire" is not wanting, and at the end, in the Envoy, he has not omitted his favourite request to "correct" his poem, if "any thing be missaid in it."

Lastly, the entire atmosphere of the poem, the framework of a vision, the allegories, the whole range of ideas, and the *motifs* borrowed from Chaucer, Gower, the "Roman de la Rose" etc., are essentially the same as in several of the monk's earlier works, particularly the *Complaint of the Black Knight*, the *Flour of Curtesie*, and his hitherto almost unnoticed best work, *Reason and Sensuality*.

CHAPTER VIII.
CHRONOLOGY OF LYDGATE'S WRITINGS.

"For myne wordes here and every parte,
I speke hem alle under correccion."—*Troilus*, III, 1282, 1283.

§ 1. *Lydgate's Life*.

THE exact dates forming the boundary-lines of Lydgate's life have never been precisely made out; nor can we affix a certain date to the greater number of his works. Still there is in his case comparatively less ground for complaint than in other instances, with regard to the scantiness of information accessible to us; for it has been at least possible to fix approximately the dates of the longer writings of Lydgate's second period, and no doubt, after a careful collection and investigation of the materials extant, many more points connected with chronological questions will be brought to light.

It is in view of assigning to the *Temple of Glas* its proper place amongst Lydgate's other writings, and also, I hope, of offering some help to the investigator of particular works of the monk's, that I here attempt a rough outline of his life and his most important works, in chronological order—with great mistrust in more than one point, I confess, and always "under correccioun."

We know that the monk was born at Lydgate[1] (near Newmarket),

[1] *Falls of Princes*, fol. 217 *d*:
"Borne in a village which called is Lidgate,
By olde time a famous castel toune;
In Danes time it was beat[e] doune,
Time whan saint Edmund, martir, maid, & king
Was slaine at Oxone, record of writing."
ib., 176 *d*: "I was borne in Lydgate,
Where Bacchus licour doth ful scarsly flete."
Æsop, Prol. 32: "Have me excused, I was boru in Lydegate."

lxxxvi *Chapter VIII.—Chronology of Lydgate's Writings.*

whence he derived his name. But there has been much dispute as to the year of his birth. Bale says of him (*Catalogus*, 1557, p. 587): "*Claruit* sexagenarius, anno . . . 1440."[1] Pits, "illius pro more exscriptor," makes of this (cap. 820): "(Buriæ tandem) circiter sexagenarius *mortuus & sepultus est* circa annum . . . . 1440", adding in brackets : " malè etenim vitam eius producit Iosephus Pamphilus vsque ad annum Domini 1482."

This censure is well-deserved by Pamphilus, who seems to confuse Lydgate with the Augustinian (or Ipswich Carmelite?) John of Bury, as has been remarked above in the footnote on page lxxvii. The exact words of Pamphilus concerning Lydgate are (*Chronica ordinis fratrum sancti Augustini*, p. 88) : " Claruit Buriæ, vbi tandem decessit, anno. 1482." This date has also been wrongly defended in the *Catalogue of the Harleian MSS.*, No. 2251, Article 3, on the grounds that a stanza on King Edward IV. is, in that MS., added to Lydgate's stanzas on the Lives of the English Kings. Again, Ghilini, dependent on Pits, says : " Finalmente nell' età di 60. anni, passò all' altra vita nel suo Monasterio di Sant' Edmondo, circa l'Anno 1440 " (Teatro d'Huomini Letterati, II, 131), and Papadopoli, following him, has : " Decessit in patria an. MCDXL. aetat. LX" (Historia Gymnasii Patavini, II, 165). Papadopoli had evidently well mastered the first rules of arithmetic; for, from Ghilini's evidence, he has been able to make out the date of Lydgate's birth, which he is the first to state expressly as 1380. This year, however, is certainly too late. It has since been concluded from more than one reason that the monk must have been born some ten years earlier.

The facts which are of first importance to us in attempting to settle this much disputed point, are contained in the extracts from certain MSS. quoted by Tanner in his *Bibliotheca Britannico-Hibernica*, p. 489. The dates we gather from these extracts, are the following :

March 13th, 1388 (I suppose 1389, according to the new style): " fr[ater] Joh[annes] Lidgate monachus de Bury ord[inatus] ad omnes ordines in ecclesia de Hadham."

This entry is from the register of Robert Braybrook, Bishop of London from 1381—1404; it certainly has reference to the four minor ecclesiastical orders. The next three entries, which I have had the opportunity of examining myself, are contained in MS.

---

[1] In the first edition, however (1548, folio 203 *a*), Bale wrote : "Claruit ab incarnato Dei verbo. 1470. sub rege Edwardo quarto."

Chapter VIII.—Chronology of Lydgate's Writings. lxxxvii

Cotton Tib. B. ix, the register of William Cratfield, abbot of Bury St. Edmunds from 1389—1414. According to them, the young monk of Bury received letters dismissory for the office of subdeacon on [Dec. ?][1] 17th, 1389 (Cotton Tib. B. ix, fol. 35 b); for that of deacon on May 28th, 1393 (ib., fol. 69 b); for the order of priesthood on April 4th, 1397 (ib., fol. 85 b). According to a MS.-note[2] in Tyrwhitt's copy of Wayland's *Falls of Princes* (now in the British Museum, marked 838. m. 17), Lydgate was ordained priest by John Fordham, Bishop of Ely, on Saturday, April 7th, 1397, in the chapel of the manor at Dounham.

From these dates it has been reasoned backwards that Lydgate must have been born about 1370. So by Ward, *Catalogue of the Romances in the British Museum*, I, 75, and by H. Morley, *English Writers*, II, 421. Tame, *Life of our Lady*, p. III, and Th. Arnold, *A Manual of English Literature*, 6th ed., p. 134, conclude the date to be 1368; but this date does not agree so well with certain allusions to his age made by Lydgate himself in several of his works, allusions which will be discussed in full below.

Nothing seems to be known about his family,[3] or as to how he came from his native village of Lydgate to the Monastery of Bury St. Edmunds. Papadopoli, indeed, has: "A puero Monasticam D. Benedicti regulam professus est, primasque literas didicit in cœnobio," which is not unlikely at all; but, in Papadopoli, this statement seems merely to be a guess, and not drawn from any older reliable authority.

If I interpret the passages in Lydgate's *Testament* rightly, this poem would seem to warrant the conclusion that he was received into the monastery as a "child," "within 15 yeares age," although the lines in question are not very clearly put. He says that

---

[1] The month is wanting in the MS., owing to its being much damaged by fire. Tanner has December. The date immediately preceding in the MS. is Oct. 26th, 1389.

[2] Printed in A. Hortis, *Studj sulle opere latine del Boccaccio*, p. 641, note 2, not always quite correctly. It runs as follows: "Frater Iohannes Lydgate Monachus de Bury, ordinatus Presbiter per Iohannem ffordham Episcopum Eliensem in Capellâ magni Manerii de Dounham, die Sabat. 7° April. 1397." The passage professes to be transcribed from a Register of Bishop Fordham of Ely, which was in 1728 in the hands of "ffr[ancis] Blomefield de Hersfield."

[3] In his *Testament* (*Halliwell*, p. 255) he says of himself (speaking of his school-days):
"Made my freendys ther good to spende in ydil";
and, further on, p. 256:
"Snybbyd of my frendys such techchys for tamende,
Made delfe ere, lyst nat to them attende."

Chapter VIII.—Chronology of Lydgate's Writings.

"Duryng the tyme . . . of my yeerys greene,
Gynnyng fro childhood stretchithe up so fere,
To the yeerys accountyd ful fifteene,"

he was a naughty, mischievous boy, "loth toward scole," "straunge to spelle or reede"; then he tells us that he entered the monastery as a novice:

"Entryng this tyme into religioun,
Unto the plouhe I putte forth myn hoond,[1]
A yeer compleet made my professioun ;"

but he did not like much to follow "blessed Benet's doctrine,"

"Which now remembryng in my latter age,
Tyme of my childhood, as I reherse shal,
Witheyne fifteene holdyng my passage,
Mid of a cloistre depict upon a wal
I sauhe a crucifix."

This would go very well with *Temple of Glas*, ll. 196, etc. I believe that Lydgate was certainly thinking of himself when he wrote those lines, and that he also was "entered in childhood into religion before he had years of discretion." Certain is that in the extracts referred to above, the dates of which range from 1388 to 1397, Lydgate is always called a "monachus de Bury."

Besides the instruction which he would thus have received during a considerable number of years in the monastery, Lydgate seems to have enjoyed the benefit of a University education. Bale says of the monk in his *Catalogus*, p. 586:

"Didici tamen, post perlustratas Anglorum academias, Galliam & Italiam, discendarum linguarum gratia, petijsse illum."

His statement, which I do not consider very trustworthy in itself, is, so far as Oxford is concerned, corroborated by an entry in MS. Ashmole 59, where we have, on fol. 24 *b*, in Shirley's handwriting, the following title to part of Lydgate's *Æsop:*

"Here begynneþe . a notable proverbe of Ysopus Ethiopyen in balad . by Daun Iohan Liedegate made in Oxenford."

Of course, it does not follow from this passage that Lydgate was then studying at Oxford, as a member of the University; still, I think, this would be the most natural interpretation.[2] According to Tanne,

---

[1] This expression, taken from the Bible, occurs also in the *Pilgrimage*, fol. 296 *b*: "I sette myn hand vnto the plough."

[2] Is it a grateful reminiscence of Oxford, when he, in his old age, writes in the *Secreta Secretorum* (MS. Ashmole 46, fol. 123 *b*):

"As the sonne shewyth in his guyse
Mong smale sterrys with his beemys bryght,
Right so in the same maneer wyse
An vniuersite shewith out his lyght,
In a kyndoom, as it shulde be of ryght"?

But see also his verses on the foundation of the town and University of Cambridge, printed in the *Retrospective Review*, 2nd series, vol. I, p. 498.

Chapter VIII.—Chronology of Lydgate's Writings.

Lydgate would then have been attached to Gloucester Hall, where the Benedictines used to send their pupils.

After finishing his academic studies in his native country, a tradition, repeated from Bale downwards, supposes Lydgate to have travelled abroad and studied in France and Italy. That the monk was at one time at Paris, we shall see presently; but whether he was there in his youth, for the purpose of study, seems doubtful enough. His translation of Deguileville's *First Pilgrimage* would have afforded him an opportunity of showing off his knowledge of Paris University-life; but in the passage in question he adds hardly anything of his own to Deguileville's words. The original reads (Barthole and Petit's print, fol. 50 b):

"Car se aux escolles a paris
Auoit par quarante ans apris
Ung poure / qui mal vestu fust"...

Lydgate translates (Cott. Vit. C. XIII, fol. 176 a):

"Thogh a man wer neuere so wys,
And hadde lernyd at parys,
Thys thrytty yer at scole be
In that noble vnyuersyte,
And hadde ful experyence
Off euery wysdam & seyence,
& koude expounen euery doute,
And wer but porely clad with-oute"...

It is even more doubtful whether he was ever in Italy. Papadopoli, *Historia gymnasii Patavini*, II, 165, has: "Joannes Ligdat (*sic*) unus est ex antiquissimis alumnis Patavini lycæi. Ejus in monumentis gymnasticis vix obiter semel mentio est, memoratur attamen à Ghilino, ut diuturnus hospes Patavii." I wish Papadopoli had given in full the reference he alludes to from the "monumenta gymnastica," instead of quoting Ghilini.—Or is it a mere creation of his own imagination? "Vix obiter semel" is a very suspicious expression.[1]

In one of his poems in MS. Harl. 2255 (fol. 148 a—150 a)—the genuineness of it is vouched for by the "Explicit quod Lydgate" of the MS.—Lydgate says:

"I haue been offte in dyvers londys
And in many dyvers Regiouns,
Haue eskapyd fro my foois hondys,
In Citees, Castellys, and in touns;
Among folk of sundry naciouns
Wente ay forth, and took noon hede:
I askyd no manere of protecciouns;
God was myn helpe ageyn al drede."[2]

---

[1] In Jacopo Facciolati's *Fasti Gymnasii Patavini*, Patavii 1757, I do not find Lydgate's name. [2] Also printed by Tame, *Life of our Lady*, p. viii.

The first line of this stanza is quoted in Warton-Hazlitt (III, 53, note 2), and again referred to by Koeppel, *Falls of Princes*, p. 76. It is, however, not the first line of the whole poem, as Koeppel was led to suppose from Warton-Hazlitt, but it stands in the middle of it (MS. Harl. 2255, fol. 149 a, top). The last line, as given above, forms, with slight variations, the refrain throughout the poem, which is, in fact, an illustration of this burden. We cannot draw much in the way of a definite conclusion from these lines.

The last support which I can bring forward for the hypothesis that Lydgate was ever in Italy, is contained in the following passage from Papadopoli, *Historia Gymnasii Patavini*, II, 165, in which the author expresses his belief that a certain *Joannes Anglus*, mentioned by Salomoni, must be identical with our John Lydgate, not with Duns Scotus, as Salomoni had imagined. Papadopoli says of Lydgate:

" nec alius sit à Joanne Anglo, quem à se in antiquissimis quibusdam albis Salomonius inventum, notatumque scribit, ac vir bonus Joannem Scotum principem Scotistarum existimavit: cum nedum patria, quæ Scoto Caledonia, Anglo Anglia, & Ordo sacræ Familiæ, quæ Anglo Benedictina, Scoto Franciscana fuit, alterum ab altero discriminent, sed etiam ætas, quæ Scoto annum MCCCVIII. emortualem præstituit, natalem Anglo MCCCLXXX."

I do not know whether Papadopoli refers to Giacopo Salomoni's *Agri Patavini inscriptiones sacræ et prophanæ*, Patavii 1696—1708; I certainly have not been able to find the reference in this work. With regard to the question before us, everything depends upon whether this Joannes Anglus was stated by Salomoni himself, on the authority of old documents, to be a Benedictine, born in 1380. I am hardly inclined to believe it; the documents would scarcely have given the wrong date, 1380, for Lydgate's birth, which was suggested to Papadopoli by the statements of his principal authority, Ghilini. If Salomoni himself does not call this Joannes Anglus a Benedictine, born in 1380, I should then prefer to believe that his Joannes Anglus might have been some other Englishman, perhaps the distinguished Earl of Worcester, John Tiptoft (executed in 1470), who, according to *Warton-Hazlitt*, III, 337, note 1, occupied a professorship at Padua for some time. As I know of no further evidence which could supply us with information concerning this period of Lydgate's life, I am inclined to acquiesce in Koeppel's opinion concerning the monk's relations to Italy (*Falls of Princes*, p. 82), namely, that he was never in the country, and knew nothing of its literature in the *lingua volgare*.

Chapter VIII.—Chronology of Lydgate's Writings.

Of our monk's successive advances in the priestly office we have spoken above. From 1397 to 1415 we lose sight of him and his outward life, nor do we know, with one exception, a precise and certain date for any of his writings before the *Troy-Book*. Bale, followed by Pits, Ghilini, Papadopoli, Fuller, Winstanley, etc., says that after returning from his travels and studies abroad Lydgate opened a school for the sons of noblemen; later writers (from Warton downwards) have made this school to be in the monastery of Bury, others (Berkenhout, copied by Burrowes's *Encyclopædia*) in London. However that may be, it seems to me not unlikely that, about this time, Lydgate was in London. He evidently knew London-life very well from his own experience, a fact which would be amply proved by his *London Lick-penny* alone.[1]

Whether Lydgate knew Chaucer personally, can, I think, neither be proved satisfactorily, nor entirely disproved. On the one hand he frequently mentions Chaucer, as the note to l. 110 will show, usually with the epithet "my maister." In the *Troy-Book*, 1513, fol. N, a, we read:

"And Chauncer now, alas, is nat alyue,
Me to refourme, or to be my rede,
For lacke of whom slower is my spede";

in the *Life of our Lady*, fol. e, b:

"For want of hym now in my grete nede,
That shold, allas, conneye and dyrecte,
And with his supporte amende and correcte
The wronge traces of my rude penne,
There as I erre and goo not lyne right;
But for that[2] he ne may me not kenne,
I can nomore"... (but pray for him).

Chorl and Bird is dedicated to his "maister," who, I suppose, can hardly be anybody else but Chaucer, with the following lines:

"Go, gentille quayer! and recommaunde me
Unto my maister with humble affeccioun[3];
Beseke hym lowly, of mercy and pite,
Of this rude makyng to haue compassion."

But compare, on the other hand, the quotation on p. lvi, where Lydgate says he had "no guide to reduce him, when he went a-wrong," and the end of the *Troy-Book*, MS. Cotton Augustus A. IV, fol. 153 a:

[1] Stowe, in his Add. MS. 29729, fol. 166 a, has the entry: "And now here foloweth an ordenaunce of a presesyon of ye feste of corpus cristie made in london by daune (MS. *dame*) John Lydegate." See the poem in Halliwell, *M. P.*, p. 95—103.
[2] Thus in MS. Harl. 629; Caxton has *that for*.
[3] Halliwell (from MS. Harl. 116) *effection*.

xcii *Chapter VIII.—Chronology of Lydgate's Writings.*

> "My maister Chaucer, þat founde ful many spot,
> Hym liste nat pinche nor gruche at euery blot,
> Nor meue hym silf to perturbe his reste,
> I haue herde telle, but seide alweie þe best."

Nor does the epithet "my maister," which Lydgate is so fond of bestowing on Chaucer, go to prove much; King James, and even Gawain Douglas, call Chaucer also their master.

Tanner adduces MS.-evidence that, in 1415, Lydgate lived at Bury, "ubi electioni Gul. Excestr. adfuit"; his statement is taken from the Register of William of Exeter, who was elected abbot of Bury St. Edmunds after the death of Cratfield in 1414. We meet again with Lydgate's name in one of the Minutes of the Privy Council, dated Feb. 21st, 1423. We read there (*Proceedings of the Privy Council*,[1] ed. by Sir Harris Nicolas, III, 41, taken from MS. Cotton Cleopatra F. IV, fol. 7 a) the decree that all the lands appertaining to the Priory of St. Fides of Longville are to be let to farm[2] to certain persons named by Sir Ralph Rocheford, among which a monk John Lydgate figures, who is, no doubt, our Benedictine. Compare also Sir Harris Nicolas's *Preface*, p. lxix.

In June 1423 Lydgate was elected Prior of Hatfield Broadoke (also called Hatfield Regis), see Tanner; and, on April 8th, 1434,[3] he received permission from "Prior Johannes"[4] to go back to Bury "propter frugem melioris vitae captandam." See again Tanner, and particularly, the above-mentioned MS.-note in Tyrwhitt's copy of Wayland's *Falls of Princes*, where the whole Dimissio is quoted in full from the Register of abbot Curteys (1429—1445).[5]

In the meantime, our monk must have been for some time in Paris. In MS. Harl. 7333, fol. 31 a, occurs the following heading to a poem:

---

[1] My attention was drawn to this, as well as to another passage (given lower down) from the *Proceedings*, etc., by Dr. Furnivall.

[2] ".... dimittantur modo ad firmam dompno Iohanni Lidgate & Iohanni de Tofte monachis. Iohanni Glastoñ & Williamo Maltoñ Cappellanis ad nominacionem prefati Radulphi Rocheford, etc. ...."

[3] Tame, *Life of our Lady*, p. ix, says that Lydgate had leave to return to his monastery again in the following year, 1424, and quotes MS. Cott. Tib. B. IX (not, however, the folio). This must be one of Tame's mistakes; it seems that he misread Tanner's date MCCCCXXXIV as MCCCCXXIV.

[4] There is a gap in the list of the Priors of Hatfield Broadoke, as given in Dugdale, *Monasticon Anglicanum*, IV, 433, between William Gulle, elected prior in 1395 (and, it seems, mentioned again in 1413), and John Derham, who is named as being prior in 1430 and 1432. The latter must be our "Prior Johannes."

[5] This note has also been printed by A. Hortis, in his *Studj sulle opere latine del Boccaccio*, p. 641, note 2.

Chapter VIII.—Chronology of Lydgate's Writings. xciii

" Here begynneth A remembraunce of a pee deugre how that the kyng of Englond, Henry the sext, is truly borne heir vnto the Corone of ffraunce by lynyall Successioun. als wele on his ffader side Henry the fifth. whom god assoill as by Kateryne quene of Englond, his modir. whom god assoile. made by Lydygate John the monke of Bury at Parys. by þe instaunce of my lord of Warrewyk."

This says clearly that Lydgate was in Paris, at a time not earlier than 1421, in which year Henry VI. was born. We are even able to determine the date still more exactly. The poem, besides alluding to contemporary events, mentions the king as

"Henry the sext of Age ny fyve yere reñ";

it was begun on July 28th, I suppose in 1426.[1] The poem itself says:

"I meved was .. by .. commaundement
Of .. My lord of Warrewyk....
Beyng present that tyme at parys,
Whañ he was thañ repaired agein
From seint luliañ of mavus oute of Mayñ."

" My lord of Warrewyk" is, of course, Richard de Beauchamp, Earl of Warwick, who was then Regent of France during the absence of the Duke of Bedford. Evidently the leaders of state-affairs wished to proclaim in every possible way that Henry was the true king of France, so the Duke of Bedford commanded Laurence Callot to compose a poetical pedigree which should serve this purpose, and the Earl of Warwick employed the pen of our monk to translate it. That the notice in the Harleian MS., which ascribes the poem to Lydgate and makes him be in France about 1426, is correct, is borne out by a passage in Lydgate's writings themselves. In the beginning of his *Dance of Macabre* the monk says (Tottel's edition of the *Falls of Pr.*, fol. 220 a):

"Like thensample which that at Parise
I fonde depict ones in a wal,"

and again, at the end (fol. 224 d):

"And from Paris to England it sent."

Henry V. is called the conqueror of France in this poem, which would go very well with the above-given dates. Mention is also made in it, on fol. 224 a, of the death of Master John Rikil, whilom "Tregetour" of Henry V., the date of whose death is, however, unknown to me. We may further compare Miss Yonge's *Cameos from*

---

[1] I should express myself with greater certainty were I sure what the "reñ" in the MS. means. An astronomical calculation based on the detailed description of the position of the principal planets, given towards the end of the poem, would no doubt settle the year precisely.

English History, II, 357, where she says that in 1424, for more than six months, the *Dance of Death* was acted out by living performers in Paris.

To strengthen this argument, we might also adduce here another passage taken from the prologue to Lydgate's translation of Deguileville's *First Pilgrimage* (MS. Cotton Vit. C. XIII, fol. 4 a):

> "And of the tyme playnly & of the date,
> Whan I be-gan thys book to translate,
> Yt was . . . [1426] . . . .
> My lord that tyme beyng at Parys,
> Wych gaff me charge, by hys dyscrete avys,
> As I seyde erst, to sette myn entent
> Vp-on thys book to be dyllygent,
> And to be-gynne vp-on thys labour."

This passage, of course, only says that Lord Salisbury was at Paris in 1426; but it may indeed have been that Lord Salisbury personally gave the monk the commission

> "Thys seyde book in englyssh for to make,"

as the date 1426 (expressed in a very circumlocutory way) tallies exactly with what has been said above.

Still this sojourn at Paris, and Lydgate's priorate at Hatfield Regis, give rise to several questions which I am not able to solve. When did Lydgate return from Paris, and where was he after his return? One would think that he wrote his *Life of St. Edmund* (in 1433; see below) at Bury, or at least saw King Henry VI. there; but his "Dimissio" from Hatfield is dated April 8th, 1434. What induced or compelled him to go to Paris? When did he give up his office of Prior of Hatfield Regis? I suppose when he went to Paris; most likely Derham was then chosen in his stead.

From 1434 until his death, Lydgate seems to have lived again at Bury St. Edmunds, where he certainly was buried (cf. Bale and *Archæologia*, IV, 131). The precise date of his death has never been made out. The year 1482 we have already discarded as being quite impossible. Nor is there any certain fact warranting the supposition that Lydgate did not die before the accession of Edward IV. in 1461. In favour of this theory it has been adduced (for instance in the *Catalogue of the Harleian MSS.*, under No. 2251, art. 3) that among Lydgate's stanzas on the kings of England occurs one on Edward IV. Halliwell already (*Minor Poems*, p. vi) has pointed out this argument to be a delusion; in the older copies such a stanza does not appear. I mention only the one in MS. Ashmole 59, in which case we know very well why Henry VI. is the last king mentioned. For this copy is written by Shirley, who died himself in 1456. Nevertheless, the verses existed then already. So the stanza on Edward is evidently spurious, a fact further certified by its being written in the 8-line stanza, whilst the others are all in the 7-line stanza (MS. Harl. 2251, fol. 4 a).[1] By this mode of argumentation we might easily prove that Lydgate became not only 112 years old, but even some 180; for in MS. Royal 18 D. II (and, I think, in the print by Wynken de Worde), a stanza on Henry VIII. is added. In this recension the earlier stanzas also deviate greatly from the original text, although we can clearly see that they have been built upon Lydgate's groundwork.

Very much the same holds good with respect to the poem " Ab inimicis nostris " . . ., quoted by *Warton-Hazlitt*, III, 53, note 1, for the same purpose. The greater part of the poem may be genuine, the last stanza in MS. Harl. 2251, fol. 11 a, recommending King Edward IV. and his mother to God, is certainly not so. The refrain in this stanza differs also slightly from that employed in the preceding ones.

A proof that Lydgate was alive in 1446, is adduced by *Warton-Hazlitt*, III, 53, note 1. We there find the assertion that Lydgate in his poem *Philomela* mentions the death of Henry Lord Warwick, "who died in 1446," and are referred to MS. Harl. 2251, fol. 255. Now it is true that at this place in the MS. in question (new pagination, fol. 229 a) there is a poem by Lydgate, entitled (by Stowe) " A sayenge of the nyghtyngale,"[2] but I cannot find the reference to Henry of Warwick. In MS. Cotton Caligula A. II (fol. 59 a—64 a), however, is also a poem " The nightyngale," and this contains, on fol. 63 a, the following stanza :

"A myghty prince, lusty, yonge & fiers,
Amonge the peple sore lamented ys :
The Duc of Warwyk—entryng the oure of tierce,
Deth toke hym to—whom mony sore shall mysse :
All-myghty Ihesu, receyue his soule to blisse.
Both hye & lowe, thenk well that ye shall henne :
Deth wyll you trise, ye wot not, how ne whenne."[3]

This stanza was, of course, written after the death of Henry of Warwick—brother-in-law of the kingmaker—which, however, accord-

---

[1] The *Catalogue of the Harleian MSS.* itself says (No. 2251, article 3) that the stanza relating to K. Henry VI. looks as if it were written in that king's prosperity.

[2] This poem occurs also in Stowe's MS. Add. 29729, fol. 161 a.

[3] This latter poem has 57 stanzas (in rhyme royal); Lydgate's poem (MS. Harl. 2251, fol. 229 a—234 b, and Add. 29729, fol. 161) has 54 stanzas. It is unfinished ; the Harl. MS. has the colophon :

"Of this Balade Dan Johñ Lydgate made nomore."

ing to the *Nouvelle Biographie générale*, took place on June 11th, 1445, not in 1446. But it seems that these two poems are by different authors; their subject only is the same, namely, an allegorizing interpretation of the nightingale's song. Both poems are perhaps independent treatments of John of Hoveden's *Philomela* (see *Warton-Hazlitt*, II, 33 top, and II, 93 note), which I cannot investigate at present.

Again, there is an *Epitaphium ducis Gloucestrie* (MS. Harl. 2251, fol. 7 *a* to 8 *b*), attributed to Lydgate by Ritson, No. 139, and in *Warton-Hazlitt*, III, 50, note 8. This would bring us down to 1447. But it must first be proved that the poem is genuine. I am inclined to believe that the internal evidence is against its being so; of external evidence I am ignorant: Ritson's opinion as to the authorship of the poem is, of course, worthless.

But we have fortunately two or three certain dates for these latter years of Lydgate's life. The first of them is already referred to in *Warton* (ed. Hazlitt III, 54, note 1); it is contained in a notice of Stowe's, in his *Annals of England*, 1615, p. 385, which states that Lydgate made the verses for the pageants exhibited at Queen Margaret's entry into London. This was in 1445. Further, Lydgate is mentioned as living by Bokenam, in his *Legend of St. Elizabeth*, with the following words (13, 1075):

"For, þow I had kunnyng for to ryme,
And eck to endyten as copyously,
As had Gower & Chauncers in þer tyme,
Or *as now hath* þe munk of Bery,
Joon Lytgate, yet cowd not I . . . ."

Bokenam's *Legends* were written between 1443 and 1447; that of Elizabeth appears to have been the last in order of time, and was, according to Horstmann's *Introduction*, p. viii (at the top), written in 1446.

On viewing the above facts, it however becomes clear to us that we reach the last *certain* date connected with Lydgate's life by means of a document published by Professor Zupitza in *Anglia*, III, 532. This is a receipt signed by John Baret for a sum of £3 16s. 8d. received by him for himself and for our monk, as a half-yearly instalment of a pension granted to them jointly. That such a pension was given[1] to

---

[1] Perhaps in compliance with his request to Duke Humphrey at the end of the *Falls of Princes* (finished about 1438, or 1439 ?), fol. 217 *b*:

"Trusting ageynward, your liberal largesse
Of thys quotidian shall relenen me . . .
[Hope] Sayd, ye, my lord, should haue compassion,
Of royal pitye support me in mine age."

Lydgate and John Baret had already been known from the *Proceedings*[1] *of the Privy Council*, 1835 (ed. Sir Harris Nicolas), V, 156, from which we gather that there were at first some formal difficulties as to the payment (cf. also Sir H. Nicolas's *Introduction*, p. clvii). The entry in the *Proceedings*, taken from MS. Add. 4609, art. 27 (fol. 64), is dated Nov. 14th, 1441, the document published by Zupitza, Oct. 2nd, 1446. So far we can follow our monk, the latter being the latest certain date which we have concerning Lydgate's life. We may suppose that he died soon after this; several of the MSS. of the *Secreta Secretorum*, his last work, mention his death. In whatever year he may have died, certain it is that, for his literary fame with posterity, he lived some thirty or thirty-five years too long. Had he died before 1412, or at least written no more, the epithet of a poet—*cum grano salis*, of course—might have been given him less hesitatingly by our generation.

I have already indicated above that we know little of Lydgate's private life,[2] and nothing of his family. They were, I suppose, village-folk, and the boy most likely attracted the notice of the neighbouring monastery by his natural gifts. Considering that he passed the greater part of his life in the monastery, and moreover received frequent commissions for literary work from the highest personages in the land, it seems rather strange that we hear him so often complain of his straitened circumstances and the emptiness of his purse. We should have supposed that many of Lydgate's complaints on this score were only humoristic; for instance, his frequent hints that an occasional glass of Bacchus' finest gift would be a most desirable incentive to spur on a poet's flagging imagination. Some such passages are:

Falls of Princes, fol. 176 *d*:
"I was borne in Lydgate,
Where Bacchus licour doth ful scarsly flete,
My drie soule for to dewe and wete."

Ib., fol. 90 *c*, the monk tells us that poets should

"eschew all ydlenes,
Walke by riuers and welles christalline,
To hic mountaines a-morow ther cours dresse,
The mist defied whan Phebus first doth shine,"

---

[1] See *supra*, p. xcii, note 1.
[2] Those who care to know it may be informed that our monk wore spectacles:
"Myne yien misted and darked by spectacle" (*Falls of Princes*, fol. 217 *a*).
It was, I suppose, in imitation of his brother-poet that Bokenam also took to spectacles; cp. his *Legend of Margarete* (1,656):
. . . "myn handys gynne to feynte,
My wyt to dullyn, and myn eyne bleynte
Shuld be, ner helpe of a spectacle."

and, especially,

"Drinke wine among to quick(en) their diligence."

Ib., fol. 217 *a*, he speaks of a "thrustlew axesse" as "cause of his langour," because "of Bachus seared were the vines," and complains of the "ebbes of constrained indigence," and that there is in him

"None egal peyse : heart heauy and purs light."

Of his life in the monastery, he says in his *Testament* (*Halliwell*, p. 258):

"I savouryd mor in good wyn that was cleer
And every hour my passage for to dresse,
As I seide erst, to ryot or excesse."

The monk seems to have been of a kindred spirit to Heraclius, of whom he says (*Falls of Princes*, fol. 200 *a*):

"And therwithall he had a froward lust
Euer to drinke, and euer he was athurst."

As we have said, we should be inclined to look at this entirely from the humoristic side, although we might possibly find in it grounds for the suspicion that our monk belonged to the confraternity of "bibuli," in which the thirstier souls of the monastery may have been united in Lydgate's time as in the days of grand old Abbot Samson.[1]

There is further Lydgate's "Litera ad ducem Gloucestrie pro oportunitate pecunie in tempore translacionis Bochasii" (printed in *Halliwell*, p. 49), in which he asks the Duke

"To se thentent of this litel bille,"

in which "*nichil habet* is cause of the compleynt." This again might be interpreted, from its humoristic tone, as a mere imitation— playful or pedantic, however we choose to call it—of Chaucer's *Compleint to his Purse*. That the literal interpretation is, however, the right one, is confirmed by a passage in the *Falls of Princes* (fol. 67 *d*), in which Lydgate thanks the Duke for his liberality:

"My lordes fredom and bounteous largesse
Into mine heart brought in suche gladnes,
That through releuyng of his benigne grace
False indigence list me nomore manace ;"

further, by the wording of his "Dimissio" from Hatfield Broad-oak,

---

[1] See *Jocelyn de Brakelond* and Carlyle's *Past and Present*. With respect to Lydgate's time compare a passage in Dr. Logeman's Introduction to his edition of the *Rule of S. Benet*, p. xvii: "About the year 1421 we find that degeneration had again set in, and that a reform was contemplated. At a meeting in Westminster Abbey between King Henry V and the Abbots and prelates of the Order of Black Monks, more than 360 in number, a reform was decided upon."

which was granted him "propter frugem melioris vitae captandam" (see above); also by his petition to the king for the confirmation of a grant, in which he calls himself "youre pouere and perpetuell Oratour John Lydgate" (see above, p. xcvii), and lastly by two passages from Shirley, namely the one given above on page lxxxiii (last line), and the following one from Addit. MS. 29729, fol. 178 a (copied by Stowe from Shirley):

> "Yet for all his much konnynge,
> Which were gret tresore to a kynge—
> I meane this Lidgate, munke danne (MS. dame) Iohn—
> His nobles bene spent, I leue yehon,
> And eke his shylinges nyghe by :
> His thred-bare coule woll not ly.
> Ellas! ye lordes, why nill ye se,
> And rewaid his pouerte?"

These lines betray, however, a reminiscence of the Prologue of the *Story of Thebes*, with its humoristic description of the monk's shabby appearance, which makes it questionable whether Shirley had more resources to draw from than the passage alluded to and his own poetical inspiration.

§ 2. *Chronological sequence of Lydgate's writings.*

Lydgate's writings seem naturally to group themselves into two periods, that of his early works up to 1412, and that of his long translations—of the *Stories of Troy*, *of Thebes*, and the *Falls of Princes*, together with Deguileville's *First Pilgrimage*—as well as the legends and minor poems of his old age, a period lasting from 1412 to his death.

We have already spoken of Lydgate's sojourn at Oxford, which was most likely devoted to study in that University. It seems that when there he wrote his *Æsop*, which gives a very drawled-out version of some six or seven Æsopian fables, which have been printed by Sauerstein in *Anglia* IX, p. 1, etc., and again by Zupitza, in the *Archiv*, vol. 85, p. 1, etc., from a different MS., with important additions, and corrections of Sauerstein's mistakes. The date of this *Æsop* would then be about 1387; but there still appears to me to be room for some doubt in the matter.

The first certain date for any of Lydgate's writings has been made known to us by Miss Toulmin Smith; it is the date for the prose-work, *The Serpent of Division*, or, *The Damage and Destruction in Realms*. According to vol. 35 of Lord Calthorpe's Yelverton MSS., this tract was composed by Lydgate in 1400 (December?); see Miss Toulmin Smith's edition of *Gorboduc*, p. xx, etc.

A poem which, I think, we must not place later than 1400, is *Chorl and Bird*. The Envoy of it is directed "Unto my maister with humble affeccioun," praying him to correct and amend it. As far as I am aware, Lydgate calls no one his master, except Chaucer, and I think this envoy can be addressed to none other than him. Chaucer, of course, must have been still living then, so that the latest date we can assign to it would be 1400.

Certainly the influence of Chaucer, whom he may have known personally, is most perceptible in Lydgate during this period, to which we may assign those works most clearly impregnated with the ideas of his great master, dimmed and diluted as they may be after having gone through the alembic of Lydgate's mind. To this category belong the *Flour of Curtesie*, the *Black Knight*, the *Temple of Glas*, as well as *Reason and Sensuality*, the *chef-d'œuvre* of this period, as it is of all Lydgate's writings. It is a great pity that we have not one certain date for any poetical work of this period, which more than any other does credit to Lydgate's poetical faculties. The *Flour of Curtesie*, however, must have been written after Chaucer's death, as its Envoy proves, and the *Temple of Glas* not far from 1400, as I hope to show is probable in § 3 of this chapter. The *Black Knight* is a palpable imitation of the *Book of the Duchesse*, and may come before the *Temple of Glas*, as this last-named poem is evidently a more ambitious effort, in which Lydgate stands, it seems, for the first time, upon his own feet, the invention of the whole work originating entirely with him. Thus I believe that the three works, the *Flour of Curtesie*, the *Black Knight*, and the *Temple of Glas* were written in this sequence, most likely between 1400 and 1403.

I have little doubt that between this time and the translation of the *Troy-Book*, *Reason and Sensuality* was written, as well as the *Life of our Lady*. But as there are no certain dates recorded for these comprehensive works, and our reasons for placing them here, will become all the more evident later on, we will now, by a considerable jump, proceed at once to the lengthy works of the second period, which we may date from the year 1412.

There is, first of all, the *Troy-Book*. We have fortunately a certain knowledge of the approximate dates[1] for this work, which

---

[1] A chronological discussion of the three best-known works of Lydgate—best-known by name only, of course—forms the introduction to Koeppel's treatise

Chapter VIII.—Chronology of Lydgate's Writings. ci

heads the series of those long, spun-out and entirely unoriginal writings which have so justly discredited Lydgate's Muse. From the Prologue to that work we easily gather that Lydgate must have begun it in October 1412. With the same preciseness we know that it was finished in 1420. For we have in Pynson's *Troy-Book* (1513), sign. Dd₂ d :

> "And tyme complet of this translacyon . . . .
> Was a thousande and foure hondred yere,
> And twenty nere—I knowe it out of drede . . .
> The eyghte yere, by computacyon,
> Suynge after the Coronacyon
> Of hym . . . . Herry the fyfthe,"

the reading of MS. Cotton Aug. A. IV, fol. 152 b, agreeing word for word with this. To Koeppel, only the modernization of the *Troy-Book*, printed in 1614 by Th. Purfoot, was available. In this the passage is different, and points to 1421 as the date of the conclusion of the poem. Perhaps the expression "twenty nere" warrants the inference that the *Troy Book* was finished between March 21st and March 25th, 1420 (new style). Henry V's eighth year lasted from March 21st, 1420, until March 21st, 1421 ; so the date must be after March 21st, 1420 (old style, 1419), and if we have to interpret "nere" as meaning "nearly," "not quite," it must be before March 25th, 1420 : the days from March 21—25, 1419 (new style, 1420), lie in the eighth year of Henry V, and are "near" the year 1420, from Lydgate's standpoint. I believe, therefore, that the *Troy-Book* was begun in the autumn of 1412, and finished in the spring of 1420.

The work we have next to discuss is the English prose-translation of Deguileville's *Second Pilgrimage*, i. e. of the Soul, printed by Caxton in 1483. We know—for instance, from Caxton's colophon and MS. Egerton 615—that this translation was made in 1413, but the great question is whether it was done by Lydgate. It has several times been alleged, as a proof for Lydgate's authorship, that Chapter XXXIV of the *Life of our Lady*, and Chapter XXXIV of the *Pilgrimage* are one and the same. It is curious to compare the wording of these assertions. We read in the *Catalogus Bibliothecæ Harleianæ*, 1744, III, 126 : "This is remarkable, that the 34th Chapter of that Poet's [Lydgate's] *Life of the Virgin* Mary is a Digression in Praise of *Chaucer* . . . and

---

on the sources of the *Story of Thebes*. His dating of the *Troy-Book* and the *Story of Thebes* are certainly in the main successful ; with respect to the *Falls of Princes* I shall be obliged to somewhat modify his results. It will be seen that the conclusions I have arrived at concerning these works tally more closely with those obtained by Ward, *Catalogue of the Romances*, I, 75.

that the 34th Chapter of the Second Book of this *Pilgremage* should be the same Poem." There is, indeed, a panegyric on Chaucer in the 34th Chapter of the *Life of our Lady*, as is very well known; but the second part of the above statement is not correct. There is no 34th Chapter at all in the second book of Caxton's print of the *Pilgrimage*, as the numbers of the chapters go on without a break through the first two books (1—39 being contained in the first book, 40—65 in the second). Chapter XXXIV of the first book contains the "Charter of Mercy" for the pilgrim, but no eulogy on Chaucer. Again, Miss Cust, in *The Booke of the Pylgremage of the Sowle translated from De Guileville*, 1859, p. iv, says: 'The translator, or at least the author of the "additions," was in all probability Lydgate; for the 34th chapter of Lydgate's metrical "Life of the Virgin Mary" is literally repeated in the 34th chapter of this translation of "The Charter of Mercy."' Very much the same thing is stated in *Warton-Hazlitt* III, 67. It is quite true that the 34th, or rather 35th, Chapter of the *Pilgrimage* (Caxton's numbering is not quite correct) contains the *Charter of Mercy*, but not so the 34th Chapter of the *Life of our Lady*. The part of the *Life of our Lady*, which somewhat recalls this *Charter of Mercy* in the *Pilgrimage*, is Chapters XI —XIV, which contain the dispute between "Mercy, Pees, Rightwysnes and Trouthe, for the redempcion of mankynde"; but there again, I cannot find any verbal coincidences. It may be that some of the stanzas, interspersed between the prose of the *Pilgrimage*, can be identified with others in the *Life of our Lady*; but I must add, that a comparison of the French and English texts of the *Pilgrimage* shows the English stanzas to be in all cases renderings of the French original.[1]

In perusing this translation of the *Second Pilgrimage*, nothing in the way of internal evidence has struck me which points decidedly to Lydgate as the author, either in the prose or even in the stanzas, and yet Lydgate is, as a rule, easily enough detected. Further, it seems to me highly improbable that Lydgate, just after having begun the translation of the *Troy-Book*, at the command of

---

[1] Even if a more careful investigation than I am at present able to carry out, should after all identify some of the stanzas in the two works, this would not necessarily be a proof of Lydgate's authorship; the case would then be exactly parallel to the intended insertion of Chaucer's *A B C* in Lydgate's verse-translation of the *First Pilgrimage*. For later on I hope to make it probable that the *Life of our Lady* was written before 1413, and could thus have been made use of by anybody.

Chapter VIII.—Chronology of Lydgate's Writings. ciii

Prince Henry—in 1413, King Henry V.—should only a few months later have started a translation of another work of by no means contemptible dimensions (I should think, some 10,000 lines in the original). Moreover, in his Prologue to the verse-translation of the *First Pilgrimage* (that of Man), begun by him in 1426, he would scarcely have omitted some reference to his former rendering of Deguileville's *Second Pilgrimage*. I am, at present, aware of only one passage which could possibly be construed into a proof that Lydgate was the author of this translation of the *Second Pilgrimage* in prose. I mean the following lines from Stowe's MS. Add. 29729, fol. 178 a, which have been copied by Stowe from one of Shirley's "poetical" lists of the contents of one of his MSS. :

"First yᵉ humayne pilgrymage,
Sayd all by proose in fayre laugage :
And many a roundell and balade,
Which yᵉ munke of bury hath made."

But then this seems to refer to Shirley's Sion College MS. Archives 2. 23, which contains a prose-rendering of the *First Pilgrimage*, called in one of the headlines of the MS., "þe pilgrymage humayne."[1] I suppose this prose-translation in the Sion College MS. is essentially the same as the one published by W. Aldis Wright for the Roxburghe Club in 1869, from MS. Ff. 5. 30 in the University Library, Cambridge. The title "humayne pilgrymage," *if taken literally*, only applies to the *First Pilgrimage*, the "pèlerinage de la vie humaine," which Lydgate later on translated in verse. No one would suppose Lydgate to have translated the same work twice over, first in prose, then in verse, all the less as no decided authority can be adduced for such a supposition. Although I have not been able to examine the Sion College MS. personally, yet I should think that the last line from Shirley given above can only mean that Lydgate was the author of "many a roundell and balade" in this MS., but not so of the "humayne pilgrymage."

Thus I believe that Lydgate certainly translated Deguileville's *First Pilgrimage* in verse, in 1426, etc., but he neither made the prose-translation of the *Second Pilgrimage* in 1413, nor (as scarcely any one will assume) translated the *First Pilgrimage* in prose.

Lydgate's next large work, after the *Troy-Book*, is the *Story of Thebes*. The monk was " nie fiftie yere of age " when he wrote the

[1] See Dr. Furnivall's *Odd Texts*, pp. 65 and 78 ; compare also his *Trial-Forewords*, p. 13.

prologue to this work, which opens with a description of spring. We may therefore fairly assume that Lydgate began the work in the spring of 1420, after having finished the *Troy-Book;* the expression, "Mid of April,"[1] in the Prologue to the *Story of Thebes,* would tally very well with the end-date for the *Troy-Book.* Taking one consideration with another, it seems to me most likely that the *Story of Thebes* was begun in April 1420. For this would also agree best with the "nie fiftie yere of age" of the Prologue; if Lydgate was born in 1371—we scarcely can make it later—he was in 1420 exactly 49 years old. If he was *very* "near fiftie," he might have been born early in 1371, or better still for our chronology, towards the end of 1370. As regards the end-date for the *Story of Thebes,* Koeppel rightly points out that Lydgate would not have omitted in his Epilogue to lament the death of Henry V., after the 31st August 1422, on which day that monarch died. At all events, we cannot be very far wrong if we say that the *Story of Thebes* was written between 1420 and 1422.

It would seem also that *Guy of Warwick* belongs to this time; Prof. Zupitza has conjectured its date to be 1420. Perhaps it was written shortly after the *Story of Thebes,* when the monk appears to have had more leisure after the completion of his two large translations.

With respect to the *Troy-Book* and the *Story of Thebes,* I agree in the main with Dr. Koeppel, as to the dating of them; making only the slight change of 1421 to 1420, which change is warranted by texts of the *Troy-Book* of better authority than the one which was accessible to Koeppel. But I can no longer share his opinion as to the date of the *Falls of Princes.* On the strength of two passages in that work, Koeppel came to the conclusion that it must have been written from 1424 to about 1433. Now we shall presently show that, in 1426, Lydgate undertook the translation of Deguileville's *First Pilgrimage* for the Earl of Salisbury. This work has more than 20,000 lines, and thus it would seem unlikely that the *Falls of Princes,* being done at the command of the Regent of England and uncle of the king, should be broken off for an indefinite time for another big undertaking. Still, we should nevertheless be forced to assume that such was the case, if the date 1424 could be inferred unmistakably

---

[1] Compare, however, Wülcker, in *Altenglisches Lesebuch* II, 270, who thinks that this statement as to the time is simply made by Lydgate in accordance with the beginning of the *Canterbury Tales.*

from Lydgate's own words in the Prologue to the *Falls of Princes*. We should then assume that Lydgate, after having written the two first books of the *Falls of Princes* from 1424—1426, wrote, in the course of the next years, the translation of the *Pilgrimage*, and then returned to his former and much duller work. Thus his deep sighs in the Prologue to the 3rd book would be all the more understandable :

> "Thus my self remembryng on this boke,
> It to translate how I had vndertake,
> Full pale of chere, astonyed in my loke,
> Mine hand gan tremble, my penne I felt[e] quake . . .
> I stode chekmate for feare whan I gan see,
> In my way how litle I had runne" (*F. Pr.* fol. 67 d).

Indeed, there was reason for "trembling and standing checkmate :" 11,627 lines, and only two out of nine books done ! Surely, his breast must be girt with "robur et æs triplex" who could be impervious to all feelings of pity for our sorely-tried monk.

But, as I have said, the *Falls of Princes* was not begun in 1424. The passage adduced by Koeppel for this conclusion is wrongly interpreted (see also Ward, *Catalogue* I, 75, and Th. Arnold, *A Manual of English Literature*, 6th ed., p. 137, note). The lines in question, from the Prologue to the *Falls of Princes*, fol. A_3 a (Koeppel, *Story of Thebes*, p. 14), are as follows (the punctuation is mine) :

> "Eke in this land, I dare affirme a thing,
> There is a prince, ful mighty of puissaunce :
> A kinges sonne, & vnkle to the king—
> Henry the sixth, which now is in fraunce—
> And is lieftenant & hath the gouernaunce
> Of our Britayn . . . .
> Duke of gloucester men this prince cal."

The relative sentence, "which now is in fraunce," must certainly refer to Henry VI., an assumption which at once makes everything clear. Henry VI. was in France from April 1430 to the end of 1431 ; it will tally best with the other evidence to assume that the Prologue to the *Falls of Princes* was written in 1430.

But, before his *Falls of Princes*, Lydgate made another lengthy translation for a famous English nobleman. As I have already said, the Englishing of Deguileville's *Pèlerinage de la vie humaine*, in four-beat couplets, was undertaken by him, in 1426, for Thomas de Montacute, Earl of Salisbury. I should think that the monk finished it between the years 1426 and 1430, at his average rate of producing 4000 or 5000 lines a year.[1] In my opinion, not the slightest doubt

---

[1] The Earl of Salisbury, as is well known, had fallen in the meantime, being shot in the siege of Orleans. Lydgate, however, does not allude to the event

remains as to its genuineness; the Prologue (in heroic couplets) is thoroughly Lydgatian; there is the allusion to his master Chaucer (fol. 256 b), and to the niggardliness of "Jove's butler Ganymede" to our monk (fol. 4 b); we have further the authority of Speght (see No. 3 of the Lydgate-list in the Chaucer-edition of 1598, fol. 394 a), and thus also, I think, indirectly, of Stowe, who supplied many missing headings in the MS. Cotton Vit. C. XIII. The language,[1] the manner of translating, &c., are entirely those of Lydgate.

The next work to which we can assign a certain date is the short *Legend of St. Margaret*. According to the Durham MS., this little work was written " A° VIII° h[enrici] VI,"[2] *i. e.* between Aug. 31st (on which day Henry V. died in 1422), 1429, and August 31st, 1430. It evidently stands between the *Pilgrimage of Man* and the *Falls of Princes*.

The Prologue to this latter work, as has already been pointed out, must have been written in 1430 or 1431. The monk seems first to have finished Books 1 and 2, after which a break of a few months must have occurred. For in 1433 Lydgate certainly wrote the *Legend of St. Edmund and Fremund*. He says himself in that poem .that Abbot William [Curteys] commanded him to write the life of the patron-saint of his monastery during the visit of King Henry VI. to the shrine and convent of St. Edmund (I. 187, &c.). This visit lasted from Christmas 1432 to Easter 1433. Lydgate's own words as to his beginning the poem are not quite clear: from l. 134, &c., in the Prologue, it might appear that he began the poem at Christmas (1432); but lines 151, &c., of the Prologue were clearly written after the king's departure. There can be no doubt however that the main part of the *Legend* was written in 1433. In this case we need not wonder that the monk stopped short in his translation of the *Falls of Princes* for Duke Humphrey; for *Edmund* was written for the king himself. Lydgate brought great zeal to bear on his treatment of this *Legend*, and the work is by no means his worst. For the last time we get a glimpse of something like poetry in the

in the course of this work; but we have a reference to the Earl's death in his *Minor Poems*, Halliwell, p. 126.
[1] Note particularly the not unfrequent use of the word "chaumpartie," used in a sense which seems to have originated in Lydgate's misunderstanding of a line in Chaucer. See note to l. 1164. Other favourite expressions of Lydgate's are of frequent occurrence in the *Pilgrimage*, as the notes will to some extent show.
[2] See the edition of this Legend in Horstmann's *Altenglische Legenden, Neue Folge*, p. 446.

now aging monk, when it devolved upon him to shed all possible lustre upon his glorious martyr-king. For in true piety, which comes straight from the heart, there always lies a touch of poetry.

After this labour of love, our poor monk went on—amid the deep sighs and groans described above—with his *Tragedies of Iohn Bochas on the Falls of Princes*. "Tragedies" indeed, inspiring the Aristotelian terror and pity in no common degree: terror by their bulk, and pity for their author—and ourselves into the bargain, when we feel bound to wade through them. This time the monk went right through to the bitter end. In the Prologue to the 8th book,[1] Lydgate complains of his great age, which is "more than three-score years," and of his trembling joints. We may suppose that this passage was written about 1436, at which time Lydgate was sixty-five years old. I should think that the monk finished this dreary compilation in 1438 or 1439, and I readily believe that he said a very heartfelt "Deo gratias" after it. He need not in his next work have expressly drawn our attention to the fact that his wit was irretrievably "fordulled."

In 1439, abbot Whethamstede of St. Albans wished to see the patron-saint of his monastery and protomartyr of England glorified in the same way as St. Edmund had been. Lydgate was again chosen to carry out this work, and he thus wrote a *Life of Albon and Amphabel*, on a similar plan to the *Life of St. Edmund*, but, as may be easily understood, inferior to it in every respect.

After 1439 we hear little of any poetical efforts of our monk. Still his fame had not died before him; for in one of his last years, 1445, he was called upon to write the verses for some pageants exhibited on Queen Margaret's entry into London. About the same time he was engaged in commemorating in verse certain miracles, wrought by St. Edmund in 1441, and again in 1444, the which verses are printed by Horstmann at the end of his edition of Lydgate's *St. Edmund* (*Altenglische Legenden*, *Neue Folge*, p. 440, &c.). We may also suppose that Lydgate's *Testament* belongs to this time. We know with certainty that he died when in course of writing the

---

[1] Ward, *Catalogue of the Romances*, I, 75, says that this passage occurs in the contemporary MS. Harley 1766, on folio 184, in the middle of the 6th book. This is quite correct; but the passage stands in reality in the same place as in Tottel's print, the numbering of the books in the Harl. MS. being in great confusion. It counts only eight books, whereas Boccaccio's work has nine; and from the very passage in question, as it stands in Tottel as well as in the Harleian MS., we gather that this Prologue was to be followed immediately by "two books."

Secreta Secretorum, which was finished by Bennet Burgh. Lydgate's part ends with the line—

"Deth al consumyth, whych may nat be denyed,"

which may have been the last verse that came from the monk's pen. Immediately after it the MSS. have the rubric: "Here deyed this translatour and nobyl poete / And the yonge folwere gan his prologe on this wyse" (MS. Ashmole 46, fol. 131 a).

We must now return to certain works of Lydgate's, the classification of which we postponed until we should find ourselves on firmer ground. We will first consider the *Life of our Lady*. I have little doubt that this was the last important work of Lydgate's first period, before he began the translation of the *Troy-Book* in 1412. For we know that it was undertaken at the command of Henry V. Now we have seen that Lydgate, from 1412—1422, was occupied with the *Troy-Book* and the *Story of Thebes*. Therefore, it seems most natural that the *Life of our Lady* should have been written before these works. Moreover, we have an astronomical datum in the work. On folio i_4 b, we hear that our monk made a certain prayer when "Lucina was passed late from Phebus," and the statement seems to refer to the first of January. There was a new moon, in 1410, on the 26th of December (see *infra*, p. cxiv), which agrees very well with this statement. I should think that the *Life of our Lady* was written about 1409—1411. The poem, with its comparative freshness—at least in some parts—still belongs to Lydgate's better works.

For *Reason and Sensuality* I know of no external evidence which would warrant a certain date for the year of its composition. The work is of considerable length (about 7400 four-beat lines), and there remain only three periods in which Lydgate could possibly have found time to write it, namely, 1422—1426, 1439—1445, and the time immediately before 1409. I believe that 1422—1426, and still more 1439—1445, are quite impossible dates; the monk was much too "fordulled" at that time, and had sunk from what was, at any rate, some approach to a poet, to a mere rhymester and unoriginal translator. He can only, I believe, have written the best production of his life in his prime, and I consider the *Flour of Curtesie*, the *Black Knight*, the *Temple of Glas*, as works which lead up to the only one of Lydgate's poems which we can read with real interest and enjoyment. Thus we are, perhaps, not far wrong in believing that *Reason and Sensuality* was written between 1406 and 1408.

Chapter VIII.—Chronology of Lydgate's Writings.

Of the monk's larger works, *Horse, goose, and sheep, De duobus Mercatoribus*, the *Assembly of Gods*, and the *Court of Sapience* remain. With respect to the chronology of these I feel extremely doubtful. The least thing which I should feel it incumbent upon me to do before venturing on any definite opinion as to their dates, would be to read them again carefully, which I have at present no opportunity of doing. The first of these poems has the approximate date, 1470, in the *N. E. Dictionary* (under *bouge*), which, of course, is absolutely impossible. Lydgate cannot have written it after his death. Of the *Assembly of Gods*, otherwise called *Assemble de dyeus*, or *Banquet of Gods*, we have a late MS., Royal 18 D II; and the poem was printed by Wynken, Pynson, and Redman (it would seem, altogether five times; see Hazlitt, *Handbook*, p. 358). The MS. is later than Wynken's first print;[1] its text follows Wynken de Worde's print (C. 13. a. 21 in the British Museum) very closely; indeed, it seems to be a copy of it. Prefixed to the poem itself we find in the prints the *Interpretation of the names of gods and goddesses*, enumerating the principal heathen deities, and also indicating their respective spheres of action (for instance, Pluto = God of helle, Morpleus (*sic*) = Shewer of dremes, &c.). This *Interpretation* has often been mistaken for a separate work, which it is not; it seems only to be Wynken's addition to make the poem more easily understood by those of his readers who were less versed than he in classic mythology. In the MS. it does not appear. The metre of the prints and the MS. is exceedingly irregular, much more so than in any other poem of Lydgate's; but as the lines on the Kings of England in the Royal MS. show the same metrical corruption, besides great arbitrary changes, I am inclined to believe that this *Assembly of Gods* may have been tampered with in a similar way. Still it is not absolutely certain that Lydgate was the author; but I suppose the following item in Hawes's list of Lydgate's works (*Pastime of Pleasure*, Chapter XIV) can only mean our work:

"And betwene vertue and the lyfe vycyous,
Of goddes and goddes[ses] a boke solacyous
He did compyle"...

Further, Bale mentions *De nominibus Deorum* among the writings

[1] That is to say, the second half of it; the first part, containing the *Troy-Book* and the *Story of Thebes*, with beautiful illuminations, is in a much older handwriting. The second hand (beginning of the 16th century) has written the *Assembly of Gods*, further, a poem by Skelton, Lydgate's *Testament*, and his *Stanzas on the Kings of England*, the latter with additional stanzas down to Henry VIII. (also copied from a print by Wynken.?). See Dyce's *Skelton*, p. x.

of Lydgate; so also, following him, Pits, Ghilini, &c. It may, however, be that Bale simply drew his statement from a title-page of Wynken de Worde's, as found in the copy of the British Museum, marked C. 13. a. 21, which seems to have been a joint issue of Lydgate's *Story of Thebes, Assembly of Gods,* and *Temple of Glas* (see Hazlitt, *Handbook,* p. 358). The first stanza reminds one strikingly in its tone of the beginning of *Piers Ploughman:*

> "Whan Phebus in the crabbe had nere his cours ronne,
> And toward the Leon his Iourney gan take,
> To loke on Pyctagoras spere I had b[e]gonne,
> Syttyng all solytary allone besyde a lake,
> Musyng on a maneer how that I myght make
> Reason and sensualyte in one to accorde:
> But I coude not bryng about that monacorde."

The poem certainly deserves a re-edition.

I feel almost certain that the date of the *Court of Sapience* could be made out by a careful investigation. As to its genuineness I have not the slightest doubt; Blades's scruples on this score, as brought forward against the opinion of W. Oldys (*Caxton,* II, 115), are hardly justifiable. Blades would consider the *Court of Sapience* Lydgate's finest work, if it were his, and wonders that such a remarkable poem should be so scarce then, compared with the monk's other writings. But it cannot be said that the poem is so very scarce; for we have, besides Caxton's print, and the Trinity College MS., a print by Wynken de Worde, of the year 1510, and further, Addit. MS. 29729, which was copied out by John Stowe (from Shirley, or a print?). Moreover, the first part of it, the pleading between Mercy, Truth, Right, and Peace, occurs at the end of MS. Harl. 2251, and some stanzas of it found their way into the Chaucer-print of 1561 (see Chapter XII). We have, moreover, Hawes's (*Pastime of Pleasure,* Chapter XIV) and Stowe's plain testimony that Lydgate was the author. Stowe's testimony (in MS. Addit. 29729, fol. 87 a, in the Trinity College MS., and in the list contained in Speght's *Chaucer,* 1598) perhaps goes back to Shirley, not to Hawes, as Blades supposes.

I feel far less certain as to its date. The poem in MS. Harl. 2255, fol. 21 (" Mercy and trouthe mette on an hih mounteyn," etc.), written after Henry V.'s death, or the passage in *Pur le Roy* (about 1432), *Halliwell,* p. 11 &c., or the first book of the prose-translation of the *Pilgrimage of the Soule* (1413), have hardly any direct contact with the *Court of Sapience.* Who is the "sovoraign," by whom the author was "constrained to write"? So far as I am aware at

present, this question of the date requires us to take into especial consideration the following line of the prologue:
"Let ignoraunce and chyldhode haue the wyte."
But was Lydgate favoured so early by the Court? By Henry IV.? Or is the word *chyldhode* here not to be taken in its natural and usual sense referring to age? Some critics even feel inclined to believe that this Prologue is not by Lydgate, but was added by somebody else, perhaps Caxton. I repeat that a careful investigation must almost certainly lead to a definite solution of these questions, which will make a re-edition of the poem all the more interesting.

Speaking generally, I believe that further observations will disclose more and more decisive characteristics, from which we may ascribe an earlier or later origin for those works to which we have as yet the most difficulty in assigning a place. For as Koeppel truly remarks, we still stand "in den Anfängen der Lydgate-Forschung," and only gradually, by careful investigations and editions of each separate work, shall we be able once and for all to disperse the doubts and solve the questions which attach to all the more interesting works of Lydgate. Until now, with hardly a single exception, Lydgate's dullest works alone have been treated of by Historians of Literature.

At present we can only with certainty say this much, that there is a wide difference in poetical value, in tone and style, between the more imaginative writings of his earlier time, and the dry, monotonous translations spun out through thousands and thousands of lines in his later days; between the jovial humour, or keen enjoyment of nature in the first period, and the cumbersome and dismal pages of the *Falls of Princes*, or the philistine rules—often disgracefully devoid of taste—for the health, diet, and general conduct of a prince in the *Secreta Secretorum*. We may safely say, that, after our monk had reached the zenith of his power in *Reason and Sensuality*, the poetical value of his works decreases in direct proportion to the distance from this better time.

Whether the same is true of his metre, further investigations have to establish. As regards versification, the *Story of Thebes* is indeed, of all his works, generally made out to be the scape-grace of the family, whilst the metre of the *Falls of Princes* is applauded as being far superior. True enough, if we take the two texts as they stand, the one in the Chaucer-Print of 1561, the other in Tottel's edition of 1554. But I should not be astonished if Dr. Erdmann's forthcoming edition of the *Story of Thebes* proves that its black-letter text is much more corrupted than that of the *Falls of Princes*; for Tottel gives us to understand on his title-page that he used more than one MS. for the construction of his text. Still I must not omit to say that Lydgate's five-beat line always seems more regularly built in the seven-line stanza than in the heroic couplet.

Lydgate's style, at all events, changes considerably in the course of time, and, as he grows older, he entirely forgets some of his favourite expressions. His pen certainly had still ample occasion to "quake" in the *Falls of Princes*, and the invocations to the Furies are frequent enough; but the pretty descriptions of nature, his humour, in short, the brighter side of his poetry, is almost entirely gone; his "fresh, fair" ladies have become very scarce, and those with "hair like gold wire" have vanished for ever.

It will perhaps not be amiss to subjoin a short synoptical table of the dates—known and conjectural—of Lydgate's life and works.

1370 (or 1371)?, born at Lydgate.
1387? studying in Oxford; his *Æsop*. Travels abroad??
March 13, 1388 (new style 1389?), receives the four lower orders of the Church.
Dec. (?) 17, 1389, receives Letters dismissory for the order of subdeacon.
May 28, 1393, ditto for deacon.
April 4, 1397, ditto for the order of priest.
April 7, 1397, ordained priest.
1398 (?), *Chorl and Bird*.
  ,,   *Horse, Goose, and Sheep*(??).
1400, *Serpent of Division*.
1400—1402 (?), *Flour of Curtesie, Black Knight*.
1403 (?), *Temple of Glas*.
  ,,   [*Assemble of Gods*?? *Court of Sapience*??]
1406—1408 (?), *Reason and Sensuality*.
1409—1411 (?), *Life of our Lady*.
1412—1420, *Troy-Book*.
[1413, Prose *Pilgrimage* hardly genuine.]
1415, Lydgate living at Bury.

1420—1422 (?), *Story of Thebes*.
Feb. 21, 1423, Lydgate mentioned in the Minutes of the Privy Council.
June 1423, elected Prior of Hatfield Broadoak.
1423 (?), *Guy of Warwick*.
1424—1426, Lydgate in France?
1425 (?), *Dance of Macabre*.
1426—1430 (?), *Pilgrimage de mounde* (in verse).
1430, *Legend of St. Margaret*.
1430—1438 (?), *Falls of Princes*.
1432, *Pur le Roy*.
1433, *Legend of St. Edmund and Fremund*.
April 8, 1434, licensed to go back to Bury from Hatfield.
1439, *Legend of St. Albon and Amphabel*.
1441, legal difficulties concerning the payment of a royal grant to Lydgate.
1444, *Miracles of St. Edmund*.
1445, *Verses for Queen Margaret's entry into London*.
1445 (?), *Testament*.
1446 (?), *Secreta Secretorum*.
Dies between 1446 and 1450?

Many of the monk's smaller poems can be dated; the above list comprises only the more extensive works. I repeat that this attempt at making out the sequence of Lydgate's writings, is merely a temporary one, given in the hope that, with all its shortcomings, it may throw more light upon the matter, and may be welcome to the

Chapter VIII.—Chronology of Lydgate's Writings. cxiii

investigator of special works of Lydgate. I shall only be glad if a more thorough study of his particular writings removes any of the above notes of interrogation or assigns the right date to a work possibly inserted in a wrong place.

§ 3. *Date of the Temple of Glas.*

Unfortunately there is not sufficient evidence to afford us a precise date for the composition of the *Temple of Glas.* That it, however, belongs to Lydgate's first period, and was produced before the interminable rhymes of his middle and old age, is proved by the MS. T, which is scarcely much later than 1400. The next-oldest MS., G, seems to have been written about 1430; it exhibits, with S, extensive deviations from the other texts; and the common original of G and S may be some years earlier. This external evidence agrees very well with the classification given above in § 2, and even serves to justify it; the *Temple of Glas* certainly bears in its composition, its style, and its general tenor, the marks of the early period, as alluded to above. Lydgate's inveighing against the enforced monastic life (ll. 201—208) strengthens this supposition of an early origin; we know from his *Testament* that, in his youth, he himself felt little vocation for the cloister. Neither, unfortunately, do the sources the author used advance us much further, nor yet does Shirley's assertion that the poem was written "a la request dun amoreux." Whether this statement of Shirley's was in itself merely a bad guess,[1] must remain a matter of uncertainty; nor have I been able to find anywhere the motto of the lady: "de mieulx en mieulx magre" (in the second version: "humblement magre"). Should, however, the hypothesis that the poem was written somewhere between 1400 and 1415 be correct, then a more precise date within the limits of this period may be assigned to it, or rather we may set on one side certain years in which it cannot have been written. At the opening of the poem is an astronomical statement concerning the

---

[1] Thomas Feylde, also an admirer of Lydgate, addresses his poem *Controversy between a lover and a jay* in the Envoy thus:

"For made thou was of shorte aduysement
Be mernayllous instaunce of a louer verament."

But at the end of the Envoy he has:

"Suche grete vnkyndnesse ...
Was shewed to a louer called, F. T.,
Her name also begynneth with, A. B."

F. T. are doubtlessly meant to represent his own initials. Feylde cites in this poem a great many famous couples of lovers; those of the *Temple of Glas* are also all in it.

time of the dream which Lydgate feigns to have had. It says that he had gone to bed one night

> "Whan þat Lucina wiþ hir pale liȝt
> Was Ioyned last wiþ Phebus in aquarie,
> Amyd decembre, when of Ianuarie
> Ther be kalendes, of þe nwe yere."

The first two lines, of course, refer to the conjunction of Sun and Moon; the key to the exact meaning of the last two we find in Lydgate's poem, *Pur le Roy* (in Halliwell's edition of the *Minor Poems*, p. 2), of which the first stanza runs:

> "Toward the ende of wyndy Februarie,
> Whan Phebus whas in the ffysshe croune,
> Out of the signe, wiche callyd is aquary,
> New kalendys were enteryd and begone
> Of Marchis komyng, and the mery sone
> Upon a Thursday shed his bemys bryght
> Upon Londone, to make them glad and lyght."[1]

The date here referred to is February 21st, 1432, relating to King Henry VI's entry into London after his return from France. The above method of fixing the date has, of course, reference to the ancient calendar, according to which, after the Ides of the month, the reckoning would be made by the kalends of the next month. Thus the meaning of ll. 6 and 7 of the *Temple of Glas* is: in the middle of December, when the new "Kalendæ Ianuariæ" have begun, *i. e.* at the earliest on December 14th, which is the 19th day "ante Kalendas Ianuarias." Now, Professor Tietjen, of the Berlin University, has been kind enough to give me a list of new moons in the December of the years 1400—1420. According to it, there was a new moon in 1400, on December 16th, at 2 a.m.; 1402 on the 24th, 1403 on the 14th, at 9 a. m., 1405 on the 21st, 1407 on the 29th, 1408 on the 17th, 1410 on the 26th, 1411 on the 15th, 1413 on the 23rd, 1416 on the 19th, 1418 on the 27th, 1419 on the 17th; the other new moons all occur before December 14th. Now we must not lose sight of the possibility that Lydgate did not mean the above-quoted words to be interpreted literally; but if we do so, I should think that the two years 1400 and 1403 are of all the most likely, as the date of their new moon agrees so well with the "*Amyd decembre*" of the poem. And if we have to choose between the two, I think we must choose 1403 as the more probable. For two

---

[1] We have also a close parallel to the above lines in MS. Cott. Calig. A II, fol. 59 a:

> "And on a nyght in Aprile as y lay
> Wery of sleep & of my bed all so,
> Whene that the kalendes entred were of May."

reasons. It seems that the *Flour of Curtesie* (evidently imitated from the *Parlement of Foules*), and the *Black Knight* (imitated from the *Book of the Duchesse*) precede our more ambitious *Temple of Glas.* But the *Flour of Curtesie* was certainly written after the death of Chaucer, which is proved by its envoy. Secondly, I believe that Lydgate, in December 1400, would have mentioned Chaucer with warmer words than the bare mention of his name in l. 110. For scarcely two months had then elapsed since his beloved master had been laid in the grave.

CHAPTER IX.

THE SOURCES OF THE POEM.

§ 1. *Lydgate's learning in general.*

WE are, indeed, obliged to bring forward a strong protest against certain old admirers of Lydgate, when their effusive eulogies are too freely bestowed on his poetical powers. But we can agree more readily with these ancient *literati* when they commend our monk's wide learning.[1] Although we moderns perceive at once that it is— like much of the erudition of the Middle Ages—more extensive than deep or accurate, yet we must not deny Lydgate the epithet of "learned," which he received for several centuries, and with which he was still honoured, in the midst of the glories of the Elizabethan era, by no meaner poet than Beaumont. Still, even here we must make the necessary deductions from the wholesale eulogies of Bale, Pits, and other early writers, and some of the accomplishments attributed to him all too lavishly by them, we shall do well to strike out altogether from their lists. Thus, if Pits speaks of him as " non solum elegans Poëta, & Rhetor disertus, verum etiam *Mathematicus expertus,* Philosophus acutus, & Theologus non contemnendus,"[2] we prefer to believe Lydgate's own words, when he says (*Troy-Book,* F₁ a):

"For douteles / I radde neuer Euclyde."

---

[1] And we may perhaps add, his command of language. Bale praises him thus: "Tantæ enim eloquentiæ & eruditionis homo iste fuit, ut nunquam satis admirari possim, unde illi in ætate tam rudi, tanta accreuerit facundia;" further on: "fuitque post dictum Chaucerum, Anglici sermonis illustrator planè maximus" (*Catalogus,* p. 586).
[2] Pits evidently derives his information from the first edition of Bale (*Summarium,* 1548, fol. 202 b), which reads: "Rhetorem certe, philosophum, mathematicum, ac theologum cum extitisse, scripta eius luculenter ostendunt." Bale himself thought good to omit this questionable account of Lydgate's versatility in his *Catalogus,* whilst Pits was copied by Ghilini, Papadopoli, etc.

cxvi *Chapter IX.—The Sources of The Temple of Glas.*

After this confession we need not wonder that the history of mathematics is silent concerning any "Theorem of Lydgate." [1]

Similarly, we must not let pass unchallenged Bale's random guess concerning the authors who served as Lydgate's chief models. Bale asserts—and his assertion has been adopted even by Warton without due criticism—that Dante, Alanus, and Chaucer were the principal poets whom Lydgate studied and imitated. But of Dante he does not seem to have known much more than the mere name and the title of his great work; further, if by Alanus, Bale meant Alanus ab Insulis, then *Reason and Sensuality* alone would fully justify the tradition; but he evidently means Alain Chartier, and I must confess that, beyond a general likeness of *motifs*, etc., current at the time, I am unable, so far as my knowledge goes, to trace any actual interdependence between the two. Some works of Chartier were, indeed, translated into English in the 15th century; but we must note that Lydgate is at least twenty-five years older than Chartier, and can thus have learnt little from him. With respect to the third poet mentioned by Bale, there is no doubt that Lydgate knew Chaucer well, and the present poem would strongly confirm this statement, did it need confirmation. Bale's authority is here, as unfortunately also in many other instances, altogether unreliable; he evidently chose haphazard three representative poets of Italy, France, and England, and thus two-thirds of his statements are incorrect.

The sources of two of Lydgate's best known works, the *Falls of Princes* and the *Story of Thebes*, have been ably treated in Dr. Koeppel's two excellent treatises, which, although the two works in question are more or less only translations or paraphrases, yet throw

---

[1] Moreover, let any one who may have imagined Lydgate to be a connoisseur of jewelry, correct his error at once; for he himself tells us in the *Secreta Secretorum* (MS. Ashmole 46, fol. 109 a):
"I was nevir noon expert Ioweleere."

Nevertheless we may not inaptly apply to the monk Hazlitt's remark on Herrick, that "from his frequent allusion to pearls and rubies, one might take him for a lapidary instead of a poet" (*Lectures on the Dramatic Literature of the age of Elizabeth*, Lecture VI).—Concerning Lydgate's geometry we must, however, in justice add, that he evidently knew the value $3\frac{1}{7}$ for π (see note to l. 36). But again, his "Tractatus de Geometryen" in the *Court of Sapience*, fol. $f_2 b$ to $f_3 b$, does not prove him to have been a great adept in the mysteries of Euclid's science. Cp. also the following passage from the *Pilgrimage of Man*, fol. 182a, the purport of which we do not mean to gainsay:

"And many on that thow dost sen,
Ys nat ther-for A Geometryen,
With-In a compas—ha thys in mynde—
Thogh he konne out the centre fynde."

Chapter IX.—The Sources of The Temple of Glas.

considerable light upon Lydgate's general knowledge and the manner in which he makes use of it in enlarging upon his originals. Koeppel shows, I think conclusively, that Lydgate knew no Greek nor Italian, but Latin and French tolerably. In his so-called translations, the monk usually renders his original in a paraphrastic manner, and puts in many additions foreign to it. He is fond of quoting authorities for his statements; but often enough, he does so—like his great master Chaucer—quite incorrectly and at random. Some investigations have also been made into the sources of certain of his smaller poems; I mention especially *Guy of Warwick*. But much still remains to be done to make clear his attitude towards the sources whence he derived his other principal works. Thus a treatise on the sources of the *Troy-Book* would be a very meritorious *pendant* to Koeppel's comparison of Boccaccio, Laurent de Premierfait, and Lydgate; it would have to elucidate the manner in which Lydgate follows Guido di Colonna, and how far he deviates from the Sicilian's famous work. The investigator of Lydgate's *Secreta Secretorum* would have to define the exact relation between this work and the pseudo-Aristotelian tract of that title; and also to show how it is connected with Occleve's *De Regimine Principum* or Gower's *Confessio Amantis*, Book VII. An enquiry into the sources of the *Court of Sapience* will, so far as it deals with the first part of the poem, lead back to the Pleading between Mercy, Truth, Right, and Peace, so often treated in the Middle Ages.[1] In the later parts of the *Court of Sapience*, the inquirer will have ample opportunity to show his own erudition whilst discussing that of Lydgate. Not the least interesting of such investigations would be that of *Reason and Sensuality;* Alanus ab Insulis' work *De Planctu Naturæ*, the *Roman de la Rose*, and the moralizations on the game of chess would be found to play a prominent part in it.

If I am not much mistaken, the groundwork of the *Assembly of Gods* must go back in some way to the *Psychomachia* of Prudentius, and more than one of Lydgate's stories appear to be derived from

---

[1] By Lydgate himself in the *Court of Sapience*, 1st part, in *Life of Our Lady*, cap. 11—14; it occurs also in Deguileville's *Second Pilgrimage*, books I and IV of the English prose-translation in Caxton. In book I the Charter of Mercy has reference only to the soul of the individual pilgrim only; in the IVth to mankind in general. Further treatments of, or allusions to, this Pleading are found in a homily of St. Bernard's, in Grosseteste's *Castel d' amour* (English version, ed. Weymouth, l. 275 etc.), in the *Cursor Mundi*, ed. Morris, p. 548—561 (ll. 9517—9752); in *Piers Plowman*, C-text, XXI, 118 etc.; see ten Brink, *Geschichte der engl. Litt.*, I, 444, and particularly, Skeat's note to the passage in *Piers Plowman*.

the *Disciplina clericalis*, or a French translation of it.[1] Inquiries of the kind indicated would be valuable contributions to the history of English literature in the 15th century, and I should be glad if these discussions instigate other workers in this field to undertake an elucidation of some of the questions set forth above.

§ 2. *Current "motifs" used in the Temple of Glas.*

Whereas Sandras, some thirty years ago, spoke of Chaucer's works as "*véritables mosaïques*" of ideas, gathered together from various quarters, a better knowledge of the poet has made it clear to us that Chaucer, although drawing from many foreign sources, still preserved the originality of his singular genius and impressed each of his genuine works with the stamp of his own personality. Later researches have shown that the works to which this remark of Sandras particularly applies, are mostly not genuine, but, as a rule, belong to a post-Chaucerian school of poets, who had learnt their *technique* of, and borrowed their ideas from, the great master-poet. But if this remark is not appropriate in the case of Chaucer's genuine works, it is certainly applicable to the earlier compositions of Lydgate, and particularly to our poem. For although the *Temple of Glas* may be said to be an original production with regard to its action and composition, yet the most prominent *motifs* which form the component parts of the story, and serve as vehicles to set the action working, are the common property of the time, heirlooms, some of them, of olden days, modified and enlarged upon by generations of writers.

Thus we have in our *Temple of Glas* the framework of a vision. We can clearly distinguish in the literature of the Middle Ages two separate, yet closely related currents, which represent two different forms of the vision. First we have the vision proper, the religious trance, opening Heaven, Purgatory, and Hell to man's ecstatic gaze. For the origin of this species of the mediæval vision we must turn to the Bible, namely to the visions of Ezekiel and Daniel, the trance of St. Paul, and the Apocalypse of St. John.[2] Again, in the earlier

[1] So *Chorl and Bird* and *De duobus Mercatoribus*. For the latter see Ward, *Catalogue of the Romances*, I. 929, and Zupitza, in his *Archiv*, vol. 84, 130 etc.

[2] There are also heathen parallels, describing either descents into the lower world, or visions of a life beyond the grave; the 11th book of the *Odyssey* and the 6th of the *Aeneid*, the *Culex*, and particularly the *Somnium Scipionis*. In the *Mahābhārata* occurs a famous episode, the *Indralokāgamana*, describing the ascent of Arjuna to Indra's heaven. The popularity of these fictions was so great that it produced parodies and burlesques; two well-known instances are

Chapter IX.—The Sources of The Temple of Glas. cxix

centuries of the Middle Ages, many privileged mortals, mostly canonized saints, were credited with having beheld such visions, in body or in spirit; for the historian of literature the names of St. Patrick, St. Brandan, Alberic, Tundalus, and the apocryphal gospel of Nicodemus are of particular interest.[1] The *Sólar-Ljóð*, Raoul de Houdenc's *Songe d'Enfer* and *Voie de Paradis*, Hampole's *Pricke of Conscience*, Dunbar's *Dance of the seven Deadly Sins*, Lyndsay's *Dream*, the poem of the *Pearl*, Deguileville's *Pilgrimages*, and Alanus' *Anticlaudianus*, which latter had certainly no small influence on the conception of the *Hous of Fame*, are interesting enough as turning the vision of other worlds into a poetic theme; but it is, of course, the *Divina Commedia*, which shows in its peerless magnificence what a poet of Dante's tremendous powers could make of the vision of the Inferno, Purgatorio, and Paradiso.

On the other hand, the vision is often used more or less as a poetical framework only; in this case, it usually presents itself to the poet either in a dream, or when walking forth into the fields on some fair morning. This secular form of the vision no doubt sprang from the religious type; the frequent occurrence of the dream-*motif* appears moreover to have been partly due to the *Somnium Scipionis*, with its widespread popularity in the Middle Ages.[2] As famous examples of this species of the vision in Romance literature we may mention the popular work of Boethius, *De Consolatione Philosophiae*, Petrarca's *Trionfi*, Boccaccio's numerous visions, and—of great influence upon Chaucer and his school—the *Roman de la Rose*, and Alanus' *De Planctu Naturæ*. This type of vision, rather than the preceding, is also exhibited in *Piers Ploughman*, and Chaucer made use of it in more than one of his works, as in the *Hous of Fame*, the *Parlement of Foules* (in this case following directly the *Somnium Scipionis*), in the *Book of the Duchesse*, and the Prologue to the *Legend of Good Women*. It occurs in the pseudo-Chaucerian poems, *The Isle of Ladies*, *The Assembly of Ladies*, and *Cuckow and Nightingale*; in

---

the Μένιππος ἢ Νεκυομαντεία, attributed to Lucian, and, it would seem, contemporary with Lydgate, the Scandinavian *Skiða-Ríma* by Einar Fostri (see Vigfússon, *Corpus Poeticum Boreale*, II, 396, etc.).

[1] For the subject of visions see particularly Th. Wright, *St. Patrick's Purgatory*; Hammerich, *Aelteste christliche Epik*, p. 181; Ebert, *Allgemeine Geschichte der Literatur des Mittelalters*, passim; and C. Fritzsche, *Die lateinischen Visionen des Mittelalters bis zur Mitte des 12. Jahrhunderts*, in Vollmöller's *Romanische Forschungen*, II, 247 etc.; III, 337 etc.

[2] Cp. Warton-Hazlitt III, 65; Sandras, p. 67; Ward, *Hist. of Engl. Dram. Lit.* I, 57; ten Brink, *Geschichte der engl. Litteratur* II, 86.

cxx *Chapter IX.—The Sources of The Temple of Glas.*

Gower's *Vox clamantis*, in Skelton's *Garland of Laurel* and *Bowge of Court*, in the *Kingis Quair*, in Dunbar's *Golden Targe*, Henryson's *Æsop* (Introduction), Douglas's *Palice of Honour;* in Machault, Alain Chartier, etc., etc. Lydgate, who certainly knew Chaucer, Boccaccio, Deguileville, and the *Roman de la Rose*, is not less fond of this particular framework than his contemporaries; he has it, in different forms, besides in the *Temple of Glas*, in the *Assemble de Dieus*, the *Court of Sapience*, the *Complaint of the Black Knight*, and, in a certain degree, also in the *Falls of Princes*.

The vision of some stately building, a palace or a temple, is common, as the very titles show: *Palaces of Honour*, *Houses of Fame*, *Temples of Glory*, etc., occurring frequently in the English and the Romance literatures. Temples of Venus—for so our *Temple of Glas* turns out to be—are found amongst Chaucer's works, in the *Knightes Tale* (l. 1060 etc.), the *Hous of Fame* (l. 130 etc.), and the *Parlement of Foules* (l. 230 etc.), from all of which works Lydgate seems to have taken various hints for the present poem. The particular title, *The Temple of Glas*, may have suggested itself to Lydgate from ll. 119 and 120 of Chaucer's *Hous of Fame*, which run thus:
"But as I sleep, me mette I was
Within a temple y-mad of glas."

The temple spoken of in this passage of the *Hous of Fame* is also a Temple of Venus.

Further, the enumeration of famous names, and particularly of famous lovers, is a very common feature in works of the aforementioned category. These names are naturally most numerous in poems which make the representation and portraiture of personages seen in a vision their primary object, such as Chaucer's *Hous of Fame*, Douglas's *Palice of Honour*, Petrarca's *Trionfi*, Boccaccio's *Amorosa Visione*, the *Intelligenza*,[1] not to mention the *Divina*

[1] This list is interesting as giving, amongst others, the following pair of lovers (stanza 75, l. 2):
La bella *Analida* e lo bono *Ivano*.
This seems to point to one of the Romances treating of *Iwain* and the *Round Table*, for the origin of the name *Anelida*, which would at once upset Bradshaw's and Prof. Cowell's ingenious etymologies from 'Αναιτις and *Anahita;* for I do not believe that both the poet of the *Intelligenza* and Chaucer mistook a *t* for an *l*. We have also in Froissart's *Dit du bleu chevalier* the line (ten Brink, *Chaucer-Studien*, p. 213):
"Ywain le preu pour la belle Alydes."
One and the same personage is evidently indicated by the two names Analida and Alydes for Iwain's paramour; I am not, however, sufficiently acquainted with the Arthur-romances to know of the occurrence of such a name. Laudine in Chrestien's *Chevalier au Lion* is not very like it.

Chapter IX.—The Sources of The Temple of Glas. cxxi

Commedia. Our poem, however, connects itself in particular with the idea of a "Court of Love," inasmuch as it enumerates none but lovers in the *entourage* of Venus, who is represented as "Lady-president of Love"—to use a phrase of Peele's—with Cupid at her side and lovers of all ages and conditions around her. We need not seek long for Lydgate's immediate sources among the many Romance and English poems in which this fanciful idea is introduced; Chaucer's Prologue to the *Legend of Good Women* and Gower's vision of the Court of Love,[1] towards the end of the *Confessio* (ed. Pauli, III, 357 etc.), were certainly uppermost in Lydgate's mind when he wrote the part in question of the *Temple of Glas*. This is amply proved by the names which occur in our list (ll. 55—142), as well as in the two sources I have just named.[2]

Lydgate is not, perhaps, quite consistent in the representation of this Court of Love. In the latter part of the poem we find ourselves face to face with living inhabitants of the Temple, who sing the praise of Venus and otherwise join in the action of the poem; but in the beginning we hear of them—even of Venus, l. 53—only as "depainted upon every wall" (see l. 44). Both methods of introducing personages in a vision are common enough with these early "dreamers," and Warton (*History of E. P.*, ed. Hazlitt II, 192; 275, note 1; III, 63) has given us a series of examples, both from History and Fiction, in which such characters figure in pictures, statues, tapestry, etc. Warton's list itself may seem superfluous enough, and if, in addition to this, I point to *Beowulf* 994, to Úlfr Uggason's *Húsdrápa*, to Bojardo and Ariosto, to Athis and Prophilias, to Blikêr von Steinahe's *Umbehanc* (Gottfried von Strassburg, *Tristan* 4690), to the *Anticlaudian* of Alanus ab Insulis, to the *Intelligenza*, to Benoît de Ste-More, to the *Peripetasma* of Baldericus

---

[1] A Court of Love meant, of course, originally something different; but our version—Venus as queen listening to the complaints of the lovers—is already found in the 13th century, in Jean de Condé's *Des Chanoinesses et des Bernardines* (see Morley, *English Writers*, 2nd ed., V, 143); in fact, we may trace its origin as far back as the classics, for example, Ovid's *Amores* I, 2, 25 etc. We have this notion again in Petrarca's *Trionfo d'Amore*, in the pseudo-Chaucerian poem *The Court of Love*, in Douglas's *Palice of Honour*, in Rolland's *Court of Venus*, etc. Cp. also the little poem "*The Parliament of Love*," in Furnivall's *Political, Religious and Love Poems*, p. 48—51, and the passage from Hawes's *Pastime of Pleasure* in the note to l. 50.

[2] We may also refer to the list of lovers in *Parl. of F.*, 288, and to the enumeration of good women in *March. Tale* 119 etc., *Melibe*, p. 150; *Frankel. Tale* 628. In Lydgate similar lists frequently recur; for instance in the *Life of our Lady*, fol. a, b; in the poem on Duke Humphrey and Jacqueline, MS. Add. 29729, fol. 158b; in the poem entitled "Of a squyer y'e serued in loues courte," ib., fol. 157a; in the *Flour of Curtesie*, etc.

Dolensis, to Catullus' *Marriage of Peleus and Thetis* (the passage from which Titian drew some suggestions for his glorious picture "Bacchus and Ariadne" in the National Gallery), etc. etc., I willingly plead guilty to the charge of *krokyleymos*.

Further, the "Complaints" of the Lady and the Knight, as they present them to the goddess, recall to us a certain species of poetry[1] which was at one time much in vogue in England and France. These "Complaints" are usually put into the mouth of a rejected or forsaken lover, bewailing his wretched state, and calling upon his lady for pity. It is not impossible that their origin may have been influenced by Ovid's *Heroides*, which enjoyed so remarkable a popularity in the Middle Ages. We have such "Complaints" from French poets—for instance, from Rutebeuf, Christine de Pisan, and Machault; Chaucer wrote the "Complaints" of Mars, of Venus, and of Anelida (of somewhat different *genre*, the *Compleint to Pity*, and, turned jokingly, the *Compleint to his Purse*). Of Lydgate we have the *Compleint of the Black Knight*, a tangible imitation of the *Boke of the Duchesse*; the *Compleint to his Purse* has also its parallel in Lydgate, see Halliwell, *M. P.*, p. 49. Of Surrey, we have the *Complaint of a dying lover*, and, in fact, this species had not died out in Elizabethan times, witness Gascoigne's *Complaint of Philomene* and *Complaint of the green Knight*, Daniel's *Complaint of Rosamund*, Shakspere's *A Lover's Complaint*, etc.

We ought, however, to add here that the "complaints" in the *Temple of Glas*, and the prayers combined with them, have perhaps been most immediately influenced by the *Knightes Tale*, with its prayers of Arcite, Palamoun, and Emelie to Mars, Venus, and Diana.

The mode of beginning a poem with a detailed description of the time was also extensively used in those days; every one will at once recall Chaucer's beautiful descriptions of the May-morning, or the season of spring. These "dreamers" are particularly fond of embellishing their fictions by means of astronomical references; see, for instance, Petrarca's *Trionfo d'Amore*, I. 4—6, Skelton's *Garland of Laurel* and *Bowge of Court*, the *Flower and the Leaf*, the *Kingis*

---

[1] Cp. *Marchaundes Tale* 636, 637:
  "And in a letter wrot he al his sorwe,
   In maner of a compl·ynt or of a lay."
Frankeleynes Tale 219, 220:
  ". . . made he many layes,
   Songes, compleigntes, roundeletis, virrelayes."

Chapter IX.—*The Sources of The Temple of Glas.* cxxiii

Quair, Dunbar's *Golden Targe* and *Thrissill and the Rois*, Henryson's *Testament of Cryseide*, Douglas's *Palice of Honour*, Lyndsay's *Dream*, the *Pastime of Pleasure*, etc. Nor is Lydgate behind his contemporaries in this respect. His *Story of Thebes*, the *Assemble de Dieus*, the *Flour of Curtesie*, and the *Troy-Book* (fol. A₁ d), begin in a like manner to the *Temple of Glas*, and these astronomical allusions are also frequently scattered throughout some of his other works.

Lastly, we believe we hear a faint echo of the love-poetry of those times in the admonitions of Venus to the lovers. They are most of them very diluted and commonplace, but sometimes they remind us of certain laws to which the lovers were bound in the Romance *Courts of Love*, alluded to in Cupid's Code in the *Roman de la Rose* and in the English poem, *The Court of Love*. The latter poem in particular enumerates 20 statutes for lovers, of which many coincide more or less closely with some of Venus's exhortations (see further on, § 4). Naturally, in all these regulations with respect to love, we are also sometimes vaguely reminded of "Venus clerk Ovide," one of the favourite classics in mediæval times.

§ 3. *Influence of Particular Works on the Temple of Glas.*

It has been more than once alleged that the *Hous of Fame* and *Parlement of Foules* were imitated and made use of by the author of the *Temple of Glas*. Although some of the remarks in question do not seem to be more than vague guesses, yet there is at least some little truth in this statement. We have above referred to ll. 119 and 120 of the *Hous of Fame*, and intimated that Lydgate may have got the title of his poem from there. Lines 19 and 20 of the *Temple of Glas* must have been written in remembrance of ll. 1128—1130 of the *Hous of Fame:*

> "But at the laste espied I,
> And found that hit was, every del,
> A roche of yse, and not of steel."

Ll. 130—139 of the *Hous of Fame* have been made use of in several passages of the *Temple of Glas;* see particularly ll. 53 and 541. The "wicket," through which Lydgate gains access to his glass-temple (l. 39), is also found in l. 477 of the *Hous of Fame;* it occurs further in the *Romaunt of the Rose*, ll. 528, 642; similarly a "guichet" is found in Deguileville's *Pilgrimage*, etc. Finally, Chaucer also dreams in the middle of December (on the 10th), see

cxxiv   *Chapter IX.—The Sources of The Temple of Glas.*

ll. 63 and 111 of the *Hous of Fame;* it may be that Lydgate intended to imitate this.[1]

If we turn to the *Parlement of Foules*, we find there also an imaginary Temple of Venus, "peynted over al of many a story;" the names given from ll. 284—292 coincide partly with those in the *Temple of Glas*. Moreover, l. 442 of Chaucer's poem occurs almost word for word in l. 1042 of the *Temple of Glas*. In Chaucer it is the female eagle who blushes so deeply. Of course, this coincidence may be purely accidental.

This may also be the most convenient place to note that certain other ideas which appear in the *Parlement of Foules*, are found occasionally in Lydgate; thus the "pecok with his aungels fethers bright" (*P. of Foules*, l. 356)[2] occurs in *Reason and Sensuality*, 221 b; also in the *Court of Sapience*, $e_1 b$:

(*the peacock*) "That to the syght he semed euery dele
   An Archaungell donne frome the heuen sent."

"The cok that orloge is of thorpes lyte" (l. 350) appears in the *Troy-Book* $D_1 a$ as "the cok comon Astrologere"; see again $G_8 a$:

"a cocke
Syngynge his houres trewe as any clocke."

Similarly, in *Æsop* 2, 10 and 11, the cock is called

" comvne astrologere
In thropes small to make hertis light."

As to the expression "Nature, the vicaire of thalmyghty lorde" (*Parl. of F.*, l. 379, Chaucer's *A. B. C.*, l. 140, and *Doctoures Tale*, l. 20), compare:

De duobus Merc. (MS. IIh. IV. 12, fol. 70 a):

(*Nature*) "Which is of god minister and vicare;"

---

[1] Lydgate often alludes to the idea of a house of Fame, for instance, *Tr.-B.* $Q_6 b$ (Chaucer, the monk says, is to be exalted thither); *ib.* $Dd_4 a$ (the same is said of Henry V.). Add to these the instances given by Köppel. *Falls of Princes*, p. 94, and cp. the poem on Humphrey and Jacqueline, MS. Add. 29729, fol. 159 b:

" He hathe deserved thoroughe his knyghtly name (*Duke Humphrey*)
To be regystred in the hous of ffaame."

[2] The following line 357 of the *Parl. of Foules* occurs nearly word for word in MS. Gg. 4. 27, fol. 9 b:

"Þe fesaunt, scornere of þe cok
Þe nihyter tyme in frostis colde,
Þhat nestelyth lowe be sum blok
Or be sum rote of bosschis olde."

In the same poem, fol. 9 a, we have also "Qui bien ayme tard oublye" sung by the "mauys" (cf. *Parl. of F.* l. 679); this motto occurs also in the form: 'Tar · vblia · chi · bien · cima" as an inscription on one of Francia Bigio's pictures in the National Gallery; see E. T. Cook, *Handbook to the National Gallery*, 1890, p. 21.

further, *Troy-Book* D₃ d :
" For the goddesse that called is nature,
Whiche next hir lorde [hath] all thynge in cure,
Hath vertue gyue to herbe, gras and stone,
Which no man knoweth but hir selfe alone ;"

again, *Testament*, Halliwell, p. 243 :

(*Nature which is*) "undyr God ther worldly emperesse ;"

F. Princes, 93 a :

(*Nature*) " Which vnder god in heauen aboue reigning,
The world to gouerne, is called themp[e]resse ;"

R. Sens. fol. 205 b :

"For she ys lady and maistresse, (*Nature*)
And vnder god the chefe goddesse."

The same occurs nearly word for word again on fol. 210 a. See further, *Black Knight*, 491—493, and *Pur le Roy*, Halliwell, p. 6. Scipio's Dream is mentioned, *Troy-Book*, fol. R₃ d (not in Guido). The *Parlement of Foules* was evidently in great favour with Lydgate, as with all his contemporaries.

Line 703 of our poem, with the name of Cirrea, suggests line 17 of *Anelida and Arcite*. " Cirrea " occurs more than once in Lydgate's writings; see note to l. 703. The general composition of *Anelida* is also somewhat similar to the *Temple of Glas*, the epic and lyric *genre* alternating in different metres.

There are also certain points of analogy between the *Temple of Glas* and the *Boke of the Duchesse* ; the *dream-motif* occurs in both at the beginning, and the figures of the Duke and Duchess Blanche bear some resemblance to our knight and lady.

One is frequently reminded of the *Legend of Good Women*, especially of the Prologue, as the greater part of the lovers named in the *Temple of Glas* also occur there, and some of them, with their detailed history, in the Legend itself. Lydgate may also have been influenced in the portraiture of his lady by Chaucer's description of certain ladies in the Legend ; for instance, Alceste, whom Lydgate mentions in l. 74, as having been turned into a daisy. The garments of the Lady (l. 299) remind one also of Alceste's " whyt coroun " and " real habit grene," Prologue 214, etc. Line 60 of the *Temple of Glas* agrees with the *Legend of Dido*, l. 385, where Dido also exclaims :

" That I was born ! allas ! "

Compare, however, for the common occurrence of this expression, the note to l. 60. A " ballade " of similar metrical structure is inserted in both poems (*Legend*, Prol. 249—269, and *Temple of Glas*, 1341—1361).

The mention of Mars, Vulcan, and Venus, ll. 126—128, may also remind us of Chaucer's *Complaint of Mars*, and *Complaint of Venus*.

Lydgate was of course well acquainted with the *Canterbury Tales*; he himself aspired to add another to their number in his own *Story of Thebes*. The following of them are referred to in the *Temple of Glas*:

The *Knightes Tale*, in ll. 102—110, in which the monk mentions Chaucer's name expressly (l. 110). I have already said that the prayers of the three principal personages in the *Knightes Tale* bear a certain resemblance to those in the *Temple of Glas*. The conception of Lydgate's temple may have been somewhat influenced by Chaucer's description of the "theatre" built by Theseus (*Kn. Tale*, 1027 etc.); the line on Venus, *Temple of Glas* 53, is almost a literal transcript from *Kn. T.* 1098 (cp., however, also *Hous of Fame*, l. 133). Certain ideas and many lesser expressions are common to the two poems, as pointed out in the notes.[1]

Further, allusions are to be found to the *Clerkes Tale*, ll. 75 and 76, to the *Squieres Tale*, ll. 137—142;[2] to the *Frankeleynes Tale*, ll. 409 and 410, and to the *Marchauntes Tale* (ll. 184, 185), which latter has been imitated by Lydgate in his *Story of December and July* (see Halliwell, *M. P.*, p. 27).

Lastly of Chaucer's works we may mention *Troilus and Cressida*. The notes will sufficiently show that many of the standard phrases of the monk come from this poem, especially those relating to love and lovers. The monk says of this poem in his well-known list of Chaucer's works in the Prologue to the *Falls of Princes*:

> (*Chaucer*) "Gave it the name of Troylous and Cresseyde,
> Whiche for to rede lovers them delyte,
> They have therin so grete devocyon."
>   (Morris's *Chaucer*, I, 79.)

Lydgate is also indebted to Gower's *Confessio Amantis*. First, Gower's representation of the *Court of Love* seems to have been present in a general way in his mind, as has been said above. More-

---

[1] Our monk also got the epithet "armipotente" for Mars, in the invocation at the beginning of the *Troy-Book*, from the *Knightes Tale*, 1124, or *ib.* 1583 (and compare the beginning of *Anelida and Arcite*). The *Knightes Tale* is twice alluded to in the *Story of Thebes*, fol. 372 d, and 377 c.

[2] I do not think that the wording of this passage warrants the supposition that there was more of the *Squieres Tale* written than is now extant (as suggested in *Warton-Hazlitt* III, 63, note 3); see Milton's *Penseroso*, and the continuation of our story in the *Faerie Queene*, book IV, and that by John Lane.

Chapter IX.—The Sources of The Temple of Glas.

over, the allusion to the story of *Phoebus and Daphne* (ll. 111—116) seems to have been suggested by the *Confessio*, book III (ed. Pauli I. 336, etc.); so was certainly the story of *Phyllis and Demophoon*, the "filbert" tree, which seems to have been introduced by Gower (Pauli II. 30), occurring in Lydgate's poem, l. 90.¹

We have furthermore to mention Martianus Capella, whose work, *De nuptiis Philologiae et Mercurii* is referred to in ll. 129—136. It may be questioned whether Lydgate was acquainted with the original; certain it is that the book was widely known in the Middle Ages; see *Warton-Hazlitt*, III, 77. Chaucer mentions it in the *Marchaundes Tale*, 488, and in the *Hous of Fame*, 985; Lydgate refers to it again in the *Story of Thebes*; see Warton, *l. c.*, and Koeppel, *Story of Thebes*, pp. 25 and 74. Perhaps we must add to Lydgate's sources for the *Temple of Glas* Fulgentius, on account of l. 248; for in his *Troy-Book* (G_5 b) the monk tells us that this crystal shield of Pallas is a symbol of force in virtue,

"by manly hye diffence
Agayne vyces / to make resystence."

For this and other symbolical interpretations Lydgate gives "Fulgence" as his source, *ib.* G_5 c. In the same passage of the *Troy-Book*, the monk refers us also to Fulgentius with regard to the doves which he there attributes to Venus as in our *Temple of Glas*, l. 541. Cp. the notes to ll. 53, 248, 541.

§ 4. *Resemblances in Later Works to the Temple of Glas.*

After having spoken of the sources of the *Temple of Glas* and the *motifs* which it has in common with earlier works, it may not be out of place here to add a few words on some resemblances which we find to the *Temple of Glas* in certain of Lydgate's own works, and in works of later date than our poem.

Of all Lydgate's works, the *Complaint of the Black Knight* and the *Flour of Curtesie* are those which a perusal of the *Temple of Glas* recalls most vividly to our mind, both as regards tone and

---

¹ Koeppel, *Falls of Princes*, p. 97, has also pointed out an instance of Lydgate's dependence on Gower, namely in the monk's narrative of the story of Canace (*Falls of Pr.* I, 23). Lydgate mentions Gower very rarely; he does so, together with Chaucer, in the *Court of Sapience* a₂ a:
"Gower, chaucers, erthly goddes two . . .
I you honour, blysse, loue, and gloryfye."
And, again, in *Falls of Princes*, IX, 38, fol. 217 c:
"In moral matter ful notable was Gower."

Chapter IX.—*The Sources of The Temple of Glas*.

imagery. As the *Temple of Glas* represents, with its introduction of the dream-*motif*, one of the popular forms of poetical frame-work, so in the *Black Knight* we have an example of the other species, opening with a description of the May-morning, and the poet's walk into the woods and by the river. Both poems begin with astronomical allusions; the lines dedicated to " Lucifer " (*Black Knight*, ll. 5—9) have moreover a close resemblance to ll. 253, 328—331, and 1355—1358 of the *Temple of Glas*. In both poems we find to a great extent the same mythical and allegorical personages (note particularly Daunger, Malebouche, and the filbert tree in the story of Phyllis), and the same phrases concerning lovers frequently occur in both (the mischievous " false tonges," the " access " hot and cold, etc.). The figure of the Black Knight is the double of the " hero " of the *Temple of Glas;* he is introduced and described precisely like the latter, and the Complaints of the two are much in the same strain. Both poems are dedicated, in the Envoy, to the poet's lady; one line (554) of the *Black Knight* is word for word the same as one which occurs twice in the *Temple of Glas* (424 and 879); also l. 623 of the first poem is nearly the same as l. 128 of the latter. A more minute analysis of the *Black Knight*, although by no means devoid of interest, would be out of place here; I can only state my opinion briefly that the form and contents of this poem are thoroughly Lydgatian, and even without Shirley's direct evidence (see p. lxxxiii), it would be emphatically clear that the poem is by Lydgate.

The *Flour of Curtesie* also begins with a joyous greeting to the morning (this time it is St. Valentine's day), and the poet's walk into the woods. The beginning at once pleasantly reminds us of the *Parlement of Foules*, nor are the astronomical embellishments wanting here. The two principal parts of the *Flour of Curtesie* are the poet's complaint on the obstacles to his love, and the description of his ideal Lady-love, the *Flour of Curtesie*. Both are much like their analogues in the *Temple of Glas;* the latter particularly, with its profuse comparisons of rubies, roses, and stars closely resembles certain lines of the *Temple of Glas* (cp. the notes to ll. 251 and 257—261). Lydgate has again managed, in spite of the small compass of the poem, to introduce his favourite personifications from the *Roman de la Rose*, Daunger, Malebouche, False Envie, and also " false suspection " (cp. *Temple of Glas*, l. 153). The names of famous women enumerated are to a great extent the same as those in the *Temple of Glas;* I would emphasize particularly the occurrence of Alceste,

Chapter IX.—The Sources of The Temple of Glas. cxxix

Grisilde, and Dorigene. At the end of the *Flour of Curtesie*, Lydgate introduces a ballad in praise of his lady; in the *Temple of Glas* (l. 1381) he seems to express a similar intention, which, however, he does not carry out. Finally, in both poems, the monk makes mention of his master Chaucer, the closing stanzas of the *Flour of Curtesie* lamenting his death.

I will now proceed to discuss certain other works which bear some similarity to the *Temple of Glas*. We have spoken above of Stephen Hawes and his excessive admiration of Lydgate. We have also quoted Wood's assertion that he knew many of Lydgate's works by heart and could repeat them at will. Some lines of the *Temple of Glas* seem thus to have remained in his memory; there is, at least, a great resemblance between ll. 19—34 of our poem, and Hawes's lines (ed. Wright, p. 15):

"I loked about, and sawe a craggy roche . . . (cp. *T. of Glas*, l. 19)
And as I dyd then unto it approche . . . (l. 20)
. . . I sawe . . . The royall tower . . . Made of fine copper . . .
Which against Phebus shone so marveylously, (l. 21)
That for the very perfect bryghtnes,
What of the tower and of the cleare sunne,
I coulde nothyng beholde the goodlines (l. 27)
Of that palaice where as Doctrine did wonne;
Tyll at the last, with mysty wyndes donne, (l. 30)
The radiant bryghtnes of golden Phebus (l. 32)
Auster gan cover with clowde tenebrus."

Again, a good many parallels of minor importance are to be found between Hawes's poem and the *Temple of Glas*.

But, as far as I am aware, the two poems that bear the greatest family-likeness to the *Temple of Glas* are the *Court of Love* and the *Kingis Quair*. Tytler, in his edition of the *Kingis Quair*, p. 49, has already compared King James's poem to the *Court of Love*—"of Chaucer," he adds, a mistake which we can readily forgive him: he considered the spirit, not the language of the poem. If we are entitled to introduce the *Temple of Glas* into the family—as its weakest member, we willingly allow—then there would naturally also be a likeness between Lydgate's work and the *Court of Love*. And a comparison of the two latter poems proves this to be the case. The structure and extent of the *Court of Love*, the metre adopted, the allegories introduced, the progress of the action, and a great many direct verbal resemblances, remind us frequently of the *Temple of Glas*. Philogenet, the poet and hero of the *Court of Love*, enters the magnificent castle, where the King and Queen of Love, Admetus and Alcestis, have their residence. In it he finds a great throng of young

cxxx Chapter IX.—The Sources of The Temple of Glas.

and old people (ll. 110 and 111), servants to Love. Within this castle is the "temple" (l. 229), or "tabernacle" (l. 222), of Venus and Cupid, which shines "with wyndowes all of glasse" (l. 229), "bright as the day with many a feire ymage" (cp. *Temple of Glas*, l. 45): Dido and Aeneas, and Anelida and Arcite are given as representatives, of which Dido and Aeneas occur also in the *Temple of Glas*, the false Arcite of Thebes in the closely allied poem of the *Black Knight* (l. 379). Philogenet is "sore abasshed" to see such a crowd of people, who, "in here guyse" (*Court of Love*, l. 245, *Temple of Glas*, l. 537), sacrifice to Venus and Cupid (cp. *Temple of Glas*, ll. 531—544). He finds a beautiful lady, Rosiall (l. 767), whose description at once reminds one of the Lady in the *Temple of Glas*; Rosiall also, like the Lady, has on the *green* garments to which one of the scribes of our poem seems to have had an objection (*Court of Love*, l. 816, *Temple of Glas*, l. 299). Philogenet's prayer to Venus, l. 631, etc., and his "bille" to Rosiall, l. 841, etc., recall at once the Knight's prayer to Venus and his suit to the Lady. Rosiall's answer (ll. 890 and 891):

> "Truly gramercy, frende, of your gode wille,
> And of youre profer in youre humble wise"

has a verbal resemblance to that of the Lady in the *Temple of Glas*, l. 1060; lines 1016—1019 also, describing Rosiall's blushing, resemble *Temple of Glas*, ll. 1042 and 1043. The praise of Venus by the fortunate lovers (ll. 591—623) has the same ring as the joyous ballad at the end of the *Temple of Glas*. The various complaints of the lovers in the *Court of Love* are in part identical with those in the *Temple of Glas*; such as the complaints on "Poverte" (*Court of Love*, ll. 1137—1148, *Temple of Glas*, l. 159, etc.), and, particularly, the complaints of the priests, monks, and nuns (*Court of Love*, ll. 253—258, 1095, etc., *Temple of Glas*, ll. 196—208). The latter are sometimes worded similarly in the two poems; cp. *Court of Love*, ll. 1116 ("copes wide") and 1104—1106:

> "'Alas,' thay sayn, 'we fayne perfeccion,
> In clothes wide, and lake oure libertie;
> But all the synne mote on oure frendes be'"

with *Temple of Glas*, ll. 204 and 208. Lines 50—52 of the *Temple of Glas* should also be compared with ll. 575—581 of the *Court of Love*, and stanzas 25 *b* and 25 *c* (most likely spurious) in the first poem with ll. 582, etc. of the latter. Some of the allegorical figures in the *Court of Love* are identical with those in the *Temple of Glas*. So

Chapter IX.—The Sources of The Temple of Glas.

Daunger and Disdeyne, mentioned together in l. 156 of Lydgate's poem, stand, in the *Court of Love*, near the King and Queen as attendants (ll. 129 and 130); further, Envie, mentioned in *T. of Glas*, l. 147, is described in two stanzas of the *Court of Love* (ll. 1254—1267); lastly, the dispute between Hope and Dispeyre, *T. of Glas*, ll. 641—661, has its parallel in the *Court of Love*, l. 1036, etc.

But as I have already indicated at the end of § 2, it is in particular the Statutes of the Court of Love which recur in a diluted form in the *Temple of Glas*, mostly in the exhortations given by Venus to the Knight, *T. of Glas*, ll. 1152—1213. The lover is admonished in the third of these statutes to be constant, true and faithful to his lady, and never "to take another love" (*Court of Love*, l. 316, etc.); the same injunction we find frequently in the *T. of Glas*; see ll. 1152—1158, 1124—1130; 1188; 1201; cp. also 999, 1005. The second of the statutes enjoins secrecy in love (*C. of Love* 309); cp. *T. of Glas* 1005, 1154; the fifth commands the lover "to turne and walowe" in bed and weep; cp. *T. of Glas*, ll. 1—3 and 12; the 6th, to wander alone and to be reckless of life and death; see *T. of Glas*, 550 etc. and 939; the 7th, to be patient; see *T. of Glas* 1203 and 1267, and lowly to obey his mistress (*T. of Glas* 1007, 1145 etc.); the ninth, never to be overbold or offend his lady (ll. 1013, 1025); the tenth, to ask everything from the mercy and pity of his lady, and never to demand anything as his right (*T. of Glas* 800 and 979); the 12th, to suffer mortal wounds (ll. 170, 1014); the 14th, to believe no "tales" (*T. of Glas* 1182); lastly, the 18th, not to be "sluttish," but always clean, "fresh," and courteous (*T. of Glas* 1166, 1167).

If thus the *Court of Love*, concerning the author and exact date of which we are so sorely puzzled, reminds us in many particulars of the *Temple of Glas*, the *Kingis Quair*, written, it would seem, some twenty years later than our poem, does so perhaps even more forcibly and directly.

This poem, justly famous for its intrinsic worth and the associations connected with it, nevertheless presents two different aspects of poetry, which illustrate in a striking manner the poetical currents of the time. We almost imagine, in the first part of the poem, and again at the end, that we hear Chaucer's own melodious voice once more, speaking to us of beauteous ladies, of the fresh May-morning, and the delightful song of the birds, whose charms alone could lure him away from his beloved books. But the more we feel delight cxxxii Chapter IX.—The Sources of The Temple of Glas.

in King James's poetry in the first part of his famous work, so much the more are we reminded, in the second part, of Goethe's famous words:
"Weh dir, dass du ein Enkel bist!"
This part, decidedly inferior to the first, is blighted throughout by the baneful influence of the allegorical plots so much in vogue at that day—from which, however, Chaucer wisely kept aloof in his ripest works—and even King James's brilliant genius could not take free flight under the pressure of those leaden wings. This part does not recall Chaucer, but Gower and Lydgate. It is true that, besides Chaucer, King James mentions Gower alone as entitled to his thanks;[1] but my impression is that he must also have read Lydgate. If I remember rightly, some resemblances are found in *Reason and Sensuality* to the *Kingis Quair*;[2] but, of all Lydgate's writings, it is the *Temple of Glas* of which we are especially reminded in reading King James's poem. The very first lines of it contain an expression which Lydgate seems to have originated, and perhaps, indeed, just in our present poem. We read in the *Kingis Quair*, stanza 1, ll. 3 and 4:
"And, In Aquary, Citherea the clere
Rynsid hir tressis like the goldin wyre."
Skeat, in his notes, cites many instances of the notion of golden hair, but none which contains the exact comparison of hair to "golden wire." The latter is, however, a favourite phrase of Lydgate's, as the note to l. 271 will amply show, and, once started, this expression lived a long life down to the Elizabethan period, from Lydgate and King James through Hawes and popular ballads down to Spenser, Peele, and perhaps even Shakspere. I do not think it probable that such an expression should have been started twice independently. Unless, therefore, earlier instances of it come to light, I am inclined to believe that King James borrowed it from Lydgate.

[1] Prof. Schipper evidently quotes from memory in stating the contrary, see his *Dunbar*, p. 29. Henry Morley, indeed, makes King James finish up with an additional stanza in honour of Lydgate (*English Writers*, II, 453). Skeat, however, on p. 94 of his edition of the *Kingis Quair*, rejects this stanza, as obviously belonging "to some other poem"; and rightly so, for it is the closing stanza of Hawes's *Pastime of Pleasure*.
[2] Henry Wood, in *Chaucer's Influence upon King James I.*, p. 25 (also in *Anglia*, vol. III, 223 etc.), compares *Kingis Quair*, stanza 116, and *Troy-Book*, lib. III, cap. 24 (beginning):
"Whan Aurom the syluer droppes shene,
Her teares, shad vpon the freshe grene;
Conplaynyng aye in weping and in sorow
Her chyldrens death euery somer morowe."
He also points out (p. 31) a general likeness between *Kingis Quair*, stanza 154—158$_2$, and *Black Knight*, l. 36 etc.

Chapter IX.—The Sources of The Temple of Glas. cxxxiii

But, more than this, there is in part of the *Kingis Quair* great resemblance of subject-matter to the *Temple of Glas*. This similarity begins at stanza 73, where King James feigns to have been carried up to the Temple of Venus, an episode much resembling part of our poem. Stanzas 82—93, in particular, cover the same ground as ll. 143—246 of the *Temple of Glas*, both passages containing the complaints of various conditions of lovers, who present their "billes" to Venus. King James's complaint to Venus and her answer to him are much in the same style as the complaint of our Knight and Lady to the goddess and Venus's reply. Portions also of Minerva's answer to King James recall expressions used by Venus in the *Temple of Glas*; compare, for instance, *Kingis Quair*, 129, with stanza 55 of Lydgate's poem.

Further, special instances of resemblance occur in the following passages: Stanzas 88—90 of the *Kingis Quair*, and lines 196—206 of the *Temple of Glas*; particularly stanza 90 and ll. 207 and 208; stanzas 91 and 92 and ll. 209—214; stanza 93 and l. 151; stanza 134 and ll. 215—222; stanza 137 and ll. 167 and 168; stanza 144, 1 and 2, and ll. 1061 and 1062. Many more verbal resemblances will be pointed out in the *Notes*; I would only observe here that "gude hope" is James's guide to Minerva (cp. *Temple of Glas*, 892 and 1197).[1]

The names of the lovers in the Temple of Venus, enumerated in Lydgate's poem from ll. 55 to 142, are not given by King James, as, to use his own words, of their

"chancis maid is menciou*n*
In diuerse bukis, quho thame list to se;
And therefore here thaire namys lat I be."
(*Kingis Quair*, 78, 5—7.)

As instances of the "*diuerse* bukis" which King James had in mind, Professor Skeat mentions, besides Ovid, the three well-known lists in the *Man of Law's Prologue*, the *Legend of Good Women*, and in Gower's *Confessio Amantis* (ed. Pauli III, 359). I think we may boldly add the *Temple of Glas* to the books enumerated by the learned commentator of the *Kingis Quair*.

---

[1] If King James wrongly inferred from *Troilus* (1st stanza of Canto 1 and last stanza of Canto III) that Tisiphone was a Muse, Lydgate's frequent invocation of that "Muse" was quite calculated to keep this error awake; see *Temple of Glas*, l. 958 and Note.

CHAPTER X.

STYLE OF THE *TEMPLE OF GLAS*.

I PURPOSE, in this chapter, to treat of certain characteristics of Lydgate's, which I would handle collectively under the comprehensive heading "Style," although some of them might more properly be assigned a place in Chapter VI on the language, or Chapter IX on the sources and borrowed *motifs* of the *Temple of Glas*.

We have already stated, in discussing the authorship of the *Temple of Glas* (see p. lxxxiv), that the style of this poem is essentially the same as that of Lydgate's other works. Drawled-out and incompact, are the first epithets which one would most readily apply to the style of the monk's productions. His sentences run on aimlessly, without definite stop, and it is often difficult to say where a particular idea begins or ends. One certainly has the impression that the monk never knew himself, when he began a sentence, how the end of it would turn out. He knows little of logic connection, or distinct limitation of his sentences, and the notion of artistic structure, by which all ideas form, in mutual interdependence, an organic whole, is entirely foreign to him: what is uppermost in his mind comes to the surface without further consideration of the context; for a moment he may lose sight of the first idea when something fresh turns up, to resume it again as soon as his new thought leaves him. Compare, for instance, the list of the lovers, from ll. 55—142. In his enumeration, he is evidently only guided by the inspiration of the moment, according to which he either gives a brief summary of the story, or merely indicates it. After line 77, and particularly after 91, one imagines that he is about to close his list, as we find an apparently concluding phrase; but the expected finale turns out to be a delusion, for meanwhile Paris and Helen have flashed across his mind, which sets him going once more in the old strain, on the principle of "The more, the merrier." The same applies to the lengthy list of the complaints of the various lovers, from l. 143—246. He adds one set of complaints after another, just as they occur to him, and as the rhyme may require, so long as he can think of any; nor does it matter much to him if he says similar things twice over.

He is especially in his own element whenever he can bring in long sermons and moralizations. Then showers of commonplaces, proverbs, and admonitions rain down upon us, the fruits of his extensive reading swelling the vast store of his own commonplaces. In our poem, this natural propensity of the monk is most apparent in the speeches of Venus, who, in this character of a pedantic moralizer, occasionally appears to us in a very philistine aspect.[1] More commendable, however, is the zeal with which our monk allows his pen free flight, when he comes to a passage which inspires him with unusual fervour. Then he lets loose the floodgates of his eloquence, and a whole deluge of epithets and images is showered down upon us. Such is usually the case when he comes to a turning-point in his story, or when he wishes to present us with a lively description of Nature, or a portrait of a personage in whom he is especially interested. In our poem, he found unfortunately no opportunity for bringing in one of his famous pictures of Nature, but he more than makes up for it in what he evidently considered the *chef-d'œuvre* of his poem, the description of his lady. For this, every imaginable simile and comparison is raked up from every possible quarter, and he heaps together sun and stars, May, roses, balm and rubies; it is a wonder how ever Nature could make such an angelic creature; her hair shines like Phœbus' beams, and the entire temple is illumined by her; and, in addition to all this, he winds up with a whole string of womanly charms and virtues in her praise. The "πλέον ἥμισυ παντός" evidently never dawned upon our monk.

It is nevertheless in this vitiated, overwrought style that he is at his best, as the good intention of heaping every beauty and virtue upon his ideal lady, or his sincere love of Nature, makes him sometimes really a poet. The worst of it is that he often loses his way and becomes entangled in his own sentences, by reason of overmuch zeal in setting forth what impresses his mind most strongly. The consequence is that the anacoluthon is exceedingly common in all Lydgate's writings. Now, an anacoluthon may be a fine thing—I have always, for instance, admired the one in *Hamlet*, before the Prince first sees his father's ghost;—but, in Lydgate, it does not usually heighten the beauty of the passage—at all events, if it ever

---

[1] Brugari, in a little pamphlet on Chaucer, has a quaint remark concerning the position of Venus in certain poems of this period: "Venere in tutta questa letteratura è degradata e rassomiglia ad una vecchia *douairière* pensionata e collocata a riposo" (*Jeffrey Chaucer e la Letteratura Inglese del secolo xiv*, p. 13). Similarly Godwin, *Life of Chaucer*, III, 256, has: [The poets of chivalry] "superannuated her [*Venus*], and substituted another [*Alcestis*], as the active and administering divinity, in her room."

does, it must be by a tremendous fluke. What it certainly does, is to make the punctuation very difficult for the editor, especially as it is often impossible, in the monk's interminable sentences, to define with certainty whether we have to do with an anacoluthon. An undoubted oversight of this kind has, however, crept in unawares into his masterpiece, the portraiture of his lady; for it seems impossible to construe ll. 271 etc. grammatically. The same may be said of ll. 548 etc., 563 etc., 603 etc., 614 etc.; stanzas 42, 43, 44, 50, etc. There is, however, no instance of the anacoluthon in our poem quite so bad as the beginning of *Guy of Warwick*, where, as Professor Zupitza says (*Sitzungsberichte der Wiener Akademie, Phil.-Hist. Klasse*, 1873, vol. 74, p. 665), not only the predicate of the sentence is wanting, but the subject as well.

We may also note here that sometimes direct and indirect speech flow together in a very careless manner, as in ll. 509 and 510, and in ll. 376 and 377. Our monk apparently here at first intended to give only a few words of reply, for which indirect speech might conveniently be employed; but he changed his mind, and when once in full swing, it is no easy matter to stop him.

Parallel to this carelessness in language, is the monk's inconsistency in depicting his ideas. Thus we first hear of his assemblage of lovers as being painted on the wall, whilst later on we have clearly to do with living personages. Venus herself is first spoken of as "fleting in þe se," evidently in a picture on the wall (l. 53); then, in l. 249, her "statue set on height" is mentioned, before which the Lady kneels to pray, and, throughout the rest of the poem, we find her addressed as a living being, and speaking and acting as such. If we had to do with a poet who can hold his ideas together, we might try and reconcile the discrepancy; but, in the present case, it arises simply from Lydgate's well-known *laisser-aller* and general muddle-patedness.—In the same manner, also, his mode of expression in the last lines of the poem is unclear, and of the several "treatises" mentioned in ll. 1380 and 1387, it is difficult to know which is which. Such a slight inconsistency as the ὕστερον πρότερον in ll. 33 and 39, where he sees the inside of the temple before entering it, of course hardly counts with our monk.

If, however, heathen and Christian ideas are heaped together in a very incongruous medley, the monk is less to blame for it than the general taste of that period. For this feature is exceedingly common throughout the Middle Ages, and is especially in accordance with the

Chapter X.—Style of The Temple of Glas. cxxxvii

notions prevailing at the time of the Renaissance. We meet with more or less grotesque confusion of this kind in Dante, Boccaccio, the Italian Humanists, Chaucer, Gower, Camões, etc. In the same way it mattered little to our monk whether he invoked a saint, the Virgin Mary, or a heathen goddess; he did it all in one and the same strain. In our poem Lydgate speaks of "orisouns" to Venus (l. 460), of an "oratory" in her temple (l. 696), and when the scribe of the Pepys MS. once (l. 577) changes *tempil* into *cherche*, the alteration is not out of keeping with the general tenour of the poem. The greatest absurdity, however, committed by our monk himself, is that Venus cites the example of "holy saints," who won heaven through their suffering; but this is more than matched by the *Kingis Quair*, in which Minerva quotes *Ecclesiastes* (see the passage in the Note to l. 1203), or by Bishop Gawain Douglas, in whose *Palice of Honour* a nymph of Calliope's train expounds the scheme of redemption.[1]

We need not be greatly astonished that a rhyme-maker of Lydgate's order of mind should make ample use of expletives, pleonasms and certain stock-phrases occurring again and again; in fact, if we consider how often a poet like Chaucer has recourse to such means, we wonder that Lydgate does not go still further in that respect. Some of the expressions he uses as a make-shift to fill up the line— mostly also Chaucerian—are the following : Shortli in a clause, 536 ; shortli to conclude, 545 ; forto reken all, 579 ; if I shal not lie, 73 ; if I shal not feine, 911 ; what shal I lenger tarie, 1297 ; þer is no more to sein, 1325 ; some of his set phrases : for wele or (for) wo, 517, 783 ; hoþe in cold and hete, 512 ; doumb as eny ston, 1184 ; stil as eni stone, 689 ; trw as eny stele, 866 ; constant as a walle, 1153 ; favour or be foo, 519. Sometimes he repeats whole lines which form favourite stock-phrases ; thus l. 385 is the same as 1295, and l. 424 the same as 879. Paraphrases by means of a relative—

[1] Other incongruities and anachronisms, at which we cannot forbear a smile, occur in the following passages, where Lydgate calls Orpheus a "poet laureate" (*Falls of Princes*, 32 c), and Gabriel the "secretary of God" (*Life of our Lady*, fol. e₃ b) ; the Parcæ are made to keep the library of Jove (*Falls of Princes*, 27 d) ; Mercury is chamberlain, secretary and chief notary to Phœbus (*R. & Sens.*, 225 a) ; Pythagoras is chief clerk to govern the library of "Arsmetryk" (*Pur le Roy*, Halliwell, p. 11) ; Ganymede, Jove's "butler," and of Venus the monk says (*R. & Sens.*, 222 a) :

"For she doth leden and eke guye
The amerouse constablerye."

Sometimes, however, I believe Lydgate must have seen the joke himself, as Chaucer certainly did when he made Pluto quote Solomon (*Marchauudes Tale* 998).

for instance: *stormes þat be kene* for *kene stormes* (l. 515); *cloudes þat ben blake* (l. 613)—often help him through, and meaningless little words, such as *so, as, gan* and other similar stop-gaps, also serve to fill up his line.

To return, however, to points of more general and further-reaching interest than the monk's individual make-shifts to get his lines right, we must first notice the traces found in the *Temple of Glas* of the allegorical style so much in vogue at that time. Professor Ward, in his *History of Dramatic Literature*, I, 56, calls the English an allegory-loving people, and rightly so, no doubt, if we bear in mind Piers Ploughman, Chaucer and his school, Hawes, the Moralities, and above all Spenser, Bunyan, and Swift. Lydgate certainly was acquainted with those of the above-mentioned works which existed at his time; all the instances, however, of allegory, or rather personification, in our present poem, seem to go back, more or less directly, to the *Roman de la Rose*.[1] In that poem excessive prosopopœia forms a distinctive feature, and many of its personifications became exceedingly popular with the English poets. So, in numerous passages of our poem (ll. 156, 646, 652, 739, 776), we meet with the great bugbear of the *Roman de la Rose*, Dangier, who guards the rose-tree from all assailants; in l. 153 we have also a distinct allusion to Dangier's comrade, Malebouche, called Wikked-Tonge in the English translation (see also stanza 25 *b*, l. 7). Other such personifications—nearly all of them started by the *Roman de la Rose*—are the following: Hope (641—686, 736, 892, 1119, 1197) and its opponents Drede (631—686, 893, 1119, 1198), Dispeire (656, 895, 1198), Wanhope (673, 895), and Disdain (156, 218); further, Reason

---

[1] *Reason and Sensuality*, especially, has in many points a distinct connection with the *Roman de la Rose*; the French poem is directly named on folio 268 *b*, etc. (MS. Fairfax 16), and the monk says of its author:
"He compiled the romaunce,
Callyd the Romavnce of the Rose,
And gañ his processe so dispose,
That neuer yet was rad noo (read *nor*) songe
Swich a nother in that tonge,
Nor nooñ that in comparysouñ
Was so worthy of renouñ,
To spekyñ of Philosophie,
Nor of profounde poetrie:
For sothly yet it doth excelle
Al that ever I herd of telle."

This admiration, in his earlier days, for the *Roman de la Rose* did not, however, prevent Lydgate from translating, without any comment of his own, Deguileville's severe censure of it in the *Pèlerinage de la vie humaine*, MS. Cott. Vit. C. XIII, fol. 201 *a*, etc.

(878); Riches 175, Tresour 176, Poverte 159; Mirth and Gladnes 190; croked Elde 182, 187; þe serpent of fals Ielousie 148 (see also stanza 3 b, and 25 a, l. 7); Suspecioun 153; Envie 147;[1] Covetise 244, Slouth 244, Hastines 245, Reklesnes 246; see also, particularly, stanza 58 and 59. In more than one of the above instances it is, however, difficult to say whether we have to do with a distinct and conscious prosopopœia.

Another feature of some prominence in our poem is the occurrence of expressions which had arisen from the astrological beliefs of the time. Every planet was supposed to be guided by the heathen god whose name it bore, and star and god were, in the language of the period, often entirely identified. So Venus in our poem is directly addressed or spoken of as a "star" or "planet," etc., see ll. 326, 328, 715, 835, 1097, 1341, 1348, 1355. The "aspects" of the planets are described as "benign," l. 449, or "fierce," l. 1236, and their effect is accordingly beneficial or pernicious. The proper word to express the working of the planets upon human destiny is the word *influence*, of particularly common occurrence throughout these centuries; so also in the *Temple of Glas*, ll. 718, 885, 1330; Chaucer, in one place (*Man of Law's Tale*, l. 207), introduces the corresponding Arabic word *at-ta'thīr* (infinitive of second stem of *'athara*, with prefixed article).

Quite in accordance with the style of the age are likewise the portions of the poem referring to love and lovers. As already indicated, the idea of a Court of Love runs through the whole poem; Cupid deals his dreadful stroke (l. 984), and Cupid and Venus keep the books (ll. 1238, 1136, 1234) in which the good and evil deeds of every lover are registered. The poor lover has, indeed, a hard time of it. He is the "man" and "servant" of his lady, and desires to be nothing beyond that; the wounds inflicted by his lady's "casting of an eye" are always fresh and "green"; his blood rushes to his heart, making him "pale and wan"—the favourite aspect of a man "daunted" by Cupid; he is in a continual "access," now hot, now cold, constantly swoons and falls down, and is altogether nearly killed. In fact, we hear from the mouth of our lover himself (l. 634) that he is murdered and slain *at the least*. Now there is appropriateness in the hyperbole of Harpagon's "Je

---

[1] The seven deadly sins appear to have been particularly often personified at that time; Lydgate himself introduces them thus in the *Assembly of Gods*, b7 b, following, it seems, Prudentius' *Psychomachia*; and they come, of course, also in his translation of Deguileville's first *Pilgrimage*.

suis tué, je suis tué," after his money-box has been stolen, or in the cowardly "hada mhi, hada mhi" of Kâlidâsa's *Vidûshaka;* but in the case of our innocent though long-winded lover it seems hard lines that Cupid should go so far as to kill him straight off, and, indeed, murder and slay him *at the least.* We involuntarily ask, if to be murdered and slain is the least that befalls him, what would be the most?

Another similarly absurd way of putting the case is that our lover assures us—evidently with a view to refute those who might not believe it—that he has a mouth (l. 823), with which he is, however, unable to speak. Yet this ridiculous phrase seems not to have been uncommon at the time; see note to l. 823. But among all these absurdities, the palm must certainly be awarded to line 117, where the monk represents

"Κρονίωνα κερασφόρον ἅρπαγα νύμφης"

as changing his "cope" for the purpose alluded to. Leopold von Schroeder, in his *History of Sanskrit-Literature,* has aptly drawn our attention to the significant fact that all nations represent their gods as being similar to themselves in appearance and occupation, and he adduces the characteristic instance of the compilers of the *Yajur-Veda,* who, impressed with the all-importance of their interminable sacrifices, finally make their own gods priests operating with the sacrificial ladle. So our monk, being himself vested in the black cope (see the Prologue to the *Story of Thebes*), would clothe the "father of gods and men" with the same garment, and the outcome of this "false analogy" is, mighty Jove enthroned on Olympus in a monk's cope.

Another feature characteristic of Lydgate is his self-deprecatory vein. He very frequently introduces modest excuses and phrases; he willingly grants that the Muses did not preside over his cradle, that he knows nothing of the flowers of Tully, that Jove's butler, Ganymede, deals his liquor very sparingly to him (Prologue to the *Pilgrimage of Man,* and Envoy to *Edmund*), and that he never slept on the hill of Parnassus; he complains of his "dulnesse" and asks Calliope to "redress" it; he excuses himself that he is "born in Lydegate,"[1] and that thus his English is not the best; his metre, also, he is afraid, may be found wanting, and he even does not

---

[1] "I wil procede furth with white and black,
And where I faile, let Lidgate beare yᵉ lack."
Falls of Princes, 217 d.

hesitate to run down his own character and manner of life.[1] I have already alluded to his particular mania of ending his poems by an appeal to the reader, or the addressee of his envoy, to correct his poem; for he knows well, as he himself says at the end of the *Troy-Book* (fol. Dd, b), that

"moche thynge is wronge
Falsely metryd / bothe of short and longe."

Similar requests to correct his verses are found, besides in the *Troy-Book*, in our *Temple of Glas*, in the *Æsop* (Anglia, IX, 2, 46), in the *Legend of Austin* (Halliwell, p. 149), and elsewhere; see note to l. 1400. In one case he says:

"If ought be mysse in worde, sillable or dede,
Put all defaute upon John Lidgate."[2]

Similarly in *Guy of Warwick*, 73, 7. 8, he has:

"Yif ought be wrong in metre or in substaunce,
Putteth the wyte for dulnesse on Lydgate."

Yes, certainly, on whom else?

Almost invariably hand in hand with the demand to correct him, goes the expression "litel boke" bestowed by the monk on his poems in the envoys. Lydgate forgot many a favourite phrase of his youth, when, in later years, the *Falls of Princes* too sorely tried his spirits; but to this particular one he clung most tenaciously. We should have thought the monk might have been content to call the 20,000 lines of the *Pilgrimage*,[3] or the 30,000 of the *Troy-Book* a "litel boke." But no; after he has tired us out with nearly four myriads of verses of the dullest description in his *Falls of Princes*, he has once more, at the end, the coolness to say in his envoy (fol. 218 c):

"With letters and leaues goe *litle* booke tremblyng."

I need hardly add a word on our envoy (ll. 1393—1403), as such terminations occur in dozens and dozens of poems of the time. Nor is indeed self-deprecation, even in its absurd exaggeration, uncommon

---

[1] Cp. his *Testament*, and *Troy-Book*, Dd, b :

"Monke of Burye by professyon,
Usynge an habyte of perfeccyon,
Albe my lyfe accorde nat therto.
I feyne nat, I wot well it is so ;
It nedeth nat wytnesse for to calle :
Recorde I take of my brethren alle,
That wyll nat fayle at so great a nede."

[2] *Stans Puer ad Mensam*. I have not yet seen the paper by F. Burhenne, which undertakes to prove that this poem is spurious (s. *Mitteilungen zur Anglia*, 1890, p. 221).

[3] See MS. Cott. Vit. C. XIII, fol. 257 a.

in those days. Skeat, *Man of Law's Tale*, p. xxv, quotes Dunlop's *History of Fiction* (3rd ed. 1845, p. 247), who says of Ser Giovanni's *Pecorone* (the "Dunce"): "a title which the author assumed, as some Italian academicians styled themselves, Insensati, Stolidi, &c., appellations in which there was not always so much irony as they imagined." The immediate sources, however, of Lydgate's self-deprecatory phrases seem to be Chaucer's humoristic excuses for possible shortcomings; for instance, the familiar ones in the *Hous of Fame*, l. 1098, and at the end of *Troilus* (V, 1872), and I may add, Lydgate's personal modesty, especially when he measures himself with his great master. We have seen above how Lydgate himself is apt to fall into absurdities in his handling of these phrases; but they come to sheer stupidity in their treatment by Lydgate's imitators. Thus one of them (MS. Fairfax 16, fol. 309 *a*) complains that the Pierides do not favour him "dull ass." Chaucer is here, as always, the graceful humourist, Lydgate the ungraceful imitator, and our anonymous aspirant at the laurels of Parnassus—"such as he said he was."

CHAPTER XI.
CONCLUDING REMARKS.

AFTER these strictures on Lydgate's absurdities it is only fair that we should also hear the other side. If we needed only the laudatory testimony of a successive line of poets, historians, and critics to prove that Lydgate was a great poet, we could, indeed, for this purpose marshal a long and proud array of names. I have spoken above of Hawes's craze for his favourite author, and of Shirley's verses in honour of Lydgate; I may further mention, among the less conspicuous admirers of Lydgate, Bennet Burgh, the continuator of the *Secreta Secretorum*, Bradshaw (*Life of Saint Werburge* II, 2023), Feylde (*Controversy between a lover and a jay*, Prol. 19—21), Bokenam (*Legends* I, 177; II, 4, 612; VI, 24; XIII, 1078) and Ashby, *Active Policy of a Prince* (see Morley, *English Writers*, 2nd ed., VI, 161). To proceed to greater names, King James I. was, as we attempted above to make probable, acquainted with his writings; Skelton frequently introduces him together with Chaucer and Gower (*Philip Sparrow* 804—812; *Garland of Laurel* 390, 428—441, 1101); Sir Thomas More evidently imitated him in his early poems, and the great triad of later Scotch poets never fail to mention him in connexion with Chaucer (cp. Dunbar, *Golden Targe* 262—270, and

Chapter XI.—Concluding Remarks.

Lament for the Makaris 51; Douglas, *Palice of Honour*, ed. Small, I, 36, 11; Lyndsay, *Papyngo*, Prol. 12). In the Elizabethan times, even at the close of the period, Lydgate's name was far from being forgotten. In Tarlton's *Seven Deadly Sins* he appeared before the Elizabethan public as speaker or chorus (like Gower in *Pericles*), see Boswell's *Malone*, 1821, III, 348 etc.; Richard Robinson, in the *Reward of Wickednesse*, 1574, places Googe on Helicon with Lydgate, Skelton and others (*Dictionary of National Biography*, under Googe); later on, John Lane, in his continuation of *Guy of Warwick*, again introduces Lydgate as speaker of the prologue and epilogue. Camden praises him very highly indeed,[1] the *Polimanteia* (fol. R_3 *a*) and Beaumont (Chaucer, ed. Speght, 1598) mention him honourably, and but little doubt can be entertained that even Shakspere himself read Lydgate. The *Story of Thebes* was repeatedly printed between 1561 and 1687, together with Chaucer's works, and even the two longest poems of the monk were reprinted after the middle of the 16th century (the *Troy-Book* in 1555 by Marsh, the *Falls of Princes*, 1554, by Tottel, and again, 1558 (?) by Wayland). The authors of the *Mirror for Magistrates* continue his longest and dullest production, and the man who, in 1614, took the trouble to re-write the *Troy-Book* in six-line stanzas, and the publishers who issued it, must have had no mean opinion of the value of that book. Nay, even a hundred years later, we find the highest compliments paid to Lydgate. Dart, the modernizer of the *Black Knight*—which he, it is true, believes to be Chaucer's—says in his preface (1718) that he thinks this Complaint " the best design'd of any extant, either Antient or Modern, . . . the Thoughts in the Speech natural, soft, and easy, and the Hint for Invoking *Venus*, and the Invocation inimitable." It even seems that this Complaint of our "inimitable" Lydgate biassed Dart not a little in proclaiming its supposed author to be "the greatest Poet that *England* (or perhaps the World) ever produc'd."

More than one name of good repute might also be adduced to testify that the *Temple of Glas* is far from being the meanest work of our "*brillant* (sic) *disciple de Chaucer*."[2] I have above quoted

---

[1] "Nec procul dissitus est *Lidgate* viculus, qui hoc nomine neutiquam tacendus, quòd in lucem Ioannem *Lidgate* monachum ædiderit, cuius ingenium ab ipsis Musis effictum videatur, ita omnes Veneres & elegantiæ in suis Anglicis carminibus renident" (*Britannia*, 1607, p. 336).

[2] So is he called by L. Constans, *La Légende d'Œdipe*, p. 368. Tame also, *Life of Our Lady*, p. iv, speaks of his "brilliant genius."

the excessive praise bestowed upon this poem by a poet laureate (see p. xiii). Warton's criticism was fully endorsed by Dibdin I, 309 note: "Whoever may be the author of it (the *Temple of Glas*), its intrinsic merits are very great; as the reader will be convinced by a careful perusal of the brilliant extracts given by Warton." Hill, *De Guileville ... compared with ... Bunyan*, p. 35, finds a "decided similarity" between the preamble of the *Temple of Glas* and Dante's *Inferno*. He compares, in particular, l. 14 to Dante's words:

> "I' non so ben ridir com' io v' entrai;
> Tant' era pien di sonno..."—(*Inferno* I, 10).

I must confess that in reading the poem for the first time, I myself was also vaguely reminded, by certain lines such as stanza 1, 2, 117—119, l. 716, of the *Divina Commedia*. But this does not go to prove much for the value of the poem, and even less for the supposition that Lydgate had read the *Divina Commedia;* for such lines as 329, 330; 1355, 1356 also reminded me vaguely of the hymns to the Açvins in the Veda, which latter were, *most likely*, unknown to Lydgate. Further, Mrs. Browning says that the *Temple of Glas* forms, with *Piers Ploughman*, the *Hous of Fame*, and Hawes's *Pastime of Pleasure*, one of the "four columnar marbles, on whose foundation is exalted into light the great allegorical poem of the world, Spenser's *Faerie Queene* (Book of the Poets, in E. B. Browning's *Greek Christian Poets and English Poets*, p. 123). I do not think that the text of our poem bears out this statement; if any one of Lydgate's writings may be regarded as a forerunner to the *Faerie Queene*, it would be the *Court of Sapience*, which seems to have served Hawes as a model.[1]

I do not claim such a high place for the *Temple of Glas* as Warton and Mrs. Browning. But I think we may fairly allow it some small amount of poetical merit. It may be that Shirley is right in his statement that Lydgate wrote the poem "a la request dun amoreux;" for the monk had, all his life, patrons enough: Henry V., Henry VI., Humphrey of Gloucester, the Earl of Warwick, the Earl of Salisbury, Lady March, etc., representing the proudest names among them. And if it is true that our monk wrote the poem with the view of celebrating the union of a certain knight and his lady, we must admit that the machinery he introduces is prettily conceived. The poet takes up the current *motif* of a vision, and by this means brings his

---

[1] By a closer investigation the following pedigree might perhaps be made out—of course, with regard to certain features only—: *Martianus Capella—Anticlaudianus—Court of Sapience—Pastime of Pleasure—Faerie Queene.*

knight and lady, as the most prominent pair among the famous lovers of history and mythology, into the magnificent temple of Venus, where the goddess of Love herself unites them. Of course, our monk does not omit to adorn both with all imaginable excellences, and the picture of the Lady is one of the brightest of any in Lydgate's works. The rejoicing in the Court of Venus, ending in a ballad which makes the whole temple resound with the praises of Venus Urania for her graciousness to the lovers, leaves an impression at once vivid and pleasing upon the reader's mind. We can at all events understand the long-enjoyed popularity of our poem in an age which fully appreciated this its brighter side, and perhaps even found the weaker parts to its taste. If I add to this that our poem belongs to the few of Lydgate's works which are not directly taken from a foreign source, but that it exhibits, at the most, some traces of the poetical currents of the day, and especially of Chaucer's genial influence, I think I have said about all that can be brought forward in its praise.

I have above pointed to a general family-likeness, and a number of minor resemblances between the *Temple of Glas* and the *Kingis Quair*. I must not be understood, however, to wish for one moment to compare the *Kingis Quair* and its right royal author to our monk and his glass-temple. For although the second part of the *Kingis Quair* reminds one of Lydgate, and although many passages could be adduced from certain writings of Lydgate which would almost be a match for some of the finer parts of King James's poem, yet I know full well that there is another side to be considered in this question, namely, the subjective as well as the objective. Two-thirds of the poetry of the *Kingis Quair* lie in King James himself, his person and fate, his capture, his love, and death. Manly strength and undaunted courage—exhibited in the cause of justice—have seldom been combined in one man with that exquisite tenderness of feeling with which the royal Stuart wooed and won his lady, and the graceful gift of song with which he immortalized it. It is the consciousness of its reality and of a tragic fate lurking behind its sunny pages that gives the *Kingis Quair* an incomparable interest, and raises many a passage into poetry which otherwise would be flat and meaningless. In what light has subsequent history placed the following passage from it:

"And thus this floure, I can seye [3ou] no more,
So hertly has vnto my help attendit,
That from the deth hir man sche has defendit" (*Kg. Qu.*, 187, 5—7).

the absurd counterpart of which we had to criticize severely in Lydgate! It is this personal interest which appeals to us so strongly in the *Kingis Quair:* the royal poet has in reality loved the beauteous lady of whom he sings, he has made her his queen, and she has defended him in that last terrible struggle, when the "noblest of the Stuarts" had to fight for his life. And, moreover, the kindly feeling displayed by the noble prince towards everything surrounding him, animate and inanimate Nature, and the gratefulness with which he thanks the nightingale, the roses, the hedges, Gower, Chaucer, and all the saints of March for their help, win our hearts irresistibly. All these qualities would alone be sufficient to make the *Kingis Quair* a book of uncommon interest, and as the poetry is occasionally truly beautiful, it will remain a pearl in English literature for ever and ever.

Pour revenir à nos moutons! Although the two poems, in spite of many resemblances, are not for one moment to be compared as regards poetical value or interesting associations, the above discussions have I hope at least shown that a better knowledge of Lydgate's works would greatly contribute to the elucidation of the more illustrious of his contemporaries, "who sang together at the bright dawning of British poesy." The monk's name will certainly be of frequent occurrence in commentaries on Chaucer, Gower, and King James, when the principal of his works are more easily accessible. There is, in the investigation of Lydgate, a wide field for work open to the student: editions, treatises on the sources, the language, the metrics, the text-criticism, the chronology, and also the genuineness of certain poems affording ample material to the philologist, whatever his particular bent may be.

I have spoken above, in the preliminary remarks, of the most important work done in this direction, and, in Chapter IX, § 1, have also pointed to some *desiderata* towards the elucidation of the monk's sources. I may add here that a re-publication of the smaller poems, as edited by Halliwell, would be very welcome; it would have to omit the spurious poems[1] given by Halliwell, and to collect those not contained in this first edition; its text, of course, would have to be based throughout on critical principles. A not uninteresting col-

---

[1] Also those that form part of larger works of Lydgate's, as the "*Moral of the Legend of Dido*" (Halliwell, p. 69), which is identical with the Envoy to Chapter II, 13 of the *Falls of Princes*, and "*A Poem against Idleness*" (Halliwell, pp. 84—94), which consists of *Falls of Princes* II, 15 (beginning with the second stanza), followed by II, 14 and closing with the Envoy to II, 15.

lective volume might then be formed by a *critical* edition of Lydgate's somewhat longer poems in the epic, or lyric-epic *genre*, such as the *Black Knight, Chorl and Bird, Horse, Goose, and Sheep*, etc.; of the latter Halliwell (*Minor Poems*, pp. 117—121) and Furnivall (*Political, Religious and Love Poems*, pp. 15—22) unfortunately only give parts, and the reprint of the whole for the Roxburghe Club from a faulty print, is scarce enough. The *Æsop, Guy of Warwick*, and the story, *De duobus Mercatoribus*, belong also to this class. A good critical edition of the *Dance of Macabre*, or of the *Testament*, would likewise be very desirable.

To speak of Lydgate's larger works, I should consider an editor of *Reason and Sensuality*[1] as more fortunate than myself; for this poem appears to me to be by far the finest of all Lydgate's productions. The editor would have to settle definitely the question of the authorship; I can only mention here that there is amongst others Stowe's evidence for its being Lydgate's. The text-criticism would be very simple, as there are apparently only two MSS., Fairfax 16 and Stowe's Add. 29729, of which the first presents a very fair text indeed. The investigation of its sources would be highly interesting, and, if anything definite could be brought to light as to the time of its origin, such a date would be of great importance for the right understanding of Lydgate's development as a poet. Another important contribution would be a treatise on the *Troy-Book*, with respect to which many questions have to be settled: the classification of the numerous MSS. and Prints, the way in which Lydgate follows Guido di Colonna, the assignment to it of its right place in the literature of the mediæval Troy-Saga; its popularity in the Elizabethan time, the authorship of its modernized form, as printed in 1614, and the question as to exactly how much Shakspere took from it, furnishing ample material for research. The Prolegomena would, I suppose, be a good deal more interesting than the edition itself; but, perhaps, some unusually courageous philologist will also one day undertake this; and then he had better at once set about the *Falls of Princes* into the bargain. Previous researches in the text-criticism of at least parts of these two big works would make the matter considerably easier, and not tax the patience of one individual too sorely.

Further, it would be no thankless task to compile a good and clearly-put treatise on the two *Pilgrimages*, and to settle their author-

[1] Skeat, *M. P.*, p. xli, l. 9, means this poem, and quotes from it on p. 349, where he has the title.

ship, their relation to the French original, etc. Lydgate's last work, the *Secreta Secretorum*, with its curious lore—not poetry, I must add—might induce a scientist among the philologists to publish it and compare it with other poems based on the same grounds. Perhaps Dr. Horstmann will one day reprint the *Life of our Lady* in full, and tell us something definite about its date. An edition of the *Serpent of Division* would be interesting as a specimen of Lydgate's prose, and even more in its connection with Gorboduc; perhaps the careful investigator would find that it was not unknown to Shakspere.—Of the forthcoming editions of the *Story of Thebes*, *De duobus Mercatoribus*, and the *Court of Sapience* I have spoken above, and from the prospectus of the Early English Text Society I see too that it has an edition of the *Pilgrimages* in view.

I need hardly mention that a careful and exact bibliography is one of the greatest *desiderata* for Lydgate-literature. And now for my bone with Ritson. We are usually referred to his list of 251 "works" (*Bibliographia Poetica*, p. 66, etc.) as the "fullest and best" account and synopsis of the monk's literary productions. I call this "fullest and best" list an Augean stable of disorder, glaring mistakes and inextricable confusion. For first, this appallingly tedious medley is arranged according to no apparent principle whatever, neither of chronology, nor length, nor importance, nor *genre*, nor anything else. Ritson's intention seems, indeed, to have been to enumerate the printed works first (No. 1—36); but this is a ridiculous division, the best copies of the first numbers being, of course, also as a rule in the MSS. Moreover, this pretended classification is a mere delusion; for—to give only one or two examples—the very next number 37 is also in print, forming part of the *Falls of Princes;* No. 11 is *Parvus Catho*, No. 54 *Magnus Cato;* but in the very print by Caxton mentioned in No. 11, *Magnus Cato* is of course also included, etc. etc. The whole list is a thoughtless jumble copied without understanding from headings of MSS. and entries in Catalogues, and from earlier writers whom Ritson reviles with the utmost impertinence, whilst at the same time transcribing and distorting their statements with a coolness *sans pareil*. Ritson says he believes his list to be the completest that can be formed "without access, at least, to every manuscript library in the kingdom, which would be very difficult, if not impossible, to obtain," thus implying hypocritically that he at least consulted the libraries easily accessible to him. But a consultation of the British Museum or the Bodleian alone would have been more

Chapter XI.—Concluding Remarks.

than sufficient to prevent the incredible mistakes which I have here to expose. Indeed the worst of them he ought surely to have avoided without any library at all. Nobody but Ritson would want access to "every library in the kingdom" to know the *Canterbury Tales!* Of Bale, who has also, it is true, serious mistakes in his list, Ritson says: "but it is the constant practice of that mendacious prelate to split one book into several."[1] Let us see what Ritson himself does.

First, he has made two works of the *Secreta Secretorum*, which he mentions in No. 36; in No. 52 they come again as "*Regimen principum*," sive "*De Aristotele & Alexandro*," called also "The booke of all goode thewes, and *Secreta secretorum*." Again, he has made two works of *Albon and Amphabel*, which he mentions under No. 7; but under No. 249 he has once more: *Vita S. Albani martyris ad J. Frumentarium abbatem*. Similarly, of *Æsop's Fables* :—the "notable proverbe of Ysopus in balade, made in Oxford (*canis & umbra*)" in No. 44 is part of No. 45: "Isopes fabules." Further, of the *Testament*, which he mentions under No. 33; but in No. 214 we read: Christ a lamb offered in sacrifice: "Behold o man, lift up thy eye and se"; this is in reality part of the *Testament*, occurring in *Halliwell*, p. 259. Also of the "Dietary," Nos. 55 and 61 belonging to the same poem; see Halliwell, *M. P.*, p. 66; Skeat, *Bruce*, p. 537. Again, No. 58 "Of a gentlewoman that *lived with* (read *loved*) a man of great estate," is the same as No. 110: A love balade: "Allas i woful creature," printed by *Halliwell*, p. 220, as "A Lover's Complaint," and declared to be altogether spurious by Koeppel, *Falls of Princes*, p. 76, note. Then, No. 22 of our "learned" Ritson's list: "A balade of gode counseile, translated out of Latin verses," is identical with No. 62: "*Consulo quis quis eris*, &c." "I counceile whatsoer thow be," and No. 84 is again the same: Balade of wysdome: "Counseillyer, where that ever thou be." Besides this, our "accurate Ritson" has made three works (at least) of the *Court of Sapience;* namely, No. 12: "The werke [or Court] of Sapience," and No. 225: "The court of sapience in heaven for redemption of mankind"; further, No. 51: The vision:

---

[1] To adduce an instance, which Ritson omits to do—he almost invariably gives again in his own list these split-up books, enumerated as separate works by Bale—: Leland, *Collectanea* II, 428, has: "John Lidgate, monke of Byri, made a treatise of king Athelstan, and Gui of Warwike that slew Colbrond the Dane." Bale has, as three separate articles (pp. 586 and 587): "Vitam regis Ethelstani; Acta Guidonis Vuaruuicensis; De Guidone & Colbrando."

"All busy swymmyng in the stormy floode" (Harley MSS. 2251) is nothing else than the beginning of the *Court of Sapience*, after the Prologue. We have again three separate works made of the *Life of our Lady*, in No. 5: "The lyf of our lady"; No. 8: "Part of the life of the virgin Mary," etc., contained in the *Pilgrimage of the sowle*, printed by Caxton (on this see Introduction, Chapter VIII, p. ci); further, in No. 187 we have: On the same subject [*i. e.* In praise of the virgin Mary]: "O thoughtful herte plunged in distresse." But these words are actually the beginning of the *Life of our Lady*. Sometimes these mistakes are very complicated and difficult to unravel. Compare No. 158: "Moralisation of a fable how the trees chose them a king." Sauerstein, *Ueber Lydgate's Aesopübersetzung*, p. 13, believes that Ritson refers to the beginning of *Chorl and Bird*, a not unlikely supposition in itself. This is, however, not the right solution. Ritson saw in MS. Ashm. 59, fol. 34 *b*, the following entry by Shirley: "þan foloweþe nowe a notable moralisacion made by Lidegate of a fabul poetical. howe trees chose hem a kyng bytwene þe þe [*sic*] Ryal Cydre of þe hye mõntayne and þe thowthistell of þe lowe valeye. þis moralisacion is in þis same boke to-fore." Thus Shirley was on the point of copying over again a piece already transcribed a few pages back in his MS., namely No. 3, on fol. 16 *b*: "þis moral Epistel sent kynge Amasias to kynge Johas made by . . . . Lidegate"; but Shirley saw his error, did not transcribe a second time this epistle to[1] Amasias, and proceeded to copy a new piece. Thus Ritson's No. 158 is a mere imaginary shadow. Nor is this epistle to King Amasias itself a separate work, although Ritson, in No. 72, has put it down as one; it is nothing else but part of Book II, Chapter 16, of the *Falls of Princes*.

We have again a complete muddle in Ritson's Nos. 13, 112, and 113. No. 112 reads: "Play at the chesse between Reason and Sensualitie"; No. 113: "Banket of gods and goddesses, with a discourse of reason and sensualitie": "To all folkys vertuose" (Fairfax, MSS. 16: Royal MSS. 18 D II.); No. 13: "The interpretation of the names of the goddes and goddesses"; printed by W. de Worde. Two works are totally confused in these three numbers. MS. Fairfax 16 contains *Reason and Sensuality* (No. 112), beginning "To all[e] folkys vertuose"; Royal MS. 18 D II contains the "Assembly [or Banket] of Gods"; No. 13: "The interpretation of the names of the gods" is a printer's addition to the *Assembly of Gods*, on the

[1] Not *from* Amasias; see the *Falls of Princes* II, 16, and *Kings* II, 14, 9.

Chapter XI.—Concluding Remarks.

title-page of that work, to render the heathen names more familiar to the reader. See Chapter VIII, p. cix. So much for learned Ritson's account of Lydgate's best work, which of course he had never even seen. This number 113 is, by the bye, not the only one which exhibits a tendency of Ritson's to make up for his chorizontic work; in No. 213 also two distinct works are mixed up: "A saying of the nightingale touching Christ" : "In June whan Titan was in Crabbes hede" (Caligula. A. II. & the Harley MS. 2251); as has been said above, on p. xcv, the poems in the two MSS. are two distinct works.

But we have not yet done with Ritson's feats in "splitting up one work into several." Of the *Legend of St. Edmund and Fremund* he has made at least four works; in No. 243, "The martyrdome of saint Edmunde" is put down as one work; but No. 244: A poem on the banner and standard of St. Edmund : "Blyssyd Edmund, kyng, martyr, and vyrgyne," is equivalent to *Edmund* I, 1 (Prologue) in Horstmann's edition; No. 245, "A ballad royall of invocation to saint Edmond at thenstaunce of kynge Henry the sixt": "Glorious master [read *martir*], that of devout humblenesse" [read, of course, *humblesse*], is nothing but *Legend of Edmund*, Book III, ll. 1456, etc. No. 247, *Vita sancti Fremundi martiris*, constitutes Book III of *Edmund and Fremund*. No. 246: *Miracula S. Edmundi* may stand as a separate work; see above, p. cvii. But Ritson's masterpiece in "splitting up" is his account of the *Falls of Princes*. These are first cited as number 2 in his list. But then we have besides this, in No. 37: "*De rege Arthuro*"; in No. 38: "*De ejus mensa rotunda*"—both numbers thoughtlessly copied from Bale. They are, of course, one and the same, and form Book VIII, Chapter 24 of the *Falls of Princes;* MS. Lansdowne 699, fol. 50 *b*, gives "Arthurus Conquestor" as a separate work. That No. 72, identical with No. 158, "Morall epistle sent [from] kynge Amasias to kyng Johas" forms part of the *Falls of Princes* (II, 16), I have already mentioned. No. 93: Of poverty: "O thow povert, meke, humble, and debonayre," is I, 18 (stanza 4, etc.) of the *Falls of Princes*. No. 73 reads: "Epistle of vartuous ensines eschewing idlenesse"; this I suppose is nothing else but II, 15 of the *Falls of Princes*, also printed as "A poem against Idlenesse" by *Halliwell*, pp. 84—94 ("Two maner of folkes to put in remembraunce"); it may, however, also be that it is the same poem as Ritson's No. 141. I am not sure whether No. 117 etc. of the list are also taken from the same passage of the *Falls of Princes*. Lastly, in No. 17 we have the

"Proverbes of Lydgate" (on the *Falls of Princes*) printed by Wynken de Worde. The very title of Wynken ought to have shown Ritson that these proverbs would, in part at least, be taken from the *Falls of Princes*.[1] So the *Falls of Princes* come at least about seven or eight times in Ritson's list. We see that "mendacious" Bale's feats in splitting up are very poor performances indeed as compared with those of "accurate," "learned" Ritson.

But this is not all. Ritson ascribes to Lydgate any number of early English pieces, the titles of which he happens to have come across: thus the *Assemblee of Ladies* (No. 27), *Remedie of Love* (No. 29), *Craft of Lovers* (No. 30), *Childe of Bristow* (No. 42), *De fabro dominum reformante* (No. 44), the "*Coventry Plays*" (No. 152, see Halliwell, p. 94), "*Dantis opuscula*," "*Petrarchae quaedam*" (No. 159, 160, copied from Bale), etc., etc., are all by Lydgate! In No. 38 he attributes the *Siege of Jerusalem* to Lydgate, forgetting that on p. 24, No. 6, he had already ascribed it to Adam Davie. He sometimes also attributes spurious writings to Lydgate, and then again splits them up into two; we have noted this already in the case of No. 58 and 110; we have further in No. 53: *Vegetius de re militari*, and again in No. 144: "*De arte militari*." We also find Bennet Burgh's translation of *Cato* among Lydgate's pieces, again split up into *Parvus Catho*, No. 11, and *Liber magni Catonis*, No. 54.

But the worst is yet to come. In No. 21 we have: "Balade of the village without paintyng." This is, of course, Chaucer's *Ballade of the visage without painting*. No. 206 reads: Another [*i. e.* poem in praise of the Virgin Mary]: "Almighty and almerciable qwene." Of course, Chaucer's *A. B. C.* In No. 85, Ritson has the *Complaynt d'amour*. Prof. Skeat says that the poem is by Chaucer; it forms No. XXII. in his edition of Chaucer's *Minor Poems*. Here, indeed, it is possible that Ritson may not be wrong. But it would

---

[1] That these "Proverbes" were not entitled to be put down as a separate work of Lydgate's, the identification of the contents of Wynken's print will clearly show: "Go kysse y* steppes" . . . = *Falls of Princes*, fol. 218 c (the three last stanzas); "Sodeyne departynge" . . . = *Falls of Princes* I, 1 Envoy (5 stanzas); then follow Chaucer's *Fortune* and *Truth*; further: "The vnsure gladnesse" . . . = *Falls of Princes* I, 12 Envoy (4 stanzas); "Vertue of vertues" . . . = *Falls of Princes* IX, 31 Envoy (9 stanzas); "Myn auctour" . . . = *Falls of Princes* VI, 15, stanzas 1, 30, 39—47; "This tragedye" = *Falls of Princes* V, 25 Envoy (4 stanzas). Then follow the two poems: "I Counseyll what so euer thou be," already amply represented in Ritson's list, as No. 22, 62 and 84 (in Halliwell, *Minor Poems*, pp. 173—178, called "The Concords of Company"), and "Towarde the ende of frosty Januarye" = Ritson 99 (in Halliwell, *Minor Poems*, pp. 156—164, with the title "A Poem against Self-love").

be a rash conclusion to think that any merit in the case belongs to Ritson; he has merely copied Tanner. No. 28, "A praise of women," is printed in Morris's *Chaucer*, VI, 278; cp., however, Skeat, *Minor Poems*, p. xxvi. No. 31: "A balade teching what is gentilnes" is, I suppose, again Chaucer's work. But Ritson's supreme ignorance of Chaucer becomes most transparent, when we look at Nos. 46 and 235 of this "fullest (full, indeed!) and best" list of Lydgate's works. No. 235 reads: *Vita Sancte Cecilie:* "The ministre *of the* (read *and*) norice unto vices." Of course, this is the Second Nun's Tale! No. 46: "Tale of the crow." The precedence of "accurate, learned" Ritson also induced Sauerstein to regard this "Tale of a Crow" as a fable by Lydgate; but Zupitza, in the *Deutsche Litteraturzeitung* 1886, col. 850, showed that this "Fable," "little known and never published," was in reality Chaucer's well-known and somewhat frequently published *Maunciples Tale*. Ritson, I suppose, had heard that Lydgate's *Story of Thebes* was intended to form an additional Canterbury Tale, and so the "learned" reviler of Warton seems to have thought Lydgate must also be the author of those which one usually ascribes to Chaucer. I am in justice bound to add that "accurate" Ritson makes up for this by attributing works of Lydgate to Chaucer; but I am afraid that the *Black Knight* is but a poor compensation for some half dozen of Chaucer's poems.

And here I think I had better stop. It would go far beyond my knowledge and patience to set all Ritson's errors right, or even to find them all out; I have here merely censured his more glaring and obvious mistakes. I would only add that Ritson's references are very often faulty, and always exceedingly poor; in the case of many of the most interesting works they are only conspicuous by their absence. Of course, Ritson never even saw many of Lydgate's principal works; much less did he know anything of their contents. He found it easier to revile the monk than to know him: reviled he must be, for Warton had praised him.

Still, after all this, I owe some thanks to Ritson. It is for having himself put into my mouth the very words which constitute the truest criticism on him. I myself could have found none so appropriate as the following, with which Ritson sums up his arrogant attack on Warton, who was in every way his superior.

"I have at length, Mr. [Ritson], completed my design of exposing to the public eye a tolerable specimen of the numerous errors, falsities, and plagiarisms of which you have been guilty in the course of your celebrated ["fullest and best" list of Lydgate's works]. And, though I am conscious of having left considerable gleanings to any who may be inclined to follow me, I trust I have given you much reason to be sorry, and more to be ashamed..... Your indolence in collecting and examining materials; and, beyond every thing, your ignorance of the subject, should have prevented you from engaging in a work which [requires, if certainly no vast amount of genius, yet care, diligence, and learning]; in which, whatever might be your progress, how uninformed soever you might esteem the bulk of your readers, you were certain, at last, of encountering detection and disgrace."

These words are literally taken from Ritson's "*Observations on . . . the History of English Poetry*" (by Warton), p. 47; the words in brackets only replace such words as are, indeed, applicable to Warton's great *History of English Poetry*, but not so to Ritson's bibliographical gallimaufry.

The least thing we expect from a list of an author's works is an insight into the extent of his productions; but this is certainly impossible in Ritson's list. I should not point out the self-evident absurdity of putting little trifles of a few lines only, on a level with the *Falls of Princes* or the *Troy-Book*, if I had not, in ever so many books, met with the number 251 given as the fixed and sacrosanct number of Lydgate's "works." Such a method of proceeding gives a most inadequate idea of the monk's productions, the combined length of two particular works out of the list being more than all the remaining 249 put together. The truth is this. There are two or three works of the monk's, translated by the command of the Court, which indeed exceed all ordinary limits. I mean, of course, the *Falls of Princes*, consisting of nearly 40,000 lines, the *Troy-Book* of about 30,000, and the *Pilgrimage of Man*, of some 22,000 or 23,000. The subjoined list enumerating the monk's principal works, together with the number of lines they respectively contain, will I hope be welcome to the reader :[1]

[1] In some cases, the number of lines is only roughly estimated, by multiplying the number of pages with the approximate average number of lines contained on one. Had I counted line for line, the result would again have only been approximate, as lines are sometimes wanting in the MSS., etc.

Falls of Princes	... ...	36,316 lines (cp. Köppel, *F. Pr.*, p. 87).
Troy-Book	... ... about	30,000 ,, (Ward, *Catalogue* I, 75).
Pilgrimage of Man	... ,,	22,000 ,,
Reason and Sensuality	,,	7,400 ,,
Life of Our Lady	... ...	5,936 ,,
Albon and Amphabel	...	4,724 ,,
Story of Thebes	... ...	4,716 ,, (Ward, *Cat.* I, 87).
Edmund and Fremund	...	3,693 ,,
Court of Sapience	... ...	2,282 ,,
Assembly of Gods	... ...	2,107 ,,
Secreta Secretorum	... ...	1,484 ,, (+ 1239 by Burgh).
Temple of Glas	... ...	1,403 ,,
Æsop	...	959 ,,
De duobus Mercatoribus	...	910 ,,
Testament	...	897 ,,
Dance of Macabre	... ...	672 ,,
Horse, Goose, and Sheep	...	653 ,,
Guy of Warwick	... ...	592 ,,
Pur le Roy	...	544 ,,
Legend of St. Margaret	...	540 ,,
December and July	... ...	520 ,,
Miracles of St. Edmund	...	464 ,,
Legend of St. Austin	... ...	408 ,,
Chorl and Bird	... ...	386 ,,
Legend of St. Giles	... ...	363 ,,
Flour of Curtesie	... ...	270 ,,
	Total	130,249 lines.

Hereto we have to add the smaller poems, especially those in Halliwell, which are not comprised in the above list, and possibly also a number of pieces of doubtful authenticity. We are, however, at all events, not far from the truth, if we say that the number of lines our monk produced, is, in round numbers, 130,000—140,000. There are, as we see, three works of indeed stupendous length, which betray their origin in one of those "collegiate establishments, where the patient monk, in the ample solitude of the cloister, added page to page, and volume to volume, emulating in the productions of his brain the magnitude of the pile he inhabited."[1] There are, further, some four or five works of no mean bulk, and, again, some four or five of less significant length, some dozen of a few hundred lines only, besides numerous smaller pieces. I hope that the above synopsis I have given will at least prevent the repetition of the absurd statement that the monk wrote 251 "works." In comparison with the coryphæi of prolific production—take Lope de Vega as an example—our monk is but an innocent baby, and even among the "drivellers" of our 19th century, called Novel-Writers,[2] who are the nearest

---

[1] Washington Irving, *London Antiques*.
[2] Henry Morley, *English Writers* II, 424 note, wishes to rebut the accusation of tediousness often laid against Lydgate, with the fact that when he was one of the novel-reading "boys" in the British Museum Library, a MS. of

brethren to Lydgate I can think of, he would be one of the more harmless delinquents.

To sum up, I certainly shall not subscribe to the insipid eulogies of a Shirley, a Burgh, or a Hawes; I find Warton's praise far too high, and in some cases even ten Brink's, or Koeppel's, well-tempered commendation of Lydgate's better-known works somewhat beyond the mark. But neither, on the other hand, do I endorse the slighting remarks of Pinkerton and Pauli, and still less do I mean to act the *advocatus diaboli*, by joining in Ritson's Billingsgate. It certainly does not occur to me to claim for Lydgate a place in the realms of higher poetry; but I think we must allow that not unfrequently do we meet in his better works, especially in those of his youth, with passages which breathe true poetry, or at all events, lie on the borderlands of true poetry. There is certainly many a felicitous line and many a poetical sentiment or piece of imagery to be found in his works that would not deface the finest page of a true poet. Moreover, his love of Nature, his humour, his earnest piety,[1] his admiration of his betters or of genius beyond his reach—always tendered ungrudgingly—the love of his country, his national pride,[2] his high reverence for woman, cannot fail to win our hearts; certainly these qualities incline us to forgive much.

Ten Brink, in his *History of English Literature*, and Professor Minto in his *Characteristics of English Poets*, have some admirable remarks showing that many of the monk's most prominent faults arise from his being an epigone of greater masters; our motto at the head of the second part of the Introduction will have shown that we judge of many of Lydgate's peculiarities from the same point of view. There cannot be, moreover, the slightest doubt that Lydgate's commissions from the Court, resulting, amongst other productions, in his two most bulky works, had a baneful influence upon his further

---

Lydgate, with a long saints' legend, was as pleasant to him as *Tylney Hall* or *Peter Simple*. Sir W. Scott calls Hawes "a bad imitator of Lydgate, *ten times more tedious* than his original"—which, be it said by way of parenthesis, means not a little.

[1] Especially in the *Life of our Lady* and the *Legend of Edmund*.

[2] Compare Lydgate's amusing rebuke of Boccaccio, whom he pays out soundly for having slighted his dear Albion (the passage refers to the battle of Poitiers, and the capture of King John):

"Hys fantasye nor hys opinion [*Boccaccio's*]
Stode in that case of none auctorite:
Their king was take, their knightes did[e] flee;
Where was Bochas to help them at such nede?
Saue with his pen he made no man to blede."
Falls of Princes, fol. 216 a and b.

development. I believe that the scales will be decidedly turned in Lydgate's favour, and ten Brink's comparatively high opinion of the monk still further justified, when certain of his works which lie as yet unpublished in various libraries are made generally accessible. Then it will appear more and more clearly that, in estimating him as a poet, the stress should not so much be laid on the unoriginal and spun-out rhymes of his later age, but rather on the more spontaneous and animated productions of his earlier years. The best turn we can do Lydgate—and ourselves in studying him—is certainly to leave the nauseating tirades on Fortune in the *Falls of Princes*, and the soporific speeches in the *Troy-Book* alone, and to take up one of his earlier and more attractive works—such as *Reason and Sensuality*, which we put down with real regret at its unfinished state. Of works of the first stamp we say with Taine : " On s'en va et bâille," while those of the second are sure to engage our interest. At all events, in criticizing Lydgate's abilities, we must not lose sight of one fact which will always incline us to a mild judgment :—as Lydgate has often and justly been praised for his reverence of woman, let me express it in the words of an accomplished woman :[1] " When he ceased his singing, none sang better; there was silence in the land."

CHAPTER XII.
THE APPENDICES.

I. *The Compleynt.*

I HAVE already, in Chapter III, § 1 and Chapter IV, § 1, sufficiently expressed my opinion concerning these lines which MSS. G and S give as a continuation of the *Temple of Glas*. I ought perhaps to apologize for the publication of such worthless rhymes; but I need hardly assure the reader that it was not as a pleasure that I resolved upon the printing of them. When I first came upon this *Compleynt* in the London MS., it was, I confess, with many a deeply-heaved sigh to Apollon Apotropaios that I perused it; but the piece turned up again in the Cambridge MS. Gg. 4. 27, which, with S, formed a conspicuous group by itself, and therefore it had to be printed, were it only for the sake of the text-criticism.

The date of this " *Compleynt* " cannot be much later than that of the *Temple of Glas;* I should think, it is about 1420 or 1430.

[1] El. Barrett-Browning, *Book of the Poets*, 1863, p. 121.

Chapter XII.—The Appendices.

Later than 1430 we cannot make it, since it occurs in MS. G, which is one of our oldest texts, and supposed to be written about that date. We have also distinct reminiscences of Chaucer in the poem. I mean the allusion, in ll. 394—437, to the worship of the daisy-flower, which reminds us at once of the Prologue to the *Legend of Good Women.*

Line 575 may also be a reminiscence from *Anelida* 211:

"So thirleth with the poynt of remembraunce"...

The evidence of the language is quite in accordance with the above date. In fact I do not see any remarkable discrepancy between the language of the *Compleynt* and that of Lydgate. The rhymes, although often faulty from Chaucer's standpoint, nevertheless agree with Lydgate's principles of rhyming. That the poem is not northern, we see at once by rhymes like abod : stod, 207 ; oones : sones, 619. We have further the rhyme *y* : *ie* in l. 86 : mercy : dye ; l. 447 : dayesye : pryvyly ; further, trespas : grace 603 ; mynde : finde 39 ; but also mynde : ende 287 ; fyr : cler 607 ; deye : preye 625 ; eye : espye 183 ; recure : endure 93 ; further, dysdeyn : peyne 89 ; ageyn : peyne 407 ; seyn : peyne 615 ; holde : cold 305 ; among : vndyrfonge 171 (or have we to read amongë? cf. stanza 25 *c*, l. 6) ; whether sloo : foo, l. 295, is a Lydgatian rhyme, I am at present unable to say.[1] In ll. 395, 396 we have only an assonance ; Shirley's reading, however, differs here from G.

Moreover, the inflexions, as shown by the metre in the middle of the line also, are exactly the same as in Lydgate. The ratio of the number of instances in which the final *e* is sounded, to those of its apocope, at the end of nouns—of Teutonic or Romance origin—and in the conjugation of the verb is very much the same as in the *Temple of Glas.* I speak with diffidence of the metre, as I have not analyzed Lydgate's four-beat line with the same care as his five-beat one. If there are many more monosyllabic first measures in the *Compleynt* than in the *Temple of Glas*, this need not surprise us ; for in the four-beat line a trochaic beginning has not an unpleasant effect on the ear, and consequently it is also frequently used by poets with an unmistakably fine perception for rhythm. Lydgate himself has this acephalous type very often, as the perusal of any one page of *Reason and Sensuality* will amply show.

But in spite of all this I cannot help thinking that the *Compleynt*

[1] The form *sloo* occurs in the rhyme in the *Siege of Jerusalem*, and more than once in the *Romaunt of the Rose* (ll. 1953, 2593, 3150, 4592).

not only has nothing to do with the *Temple of Glas*, but that it is not Lydgate's production at all. The piece is so thoroughly stupid. Now Lydgate's poetry was, it is certain, only occasionally inspired by Apollo and the Muses, but I do not think that I have read anything so wretchedly poor as this in his acknowledged works. The only piece of Lydgate's that reminded me slightly of it, is the poem on Thomas Chaucer's departure for France.[1] But even that is not quite so miserable a production as this Compleynt, and besides, it is contained within merciful limits.

There was little doubt as to which MS. was to be chosen as the basis of the text, G being older and evidently better than S. Where G is deficient, we had to rely on S; the text is then sometimes hopelessly corrupt. In no case am I a great advocate of conjectural emendations; in the instance of these silly rhymes it would certainly have been ridiculous to deliberately sit down and try one's ingenuity in improving upon them.

I need hardly add that the principles adhered to with respect to punctuation, orthography, etc., are the same as those I have followed in the *Temple of Glas* itself. The headlines and the short summary of the contents on p. 58 were done by Dr. Furnivall.

II. *The Duodecim Abusiones.*

In the description of the Prints, in Chapter II, I have spoken of the errors and disputes which exist with respect to the Prints of the *Temple of Glas* by Caxton and Wynken de Worde. It is not always easy to see which particular print Herbert and Dibdin mean; but these *Duodecim Abusiones*, occurring in W, W$_2$, w and b, and given as specimens (with the beginning of the *Temple of Glas*) by Herbert and Dibdin, help to make their statements clearer.[2] It was therefore with the view of enabling the reader to judge for himself which print the historians of Typography meant in each respective case, that I thought it advisable to subjoin Appendix II. The text is taken from W, *i. e.* Wynken de Worde's first edition of the *Temple of Glas*, which has been faithfully reproduced, with the addition of stops only. All the variations of W$_2$, w and b are given, including even those of mere orthography.

[1] I fully concur in Dr. Furnivall's opinion that Thomas Chaucer was not the son of Geoffrey, as expressed in *Notes and Queries*, 1872, May, p. 381 etc. Lydgate would not have let this opportunity slip of introducing an allusion to his " master."

[2] Unfortunately, their orthography (even Herbert's) seems anyhow to be somewhat incorrect, whatever print they used.

Chapter XII.—The Appendices.

But I hope the present reprint will also serve another purpose. A very important task of Chaucer-philology is the critical analysis of Stowe's Chaucer-print of 1561, the object of which must be to eliminate the supposititious works, and to assign, as far as possible, each of the spurious pieces to its real author. Now these *Duodecim Abusiones* appear also in this Chaucer-print (on folio 336 d), that is to say, the two English stanzas only without the Latin text. They have been reprinted in Bell's *Chaucer*, ed. Skeat IV, 421, and again in Prof. Skeat's edition of Chaucer's *Minor Poems*, Introduction p. xxix. Skeat has pronounced his opinion as to the authorship with great decision: "Surely it must be Lydgate's," and I think he is right. The appearance of the *Abusiones* in the above-mentioned prints, annexed as they are to a work of Lydgate's, can only tend to strengthen the learned Professor's supposition.[1] I have added the few variations of importance (not the orthographical ones) of the earlier Chaucer-prints.

There are similar pieces to these *Duodecim Abusiones* in earlier English literature (see ten Brink, *Geschichte der englischen Lit.*, I, 268, and note). The "twelf unþeawas" existed also in Old-English; a homily on them is printed in Morris, *Old English Homilies*, p. 101—119. It is based on the Latin Homily, "De octo viciis et de duodecim abusivis huius sæculi," attributed to St. Cyprian or St. Patrick; see Dietrich in Niedner's *Zeitschrift für historische Theologie*, 1855, p. 518; Wanley's *Catalogus*, passim (cp. the Index *sub voce* Patrick). In the Middle-English period we meet again with more or less of these "Abusions"; see Morris, *Old English Miscellany*, p. 185 (11 Abusions); Furnivall, *Early English Poems*, Berlin 1862 (Philological Society), p. 161: "Five evil things"; Wright and Halliwell, *Reliquiæ Antiquæ*, I, 316 and II, 14.

[1] In another case, which concerns a work of Lydgate's in Stowe's Chaucer-print, Skeat is on the right track, without however arriving at the ultimate conclusion. I mean the passage in *M. P.* XLVI, top of page. The poem on the "Fall of Man" in MS. Harl. 2251 is part of Lydgate's *Court of Sapience*.

The Temple of Glas.

For thou3t, constreint, and greuous heuines,	In heaviness and distress
For pensifhede, and for hei3 distres,	I went to bed the other night,
To bed I went nov þis oþir ny3t,	
Whan þat Lucina wiþ hir pale li3t	4 when Sun and Moon were
Was Ioyned last wiþ Phebus in aquarie,	last in conjunction in
Amyd decembre, when of Ianuarie	mid-December.
Ther be kalendes of þe nwe yere,	
And derk Diane, ihorned, noþing clere,	8
Had [hid] hir bemys vndir a mysty cloude:	
Wiþin my bed for sore I gan me shroude,	
Al desolate for constreint of my wo,	
The long[e] ny3t waloing to and fro,	12 A long while restless,
Til at[te] last, er I gan taken kepe,	I at last fell into a deep
Me did oppresse a sodein dedeli slepe,	sleep,
Wiþ-in þe which me þou3t[e] þat I was	in which I was carried in
Rauysshid in spirit in [a] temple of glas—	16 spirit into a Temple of
I nyst[e] how, ful fer in wildirnes—	glass, far in a wil-
That foundid was, as bi lik[ly]nesse,	derness, on a craggy rock,
Not opon stele, but on a craggy roche,	frozen like ice.
Like ise Ifrore. And as I did approche,	20 As I ap-
Again þe sonne that shone, me þou3t, so clere	proached, methought

For the titles in the various MSS. and Prints, see the Introduction. 1. For thou3t] For through W2. Throughe w. b. constreint] compleynt G. S. 2. pensifhede] pensyfnes w. great thought b. 2ᵈ for] om. L. Pr. distres] pensyuenesse b. 6. Amyd] Amiddes S. 7. nwe] newe come S. 8. ihorned] horned and Pr. 9. Had] om. L. b. hid] om. T. P. F. B. C. W. W2. w. 10. sore] feyr P. colde L. Pr. 13. atte] at the L. P. G. S. at T. B. Pr. cr] as S. til P. gan] began C. 14. oppresse] expresse L. dedeli] dede L. 15. þat] om. Pr. (exc. b.) 16. spirit] scripture F. in] into S. L. Pr. a] om. T. W2. w. 17. nyst] nyst nought S. ne wist L. ne wyste w. b. fulfer] fer S. Pr. in] into S. 18. as] all w. b. liklynesse] liknesse T. F. B. L. 19. on] vpon B. L. S. a] om. G. S. 20. Ifrore] afrore P. 21. that shone me þou3t] me thoughte I saw G. me thought hit shoone S. me þou3t] om. Pr. so clere] as clere G. als clere S.

TEMPLE OF GLAS.   B

the Temple shone clear as crystal against the sun;	As eny cristal, and euer nere and nere	
	As I gan neigh this grisli, dredful place,	
the light shone so dazzlingly in my face,	I wex astonyed : the liȝt so in my face	24
	Bigan to smyte, so persing euer in one	
	On euere part, where þat I gan gone,	
that I could perceive nothing,	That I ne myȝt noþing, as I would,	
	Abouten me considre and bihold,	28
	The wondre *estres, for briȝtnes of þe sonne ;	
till at last some dark clouds drifted before the sun,	Til at[te] last certein skyes donne,	
	Wiþ wind Ichaced, haue her cours I went	
	To-fore þe stremes of Titan and Iblent,	32
so that I could see all around me.	So þat I myȝt, wiþ-in and with-oute,	
	Where so I walk, biholden me aboute,	
	Forto report the fasoun and manere	
This place was circular, round in shape.	Of al þis place, þat was circulere	36
	In compaswise, Round bentaile wrouȝt.	
After I had long sought, I found a wicket, and entered quickly.	And whan þat I hade long gone & souȝt,	
	I fond a wiket, and entrid in as fast	
	Into þe temple, and myn ciȝen cast	40
I cast my eyes on every side,	On euere side, now lowe & eft aloft.	
	And riȝt anone, as I gan walken soft,	
	If I þe soth ariȝt report[e] shal,	
and saw pictured on the walls images of sundry lovers.	I sauȝe depeynt opon euere wal,	44
	From est to west, ful many a faire Image	
	Of sondri louers, lich as þei were of age	
	I-sette in ordre, aftir þei were trwe,	
	Wiþ lifli colours wondir fressh of hwe.	48

22. 1ˢᵗ nere] the nerre P. 23. gan] cam C. b. 24. wex] was L. 25. persing] passynge w. b. 26. euere part] yche apart S. gan] koude S. om. W2. w. dyde b. 28. me] me to P. *Between 28 and 29 are the following two lines in S:*

And many a story / mo þan I reken can, (= *line* 91)
Hem to rehers / I trowe þer might no man.

29. wondre] wondreful S. wonders b. estres] hestres T (hestrys L.) 30. atte] at the P. L. G. S. att B. at T. w. b. skyes] kyes P. donne] doone L. 31. Ichaced] chaeed Pr. haue] than w. and b. Iwent] went G. S. 32. To-fore] þo for S. Before b. 33. and] and eke P. S. 34. Where so] Wher that P. walk] wolde G. Pr. 35. report] report the report P. 36. þis] þat S. 37. In] I W2. w. Off P. Round] om. P. 38. þat] om. P. Pr. hade long] longe hadde G. long] longher P. long gone] goon longe S. gone] om. W2. w. b. souȝt] well sought b. 39. fond] founded L. 41. &] om. C. and now W. W2. w. b. 43. ariȝt] ryght P. 44. euere] a Pr. 45. ful] om. S. Pr. 47. I-sette in] Sett by S. aftir] lych as G. after that as P. right as S. 48. wondir] wonders b. of hwe] & new B.

Pictures of Famous Lovers. 3

And, as me þouȝt, I sauȝe somme sit & stonde,   Some sat,
And some kneling wiþ billis in hir honde,   some stood, some knelt, with 'bills' in their hands,
And some with compleint, woful & pitous,   with com-
Wiþ doleful chere to putten to Venus,   52   plaints to lay before Venus.
So as she sate fleting in þe se,
Vpon hire wo forto haue pite.
    And first of al I saugh þere of Car[ta]ge   First I saw Dido of
Dido þe quene, so goodli of visage,   56   Carthage,
That gan complein hir aduenture & caas,   complaining of the faith-
Hov she deceyued was of Eneas,   lessness of Æneas;
For al his hestis & his oþis sworne,
And said: 'alas, þat euer she was borne,'   60
Whan þat she saugh þat ded she most[e] be.
    And next I saugh the compleint of Medee,   next Medea, deceived by
Hou þat she was falsed of Iason.   Jason;
    And nygh bi Venus saugh I sit Addoun,   64   then, nigh by Venus,
And al þe maner, hov þe bore him slough,   Adonis slain by the boar.
For whom she wepte & hade pein Inouȝe.
    There saugh I also, hov Penalope,   Also Pene-
For she so long hir lord ne myȝt[e] se,   68   lope, pale with grief at her lord's
Ful oft[e] wex of colour pale & grene.   absence.
    And aldernext was þe fressh[e] quene,   Next Alcestis, who died for
I mene Alceste, the noble trw[e] wyfe,   Admetus,
And for Admete hou sho lost hir life,   72
And for hir trouth, if I shal not lie,   and was turned into a
Hou she was turnyd to a dai[e]sie.   daisy.
    There was [also] Grisildis innocence,   There was also patient
And al hir mekenes, & hir pacience.   76   Griselda,
    There was eke Isaude—& meni a noþir mo—

49. And] Right S. &] sum L. & som Pr. 51. compleint] compleyntes G. S. 54. forto] to L. 55. Cartage] Carge T. P. F (in F. corrected by Stowe). 58. deceyued] descended F (n corrected to v in different ink). 59. hestis] behestes P. 60. she was] was she G. S. 61. Whan] And when P. þat] om. S. P. Pr. she moste] most she S. 62. next] nex W2. next her w. b. 63. was falsed] falsed was Pr. falsed] Ifalsid G. Iason] Iosan L. 64. saugh I] I saw P. sit Addoun] siten doun S. 65. þe maner] manere P. hov] how that G. bore] bere P. 66. hade] made S. pein] sorwe G. S. pyne C. W. W2. w. pite b. 67. hov] how that Pr. howe feyre S. 68. so] om. S. hir lord ne myȝte] ne myght her lorde b. ne myȝte] might not S. 69. Ful ofte wex] Was Pr. wex of colour] of colour wex S. pale] bothe pale Pr. 70. And] All B. 72. And for Admete] þat for hir trouthe S. 73. for hir trouth] transfourmed S. trouth] through W2. thrughe w. 74 in S: In to þe floure / cleped Daysye. to] into P. Pr. 75. also] om. T. P. L. Pr. 76. & hir] and al hir P. and Pr. 77. eke] om. S. a noþir] other Pr.

Tristram and Isolde,	And al þe turment, and al þe cruel wo,
	That she hade for Tristram al hir liue.
Pyramus and Thisbe,	And hou þat Tesbie her hert[e] did[e] rife 80
	Wiþ þilk[e] swerd of him Piramus;
Theseus and the Minotaur,	And al þe maner, hou þat Theseus
	The Minatawre slow amyd þe hous,
	That was for-wrynkked bi craft of Dedalus, 84
	When þat he was in prison shette in Crete.
and Phyllis, who for love of Demophoon, hanged herself upon a filbert tree.	And hou þat Phillis felt of loues hete
	The grete fire of Demophon, alas,
	And for his falshed and [for] his trespas 88
	Vpon þe walles depeint men myȝt[e] se,
	Hov she was honged vpon a filbert tre.
	And mani a stori, mo þen I rekin can,
There were Paris and Helen,	Were in þe tempil, & hov þat Paris wan 92
	The faire Heleyne, þe lusti fressh[e] quene,
and Achilles slain for Polyxena.	And hov Achilles was for Policene
	I-slain vnwarli within Troi[e] toune:
	Al þis sawe I, [walkynge vp & doun. 96
There was also the story of Philomene and Progne,	Ther sawe I] writen eke þe hole tale,
	Hov Philomene into a nyȝtyngale
	Iturned was, and Progne vnto a swalow;
and the Sabines at the feast of Lucrece.	And hov þe Sabyns in hir maner halowe 100
	The fest of Lucresse ȝit in Rome tovne.
I saw also the sorrow of Palamon,	There saugh I also þe sorov of Palamoun,
	That he in prison felt, & al þe smert,
	And hov þat he, þurugh vnto his hert, 104

78. 2ᵈ al] *om.* G. S. Pr.   79. hade for Tristram al] for Trystram sufferede in G. S.   80. hou þat] howe b. her] thorowe þe S.   81. þilke] þe S.   him] hyre G.   hir S. sire C. syr W. W2. w. b.   82. þe] *om.* P.   hou] of G.   þat] Duc S.   84. for-wrynkked] for wrynkeled F. for wrinkelid B. so wrynkled G. S.   85. When] What L. W2. w.   þat] *om.* Pr.   was] *om.* P.   86. loues] loued w. loue the b.   87. fire] furye S.   of] for S. b.   88. 2ᵈ for] *om.* T. P. F. B. L. G.   89. walles depeint] wal depeuted G. S.   depeint] epeynted P.   90. was honged] was hangyn G. henge Pr. filbert] philbertis S.   92. in þe tempil] þer depeynted S.   93. The] *om.* S.   þe] a Pr. (*exc.* b.) lusti fresshe] fresche lusty G. S.   94. hov] *om.* L.   95. I-slain] Slawe G. vnwarli] vnwardly W. W2. w. b. Troie] troyes S.   96. *om.* T. (P.) F. B. L.   *In F the following line has been subsequently supplied:* by forcastyng of greit tresovne; *this has been expunged and (by Stowe) corrected to:* And in this Temple / as I Romed vp and downe. *The latter is also the reading of* P.   sawe I] I sawe S.   I say G.   97. Ther] Al þis T. F. B. L. Al thus P.   eke] also S.   99. vnto] to G. into L. S. b.   100. þe] *om.* S.   hir] a S. *om.* L.   101. ȝit] that P.   103. prison] *om. in* F; *but subsequently added by Stowe.*   104. vnto] in to S. *om.* P.

Was hurt vnwarli þurugh castinɡ of an eyȝe — his love for Emily, and his fight with his brother,
Of faire fressh, þe ȝung[e] Emelie,
And al þe strife bitwene him & his broþir,
And hou þat one fauȝt eke with þat oþir   108
Wiþ-in þe groue, til þei bi Theseus
Acordid were, as Chaucer telliþ us. — as told by Chaucer.
  And forþirmore, as I gan bihold,
I sawȝ hov Phebus with *an arow of gold   112   I saw how Phœbus was wounded by Cupid,
I-woundid was, þuruȝ oute in his side,
Onli bi envie of þe god Cupide,
And hou þat *Daphne vnto a laurer tre   — and Daphne changed into a laurel tree;
Iturned was, when she did[e] fle;   116
  And hou þat Ioue gan to chaunge his cope   — and how Jove turned himself into a bull for love of Europa,
Oonli for loue of þe faire Europe,
And into [a] bole, when he did hir sue,
List of his godhode his fourme to transmwe;   120
And hou þat he bi transmutacioun   — and took the shape of Amphitryon for Alcmene's sake.
The shap gan take of Amphitrioun
For *hir, *Almen, so passi[n]g *of beaute;
So was he hurt, for al his deite,   124
Wiþ loues dart, & myȝt it not ascape.
  There sauȝ I also hou þat Mars was take   — I saw Mars and Venus bound by Vulcan,
Of Vulcanus, and wiþ Venus found,
And wiþ þe Cheynes invisible bound.   128
  Ther was also al þe poesie   — and the wedding of Mercury with Philology,
Of him, Mercurie, and Phil[o]log[y]e,

105. hurt] hit G. wounde P. vnwarli] om. S. vnwardly W2. inwardly w. b. þurugh] thorowe þat S. for G. by Pr. 106. Of] On Pr. faire] the fayre w. b. þe] om. L. and w. b. ȝunge] lusty yong Pr. 108. eke] om. P. B. Pr. þat one] the ton G. þat oþir] the tothyr G. the othir P. 109. þei bi] that P. 110. Acordid] Arrested S. Departed P. Chaucer telliþ] telliþe Chaucer to S. 111. as] om. L. 112. hov] of G. S. an arow] anoro T. of] om. P. 113. oute in] in to P. in] om. Pr. 115. Daphne] Dane G. Done S. Diane T. P. F. B. L. Pr. vnto a] In ta G. in to a S. 116. when] whan that Pr. 117. Ioue] Iohon P. gan to chaunge] changed C. began to chaunge L. W. W2. w. b. 118. loue of þe] the love of G. 119. into a bole] Triable S. a] om. T. F. B. hir] he C. 121. hon] om. S. 122. gan] cane S. 123. hir] his T. F. B. L. he P. om. Pr. Almen] Alcumena Pr. al men T. P. L. þat was S. so] om. L. passing] passaunt G. of] was T. F. B. was with P. was of Pr. 124. in P: Aforne all othir that smyten so was hee. deite] deynte S. 125. reads in P:
  With lowes dart he myght
  he myght it noght aschape. it] om. B.
126. þat] om. Pr. 127. found] I founde B. 128. Cheynes] Cheynes of L. bound] I bounde B. 130. him] om. S. and] and al the Pr. Philologye G.] Phillogie (Philogye etc.) F. B. P. L. Pr. Philloge T. Philosophie S.

And hou þat she, for hir sapience,
I weddit was to god of eloquence, 132

and how the latter was conveyed to heaven by the Muses.
And hou þe Musis *lowli did obeie,
High into heuen þis ladi to conuei,
And with hir song hov she was magnified
With Iubiter to bein Istellified. 136

One could see, how Canace understood the language of birds,
And vppermore depeint men myȝt[e] se,
Hov with hir ring, goodli Canace
Of euere foule þe ledne & þe song
Coud vndirstond, as she welk hem among; 140

and how her brother was helped by the steed of brass.
And hou hir broþir so oft holpen was
In his myschefe bi þe stede of bras.

There were, furthermore, many thousands of lovers, ready to complain to the goddess:
And forþermore in þe tempil were
Ful mani a þousand of louers, here & þere, 144
In sondri wise redi to complein
Vnto þe goddes, of hir wo & pein,

of envy, Hou þei were hindrid, some for envie,
of jealousy, And hou þe serpent of fals Ielousie 148
Ful many a louer haþ iput o bak,
And caus[e]les on hem Ilaid a lak.

of absence and exile through wicked tongues,
And some þer were þat pleyned on absence,
That werin exiled & put oute of presence 152
Thuruȝ wikkid tungis & fals suspecioun,
[With-oute mercy or remyssyoun.]
And oþer eke her seruise spent in vain,

of 'Danger' and 'Disdain.'
Thuruȝ cruel dau*n*nger, & also bi disdain; 156
And some also þat loued, soþ to sein,
And of her ladi were not louyd again.

131. hir] his S. 132. god] the god Pr. 133. hou] om. S. lowli] only G. lwfly P. lowli did] did lowli T. 136. to] there to Pr. Istellified] stellified L. S. Pr. 138. with] that G. goodli] the goodly Pr. 139. ledne] leydons C. W. b. leydons W2. laydous w. layes L. &] and ek G. S. 2ᵈ þe] om. C. W. W2. w. 140. Coud] Cowde thenn L. welk] walked Pr. 141. hou] om. G. 142. stede] sounde S. 144. a] of P. a þousand of louers] an hundred thousand S. of] om. Pr. 145. In] Is W2. w. 146. pein] pyne P. 147 and 148 transposed in P. 147. þei] there G. for] thourgh G. by S. of P. 149. iput] put Pr. offt put S. 150. causles T. hem] hym G. S. Ilaid] leyd G. haþe leyde S. b. haue leid C. W. W2. w. he layd P. 151. þer] om. S. þat pleyned] pleynynge G. pleyning hyely S. pleyned] playne L. 152. put] om. L. 154. om. T. P. F. B; in F by a different hand:

Wyth owte answar weche was no resoun.

154. or] or any L. Pr. 155. eke] also W. W2. w. b. seruise] lwfys P. 156 and 157 om. Pr. 156. also] al P. 157. loued] lwfith P. 158. And] om. L.

And oþir eke, þat for pouerte — Others were in poverty,
Durst *in no wise hir grete aduersite   160
Discure ne open, lest þai were refusid;
And some for wanting also werin accusid, — or loved secretly, not daring to declare themselves;
And oþir eke þat loued secreli,
And of her ladi durst aske no merci,   164
Lest þat she would of hem haue despite;
And some also þat putten ful grete wite — others blamed false lovers, who hinder the faithful ones.
On double louers, þat loue þingis nwe,
Thurgh whos falsnes hindred be þe trwe.   168
And some þer were, as it is oft[e] found, — Some had endured bloody wounds in distant regions,
That for her ladi meny a blodi wounde
Endurid haþ in mani [a] regioun,
Whiles þat an oþer haþ poscessioun   172 — whilst another possessed their lady.
Al of his ladi, and beriþ awai þe fruyte
Of his labur and of al his suyte.
And oþer eke compleyned *of Riches, — Others complained against Riches, who, with Treasure, wins the field against true lovers.
Hou he with Tresour doþ his besines   176
To wynnen al, againes kynd & ryȝt,
Wher trw louers haue force noon ne myȝt.
And some þer were, as maydens ȝung of age, — Young maidens complained, that they were coupled with crooked Old Age:
That pleined sore with peping & with rage,   180
That þei were coupled, againes al nature,
Wiþ croked elde, þat mai not long endure
Forto performe þe lust of loues plai:
For it ne sit not vnto fressh[e] May   184 — for fresh May should not be coupled with old January;
Forto be coupled to oold[e] Ianuari—

159. oþir eke] also other W. W2. w. b.   160. in] on T. F. B.   161. ne] in G. S.   162. And] om. S. wanting] avaunte S.   163. oþir eke] also other W. W2. w. b.   164. And] om. L. þat S. no] ne b.   165. she would of hem] of hem she wolde S. of hem haue] haue of theim L.   166. ful] right Pr.   167. loue] lufyth P.   168. þe] om. P. L.   169. þer] that L. as] at P. found] efounde S.   170. meny a blodi] haden many a S.   171. haþ] hadde G. haue b. and S. a] om. T. F. B. S.   172. Whiles] Whyle b. þat] om. P. haþ] hath had Pr. hath the P.   174. Of his] Of al his P.   175. And] An b. eke] om. Pr. compleyned] complayneth b. of] in T. P. F. B. L.   176. he] om. B. tresour] tresouns L.   177. wynnen] wymen F. womene P. al] om. Pr. againes] agaynst al Pr.   178. Wher] Where as Pr. force noon] noo force W. W2. w. b.   no kynde S. ne] no b. myȝt] ryght P.   180. pleined] pleyneth C. playnen W. W2. playne w. b. sore] so L. Pr. peping] piping L. pipyng C. W. W2. w. popyng P. peynenge B. wepyng F. G. S. b.   181. þoi] om. G. Pr. were] om. P. coupled] compelled S. againes] agayn Pr.   182. elde] olde G. W. W2. w. b. old P.   183. lust of loues] lustis G.   184. it ne sit not] it is nat syttynge b. vnto] to S.   185. to] vnto G. with P.

Complaints of the Lovers

Old Age and Youth are so different.

Thei ben so diuers þat þei most[e] varie—
For eld is grucching & malencolious,
Ay ful of ire & suspecious, 188
And iouth entendeþ to Ioy & lustines,
To myrth & plai & to al gladnes.

'Alas! that sugar should be mixed with gall!' these young folks cried.

'Allas þat euer þat it shuld[e] fal,
*So soote sugre Icoupled be wi͏th gal!' 192
These yong[e] folk criden oft[e] siþe,
And praied Venus hir pouer forto kiþe
Vpon þis myschef, & shape remedie.

And others I heard lament with tears and piteous sounds,

And riȝt anon I herd oþir crie 196
Wi͏th sobbing teris, & wi͏th ful pitous sounc,
Tofore þe goddes, bi lamentacioun,

that had been forced to enter the monastic life in their childhood,

That *were constrayned in hir tender youþe,
And in childhode, as it is oft[e] couþe, 200
*Yentred were into religioun,
Or þei hade yeris of discresioun,

and now must feign perfection in wide copes, hiding their inwardsmart.

That al her life cannot but compleín,
In wide copis perfeccion to feine, 204
Ful couertli to curen al hir smert,
And shew þe contrarie outward of her hert.

Thus wept many a fair maid, blaming her friends.

Thus saugh I wepen many a faire maide,
*That on hir freendis al þe wite þei leide. 208
And oþer next I saugh þere in gret rage,

---

186. moste] mot nedes S. most nedes P. 187. eld] olde G. P. W. W2. w. b. grucching] grucchynd P. &] om. S. 188. Ay] Alwaye w. b. ful of ire] irefull b. of] om. L. &] and eke b. suspecious] suspicessyonous S. 189. iouth] though P. &] & to P. 190. al] gret S. 191. 2ᵈ þat] om. L. S. Pr. it] is P. ye F. om. B. shulde] shulle P. eshoulde S. fal] befall b. 192. So] þat S. So soote] To sute T. Icoupled] couplid B. Icoupled be] shoulde be coupled S. be] om. L. be wi͏th] be to C. W. W2. to be w (be *has been scratched out and* soure *written over it*). with the b. 193. These] The F. B. folk] folkys S. criden ofte siþe] of sithe weppith and cryden P. ofte] oftyn G. 194. forto] to C. W. W2. w. 195. Vpon] Vnto L. &] to S. 196. oþir] an othir P. 197. sobbing] sowing L. pytous S. wi͏th ful] om. Pr. ful] wol G. pitous] weping S. soune] swoun G. 198. Tofore] By fore S. Before b. A for P. bi] with S. with gret L. 199. That] Thaire L. were constrayned] conseiles T. counseyles F. B. counseillys L. conseylis G. concellith P. cofessen S. tender] om. Pr. 200. in] In here G. in hir S. childhode] childysh hode F. childerhod P. it] om. C. W. W2. w. ofte] oft a W2. w. 201. Yentred] Yrendred T. L. Irenderede G. were] ben S. 202. Or] Er þat S. 204. to] for to C. W. b. P. or to W2. w. 205. to curen al] for to coueren Pr. hir] they W2. 206. outward] outwardes S. om. Pr. of] in G. her] om. P. 207. Thus] This P. There b. wepen] wepyng P. where w. om. b. 207 *and* 208 *transposed in* P. 208. That] Than T. L. þe] hir S. þei] om. P. G. b. 209. oþer] ouer L. next] mo b. þere] om. P. they *altered to* them F.

That þei were maried in her tendir age,   Others had been married in their tender age,
Wiþ-oute fredom of eleccioun,   without free choice, re-
Wher loue haþ seld domynacioun: 212   gardless of inclination.
For loue, at laarge & [at] liberte,
Would freli chese, & not with such trete.
And oþer saugh I ful oft wepe & wring,   Others com-plained of
[That they in men founde swych variynge,]   216   men, who only love
To loue a seisoun, while þat beaute floureþ,   while beauty blooms,
And bi disdein so vngoodli loureþ   and when it departs,
On hir þat whilom he callid his ladi dere,   frown on their lady.
That was to him so plesaunt & entere;   220
But lust with fairnes is so ouergone,
That in her hert trouþ abideþ none.
And som also I sauȝ in teris reyne,   Some I saw in floods of tears
And pitousli on god & kynd[e] pleyne,   224   complain against God
That euer þei would on eny creature   and Nature, for endowing
So mych beaute, passing bi mesure,   a woman with such
Set on a woman, to yeue occasioun   passing beauty as to
A man to loue to his confusioun,   228   ruin a man:
And nameli þere where he shal haue no grace;
For wiþ a loke, forth-bi as he doþ pace,   for by one look a man is
Ful oft[e] falleþ, þuruȝ casting of an yȝe,   often wound-ed to the
A man is woundid, þat he most nedis deye,   232   death.
That neuer efter perauenture shal hir se.
Whi wil god don so gret a cruelte   Why does God inflict so
To eny man, or to his creature,   much woe on any man,
To maken him so mych wo endure,

210. þei] om. b. maried] murdred S. 211 and 212 transposed in L. 211. of] of fre Pr. 212. seld] seldome b. 213. 2ᵈ at] om. T. L. 214. chese] om. S. not] om. P. trete] threte L. 215. saugh I] I sawe L. I saughe P. oft] soore G. sore S. 216 om. T. F. B. In F the following line is inserted by a later hand: that weer dysayuyd / bi thaeyr wenynge. The reading of P is: That euer a man shuld so fals a thyng. variynge] vaveringe L. 217. þat] om. G. the L. 218. And] And after Pr. bi] be high P. 219. On] Vpon S. hir] hym G. þat whilom he callid] he cleped S. whilom] somtyme w. b. 220. was to him] to hym was G. S. him] hynt P. & entere] in tyre P. 221. so] sone F. B. ouergone] ouer grone P. 222. her] hys P. 224. pitousli] pituous L. pleyne] complayne b. þey pleyne S. 225. euer þei] thei euer P. þei] he b. on] in L. G. S. 227. on] in G. S. to] ȝeue] by S. 229. haue] fynd P. haue no] non corrected to hanno G. no] om. S. 230. wiþ] by B. forth-bi] forby G. S. he doþ] men do G. men doon S. 231. Ful] Wel S. þuruȝ] om. Wᶻ. w. 232. he most nedis] nedis he most P. 233. That] Whiche G. And S. Yet b. efter perauenture] perauuter after he L. Pr. perauenture shal hir] shal hir peravntre S. 234. a] om. P. b. 235. or] or els b.

Vision of the Fair Lady:

<small>for the sake of one, who will never be his own?</small> For hir percaas, whom he shal in no wise
　Reioise neuer, but so forþ in lewise
　Ledin his life, til þat he be graue.
　For he ne durst of hir no merci craue,   240
　And eke perauenture, þou3 he durst & would,
　He can not wit, where he hir find[e] shuld.
　I saugh þere eke, & þerof hade I rouþe,
<small>Some were also hindered by couetousness, by sloth or hastiness.</small> That som were hindred for couetise & slouth,   244
　And some also for her hastines,
　And oþer eke for hir reklesnes—
<small>Last of all I saw, beside Pallas, before the statue of Venus,</small> But alderlast as I walk & biheld,
　Beside Pallas wiþ hir cristal sheld,   248
　Tofore þe *statue of Venus set on height,
<small>a lady kneeling, and, as the Sun outshines all stars,</small> Hov þat þer knelid a ladi in my sy3t
　Tofore þe goddes, which ri3t as þe sonne
　Passeþ þe sterres & doþ hir stremes donne,   252
　And Lucifer, to voide þe ny3tes sorow,
　In clerenes passeþ erli bi þe morow,
<small>as May is the fairest of all months,</small> And so as Mai haþ þe souereinte
　Of euere moneþ, of fairnes & beaute,   256
<small>as the rose surpasses all flowers, balm all liquors, and the ruby all stones;</small> And as þe rose in swetnes & odoure
　Surmounteþ floures, and bawme of al licour
　Haueþ þe pris, & as þe rubie bri3t
　Of al stones in beaute & in si3t,   260
　As it is know, haþ þe regalie:
<small>so this lady</small> Ri3t so þis ladi wiþ hir goodli ci3e,

<small>237. percaas] parcas (*underlined as a proper name*) S. whom] when S. he] she P. 238. neuer] at any tyme b. forþ] sory L. in lewise] as vnwyse S. lewise] inuyse b. 239. his] this (*over erasure*) his F. þat] *om.* b. graue] in his graue W. W2. w. layde in graue b. 240. of] on P. craue] haue P. 241. eke] also W. W2. w. b. &] or G. 242. he] *om.* F. B. he hir] hir he S. hir] *om.* L. 243. eke] also W. W2. w. b. þerof] of P. therefore L. 244. hindred] hemerede G. for] thorowe S. G. by Pr. 245. for] thoroughe S. 246. eke] also W. W2. w. b. for] thoroughe S. 247. alderlast] at the last W. W2. w. b. 248. Beside] Besides L. cristal] orystall W2. w. 249. Tofore] Before b. statue] statute T. B. W. W2. w. stature P. L. b. 250. Hov þat] *om.* Pr. 251. Tofore] Byfore S. Before b. which] the whiche G. S. ri3t] *om.* P. 252. &] *om.* b. doþ hir] so thourgh G. doþ hir stremes] eke the stormys C. also the stormes W. doþ hir stremes donne] also the stormes (storme w.) W2. w. in brightnesse echone b. stremes] brightnesse S. donne] downe P. 253. And] And as b. 254. In] I W2. w. clerenes] clennesse G. cherenesse P. bi] *om.* Pr. 255. so] *om.* b. 256. of] the C. W. W2. w. in b. 258. Surmounteþ] Surmounted C. Surmounteh (*sic*) W. W2. floures] the flowres P. and] & as b. al] *om.* S. 259. &] *om.* F. bri3t] hight L. 260. Of] Bryght oll P. al] alle the G. beaute] bountee S. *Lines 261—264 are omitted in S (the rhymes* bri3t *and* si3t *occurring again in ll.* 263, 264*). P interpolates between*</small>

Her Beauty and Virtues.

And with þe stremes of hir loke so briȝt, *with her radiant looks*
Surmountеþ al þurugh beaute in my siȝte : 264 *surpassed all in beauty.*
Forto tel hir gret semelines,
Hir womanhed, hir port, & hir fairnes,
It was a meruaile, hou euer þat nature *It was a marvel how*
Coude in hir werkis make a creature 268 *Nature could make so angelic a*
So aungellike, so goodli on to se, *creature:*
So femynyn or passing of beaute,
Whos sonnyssh here, briȝter þan gold were, *her sunny hair was*
Lich Phebus bemys shynyng in his spere— 272 *brighter than goldwire,*
The goodlihed eke of hir fresshli face,
So replenysshid of beaute & of grace,
So wel ennuyd bi Nature & depeint, *in her fresh face roses and*
That Rose and lileis togedir were so meint, 276 *lilies seemed to mingle,*
So egalli bi good proporcioun,
That, as me þouȝt, in myn inspeccioun *and altogether she*
I gan meruaile, hou god, or werk of kynd, *was of such passing*
Miȝten of beaute such a tresour find, 280 *beauty and excellence,*
To yeven hir so passing excellence.
For in goode faiþ, þuruȝ hir heiȝ presence *that the whole Temple was*
The tempil was enlumynd enviroun, *illumined by her high pre-*
And forto speke of condicioun, 284 *sence.*
She was þe best þat myȝt[e] ben on lyve :
For þer was noon þat wiþ hir myȝt[e] striue, *No one could compare with*
To speke of bounte, *or of gentilles, *her in womanly*
Of womanhed, or of lowlynes, 288 *charms and virtues:*
Of curtesie, or of goodlihed,
Of spech, of chere, or of semlyhed,
Of port benygne, & of daliaunce,

ll. 260 *and* 261 : To for the goddes wheche ryght as (cf. *line* 251). 263. þe] *om.* G. 264. þurugh] *om.* B. through all P. 265. Forto] ffor forto G. That for to Pr. 266. 2ᵈ hir] hert P. 267. meruaile] meruabil P. euer þat] þat euer S. 269. aungellike] agreable G. so] or G. S. 271. sonnyssh] goodly L. Schynyng P. *om.* S. here] here heire P. clernesse S. briȝter] is bryghtere G. S. bright P. 272. bemys] by S. 273. eke] also W. W2. w. b. of] yf W2. w. fresshli] fresshe L. B. S. C. W. W2. w. fayre b. 274. replenysshid] replevisshes G. 275. ennuyd] emewed P. endewed b. coloured S. 276. That] The L. As S. Pr. Rose] roses S. so] *om.* L. S. Pr. meint] y meint F. B. b. emeynt S. 277. egalli] evenly S. bi] euen bo P. 278. as S. Pr. 279. of] or P. 281. passing] persant P. 282. heiȝ] *om.* F. 284. forto] to F. of] of her P. L. Pr. 285. best þat] *om.* P. on lyve] a lyne G. alyve S. 286. þat wiþ hir] with her that B. wiþ hir myȝte] might with hir S. 287. bounte] beute G. beautie b. or] er T. gentilles] lowlynesse S. 288. lowlynes] gentylesse S. 290 *omitted in* P. or] *om.* G. 291. Of port benygne] Beningne of port S. &] or Pr.

	The best[e] tauȝt, & þerto of plesaunce 292
she was a model and mirror, lady and mistress to all of her sex.	She was þe wel, and eke of oneste An exemplarie, & mirrour eke was she Of secrenes, of trouth, of faythfulnes,
	And to al oþer ladi & maistres, 296 To sue vertu, whoso list to lere.
So I saw this lady kneeling before Venus, clad in green and white,	And so þis ladi, benigne and humble of chere, Kneling I saugh, al clad in grene and white, Tofore Venus, goddes of al delite, 300 Enbrouded al with stones & perre
	So richeli, þat ioi it was to se,
with broideries of precious stones, and sundry 'rolls,'	Wiþ sondri rolles on hir garnement, Forto expoune þe trouth of hir entent, 304 And shew fulli, þat for hir humbilles, And for hir vertu, and hir stabilnes, That she was rote *of womanli plesaunce.
setting forth her motto: 'De mieux en mieux.'	Therfore hir woord wiþoute variaunce 308 Enbrouded was, as men myȝt[e] se : 'De mieulx en mieulx,' with stones and perre :
This is to say: she resigns her heart and will, from better to better, unto Venus.	This [is] to sein þat she, þis benigne, From bettir to bettir hir hert[e] doþ resigne, 312 And al hir wil, to Venus þe goddes, Whan þat hir list hir harmes to redresse.

292. tauȝt] thaught G. P. etaught S. &] om. w. b.   293. and eke] also S. W. W2. w. eke C. b.   294. An] And S. &] and the P. eke] also W. W2. w. b. om. S.   295. secrenes] sikurnesse S. 3ᵈ of] & G. and of P.   297. sne] shewe S. Pr. sewe *in* L *is, by a later hand, altered into* shewe.   298. ladi] om. P. benigne and] right Pr. humble] noble S. chere] her chere b.   299. al] om. Pr. al clad in grene] in blak In red G. S. and] & In G.   300. Tofore] Before b. Beseching S. al] om. F.   303. garnement] garment B. L. b.   305. And] To Pr. þat for hir] for þat hir hye S. humbilles] humblenesse L. b. noblesse S.   306. And for hir] Hir stedfast vertu S. 2ᵈ hir] for hir F. B. L. stabilnes] stablesse G. stedfastnesse b.   307. was] om. P. of] of al T. F. B. L. Pr.   309. was] om. W. W2. w. as] ther as P.   309 *and* 310 *read in* G. S:

    Was vp & doun as men myghte (mighten S) se
    In frens (ffresshly S) enbroudyt humblement magre.

310. and] of L. C. W. W2. w.   311. This] þat S. is] om. T. L. þis] is S. was L. was so Pr.   312. From] ffro P. ffor L. 312 *reads in* G. S: Hyr herte & al fully doth resigue.   313. And al hir wil to] Iu to the handys of G. S. 314. Whan] Quhame P. 1ˢᵗ hir] she P. harmes] harnes P.—*Line* 314 *reads in* b: She stode at poynt redy to expresse.—*Between* 314 *and* 315 *the following* 4 *lines are interpolated in* b:

    And her humbly of mercy for to pray
    For her dole remedy to puruaye
    Gladly she wolde the goddesse shulde attende
    Her sorowes all and harmes to amende.

For as me þouȝt sumwhat bi hir chere,
Forto compleyne she hade gret desire : 316
For in hir hond she held a litel bil,
Forto declare þe somme of al hir wil,
And to þe goddes hir quarel forto shewe,
[Theffect of which was this In wordys fewe :] 320

From her face, methought, she too had a complaint; for she had a little 'bill' in her hand, which was to this effect:

1.

'O ladi Venus, modir of Cupide, 321
That al þis *wor[l]d hast in gouernaunce,
And hertes high, *þat hauteyn [ben] of pride,
Enclynyst mekeli to þin obeissaunce,
Causer of ioie, Relese of penaunce, 325
And with þi stremes canst cueri þing discerne
*Thuruȝ heuenli fire of loue þat is eterne ; 327

'O lady Venus, mistress of all this world,

2.

O blisful sterre, persant & ful of liȝt, 328
Of bemys gladsome, devoider of derknes,
Cheif recounford after þe blak nyȝt,
To voide woful oute of her heuynes,
Take nov goode hede, ladi & goddesse, 332
So þat my bil ȝour grace may atteyne,
Redresse to finde of þat I me compleyne. 334

thou blissful star,

comfort after the black night,

let now my bill attain your grace.

3.

For I am bounde to þing þat I nold ; 335
Freli to chese þere lak I liberte ;
And so I want of þat myn hert[e] would ;

I lack liberty to choose freely;

315. þouȝt] þinkeþe S. 315 reads in b: And euermore me thought by her chere. 316. Forto] To b. gret] right great b. 317. held] had S. 318. Forto declare] Wherin was writte b. þe somme] sume part S. of] and P. al] om. S. wil] stylle W2. skylle w. b. 319 reads in b: And all that she wolde to the goddesse shewe. to] om. L. 320 om. T. B; in F Stowe supplied: hir matire was / of thes ballads fewe. This is also the reading of P; only of is wanting in the latter MS. was] foloweth b. this] om. L. Pr.
    The following headings are found before line 321: Supplicacio mulieris amantis F. B. Balade S. The copye of the supplicacion Pr. The fyrst parte of the songe L (in a later hand). 321. of] to G. S. 322. al] in C. world] word T. worde L. hast] þou hast S. in] the C. 323. And] And the b. high] om. b. hauteyn] ha doten T. hatedeyn F. hatydon B. hadoten P. haultotayn̄ L. haunteyn̄ S. ben] om. T. W. W2. w. hyȝ b. of] by Pr. 325. Causer] Cause G. Relese] releser B. P. L. G. S. 327. Thuruȝt T. fire of loue] loue of fyre b. 328. O] Olf(?) P. sterre] sterrys G. persant] passaunt G. ful] eler G. S. 329. Of] O L. devoider] the woider P. voyder S. 330. recounford] confort G. recomforter S. of recounfort P. 331. voide] wynde S. woful] woful hertes Pr. L. her] om. G. S. 333. ȝour grace may] may your grace Pr. 334. me] nowe S. 337. And] a F.

my body may not follow my thought, my outward conduct must be at variance with my heart's desire.	The bodi [is] knyt, al þouʒe my þouʒt be fre, So þat I most, of necessite, Myn hertis lust out[e]ward contrarie ; Thogh we be on, þe dede most[e] varie.	339 341

338. is] *om.* T. F. B. P. al] *om.* Pr. 339. of] of verrey L. 341. varie] nedis warie P.

Stanzas 3—7 (*ll.* 335—369) *are missing in* G. S ; *in their place the following four are found:*

3 *a.*

Deign of your benignity, to grant a remedy for wicked tongues and their cruelty.	So that ʒow lyst of ʒoure benygnete, Goodly to seen & shape remedye On wekkede tongis & on the crewelte, That they compasse thourgh maleys & envye, To quenche the venym of here felonye, Wher as they hyndere wemen gilteles : *Styntȩþe this werre & lat vs leue in pes.	1 5 7

3 *b.*

I complain also of Jealousy, the vile serpent, always grudging and suspicious,	I pleyne also vp-on Ielusye, The vile serpent, the snake tortyvous, That is so crabbit & frounynge of his ye, And euere grochynge & suspecyous, I-fret with eysel that makyth hym dispytous, Of euery thyng the werste for to deme, That ther is no thyng that may his herte queme.	1 5 7

3 *c.*

ever froward and frowning, whose reason fails in the dotage of old age.	Thus is he fryed in his owene gres, To-rent & torn with his owene rage, And euere *froward & frounynge causeles, Whos resoun faylyth in elde thourgh dotage : This is the maner of krokede fer in age, Whan they ben couplyd with ʒouthe * þey can no more, But hem werreyen, which wemen beyeth ful sore.	1 5 7

3 *d.*

Thus we are ever oppressed with torments, as you were when bound by Vulcan. Now for love of Mars and Adonis, take pity on my complaint.	Thus euere in *tourment & yre furyous We ben oppressed—allas the harde stounde !— *Rygh[t] as ʒoure selve were with Wlkanus Ageyn ʒoure wil & ʒoure herte bounde. Now for the Ioye, whilom that ʒe founde With Mars, ʒoure knyght, vp-on myn compleynt rewe, For love of Adon that was so frosch of hewe.	1 5 7

3 *a.* 3. On] Of S. 2ᵈ on] of S. 4. they] þey may S. maleys &] fals S. 5. the venym of] þeyre vemyne and S. 6. as] þat S. 7. Stynthth G.—— 3 *b.* 2. vile] wylde S. 3. crabbit] crokid S. of his ye] on hye S. 4. *om.* S. 5. dispytous] suspecious S. *In* S *the following line is marked to be inserted between* 5 *and* 6 : By al kynde þou art so envyous.——3 *c.* 3. froward] frowar G. & frounynge] groyning S. 4. in elde thourgh] nowe in olde S. 6. þey] I G. 7. werreyen] waryen S. which] *om.* S. beyeth] ben S.——3 *d.* 1. turment] tornement G. 2. the] þat S. 3. Rygh G. 4. Ageyns S. 7. Adon] yowe S.

4.

Mi worship sauf, I faile elecciou*n*,	342 To save my dignity, I forego my choice;
Again al ri3t, boþe of god and kynd,	
There to be knit vndir subieccion,	
Fro whens ferre *are boþ[e] witte & mynde;	
Mi þou3t goþe forþe, my bodi is behind :	346 in body I remain, but my thought goes forth.
For I am here, and yonde my remembraunce ;	
Atwixen two so hang I in balau*n*ce.	348

5.

Deuoide of ioie, of wo I haue plente ;	349
What I desire, þ*a*t mai I not possede ;	What I desire, I may not possess,
For þat I nold, is redi aye to me,	
And þat I loue, forto swe I drede,	and dreed to sue for what I love.
To my desire contrarie is my mede ;	353
And þus I stond, depa*r*tid euen on tweyn,	
Of wille and dede Ilaced in a chaine.	355

6.

For þou3e I brenne wit*h* feruence and wit*h* hete,	356 Although I burn with fervent heat, my heart within is cold, nor dare I unfold a word of all my pain.
Wiþ-in myn hert I mot complein of cold,	
And þuru3 myn axcesse tho3e I sweltre and swete,	
Me to complein, god wot, I am not boold,	
Vnto no wi3t, nor a woord vnfold	360
Of al my peyne, allas þe hard[e] stond !	
That hatter brenne þ*a*t closid is my wou*n*de.	362

7.

For he þ*a*t haþ myn hert[e] feiþfulli,	363 For I have no chance of being with him who, secretly, has my heart and love.
And hole my luf in al honesti,	
Wit*h*-oute chau*n*ge, al be it secreli,	
I haue no space wiþ him forto be.	
O ladi Venus, co*n*sider nov & se	367 O lady Venus, consider now

343. Again] Agaynst b.   345. Fro] For C. P.   ferre] *om*. L.   ferre are boþ*e*] for both ar C. fer both ar W. W2. w. both are farre b. are] er T. B. or F (*sign of the cæsural pause before it*). witte &] out of L. Pr.   346 *omitted in* P.   347. yonde] yond*er* W2. yonder L. w. b.   348., Atwixen] atwyen F. Bitwix L. Betwyx P. Betwene Pr. so] *om*. P.   352. swe] shewe P.   354. euen on] in Pr. on tweyn] atwayne L.   355. Ilaced] y lashed P.   356. brenne] out brenne b. feruence] feruente w. feruence and wit*h*] feruent b. 2d wit*h*] *om*. Pr.   357. mot] may w. b.   358. þuru3 myn axcesse] by excesse Pr. axcesse] act*es* L. sweltre] swelte P. Pr.   359. god wot I am not] I am nat god wote b.   360. a] one Pr.   362. That hatter] That I L. The hotter that I Pr. That the hatt*ir* P. þat closid] the closir P. In the cold*er* L. the colder Pr. 366 *and* 367 *are omitted in* w. *In their place* b *substitutes :*
    All way it must ikept and coucred be
    Wherfore lady Venus enclyne I pray the.   367. &] *om*. B.

|my com-
plaint : my
life and death
are in thy
hands.'| Vnto þe effecte and compleint of my bil,
Siþ life and deþ I put al in þi wil.' | 369 |

8.

|And then the
goddess in-
clined her
head, and
told her how
her torment
should soon
end,| And þo me þou3t þe goddes did enclyne
Mekeli hir hede, and softli gan expresse,
That in short tyme hir turment shuld[e] fyne,
And hou of him, for whom al hir distresse
Contynued had & al hir heuynes,
She *shold haue Ioy, and of hir purgatorie
Be holpen sone, and so forþ lyue in glorie. | 370

374

376 |

9.

|Saying:
'Daughter,
your faithful
meaning has
won my
hearing,

and I promise
you relief.| And seid[e]: 'Dou3ter, for þe sad[de] trouþe,
The feiþful menyng, & þe Innocence,
That planted bene, withouten eny slouþe,
In 3our persone, deuoide of al *offence,
So haue atteyned to oure audience,
That þuru3 oure grace 3e shul be wel releuyd,
I 3ov bihote of al þat haþ 3ov greued. | 377

381

383 |

10.

|As you have
been so pa-
tient in your
long adver-
sity inflicted
by Saturn,

your woe
shall now
cease.| And for þat 3e euer of oon entent,
Withoute chaunge or mutabilite,
Haue in 3our peynes ben so pacient,
To take louli 3oure aduersite,
And þat so long þuru3 þe cruelte
Of old Saturne, my fadur vnfortuned,—
Your wo shal nov no lenger be contuned. | 384

388

390 |

11.

|It will soon
be assuaged
and pass
over;| And þinkiþ þis : within a litel while
It shal asswage, and ouerpassen sone; | 391 |

368. þe effecte] affecte P. 369. I put al in] y put is in al P. al] om. B. Rubric before line 370 in F. B: Thansuere of Venus. 370. þo] than b. as G. S. me] my P. þe] that G. 371. gan] did B. 374. Contynued had] She had endured b. al] of F. b. om. L. 375. shold] would T. 376. so forþ lyue] so lyue forth Pr. lyue] om. P. 377. þe] thy L. C. W. W2. w. thi P. 378. The] Thy C. W. W2. w. feiþful] rightful S. þe] om. Pr. thi P. 380. deuoide] right voyde S. offence] defence T. vycence S. 381. haue] han they C. han W. W2. than w. haue b. 382. þuru3] with Pr. by P. shul] should S. wel] om. L. 383. þat] om. P. haþ] han G. 384. 3e] ye ben L. ye be Pr. 3e euer] euer ye P. 385. chaunge] chaunce w. eny change P. 386. Haue] And Pr. 387. To take] And takyn P. 388. þuru3] thorght F. trouth P. 389. old] youre S. 390. om. w. b reads: Ye shall of me be well rewarded. Your— lenger] Youres shal neuer more S. 391. þis within] thir within W2. ther-within w. therfore within b.

For men bi laiser passen meny a myle.
And oft also, aftir a dropping mone,
The weddir clereþ, & whan þe storme is done,   395   the sun shines all the brighter after a storm,
The sonne shineþ in his spere bri3t,
And ioy awakiþ whan wo is put to fli3t.   397

12.

Remembreþ eke, hou neuer 3it no wi3t   398
Ne came to wirship withoute some debate,
And folk also reiossh[e] more of li3t,   light gladdens the
That þei wiþ derknes were waped & amate;   more after darkness,
Non mannis chaunce is alwai fortunate,   402
Ne no wi3t preiseþ of sugre þe swetnes,   sweetness after bitter-
But þei afore haue tasted bitternes.   404   ness.

13.

Grisild[e] was assaied at[te] ful,   405   Even so with Griselda,
That turned aftir to hir encrese of Ioye;
Penalope gan eke for sorowis dul,   Penelope and Dorigen:
For þat [her] lord abode so long at Troie;
Also þe turment þere coude no man akoye   409
Of Dorigene, flour of al Britayne: Joy was the end of their
Thus euer ioy is ende and fine of paine.   411   pain;

14.

And trusteþ *þis, for conclusioun,   412
The end of sorow is ioi I-voide of drede;
For holi saintis, þuru3 her passioun,   and holy saints won
Haue heuen Iwonne for her souerain mede;   heaven through their
And plenti gladli foloiþ after nede: 416   passion:

394. also] om. Pr. droppiug] drepynge G. W. W2. w. b.   395. &] om. S.
storme] strem G.   397. awakiþ] waketh L. Pr.   398. eke] yet P. om. b.
399. Ne came to] Come to no S. some] om. w. b.   400. folk] folkes b. also
reiosshe] reioyse also C. W. W2. w. reiosshe] rechen P.   401. That] þenne S.
þei] om. b. wiþ] om. P. waped] wraped L. wrapped b. amate] mate L. P. S.
C. W. wate W2. w. b.   403. wi3t] whit G.   404. þei afore] if þai to forne S.
afore] to fore C. W. W2. w. before b.   405. assaied] assailled L. atte] at the
B. P. L. G. b. atte þe S. at T. w.   406. to] the w. hir] om. Pr. of] and P.
Ioye] her ioye b.   407. gan] cane S. became S. became b. for] for her P. sorowis dul]
sorwe dwelle G. S.   408. her] om. T. F. B.   409. turment] tornement G.
410. flour] the flour P.   411. Thus] This P.   euer] euer corrected into euere
(= euery), in different ink, T. euer ioy] euery ioyes S. ende] endid corrected
into eude T. ende and fine] fyue and S. become L. C. W. W2. w. finall ende b.
of] is S.   412. And] As F. trusteþ] truste G. þis] þus T. F. B. P. for] for
a S.   413. The] Thus S. I-voide] y woded P. voyde Pr.   415. Iwonne]
wonne G. Pr. for] by C. W. W2. w. to b.   416. foloiþ] folowed W. W2. w.
TEMPLE OF GLAS.   C

so I promise you pleasure after grief.	And so my dou3ter, after 3o*ur* greuauns, I 3ov bihote 3e shul haue ful plesaunce.	418

15.

For Love first wounds	For euer of loue þe man*er* and þe guyse Is forto hurt his seruant, and to wou*n*de ;	419
and then gives joy ;	And when þ*a*t he haþ tau3te hem his empr*is*e, He can in ioi make hem to abounde ;	
so consolation is now your due.	And siþ þat 3e haue in my lase be bound, Wiþoute grucching or rebellion, Ye most of ri3t haue consolacio*un*.	423 425

16.

	This is to sein—douteþ neu*er* a dele—	426
You shall soon possess him whom you cherish,	That 3e shal haue ful poss[ess]ion Of him þat 3e cherissh nov so wel, In honest maner, wiþ-oute offencio*un*,	
because your intent is to love him best.	Bicause I cnowe yo*ur* entencion Is truli set, in p*ar*ti and in al, To loue him best & most in special.	430 432

17.

For your chosen one shall be yours till death :	For he þ*a*t 3e haue chosen 3ow to serue, Shal he to 3ow such as 3e desire, Wiþ-oute chau*n*ge, fulli, til he sterne :	433
so have I set him afire.	So wi*th* my brond I haue him set afire, And wi*th* my grace I shal him so enspire, That he in hert shal be ry3t at 3o*ur* will, *Wherso 3e list to saue him or to spill.	 437 439

18.

His heart I will bind to you so humbly	For vnto 3ow his hert I shal so lowe, Wiþ-oute spot of eny doubelnes, That he ne shal escape fro þe bowe—	440

417. so] *om.* b. grevauns] gou*er*naunce S. 418. ful] *om.* G. S. 420. his] is P. seruant] *ser*vauntz S. and] and for L. 421. þ*a*t] *om.* S. L. Pr. hem] hym F. B. 422. ioi] no Ioye w. hem] him L. 423. þat] *om.* P. L. lase] lacys P. 426. is] *om.* F. C. douteþ] dowte it w. doute it b. dou3ter *by a second hand corrected into* douteth'L. 427. possion T. 428. him] hem G. cherissh nov] now cherisshe Pr. 429. maner] wyse F. B. G. S. offencio*un*] transgressyon b. 430. Bicause] Be cause that P. 432 *reads in* P: he shal ben> yours ryght ye wyl hym call. 434. to 3ow] right S. 435. he] ye S. 436. him] *om.* F. B. him set] sette hym C. W. W2. w. 437. him] *om.* F. B. so] *om.* W. W2. w. 438. in hert shal] only P. 439. Wherso] Wheþir T. P. W. W2. w. b. 3e] you C. 3ow G. S. 440. his hert I shal] I shal his herte Pr. I shal] shal y P. 441. spot of] sport or S. 442. he] ye F. ne shal escape] shape shal P. escape] scapen S.

Thou3 þat him list þuru3 vnstidfastnes—
I mene of Cupide, þat shal him so distres   444   that he shall
                                                   not escape
Vnto your hond, wiþ þe arow of gold,   Cupid's bow.
That he ne shal escapen þou3 he would.   446

19.

And siþe 3e list, of pite and of grace,   447
In vertu oonli his 3ouþe to cherice,
I shal, baspectes of my benygne face,   I shall make
                                                   him eschew
Make him teschwe euere synne & vice,   every sin and
                                                   vice,
So þat he shal haue no maner spice   451
In his corage to loue þingis nwe :   so that he
                                                   will ever be
He shal to 3ou so plain be found & trwe.'   453   constant to
                                                   you.'

20.

And whan þis goodli, faire, fressh of hwe,   454   When this
                                                   fair one saw
Humble and benygne, of trouth crop & rote,   how Venus
                                                   took pity on
Conceyued *had, hov Venus gan to rwe,   her,
On hir praier plainli to do bote,
To chaunge hir bitter atones into soote,   458
She fel on kneis of hei3 deuocion,   she fell on
                                                   her knees
And in þis wise bigan hir orisoun :   460   and prayed
                                                   thus:

443. him list] he wolde b. list] self C. W. W2. w. þuru3] by Pr. ‖ vnstedl-
fastne B.   444. of] om. b. þat] om. b.   445. þe] an P.   446. escapen] scapen
S.   447. 3e] you S.   449. baspectes] espectes P. be aspect G. W. W2. w. b.
by aspectaunce L. be inspect S.   450. teschwe] teshewe W. to shewe W2.
w. b. S. synne] om. P.   452. loue] lyue S. þingis] thinge P.   453. plain]
playnly P.   454. *In the margin of B in red ink:* Hic vsque verba Veneris;
in b is the heading The authour *before l.* 454. faire] ladi b. fressh] and
fresshe S.   456. had] haþ T.   457. praier] preyers S. prayer prayer P.
payne b. plainli] only G. S.   458. bitter] bitternesse S. om. P. atones]
ones b. attreynys G. om. S. into] vnto F. B. G.   459. of] by S.

---

*In MSS. F. B. G. S. the following stanza is found
between ll. 453 and 454.*

19 a.

And whi that I so sore to 3ow hym bynde,   1   I thus bind
                                                  him to you,
Is [for] that 3e so manye han forsake,   because you
Bothe wyse & worthy, & gentyl [eke] of kynde,   have refused
                                                  so many for
Pleynly refused, only for his sake :   his sake.
He shal to 3ow, wher so 3e slepe or wake,   5
Ben euene swich, vndyr hope & drede,
As 3e lyst ordeyne of 3oure womanhede.   7

19 a, 1. so sore to yow] to yow so sore F. B.   2. for that] that G. þat
for S.   3. 1st &] om. S. gentyl eke] gentyl G. eke gentil S.   5. wher so 3e]
wheþer he S.   7. 3e] you S.

C 2

21.

'Goddess of love, who by your beauty won the apple at Jupiter's feast:	'Hei3est of high, quene and Emperice, 461 Goddes of loue, of goode 3it þe best, þat þuru3 3our [beaute], with/outen eny vice, Whilom conquered þe appel at þe fest, That Iubiter þurugh [his hygh request] 465 To al þe goddesse aboue celestial Made in his paleis most imperial: 467

22.

Meekly I thank you for your gracious promise,	To 3ov my ladi, vpholder of my life, 468 Mekeli I þanke, so as I mai suffice, That 3e list nov, with hert ententif, So graciousli for me to deuyse,
and while I live I will sacrifice at your yearly feast.	That while I liue, with humble sacrifise, 472 Vpon 3our auters, 3our fest 3ere bi 3ere, I shal encense casten in þe fire. 474

23.

For I now have joy and ease,	For of 3oure grace I am ful reconsiled 475 From euere trouble vnto Ioy & ease, That sorois al from me ben exiled,
as you deign to appease my pain.	*Siþ ye, my ladi, list nov to *appese Mi peynes old, & fulli my disease 479 Vnto gladnes so sodeinli to turne, Hauyng no cause from hennes forþ to mourne. 481

24.

For as you bind him to my service who loves me best,	For siþin 3e so mekeli list to daunte 482 To my seruyce him þat louþ me best, And of 3our bounte so graciousli to graunte, That he ne shal varie, þou3e him list, Wherof myn hert is fulli brou3[t] to rest: 486

Heading in F and B before l. 461: Oracio amantis supradicte ; *in* S : La Orysoune del amant. 461. high] hight P. 462. goode] goddes P. þe] ye L. 463. þat] Though P. 3our] *om.* P. you L. beaute] *om.* T. L. vitte P. bountee S. eny] *om.* Pr. vice] wyse F. wise L. 464. Whilom] Somtyme w. b. at þe] atte C. W. W2. at w. 465. That] Whyche S. his hygh request] *om.* T. P. 466. aboue] of loue S. 469. þanke] thank you P. 470. That] What G. S. nov with hert] with hert now P. hert] her F. B. ententif] retentyff S. 471. to] vn to S. 472. while I liue] lyue whyle W2. w. 473. Autours L. 474. in] in to G. Pr. 475. of] in L. 476. euere] euer S. vnto) and to F. 477. from me ben] ben fro me P. S. Pr. 478. Siþ ye] Wiþ þe T. P. ye my ladi] þat you S. nov] *om.* w. b. thus sodeynly S. appese] peese S. haue peas T. P. 479. old] alle S. 480. Vnto] In to S. so sodeinli] so wonderfully S. to turne] to forne W2. toforne w. 481. forþ] *om.* P. 482. siþin] sith B. sithins S. 483. þat] *om.* P. louþ me] I loue F. B. G. S. b. 484. to] *om.* G. 485. varie] tary L. 486. brou3t] brou3 T. hente S. to] in F.

to Venus. 21

For nov and euer, o ladi myn benygne, | I resign my heart and will
That hert and wil to ȝow hole I resigne. 488 | to you,
. 25.
Thanking yow with al my ful hert, 489 | thanking you that you have
þat, of ȝoure grace and visitacioun, | thus sub-jected him to
So humb[e]li list him to conuert | me:
Fulli to bene at my subieccioun,
With-oute chaunge or transmutacioun, 493
Vnto his *last: [now] laude and reuerence | now laud and reverence be
Be to youre name and [to] your excellence. 495 | to your name.

487. o] now B. *om.* S.   488. wil] al F. B. G. S.   to ȝow hole I] hol I to ȝow G.   I hooly to you Pr.   hole] *om.* P.   490. of] *om.* S.   and] and god P.   492. to] *om.* w.   to bene at] in to b.   bene] ben hole P.   493. With-oute] With eny P.   494. Vnto] Now vn to S.   last now] lust T. L.   life P.   now laude] ioye S.   495. Be] Be euer b.   2ᵈ to] *om.* T. P. L.   to your] *om.* Pr.

Between 495 *and* 496 *the following three stanzas are interpolated in* F. B. G. S:
25 *a.*
And in despit platly of hem alle   1 | I shall cherish him
That ben to love so contraryous,
I shal hym cherice, what so euere falle,
That is in love so pleyn & vertuous,
Maugre alle tho that ben so desyrous   5 | spite of all who would harm us
To spekyn vs harm, thourgh grochyng & envye
Of thilke serpent I-callyd Ielosye.   7 | through Jealousy.
25 *b.*
And for hem, lady, ȝif I durste preye,   1 | I pray you
Menynge no vengeaunce, but correccyoun,
To chastyse hem with torment, or they deye, | chastise them for their untruth
For here vntrouthe & fals suspecyoun,
That deme the werste in here opynyoun,   5
With-oute desert, wherfore that ȝe vouche
To ponysshe hem dewely for here male bouche. 7 | and 'male bouche,'
25 *c.*
So that they may stondyn In repref   1 | that they may be a reproof to all lovers,
To alle loueris for here cursedenesse,
With-outyn mercy forsakyn at myschef,
Whan hem lyste best han helpe of here distresse,
And for here falshed & here doubilnesse   5 | as are jays, pies, lap-wings and owls to birds.
Had In dispit, ryght as a-mong foulys
Ben Iayis, Pyis, Lapwyngis & these Oulys. 7

25 *a.* 5. so desyrous] derysyous S.   7. thilke] þat ilk S.   I-callyd] cleped S.
25 *b.* 6. that ȝe] we S.   7. dewely] *om.* S.   25 *c.* 1. So] To S.   2. To] Un to S.   4. helpe] mercy S.   5. 2ᵈ here] for hir S.   6. Had] And S.   a-mong] amonges F.   amonge þes S.   7. Iayis Pyis] pyes Iayes F. B.   Lapwyngis] þees lapwynges S.

26.

This is the substance of my request,	This al and some & chefe of my request,	496
	And hool substaunce of *my ful entent,	
thanking you for grace to conquer him.	Yow þankyng euer of ȝour graunt & hest,	
	Boþ nou and euer, þat ȝe me grace haue sent	
	To conquere him þat neuer shal repent	500
	Me forto serue & humbli to please,	
	As final tresur *of myn hertis ease.'	502

27.

Then Venus cast down into the lady's lap hawthorn branches,	And þan anon Venus cast adoune	503
	Into hir lap, braunchis white & grene	
	Of haw[e]thorñ, þat wenten envirou*n*	
	Aboute hir hed, þat ioi it was to sene,	
	And bade hir kepe hem honestli & clene—	507
which should never fade.	Which shul not fade ne nevir wexin old,	
	If she hir bidding kepe as she haþ told.	509

28.

Saying: 'Do as these branches teach you:	'And as þese bowȝis be boþ faire & swete,	510
	Folowiþ þeffect þat þei do specifie :	
	This is to sein, boþe in cold & hete,	
Be unchanging like these leaues,	Beþ of oon hert & of o fantasie,	
	As ar þese leues, þe which mai not die	514
which no storm can kill.	Þuruȝ no dures of stormes, þat be kene,	
	No more in winter þen in somer grene.	516

496. This] This is P. L. S. of] *om.* L. 497. my] myn T. my ful] all my hole b. ful] hole T. P. hoole L. 498. Yow þankyng] Thanking yon S. euer] *om.* b. 499. me grace haue] grace me P. haue] *om.* Pr. 500. neuer shal] shal neuer S. 501. Me] and F. forto] to S. humbli] meekly S. to] for to S. L. Pr. 502. of] to T. *Between ll. 502 and 503 in* F : ffinis oracionis. 504. braunchis] Roses F. B. G. S. white] both white P. grene] rede F. B. G. S. 505. Of hawethorñ] So fressh of hewe F. B. G. And fresshe of hewe S. þat] that it G. 506 *reads in* F. B. G. S : In compas wyse even [evere F, euer B] aboute hir hede. it] *om.* Pr. 507 *omitted in* S. honestli & clene] of hir goodelyhede F. B. G. & clene] *om.* P. 508. shul] shuld P. L. shold Pr. 509. kepe] folowe F. B. G. S. she haþ] I haue G. 510 *reads in* G. S : And so as ȝe ben callyd Margarete. þese] the L. be] *om.* b. 511. þeffect] þe feythe S. þei do] it doth G. hit doþe S. 512. is] *om.* W2. w. b. &] and in L. 513. Beþ] Euer S. Be ye Pr. & of o fantasie] as is the daysye G. S. 514. As ar þese leues] I lyche fressh G. S. ar] be L. þe] *om.* S. L. Pr. which] whiche þat S. mai] many W2. 515. þuruȝ] By Pr. dures] distresse L. dures of stormes] stormys of durys G. stormes ne duresse S. þat] how it S. kene] lene G.

29.

Ri3t so bensaumple, for wele or for wo, 517 Even so, in weal and woe,
For ioy, turment, or [for] aduersite,
Wherso þat fortune fauour or be foo,
For pouert, riches, or prosperite,
That 3e youre hert kepe in oo degre 521 let your heart be constant in love for him.'
To loue him best, for noþing þat 3e feine,
Whom I haue bound so lowe vndir 3oure cheine.' 523

30.

And with þat worde þe goddes shoke hir hede, 524 Then the goddess was silent,
And was in peas, and spake as þo no more.
And þerwithal, ful femynyne of drede, and the lady answered:
Me þou3te þis ladi sighen gan ful sore,
And said again : ' Ladi þat maist restore 528 'Goddess, to do your will de mieux en mieux m' agrée.'
Hertes in Ioy from her aduersite,
To do 3oure will de mieulx en mieulx magre.' 530

Thus euer sleping and dremyng as I lay, Thus dreaming on, I saw in the temple great press of folk,
Within þe tempil me þou3t[e] þat I sey 532
Gret pres of folk, with murmur wondirful,
To *croude and *shove—þe tempil was so ful—
Euerich ful bise in his owne cause,
That I ne may shortli in a clause 536
Descriuen al þe Rithes & þe gise,
And eke I want kunnyng to deuyse,
Hou som þer were with blood, encense & mylk, making offerings

517. Ri3t so] Right B. So S. 1st for] of C. W. W2. w. 2d for] om. L. Pr.
518. turment] turnement G. for] om. T. F. B. 519. Wherso] Wheþer þat S.
Whether so Pr. þat] om. Pr. be] els b. 522. feine] seyn P. fyne S. C. 523.
Whom] Who L. so lowe vndir] om. P. 525. þo] than b. 526. ful] om. b.
as S. femynyne] memynyne P. drede] degre G. 527. þis] the w. b. sighen] to sighe b. gan] can L. 528. restore] þer fore S. 529. in] to F. B. G. S. b.
Ioy] saue S. from] for G. 530. will—magre] byddyng humblement magre
F. B. G. S. wyll (wylll w.) better & better after my gre w. b. After line 530
T and L have: Explicit prima pars (.I. parte L.). Icy commence le secund
parti (seconde party L.) de la soñge. F and B : Et cest le ffyne del primer
parte Et ycy commence la secoñde parte del songe. G: Yci comence la
secunde partye de la Chaunsoñ. S: And þus endeþe þe first partye of þe
dreem and filowyng begynneþe þe secound partye. Lines 531—596 omitted in
G. 531. Thus] This P. Thus euer] þer I was S. and] om. Pr. 532 omitted
in P. þat] om. Pr. 533. pres] preces W2. w. part S. with] om. W2. w.
534. To] Who b. To croude] So heve S. croude] bronte T. L. brounte P.
shove] showe T. 535. in his] in w. P. 536. ne may] myght P. a] om. P.
537. Descriuen] Dysceyue w. Rithes] rightes P. ry3tis B. ryte S. 538. eke
I want] al þestates þe S. 539. þer were with blood] there that blede L. om.
P. blood] golde b.

to the goddess,	And som wi*th* floures sote & soft as silk,	540
	*And some wi*th* sparovis & dovnes faire & white,	
	That forto offerin gan hem to delite	
entreating release from their pains.	Vnto þe goddes, wiþ sigh & wi*th* praier,	
	Hem to relese of þat þai most desire;	544
	That for þe prese, shortli to conclude,	
Leaving the crowd,	I went my wai for þe multitude,	
	Me to refressh oute of þe prese allone.	
	And be my self me þouȝt, as I gan gone	548
	Wiþ-in þe Estres & gan awhile tarie,	
I saw a man walking in solitude and complaining.	I saugh a man, þat welke al solitarie,	
	That as me semed for heuines and dole	
	Him to complein, þat he walk so sole,	552
	Wiþ-oute espiing of eni oþir wiȝt.	
	And if I shal descryuen him ariȝt,	
Were it not for his heaviness, he seemed the very model of a man.	Nere þat he hade ben in heuynes,	
	Me þouȝt he was, to speke of semelynes,	556
	Of shappe, of fourme, & also of stature,	
	The most passing þ*a*t euir ȝit nature	
	Made in hir werkis, & like to ben a man;	
	And þerwi*th*-al, as I reherse can,	560
	Of face and chere þe most gracious,	
	To be biloued, happi and Ewrous.	
	But as it semed outward *by his chere,	
But, for lack of his desire, he made lamentation,	That he compleyned for lak of his desire—	564
	For *by himself, as he walk vp & doune,	
	I herd him make a lamentacio*un*,	

540. floures] *om*. L.   541. And] An T.   faire &] *om*. Pr.   542. offerin] *om*.
w.   to] *om*. F. B. Pr.   543. wiþ sigh] *om*. P.   sigh] sight S.   wi*th*] *om*. Pr.
545. for] for to P.   prese] price L.   *Lines* 545—548 *read in* b:
        And shortely this thyng to conclude
        So great and huge was the multytude
        That I was fayne out of the preace to go
        And as I was alone with me no mo.
546. I] It P.   my] no P.   for þe] from þat S.   547. to] for to C. W. W2. w.
þe] *om*. w.   548. me þouȝt] *om*. S.   as] as þat S.   gan] can S.   del P.   549.
gan] I gan P.   550. I saugh] I was wel ware of S.   þat welke] *om*. S.   551.
semed] semeth W. W2.   and dole] *om*. P.   552—555 *omitted in* P.   552. þat]
om. b.   sole] hole L.   554. if] *couered by a spot in the parchment in* T.
555. Nere] þer S.   Nere þat he hade] Yf that he had not Pr.   þat] *om*. L.
557. 1st Of] aud F.   2^{d} of] and F. B. L.   fourme] striue (?) P.   558. þat euir
ȝit] yit þat S.   559. hir] hys P.   560. þerwi*th*-al] therwyth F.   561. þe]
om. B.   562. To be biloued] ffor to be lwfyd P.   563. as] *om*. b.   semed]
om. P.   outward] outwardes S.   by] in T.   565. by] in P.   by himself] bym
self T.   himself] my self L.

The Knight's Soliloquy.

And seid : 'Allas! what þing mai þis be,
That nou am bound, þat whilom was so fre, 568
And went at laarge, at myn eleccioun :
Nou am I cauȝt vnder subiecciou*n*,
Forto bicome a verre homagere
To god o[f] loue, where þat, er I come here, 572
Felt in myn hert riȝt nouȝt of loues peine ;
But nov of nwe wit*h*in his fire cheyne
I am enbraced, so þat I mai not striue
To loue and serue, whiles þat I am on lyue, 576
The goodli fressh, in þe tempil yonder
I saugh riȝt nov, þat I hade wonder,
Hou euer god, forto reken all,
Myȝt make a þing so celestial, 580
So avngellike on erþe to appere.
For wiþ þe stremes of hir eyen clere
I am Iwoundid euen to þe hert,
þat fro þe deþ, I trow, I mai not stert. 584
And most I mervaile þ*a*t so sodenli
I was Iȝolde to bene at hir merci,
Wherso *hir list, to do me lyue or deie :
Wiþ-oute more I most hir lust obeie 588
And take mekeli my sodein auentur.
For siþ my life, my deþ, and eke my cure
Is in hir hond, it would[e] not auaile
To gruch agein ; for of þis bataile 592
The palme is hires, & pleinli þe victorie.
If I rebelled, hono*ur* non ne glorie

Side notes:
and said : 'Alas! how am I, who before was so free,
now bound in Cupid's fiery chain!
Now am I forced to serue her
whom I saw in the temple yonder,
that angelic creature.
Her eyes haue wounded me to the death.
I am forced to obey her;
it avails not to murmur; for she is plainly victor in this battle.

567. þing] *om*. P. 568. That nou am] Nowe am I b. nou am] am now F. I am now B. whilom] somtyme S. so] *om*. Pr. 570. Nou am I] Nowe I am S. And now y P. subieccioun] obieccion F. B. 571. bicome] be hounde F. B. 572. god] the god b. of] o T. þat] *om*. Pr. come] kan F. 573. riȝt] *om*. Pr. 574. his] þe S. hur C. her W. W2. w. fire] verrey S. 576. loue and serue] serue and loue Pr. whiles] whyle S. L. Pr. þ*a*t] *om*. L. Pr. 577. The goodli] þat feyre S. in] wight in S. which in F. B. tempil] cherche P. 578. I saugh riȝt nov] Right nowe I saughe S. wouder] gret wonder S. 579. Hou] þat S. forto] as for to S. 580. Myȝt] Konde S. 581. on] in S. to] for to S. 582. wiþ] within W2. w. b. stremes] percyng F. B. S. 583. Iwoundid] wonndid B. S. Pr. euen] I weene S. to] vn to F. B. P. L. so to S. 584. I trow] *om*. S. Pr. stert] astert S. Pr. 586. Iȝolde] yolden S. so yolde Pr. at] in F. yn B. 587 *and* 588 *transposed in* C. 587. Wherso] Wheþer S. Whether that Pr. hir] him T. she Pr. to do me] me to Pr. 588. more l] *om*. P. most] mot S. 591. woulde] wol L. wyl P. wil Pr. not] nothyng b. 592. agein] *om*. P. of] *om*. P. 593. pleinli] playne b. 594 *reads in* S : As hole subiet / for hirs is al þe glorye. rebelled] rebell P.

	I myȝt[e] not, in no wise, acheue.	
I yield my- self: I cannot war with her.	Siþ i am yold, hou shuld I þan preue To gif a werre—I wot it wil not be— Thouȝ I be loos, at laarge I mai not fle.	596
Why dost thou wound me so, O god of love!	O god of loue, hov sharp is nov þin arowe! Hou maist þou nov so cruelli & narowe, With-oute cause, hurt[e] me and wound, And tast non hele, my soris forto sound!	600
As a bird is caught by a snare—	But lich a brid, þat fleith at hir desire, Til sodeinli within þe pantire She is Icauȝt, þouȝ she were late at laarge—	604
my barge is driven from its track by tempest.	A nwe tempest for-casteþ now my baarge, Now vp nov dovne with wind it is so blowe, So am I *possid and almost ouerþrowe, Fordriue in dirknes with many a sondri wawe. Alas! when shal þis tempest ouerdrawe, To clere þe skies of myn aduersite,	608
Alas! the lou lstar is hidden from me, nor can I foresee the end of this torment—	The lode ster when I [ne] may not se, It is so hid with cloudes þat ben blake. Alas when wil þis turment ouershake? I can not wit, for who is hurt of nwe And blediþ inward, til he wex pale of hwe,	612 616
the hurt being new and the harms of Cupid un- known to me:	And haþ his wound vnwarli fressh & grene, And is not kouþe vnto þe harmes kene Of myȝti Cupide, þat can so hertis daunte That no man may in your werre him vaunte	620

595. myȝte] might it S. not] *om.* b. no] ony Pr. wise] maner wyse b.
597. *Here G begins again.* gif] gynne F. B. G. S. gif a werre] renne awey
P'r. a werre] awerry P. I wot] y wys F. B. G. S. be] ybe S. 600. maist]
mightest S. nov] *om.* S. cruelli] pryuely S. &] and so Pr. & narowe] an
arowe P. 602. soris] sorowes L. S. Pr. forto] to P'r. sound] founde P. P'r.
605. Icauȝt] caught G. S. Pr. she were late] late she was Pr. were] was F.
late at] let a S. 606. nwe] sodeyne S. now] new F. nyw B. hath P. *om.* L.
607. it] *om.* G. so] *om.* P. 608. possid] passid T. pressid G. tossed w. b.
609 *and* 610 *are omitted in* L. 609. Fordriue] Far dryuen b. ffor throwe S.
with] of Pr. a sondri] sondry Pr. sturdy F. B. G. S. 610. þis] þe S. ouer-
drawe] to me dawe F. B. G. slake lawe S. 611. To] So S. skies] skye is S.
612. when] whan that C. what that W. W2. w. I wote b. ne] *om.* T. b.
hym P. not] *om.* C. W. W2. w. 613. ben] ben so P. 614. wil] shal F. B.
G. S. ouershake] overslake L. S. Pr. 615. for] but G. 616 *omitted in* P.
til] ryl W2. ryll w. wex] be S. 617. vnwarli] wardly W2. inwardly w. b.
618 *reads in* S: Euer vnholpen / more kene and kene. is] yt F. hit is L. P'r.
kouþe] knowen W. W2. w. b. vnto] to F. B. G. harmes] armys P. 619.
þat] which S. can] *om.* F. B. can so] cause P. daunte] daunce (?) F. 620.
may] *om.* w. b. your] his Pr. werre] werrys G. him] dare hym w. b.
vaunte] avaunte S. awaunt P. avaunce (?) F.

Soliloquy.

To gete a pris, but oonli bi mekenes— agaiust him none prevail except through meekness.
For þere ne vaileþ strif ne sturdines—
So mai I sain, þat w*ith* a loke am yold,
And haue no power to stryue þou3e I would. 624
Thus stand I euen bitwix life and deþ Thus I stand between life and death,
To loue & serue, while þ*a*t I haue breþ,
In such a place where I dar not pleyn,
Lich him þ*a*t is in t*ur*ment & in pein, 628
And knoweþ not, to whom forto discure; not knowing to whom to discover my torment.
For þere þat I haue hoolly set my cure,
I dar not wele, for drede & for daun*g*er,
And for vnknowe, tellen hou þe fire 632
Of louis brond is kindled in my brest.
Thus am I m*ur*drid & slain at þe lest
So p*r*eueli w*ith*in *myn [owne] þou3t.
O ladi Venus, whom þat I haue sou3t, 636 O lady Venus, teach me what is best to do:
So wisse me now what me is best to do,
þ*a*t *am distrau3t w*ith*in my self[en] so,
That I ne wot what way for [to] turne,
Sauf be my self soleiu forto mo*ur*ne, 640
Hanging in balau*n*ce bitwix hope & drede, I hang in the balances between Hope and Dread.
W*ith*oute comfort, remedie or rede.
For hope biddiþ p*ur*sue & assay;
And drede againward answeriþ & saiþ nai; 644
And now wiþ hope I am *set on loft, Hope lifts me up,
But drede and daunger, hard & noþing softe,
Haue ouerþrowe my trust and put adoune;
Nou at my laarge, nou feterid in prisone, 648

621. gete] grete F. a] hym S.   622. vaileþ] awalith P. 2ᵈ ne] nor b.
624. þou3e] thorgh F.   625. euen] euer L. Pr. bitwix] betwene P. S. b.
626. while] while while P. þat] om. S. C. W. W2. w. I haue] me lasteþe S.
627. dar] ne dar F. B.   629. forto] to Pr.   630. þat] as F. B. b. hoolly] hyely S.   631. wele] were P. &] ne G. Pr. & for] of foule S.   632. hou] 3ow G. S.   633. is kindled] unkyndeld S.   634. am I] y am P. at þe] atte C. W. W2. w.   635. So] Thus S. w*ith*in] with F. B. G. S. myn] my T. owne] powre P. om. T. L. Pr.   636. ladi Venus] Venus lady F. B. G. S. whom] to whom F. B. þat] om. Pr. haue] haue often P. sou3t] thought F. B.   637. 2ᵈ me] om. G. S. me is] is me P.   638. am] I am T. P. L. w*ith*in] with S. Pr. selfen] selven F. B. selvy*n* G. so] loo W2. w. lo b.   639. ne] om. P. for] om. S. b. to] om. T.   640. soleiu] sodeynly G. alone b. forto] to G.   641. bitwix] betwene G. S. b.   642. or] & G.   643. biddiþ] me bideþe B. p*ur*sue] om. P.   644. And] om. G. drede againward] agaynward drede Pr. & saiþ] om. Pr.   645. now] so now P. om. L. set] lset T. F. L.   646. hard] om. S.   647. Haue] Hath Pr.

28   *The Knight's*

   Nov in turment, nov in souerein glorie,
   Nou in paradise & nov in purgatorie,
but Dread As man dispeired in a double *were,
and Daunger
draw me Born vp wiþ hope, & þan anon daunger   652
back.   Me drawiþ abak, and seith it shal not be.
When I am For where as I, of myn aduersite,
bold to ask
mercy,   Am *bold somwhile merci to requere,
then comes þan coméþ dispeire & ginneþ me to lere   656
Despair and
dismays me. A nwe lessoun, to hope ful contrare—
   Thei be so diners þei would do me varie—
   And þus I stond dismaied in a traunce :
   For whan þat hope were likli me tauaunce,   660
   For drede I tremble and dar a woord not speke.
But indeed if And if it so be þat I not oute breke
I disclose not
my harms to To tel þe harmes, þat greuen me so sore,
her,   But in *myself encrese hem more & more,   664
   And to be slain fulli me delite,
she is not to þen of my deþ sho is noþing to wite;
blame for my
death.   For but if she my constreint pleinli knwe,
   Hou shuld she euer opon my paynis rwe!   668
Thus Hope Thus oft[e] tyme with hope I am I-mevid
oft moves me
to tell her my To tel hir al of þat I am so greued,
griefs;   And to ben hardi on me forto take
but Dread To axe merci; but drede þan doþ awake,   672
answers
back: And *þurgh wanhope answeriþ me again,
better to die þat bettir were, þen she haue disdeyne,

---

649. 2ᵈ nov] and now F. B. G. S. in souerein] soone in S. souerein] sodeyn G. 650. Nou] om. F. B. 651. man] a man P. b. double] doufull L. were] werre T. P. S. W. W2. w. b. where F. B. 652. þan] om. P. 653. not] om. F. B. 654. I] þat S. 655. bold] hold T. P. L. somwhile] sumwhat F. some tyme S. B. 656. ginneþ] begynneth W. W2. w. b. 657. ful] al S. ful the Pr. 658. would] wol L. wil Pr. 659. I stond] staund y P. 660. þat] om. P. W2. w. b. likli] like L. lyke b. tauaunce] to vaunce B. avaunce F. 661. tremble] trowe S. and] I S. b. a woord not] not on worde S. b. a] one C. W. W2. w. 662. it] om. F. B. so be] be so S. I] om. P. 664. myself] myschef T. encrese] encreoce W2. w. hem] om. P. 665. fulli] me fully L. me] my P. 666. þen] Whan L. Pr. noþing] noght F. B. 667. my] the W. W2. w. b. knwe] knowe W. W2. w. b. 668. opon] ou Pr. paynis] harmes F. B. G. 669. ofte tyme] oftymes P. ofte tymes F. B. oft tymes S. with hope I am] I am with hope G. I-mevid] moved S. C. W. W2. w. moued b. Imourned L. 670. of þat] how Pr. so greued] grevid G. Pr. agreved P. S. 672. drede þan] then drede B. þan doþ] doith than L. doth me thenne Pr. 673. þurgh] þouȝ T. thought P. than L. C. b. thenne W. W2. w. wanhope] when P. 674. were] is P. þen] that S. W. W2. w. b. haue] had F. B. S. shuld hawe P.

Soliloquy.

To deie at onys, vnknow of eny wi3t.
And þere-wit*h*[-al] *bitt hope anon ry3t   676
Me to *be bold, to prayen hir of grace;
For siþ al vertues be portreid in hir face,
It were not sitting þ*a*t merci were bihind.
And ri3t anone wit*h*in my self I finde   680
A nwe ple brou3t on me wit*h* drede,
þ*a*t me so masseþ þ*a*t I se no spede,
Bicause he seith, þ*a*t stoneiþ al my bloode,
I am so symple & she is so goode.   684
Thus hope and drede in me wil not ceasse
To plete and stryue myn harmes to encrese.
But at þe hardest 3it, or I be dede,
Of my distresse siþ i can no rede,   688
But stond[e] dovmb stil as eni stone,
Tofore þe goddes I wil me hast anone,
And complein wit*h*oute more sermon;
þou3 deth be fin & ful conclusiou*n*   692
Of my request, 3it I will assai.'
And ri3t anoñ me þou3[te] þat I say
This woful man, as I haue memorie,
Ful lowli entre into an oratorie,   696
And knelid [a]douñ in ful hu*m*ble wise
Tofore þe goddes, and gan anon deuyse
His pitous quarel wiþ a doleful chere,
Sayyng ri3t þus, anone as 3e shul here: 700

Margin glosses: than be disdained by her; Hope makes me look for mercy; but Dread urges my simpleness against her excellence. But at all events I will haste to the goddess and complain, though death result from my request.' Then methought, this man entered an oratory, and kneeling before the goddess, said:

---

675. at onys] anoon S. of eny wi3t] to my wit S. 676. al] *om.* T. P. L. bitt] bitt*ir* T. but F. L. *om.* S. ry3t] yit S. 677. to be bold] gan beholde S. be bold] bihold T. be holden P. be holde G. 2ᵈ to] and Pr. 678. For] And L. Pr. portreid] portured L. 679. merci] pyte Pr. 681. brou3t] y broght P. wit*h*] by L. 683. seith] see*þ*e S. sayd W. W2. w. b. þat] *om.* S. stoneiþ] astonyeth b. astonyed S. 684. 1ˢᵗ so] to F. B. G. S. 2ᵈ so] to F. B. knowe so S. 685. Thus] þis S. 686. to] lo w. b. encrese] peese S. 687. at—or] yit doutelesse or þat S. þe] *om.* Pr. I] *om.* P. 688. siþ] such F. 689. dovmb] doun W. W2. w. dome b. 690. Tofore] Before S. b. I will] as I P. 691. And] And me F. B. G. S. wit*h*oute more] with more pleyne S. 693. I will] wil I G. wol I hym S. 694. And] *om.* P. þou3te] þou3 T. þat] *om.* Pr. 695. woful] offulle P. deolfull S. as] as þat S. hane] haue made b. 696. *In the margin of F and B*: Verba soṁpniantis. lowli entre] lwfly entred P. into] in F. B. an] the F. B. G. S. 697. knelid] kneling S. adouñ] doun T. S. in] with S. ful] alle G. S. 698. Tofore] Before S. b. gan] *om.* P. 700. þus] this C. anone] *om.* Pr. *Before 701 the following headings are found:* Supplicacio amantis F. B. G. þe supplicacioñ of þe Loner S. The compleynt of the man Pr. Compleynt of the man (?) P (*later hand*).

31.

'O Cytherea, who gladdenest all Cirrea,
'Redresse of sorow, o Citheria, 701
That wiþ þe stremes of þi plesaunt hete
Gladest þe contre of [al] Cirrea,
Where þou hast chosen þi paleis & þi sete,

whose beams are washed in the well of Helicon: have pity on my tale.
Whos briȝt bemes ben wasshen and of[t] wete 705
In the riuer of *Elicon þe well:
Haue nou pite of þat I shal here tell. 707

32.

And, of your grace, deign to redress my mortal woe,
And not disdeyneþ of ȝour benignite, 708
Mi mortal wo, o ladi myn, goddes,
Of grace & bounte and merciful pite,
Benig[ne]li to helpen and to redresse;

though words fail me to express it.
And þouȝ so be I can not wele expresse 712
The greuous harmes þat I fele in myn hert,
Haueþ neuer þe les merci of my smert. 714

33.

Clear light of heaven,
This is to sein: o clere heuens liȝt, 715
That next þe sonne cercled haue ȝour spere,

since you hurt me by the influence of your beams,
Siþ ȝe me hurten wiþ ȝour dredful myȝt
Bi influence of ȝour bemys clere,
And þat I bie ȝour seruise nov sodere, 719

be gracious and shape a remedy.
As ȝe me brouȝt into þis maledie,
Beþ gracious and shapeþ remedie. 721

34.

For you alone can help: you know my pain.
For in ȝow hoolli liþ help of al þis case, 722
And knowe best my sorow & al my peyne:
For drede of deþ hou I ne der, allas!

701—714. *These two couplets have, in B, been closely interlined with what seem arbitrary corrections and notes, which have since been partly erased and rendered illegible.* 701. Redresser S. sorow] sorowful F. G. S. o] o thow P. 702. þe] thy F. thi P. 703. þe] al P. contre] contrees F. B. G. S. Court L. mounte Pr. al] *om.* T. P. L. 704. hast] haddest L. 2ᵈ þi] *om.* Pr. 705. briȝt] brightful S. oft] of T. *om.* Pr. 706. In] Wiþin F. B. G. S. Elicon] eleccion T. 707. here] now L. þe S. *om.* G. you Pr. 708. disdeyneþ] dysdeyn P. b. desdayne ye C. W. W2. w. 709. o] *om.* F. B. G. S. myn] and F. B. G. S. 710. merciful] of merceyful P. 711. Benigneli] Benigli T. 1ˢᵗ to] *om.* b. 2ᵈ to] *om.* F. B. G. S. 714. þe] yet the Pr. merci] pite P. 715. heuens] heuynessh F. heuenyssh B. 716. spere] light S. 718. influence] infulgence W2. w. ȝour bemys] Beemys þat been S. 720. þis] his W2. 721. Beþ] Be ye Pr. and shapeþ] to shape F. G. S. shapeþ] shape ye C. W. W2. w. shape a b. 722. hoolli] only G. al] *om.* F. B. þis] the P. case] care W. W2. w. b. 723. knowe] knowyth P. sorow] sore F. B. G. S. peyne] pyne G. P. 724. hou] now P. that B. ne der allas] alas ne dare b.

To axen merci ones ne me compleyne.
Nou wiþ ȝoure fire hire hert[e] so restreyne, 726 So constrain her heart,
With-oute more, or I deie at þe lest,   that she may understand
That she mai wete what is my requeste :   728 my request:

35.

Hov I noþing in al þis world desire,   729 how I only desire to serve her;
But forto serue, fulli to myn ende,
That goodli fressh, so womanli of chere,
With-oute chaunge, while I haue life & mynde ;
And þat ȝe *wold me such grace send   733 send me grace that she may not disdain me:
Of my scruyse, þat she not disdeyne,
Siþen hir to serue I may me not restreyne,   735

36.

And siþ þat hope haþe ȝeue me hardines   736 for Hope has emboldened me to love her best,
To loue hir best and neuer to repent,
Whiles þat I lyue, with al my bisenes
To drede and serue, þouȝ daunger neuer assent.   in spite of Danger.
And hereopon ȝe knowen myn entent,   740
Hov I haue *vowed fulli in my mynde   You know how I have
To ben hir man, þouȝ I no merci finde.   742 vowed to be her servant.

37.

For in myn hert enprentid is so sore   743 For deep in my heart are imprinted
Hir shap, hir fourme, and al hir semelines,
Hir port, hir chere, hir goodnes more & more,
Hir womanhede, & eke hir gentilnes,   all her womanly virtues
Hir trouth, hir faiþ & hir kynd[e]nes,   747
With al vertues, Iche set in his degre ;
There is no lak, saue onli of pite.   749 (she only lacks pity);

---

725. To axen] Aske b. ones] only G. ne] om. F. B. G. me] to S.   726. fire] om. b. hire] om. W. W2. w. b. herte] dart b. restreyne] constrayne Pr.   727. at þe lest] at last P. atte laste W. W2.   730. forto] to S. fulli] holly and truwely S.   732. &] or P.   733. ȝe] I P. wold] wil T. wulle P. me] om. Pr. grace] a grace F. B. G. S. send] nowe seende S.   735. I may me not] may I me nought S. me not] not me Pr. restreyne] refreyne L. F. G. Before 736 S inserts : With oute more / er I dye at þe leest (= line 727). 736. And siþ þat] Sith S. And] Alas b. haþe] haue L. haþe ȝeue me] me hath yeue Pr. (me hath yeue yeue W2)   737. neuer to repent] me neuer restreyne S.   738. Whiles] while F. B.   739. daunger] om. P. 740. ȝe knowen] to knowe P. Instead of ll. 741 and 742 S has: So let me neuer with daunger more be shent.   741. vowed] woid T. sewyd (?) P. my] om. P.   742. finde] om. P.   744. al] om. P.   746. eke] al F. B.   747. Hir trouth hir faiþ] Hire faith hire trouthe L. 3ᵈ hir] al P. all hir B. eke hir L. S. kyndenes] sikyrnesse B.   748. Iche] she P. his] her Pr. hir P.   749. saue] but F. B. G. S. sauyng C. W. W2. w. of] om. B.

38.

her grave demeanour, her benign look,	Hir sad demening, of wil not variable,	750
	Of looke benygne & roote of al plesaunce,	
	And examplaire to al þat wil be stable,	
her wit,	Discrete, prudent, of wisdom suffisaunce,	
	Mirrour of wit, ground of gouernaunce,	754
her beauty.	A world of beaute compassid in hir face,	
	Whose persant loke doþ þuruȝ myn hert[e] race;	756

39.

Besides, she is faithful, bounteous,	And ouer þis secre & wondre trwe,	757
	A welle of fredome, and riȝt bovntevous,	
	And euer encresing in vertue nwe & nwe,	
gracious and humble:	Of spech goodli and wonder gracious,	
	Deuoide of pride, to pore not dispitous,	761
	And if þat I shortli shal not feyne,	
mercy alone is wanting.	Saue opon merci I noþing can compleyne.	763

40.

No wonder then that I dread to ask grace of her.	What wonder þan þouȝ I be wiþ drede	764
	Inli supprised forto axen grace	
	Of hir þat is a quene of womanhed?	
	For wele I wot, in so heigh a place	
I will rather lowly endure my woe, till she pity me.	It wil not beñ; *þerfor I ouerpace,	768
	And take louli what wo þat I endure,	
	Til she of pite me take vnto hir cure.	770

41.

I vow, whatever she decides, to take it humbly.	But oone *avowe pleinli here I make,	771
	That wheþir so be she do me lyve or deye,	
	I wil not grucch, but humble it take,	

---

750. demening] demyng S. 751. Of] and F. B. benygne] kunnyng S. al] om. B. 752. And] An B. G. And an P. to] of S. wil be] ben F. B. G. S. 753. prudent] prudence w. kunnyng S. 754. ground] growed F. 757. And ouer þis] Et euer thus P. And euer ful S. secre & wondre] wonder secrete and Pr. wondre] wondurfully S. 758. A] om. F. B. of] om. P. 759. And euer] Alwey S. vertue] vertus P. 760. wonder] right b. 761. Deuoide] Alvoyde S. to] of G. not dispitous] folkes pitous S. 762. And] So F. B. G. S. if] om. G. if þat] þat if S. I shortli] I *corrected to* shortly I B. 763. I noþing] nothyng I b. noþing can] can no thyng G. S. can] om. F. B. Pr. 764. þan] þat S. be] om. b. 765. supprised] suppressid G. oppressed S. axen] axely w. 766. a] om. Pr. 767. wot] wot that G. S. 768. wil] wolde F. þerfor] þerfro T. F. 769. And] Et P. þat] om. P. S. Pr. 770. she] ye G. S. me take] take me P. vnto] in to G. S. to P. Pr. hir] youre G. S. 771. avowe] avove T. here] hir P. here I] I here S. 772. so be] be so P. om. S. she do] doth P. or] or ellys S.

Complaint to Venus.

And þank[e] god, & wilfulli obey;
For, be my trouth, myn hert shal not reneye, 775 *My heart shall never renounce her service.*
For life ne deþ, merci *ne daunger,
Of wil and þouȝt to ben at hir desire, 777

42.

To bene as trwe, as *was Antonyus 778 *As Antony was true to Cleopatra,*
To Cleopatre, while him lasted breþe,
Or vnto Tesbe ȝung[e] Piramus *and Pyramus to Thisbe,*
*Was feiþful found, til hem departid deþe:
Riȝt so shal I, til Antropos me sleiþe, 782 *so will I be to her, until death.*
For wele or wo, hir faithful man be found,
Vnto my last, lich as myn hert is bounde, 784

43.

To loue aswel as did Achilles 785 *As Achilles loved Polyxena,*
Vnto his last þe faire Polixene,
Or as þe gret famous Hercules, *and Hercules Dejanira,*
For Dianyre þat felt þe shottes kene—
Riȝt so shal I, y sei riȝt as I mene, 789 *so will I serve her.*
Whiles þat I lyve, hir boþe drede and serue,
For lak of merci þouȝ she do me sterve. 791

44.

Nou ladi Venus, to whom noþing vnknowe 792 *Now, lady Venus, to whom nothing in the world is unknown,*
Is in þe world, I-hid ne not mai be—
For þere nys þing, neþir heigh ne lowe,
Mai be concelid from ȝour privete—
Fro whom my menyng is not nov secre, 796
But witen fulli þat myn entent is trwe,
And lich my trowth nov on my peyn[e] rwe. 798 *take pity on my pain.*

---

774. And] Et P. wilfulli] humbelly S. wyllingly b. 775. my] om. P. shal] om. P. shal not] ne shal G. not] neuer Pr. reneye] revey B. 776. 1ˢᵗ ne] nor G. 2ᵈ ne] nor T. L. G. 777. and þouȝt to] ne trouthe but S. to] om. G. 778. was] euer was *all except G. S.* 779. lasted] lestyth G. lasteth C. 780. vnto] to P. S. Piramus] priamus P. 781. Was] That was *all except G. S.* hem] hym P. hym F. G. him B. S. 782. Antropos] Atropos b. 784. my last] last end P. 785. To] And G. S. 787. Or] Er S. 788. For—felt] Whiche felt of loue S. Dianyre] Deyanne G. þat] om. G. shottes] shott Pr. kene] sharp and keene S. 789. I, y] y P. I S. Pr. riȝt] om. P. S. cuyn b. riȝt as] om. L. as] as þat S. 790. Whiles] While G. S. Pr. þat] om. B. I lyve] lyfe P. hir] om. P. boþe drede] drede most S. 792. Nou] O P. vnknowe] is vnknowe P. 793. Is] om. P. þe] thys F. B. I-hid] hid C. hyde W. W2. w. om. b. not] naught L. nought S. Pr. 794. nys] ne is G. is no S. neþir] so S. ne] ne so S. 796. Fro] ffor G. menyng] menyng W2. w. not nov] nowe not S. 797. þat] om. P. 798. nov on] vp on G. peyne] peynes P. G. S.

TEMPLE OF GLAS. D

45.

	For more of grace þan presumpcioun	799
	I axe merci, and not of duete,	
In lowly humbleness I ask you,	Of louli humblesse, wiþoute offensioun,	
	That ȝe enclyne, of ȝour benygnyte,	
	Your audience to myn humylite,	803
of your grace, to grant me release.	To graunt[e] me, þat to ȝov clepe & calle,	
	Somdai relese ȝit of my paynes alle.	805

46.

As you hold in your hand the reward for true lovers,	And siþ ȝe haue þe guerdon & þe mede	806
	Of al louers pleinli in ȝour hond,	
	Nou of [your] grace and pite takeþ hede	
	Of my distresse, þat am vndir ȝour bond	
	So lovli bound, as ȝe wele vndirstond :	810
so let me there find my health, where first I was wounded.	Nou in þat place, where I toke first my wound,	
	Of pite sufferiþ my helth mai be found—	812

47.

	That lich as she me hurt[e] wiþ a siȝte,	813
	Riȝt so with helpe let hir me sustene,	
As the rays of her bright eyes once pierced my heart,	And as þe stremes of hir eyȝen briȝt	
	Whilom myn hert, with woundis sharp & kene,	
	Thuruȝ perced haue, and ȝit bene fressh & grene :	817
so let her now succour me.	So as she me hurt, nou let hir me socoure,	
	Or ellis certein I mai not long endure.	819

48.

For lack of speech, I can say no more;	For lak of spech I can sey nov no more :	820
	I haue mater, but [I] can not plein ;	
	Mi wit is dulle to telle al my sore ;	

799. þan] than of L. Pr.   800. not] no thing Pr.   of] om. P.   801. louli] lowe G. S.   louli humblesse] lwflynesse P.   humblesse] humblenesse L. b.   offensioun] transgression b.   803. to] vnto Pr.   804. me] hit me S.   þat to ȝov] it for whiche b.   clepe] I clepe Pr.   805. Somdai] Sumdelle (?) L (effaced).   Somdai—of] Yit ye releesse some day S.   ȝit] om. B. P. b.   806. And] An S.   808. your] om. all except G. S.   takeþ] take P.   tako ye Pr.   809. am] I am L.   810. wele] wil S.   811. Nou] om. Pr.   toke] take P.   812. Of] ffor P.   sufferiþ] suffre ye Pr.   helth] helpe G. S.   Ioy P.   found] now found P.   813. lich] om. S.   me hurte] myn herte G.   hurt me b.   hurt me first S.   814. helpe] helth Pr.   hir me] me her Pr.   815. eyȝen] euen w.   816. Whilom] Somtyme w. b.   Whilom corrected by a later hand into Entred L.   817. haue] hath P.   and] that G. S.   818. omitted in P.   she] om. L., supplied by a later hand.   1st me] om. G. S.   nou] so S.   om. Pr.   2d me] expunged in L.   socoure] sature G.   819. not long] nowhile G. S.   820. nov] om. P.   you Pr.   821. mater] gret mater S.   no mater b.   2d I] om. T.   plein] complayne b.

A mouth I haue, & ȝit for al my peyne,
For want of woordis I may not nov atteyne   824   words fail me
                                                       to tell half my
To tell[en] half þat doþ myn hert[e] greue,   heart's grief.
Merci abiding, til she me list releue.   826

49.

But þis theffecte of my mater finalle: 827   Finally, I ask
                                                        release, in
Wiþ deþ, or merci, reles forto finde.   death or
                                                        mercy;
For hert, bodi, þought, life, lust and alle,
Wiþ al my reson and alle my ful mynde,   for my whole
                                                        being is
And fiue wittes, of oon assent I bind   831   bound to her
                                                        for ever.
To hir seruice, wiþ-outen eny strife,
And make hir princesse of my deþ or life.   833

50.

And ȝov I prai of routh and eke pite,   834   O lady Venus,
O goodli planet, o ladi Venus briȝt,
That ȝe ȝoure sone of his deite—   so kindle her
                                                        heart,
Cupid I mene, þat wiþ his dredful myȝt   through your
                                                        son Cupid,
And wiþ his brond, þat is so clere of liȝte,   838
Hir hert[e] so to fire and to mark,
As ȝe me whilom brent[e] with a spark: 840   even as you
                                                        have done
                                                        mine;
51.

That euenlich, and with þe same fire,   841
She mai be het, as I nov brenne & melt,
So þat hir hert be *flaumed bi desire,   that her heart
                                                        be inflamed as
That she mai knowe bi feruence hou I swelt;   mine is;
For of pite pleinli if she felt   845   for then I
                                                        might hope
The selfe hete þat doþ myn hert enbrace,   for grace.'
I hope of rouþe she would do me grace.'   847

---

824. of] om. L.   825. half] al P. G.   826. she] ȝe G. yow S.   me list] list
me P. list S.   827. But þis] Þis is S. þis] thus L. mater] preyer G. S.   828.
or] of S.   829. þought, life, lust] lyfe lust thoght P.   life, lust] lust lyf G.
830. reson] resort P. alle] om. P. G. S.   831. fiue] myne fyve G. S. of] with
G.   833. And] To G. S.   hir] om. L., *supplied by a later hand.* of] ouer L.
or] and L. P. G. S.   834. And ȝov I prai] Beseche I yowe S. ȝov] now Pr.
of] for P. eke] of S. ek of G.   835. O] om. G. S.   836. ȝe] om. S. sone] soñ
pray P.   839. Hir] om. W2. w. Myn b. so] lyst so b. mark] make P.   840.
ȝe me whilom] whilhom ȝe me G. S. whilom] somtyme w. b. brente] henten
S.   841. euenlich] lyke wyse W. W2. w. b.   842. be het] be it w. by it b.
het] hit C. W. W2.   I] om. P.   843. flaumed] bavmed T. L. P. bi] with L.
Pr.   844. bi] wiþ G. S. I] om. L., *inserted later.*   845. For of pite] She wolde
me pitie b. of] om. W2. w.   847. would] will Pr.   *At the close of stanza* 51
F *and* B *have in the margin:* finis oracionis; *besides this,* B *has in a later
hand:* h^c vsque nescio quis.

D 2

52.

And therewith Venus looked benignly on this man,	And þerwithal Venus, as me þou3t,	848
	Toward þis man ful benyg[ne]li	
	Gan cast hir ey3e, liche as þou3 she rou3t	
and said:	Of his disease, and seid ful good[e]li :	
'Thy humble obedience deserves my help.	'Siþ it is so þat þou so humb[e]lie,	852
	Wiþ-oute grucchyng, oure hestis list obey,	
	Toward þin help I wil anoñ puruey.	854

53.

And Cupid, too, shall help,	And eke my sone Cupide, þat is so blind,	855
	He shal ben helping, fulli to perfourme	
	3our hole desire, þat noþing behind	
	Ne shal be left : so we shal refourme	
	The pitous compleint, þat makiþ þe to mourne,	859
that thy lady may relieve thy smart.	That she for whom þou soroist most in hert,	
	Shal þuru3 hir merci relese al þi smert,	861

54.

	Whan she seþ tyme þuru3 oure purueaunce.	862
Be not too hasty :	Be not to hasti, but suffre alway wele :	
	For in abidyng þuru3 lowli obeissaunce	
	Liþe ful redresse of al þat 3e nov fele,	
she will be true as steel to you, if you only bide your time.	And she shal be as trw as eny stele	866
	To 3owe allone, þuru3 oure my3t & grace,	
	3if 3e lust mekeli abide a litel space.	868

55.

But understand, all her love shall be grounded in honesty ;	But vndirstondeþ þat al hir cherisshing	869
	Shal ben grovndid opon honeste,	
	That no wi3t shal, þurugh euil compassing,	

In b, before stanza 52, is the heading: The author; in B. F: Responsio Veneris. 848. þerwithal] ther with P. Venus as] right as þat S. 849. Towardes F. B. L. S. Pr.—benygli T. benigly P. 850. hir] an P. þou3] om. G. that S. Pr. (exc. b.) rou3t] reugh P. 851. goodeli] in goodely S. 852. þou] you b. 853. obey] tobeye G. weye F. 854. Towar G. Towardes L. S. þin] your G. S. b. I wil anoñ] anon I wyl G. S. 855. eke] also W. W 2. w. b. so] om. L. G. 856. He] om. b. 857. behind] be behynd P. L. Pr. G. S. 858. left] kept S. 859. The] This Pr. þe] you b. 860. That] And b. þou soroist] ye sorowe b. 861. þi] your b. 862. seþ] seyth P. oure] your S. her w. b. 863. to] om. P. alway] althing Pr. 864. in] om. P. lowli] lwfly P. 865. ful] om. S. 867. þuru3] by Pr. oure] youre S. hyr G. 868. 3e lust mekeli abide] humbully ye byde S. mekeli abide] byde G. abyd mekly P. 869. vndirstondeþ] vnderstande ye Pr. 870. ben] be so S. so ben G. grovndid] ground P. honeste] al honestee S. 871. þurugh euil] by ony Pr. compassing] rehercyng W. W 2. w. b.

*Demen amys of hir in no degre :
For neiþer merci, roupe, ne pite   873   never shall
She shal not haue, ne take of þe non hede   she outstep
                                                    the bounds of
                                                    womanhood.
Forþer þen longiþ vnto hir womanhede.   875

56.

Beþe not astoneid of no wilfulnes,   876
Ne nou3t dispeired of þis *dilacioun ;
Lete reson bridel lust bi buxumnes,   Let reason
                                                    bridle desire ;
Withoute grucching or rebellioun ;
For ioy shal folov al þis passioun :   880
For who can suffre turment & endure,   cure crowns
                                                    patient en-
Ne mai not faile þat folov shal his cure.   882   durance.

57.

For toforn all she shal þe louen best :   883   She shall love
                                                    thee best ;
So shal I here, withoute offencioun,
Bi influence enspire[n] in hir brest,   so will I in-
                                                    fluence her
In honest wise, wiþ ful entencioun,
Forto enclyne, bi clene affeccioun,   887
Hir hert fulli on þe to haue roupe,   to pity thee.
Bicause I know þat þou menyst troupe.   889

58.

Go nov to hir, where as she stant aside,   890   Go now to
                                                    her,
Wiþ humble chere & put þe in hir grace,
And al biforne late hope be þi guide,   guided by
                                                    'Hope'—
And þou3e þat drede would[e] with þe pace,   and even
                                                    'Dread'—
It sitteþ wel ; but loke þat þou arace   894
Out of þin hert wanhop & dispaire,   but banish
                                                    'Despair.'
To hir presence er þou haue repaire.   896

872. Demen] Semen T. P. Seyen L. of hir] om. G. no] nomaner G.
873. For] But G. S. ne] nor G. Pr. 874. haue ne take] tak ne haue P.
of] at G. þe] 3ow G. S. b. 875. vnto hir] to P. 876. Beþe] But P. Be Pr.
877. Ne] Be P. Ne nou3t] Nor b. dispeired] dispayer P. þis] þe S. dilacioun]
dillusioun T. P. dissolucion L. Pr. 879. or] or ellys S. 880. filowe S. 881.
who] om. B. 882 reads in b : May nat fayle at length to optayne pleasure.
Ne] He F. B. þat] but Pr.—filowe S. felowe F. 883. For] om. S. toforn]
before b. all] alle oþer S. þe] 3ow G. S. 884. I] ye P. 885. hir] my S.
886. wiþ] and w. b. 887. clene] full P. 888. fulli] holly b. þe] 3ow G. S.
889. þat] om. P. þou menyst] 3e mene G. S. troupe] but truthe S. 890.
where] were L. om. S. as] om. L. w. b. she] he W. om. W2. stant] standes
w. standeth b. aside] side L. 891. put] pite P. 892. al] om. L. biforne] to
forn G. late] loke L. be] by L. 893. And] ffor S. þe] his P. pace] face b.
894. þou] yow P. 895. wanhop] hope P. 896. repaire] any repeyre S.

59.

'Mercy,'	And merci first shal þi wai[e] make,	897
'Honest Meaning,'	And honest menyng aforn do þi message,	
	To make merci in her hert awake;	
'Secretness' and 'Humble Port' shall smooth thy way; I, too, will favour thee.	And secrenes, to furþer þi viage,	
	Wiþ humble port to hir þat is so sage,	901
	Shul menes ben, & I myself also	
	Shal þe fortune er þi tale be do.	903

60.

Go forth at once:	Go forþe anon, & be riȝt of goode chere:	904
	For specheles noþing maist þou spede;	
	Be goode of trust, & be noþing in were,	
with my help, she shall at least grant thee a hearing.	Siþ I myself shal helpen in þis nede;	
	For at þe lest, of hir goodlihed,	908
	She shal to þe hir audience enclyne,	
	And lovli þe here, til þou þi tale fyne.	910

61.

	Fore wele þou wost, ȝif I shal not feine,	911
Thou must speak out;	Withoute spech þou maist no merci haue:	
	For who þat wil of his preve peine	
for there is no cure,	Fulli be cured, his life to help & saue,	
	He most mekeli oute of his *hertis graue	915
unless thou discover thy wound to the leech.	Discure his wound, & shew it to his lech,	
	Or ellis deie for defaute of spech.	917

62.

In mischief one must seek help;	For he þat is in myschef rekeles	918
	To sechen help, I hold him but a wrecch;	
	And she ne mai þin hert[e] bring in peas,	
	But if þi compleint to hir hert[e] strecch.	

897. shal þi waie] þy wey shal redy S.   898. menyng] mevyng G. menne w. meane b.   899. make] do P. merci] pyte Pr.   900. secrenes] sikurnesse S. to] tor P. viage] vysage S. message L.   901 *omitted in* L, *but added by a later hand.*   902. I] *om.* P.   903. fortune] forne w. forther b. er] and P. þi] al þy S. tale] calo*ur* (?) P.   904. riȝt of goode] of ryght good F. B. L. b. right good of C. W. W2. w.   905. noþing] for no thyng G. S. maist þou] may you W. W2. w. may ye b.   908. at þe] atte C. W. W2. at w. P. lest] last P.   909. to þe] the to P. to—audience] hire audience to the L.   910. lovli] lowe the C. þe] to B. *om*. G. S. þe here] to her Pr. here] hir S. til] tell b.   911. wost] knost P. wyst G. wotest w. wottest b. ȝif] yeft P.   912. þou—haue] than no m*er*cy maist hawe P.   914. Fulli] ffullyche G. be cured] to be recured P.   915. He] *om*. b. hertis] hurtis T. herte G. w. b. hert F. B. L. C. W. W2.   916. to] *om*. C. W. W2. w.   917. deie] to die P.   918. he] *om*. L. rekeles] and is rekeles b.   919. sechen] seche hym P. but] *om*. Pr. a] *om*. L.   921. if] *om*. G. S. to] vnto G. hir] thyn L. herte] erys G. S.

Wouldist þou be curid, & wilte no salue fecch,   922   without salve,
It wil not be: for no wiȝte may atteyne   thou canst
                                                        not be cured.
To come to blis, if he lust lyue in peyne.   924

63.

Therfore at ones go in humble wise   925   Therefore
Tofore þi ladi & louli knele adoun,   kneel lowly
                                                       before thy
And in al trouth þi woordis so deuyse,   lady;
That she on þe haue compassioun:
For she þat is of so heigh renoun   929   and she shall
In al vertues as quene & souerain,   have pity on
                                                       thy pain.'
Of womanhed shal rwe opon þi pein.'   931

And whan þe goddes þis lesson hade him told,   932   When the
Aboute me so as I gan bihold,   goddess
                                                       ended,
Riȝt for astoneid I stode in a traunce,
To *seen þe maner & þe covntenaunce   the counten-
And al þe chere of þis woful man,   936   ance of this
                                                       man was
That was of hwe deedli pale & wan,   woeful to see:
Wiþ drede supprised in his owne þouȝt,
Making a chere as *þouȝ he rouȝt[e] nouȝt
Of life ne deþ, ne what so him bitide: 940
So mych fere he hade on euere side,
                                                       so feared he
To put him forþe forto tel his peyne   to lay his
                                                       case before
Vnto his ladi, oþer to compleyne,   his lady.
What wo he felt, turment or disease,   944
What dedli sorov his hert[e] did[e] sense,
For rouþe of which his wo as I endite,   For very ruth
                                                       I feel my pen
Mi penne I fele quaken as I write.   quake,

922. þou] then F. wilte] lyst G. S. no] not L. B. nocht P. fecch]
seche F. 923. not be for] not be nocht be P. 924. he] him S. 925. go] go
forth Pr. 926. Tofore] By fore S. Before b. adoun] and a doun W2. þi]
this G. 928. on þe] of the may G. S. 929. of so heigh] so hye of S. 931.
opon] on Pr. of P. After 931 in F. B : Huc [Hic B] usque verba Veneris.
Heading before 932 in B. F: Verba sompniantis; in b: The author. 932.
him] om. S. Pr. 933. so as] so C. W. W2. w. as b. I gan] gan I w. gan]
cane S. 934. for] as for F. B. P. L. sore S. b. so C. W. W2. w. I] om. C.
W. W2. w. in] as in F. B. G. S. 935. seen] sein T. seyñ P. &] of L. 2ᵈ þe]
om. C. W. W2. w. covntenaunce] gouernaunce G. 937. deedli pale &] pale
and dedly S. 938. supprised] oppressid S. in his owne] inly in his G. oonly
in his S. 939. a] his S. om. Pr. þouȝ] þat T. S. he] hym G. S. rouȝte]
recched S. cared b. 940. 1ˢᵗ ne] nor F. B. P. G. 941. he] him L. on] in G.
942. him] hem S. forto] to C. 943. oþer] or els b. 944. he] him L. felt]
lete W2. ledde w. b. or] and P. b. 946. his wo as I] of his wo to S. wo as]
wooes W. W2. w. b. 947. quaken] qwakyng S. L. write] now write P.

40   The Knight's

<table>
<tr><td>as I rehearse his lamentacion,</td><td>Of him I had so gret compassioun,
Forto reherse his weymentacioun,
That, wel vnnepe pou3 with my self I striue,
I want connyng, his peynes to discryue.</td><td>948</td></tr>
<tr><td>Not the Muses, helpers in joy, may I now invoke,</td><td>Allas! to whom shal I for help[e] cal?
Not to þe Musis, for cause þat þei ar al
Help of ri3t in ioi & not in wo,
And in maters þat þei delite also,
Wherfore þei nyl directe as nov my stile,
Nor me enspiren, allas þe hard[e] while!</td><td>952

956</td></tr>
<tr><td>but Tisiphone and her sisters.</td><td>I can no ferþer but to Thesiphone
And to hir sustren forto help[e] me,
That bene goddesses of turment & of peyne.</td><td>

960</td></tr>
<tr><td>Now let your tears rain into my ink,</td><td>Nou lete 3oure teris into myn inke reyne,
With woful woordis my *paper forto blot,
This woful mater to peint[e] not, but spotte,</td><td></td></tr>
<tr><td>that I may relate the complaint of this man,</td><td>To tell þe maner of þis dredful man,
Vpon his compleint, when he first bigan
To tel his ladi, when he gan declare
His hid[de] sorois, and his euel fare,
That at his hert constreyned him so sore,</td><td>964

968</td></tr>
<tr><td>which ran thus:</td><td>Theffecte of which was þis with-oute more:</td><td></td></tr>
</table>

64.

<table>
<tr><td>'Princess of youth,</td><td>'Princes of ioupe, & flour of gentilesse,
Ensaumple of vertue, ground of curtesie,</td><td>970</td></tr>
</table>

949. Forto] þat to S. his] his gret P. weymentacioun] lamentacion b. 950, 951 *read in* b:
    Ye / though I with my selfe stryue
    Vnneth my connyng may his paynes discryue
950. wel] *om*. C. W. W2. w. vnneþe] I wot S. with my self I] I with my silf C. 951. want] lacke w. 952. to—helpe] for help to whom shall I B. 953. for cause] by cause G. b. þat] *om*. F. B. Pr. ar] *om*. S. ben Pr. al] nere all b. 954. Help] Helpynge F. B. G. Helpen S. 955—957 *om. in* P. 955. þei] *om*. F. B. G. S. 956. nyl] wil nat G. nyl not S. directe as nov] as now directe Pr. nowe dyrect S. as] *om*. G. 957. allas] but allas F. 958. I] And G. S. no] no more P.—Physyphonee S. 959. sustren—me] suster to calle help vpon C. W. W2. w. b with the rariation susters. 960. goddesses of] goddesse nt P. goddes L. 2ᵈ of] *om*. C. W. W2. w. 962. woful] peynfull S. paper] pauper T. 963. to peinte not] not to peynte B. C. b. not peynt S. but] to P. but to S. 964. dredful] woful P. 966. when] and howe b. gan] began L. 967. sorois] sorowe P. 968. That] Whiche S. at] *om*. W2. w. b. his] is W2. him] *om*. Pr. 969. þis] thus L. *After* 969 *is in* F. B *the rubric:* The supplicacion of the man to hys (his B.) lady; S *has in the margin:* Balade of þe lover. 970. Princes] Pryncisses P. 971. Ensaumple] A ensample P. Ensamplier L.

Wooing of the Lady. 41

Of beaute rote, qnene & eke maistres
To al women hou þei shul hem gie,
And sopefast myrrour to exempl:fie 974
The riʒt[e] wei of port & womanhed :
What *I shal sai of merci takeþ hede— 976   list to my request.

65.

Biseching first vnto ʒoure heigh nobles, 977   With quaking heart I beseech your help;
Wiþ quaking hert of myn inward drede,
Of grace and pite, & nouʒt of riʒtwisnes,
Of verrai rouþe, to help[en] in þis nede :
That is to saie, o wel of goodlihed, 981   I do not dread death, if only you hear me.
That I ne recch, þouʒ ʒe do me deie,
So ʒe list first [to] heren what I saie. 983

66.

The dredful stroke, þe gret[e] force & myʒt 984   Cupid has so smitten me,
Of god Cupide, þat no man mai rebel,
So inwardli þuruʒ out myn hert[e] riʒt
I-persid haþ, þat I ne mai concele   that I cannot conceal my wound.
Myn hid[de] wound, ne I ne may apele 988
Vnto no grettir : þis myʒti god so fast
Yow [for] to serue *haþ bound me to my last, 990

67.

That hert and al, wit*h*oute strife, ar yolde, 991   I have surrendered to your service,
For life or deþ, to ʒoure seruise alone,
Riʒt as þe goddes myʒti Venus would :   as Venus, on hearing my complaint, constrained
Toforne hir mekeli when I made my mone,
She me constreyned, wit*h*out chau*n*ge, anone 995

---

972. beaute] bountee S.—magistresse P. 973. shul] shuld F. B. G. 974. And] þe S. to exemplifie] goode texemplyfye S. 975. of] to þe S. &] in G. of S. and of L. Pr. 976. I shal] shal I T. L. takeþ] take ye Pr. *Between 976 and 977 no interval marking the division of the stanzas in C. W. W2. w. b. (because the same rhymes recur?).* 977. first] om. w. b. vnto] to P. heigh] gowd P. 978. inward] vnware S. 979. nouʒt] om. b. 980. in] om. W. W2. w. b. 981. That] This G. S. Pr. 983. ʒe] you S. to] om. T. 985. god] gowd P. good W2. w. om. b. þat no man] ayenst whom non P. b. 986. out] om. L. P. 987. I-persid] y presed P. concele] cancelle S. 988. hidde] hovyn S. ne] nor F. B. G. S. ne may] may not P. 989. þis myʒti god] his mightyhed S. 990. for] om. T. P. L. Pr. haþ bound me to] me haþ bound vnto T. L. hath me bound vnto Pr. me to] vnto F. B. G. S. 991. That] 'My w. b. al—ar] body hole is to you S. 992. or] and L. 993. goddes myʒti] mighty goddesse S. 994. Toforne] Before b. 995. anone] in oone F. B. G. S.

me to do,	To ȝoure seruise, & neuer forto feyne,	
	*Where so *ye list to do me ease or peyne.	997

68.

so that I can only cry mercy.	So þat I can noþing but merci crie	998
	Of ȝov my ladi—& chaungen for no nwe—	
	That ȝe list goodl[i], tofore [er þat] I deyȝe,	
	Of verrey roupe opon my peynes rwe.	
Verily, if you knew all, you would have pity.	For be my troupe, & ȝe þe soþe knwe,	1002
	What is þe cause of myn aduersite,	
	On my distres ȝe would haue pite.	1004

69.

For I will be true and humbly devoted to you,	For vnto ȝow trwe & eke secre	1005
	I wole be found, to serue as I best can,	
	And þerwith-al as lowli in ich degre	
as ever man was to his lady.	To ȝow *allone, as euir ȝit was man	
	Vnto his ladi, from þe tyme I *gan,	1009
	And shal so forþe, without͏en eny sloupe,	
	Whiles þat I lyue, bi god & be my troupe.	1011

70.

I would rather die than offend you.	For leuyr I had to dei[e]n sodeinli,	1012
	Than yow offend in any maner wise,	
	And suffre peynes inward priueli,	
	Than my seruise ȝe shuld as nov despise.	
	For I riȝt nouȝt wil asken in no wise,	1016
Take me as your servant;	But for ȝoure seruaunt ȝe would me accepte,	
	And, whan I trespace, goodli me correcte,	1018

71.

	And forto graunt, of merci, þis praier,	1019
	Oonli of grace and womanl[i] pete,	
teach me	Fro dai to dai þat I myȝt[e] lere	

997. Where so] Wheþer S. Where so euer T. P. L. Pr. ye] yow T. F. B. S. do me] me do P. me] om. L. 999. chaungen] chaunging S. 1000. ȝe] you S.—goodll T. tofore] before b. byseen S. er] om. P. er þat] om. P. 1001. rwe] knewe W2. 1002. &] yef P. if L. b. þe soþe] my peynes Pr. 1003. What is þe cause] And what the cause is b. 1004. On] Of S. L. Off P. distres] disese G. S. Pr. 1006. wole] wold P. found] bounde S. 1007. lowli] low G. S. 1008. allone] ben allone T. L. P. Pr. was] ded P. 1009. þe tyme] tyme þat S. I] the world P. gan] began T. L. P. S. Pr. 1010. shal so] so shal G. S. so] be B. 1011. Whiles] Whyle b. 1012. leuyr—to] I had lener b. 1013. offend] offence W2. w. 1014. inward] Inwardes S. 1015. mynov] as now my seruice ye shull P. ȝe shuld as nov] as now ye shold Pr. ye shulden nowe S. 1017. would] wol L. 1018. goodli me] me goodely to S. 1019. þis] the L. Pr. 1020. womanl] woman T. 1021. lere] beter lere S.

ȝow forto please, & þerwith-al þat ȝe,   how to please you;
When I do mys, list [for] to teche me,   1023
In ȝoure seruyse hou þat I mai amende   and how to amend, if I
From hens-forþe, and neuyr ȝow offende.   1025   do amiss.

72.

For vnto me it doþ inouȝ suffise,   1026   For I am content to be
That for ȝoure man ȝe would me reseyue,   your servant;
Fulli to ben, as ȝou list deuyse,
And as ferforþe *my wittes con conceyue,
And þerwithal, lich as ȝe perseyue   1030   reward or punish me as I deserve.
That I be trwe, to guerdone me of grace,
Or ellis to punyssh aftir my trespace.   1032

73.

And if so be þat I mai not atteyne   1033   And if I cannot obtain your mercy,
Vnto ȝour merci, ȝit grauntep at [þe] lest,
In ȝour seruice, for al my wo & peyne,   then let me die in your service.
That I mai deiȝen aftir my bihest.
This is al & som, þe fine of my request :   1037   This is the whole of my request.'
Oþir with merci ȝour seruant forto saue,
Or merciles þat I mai be graue.   1039

74.

And whan þis benygne, of hir entent trwe,   1040   When this benign lady heard this,
Conceyued haþ þe compleint of þis man,
Riȝt as þe fressh rodi rose nwe   she waxed red as a rose,
Of hir coloure to wexin she bigan ;
Hir bloode astonyed so from hir hert[e] *ran   1044
Into hir face, of femyny[ni]te :
Thuruȝ honest drede abaisshed so was she.   1046

1023. for] om. T. G. S. 1024. I] ye L. 1027 omitted in P. 1028. ȝou] ye G. P. W. W2. w. b. deuyse] to devise G. S. 1029. And] Ryght F. B. G. S. my] as my all except F. B. G. S. con] may F. B. G. S. P. 1030. perseyue] preue C. W. W2. w. me preue b. 1031. That I] To b. I] ye P. me of] of your G. S. 1032. to] om. G. me P. S. 1034. at þe] at T. atte F. W. W2. w. att B. me at L. P. 1035. peyne] pyne P. 1037. is] om. F. B. G. þe] and P. om. S. request] beheest S. 1038. Oþir] Outher C. Eyther W. W2. w. b. Oonly S. forto] to Pr. 1039. I] he G. S. graue] begraue Pr. grace F. P. In the margin opposite 1040 : The answere of hys lady F. 1040. And] om. S. trwe] so trewe G. S. 1041. haþ] had P. 1044. ran] it ran T. P. W. W2. w. b. 1045. femynyte T. F. B. pure femynite P. verray femynyte L. Pr. 1046. so] om. Pr.

75.

and humbly and benignly glanced at him, in abashed silence;

And humb[e]le she gan hir eizen cast　　　　1047
Towardis him, of hir benygnyte,
So þat no woord bi hir lippes past
For hast *nor drede, merci nor pite.
For so demeyned she was in honeste,　　　　1051
That vnavised noþing hir astert :
So mych of reson was compast in hir hert—　1053

76.

till at last, in pity, she spoke:

Til, at þe last, of rouþe she did abraide,　1054
When she his trouþe and menyng did[e] fele,
And vnto him ful goodli spake & seide :

'With all my heart I thank you for your offer.

'Of ȝoure [be]hest and of ȝour menyng wele,
And ȝoure seruise so feiþful eueredel,　　　1058
Which vnto me so lowli now ȝe offre,
Wiþ al my hert I þanke ȝow of ȝoure profir— 1060

77.

You must needs speed the better for your virtuous intent;

That for as mych as ȝoure entent is sette　 1061
Oonli in vertu, I-bridelid vnder drede,
Ȝe most of riȝt nedis fare þe bette
Of ȝoure request, and þe bettir spede.

but I can grant nothing more than Venus will allow;

But as for me, I mai of womanhede　　　　　　1065
No ferþir graunt to ȝov in myn entent
Thanne as my ladi Venus wil assent.　　　　 1067

78.

for I am bound to obey what she ordains.

For she wele knowiþ I am not at my laarge　1068
To done riȝt nouȝt but bi hir ordinaunce ;
So am I bound vndir hir dredful charge,
Hir lust to obey withoute variaunce.

1047. gan] began L. Pr.　1048. Towarde b. of] right of S.　1050. 1st nor] ne T. S.　2d nor] ne L. S. Pr.　1052. That] Than P.—vnaduysed C. b. vnduysed W. vndeuysed W 2. w.—no thyng no thyng P. noþing hir] hir nothyng myght G. hir astert] fro her stert Pr.　1053. compast] composed b. hir] *om.* W. W 2. w.　1054. at þe] atte C. W. W 2. w. F. at B. of rouþe] so moche b. ronþe] whiche C. W. W 2. w.　1055. his] is C. menyng] menyng w. dide] well dyd b.　1056. 1st And] That b. vnto] to G. S. spake &] thus she b.　1057. 1st Of] And of B. behest] behestes S. hest T. 2d of] *om.* G. S. Pr.　1058. ȝoure] of yowr P.　1059. vnto] to L.　1060. of] for b.　1061. That] And b. *om.* S. as mych as] so muche as L. so moche C. W. W 2. w. sette] y sette P.　1062. in] on S. b. I-bridelid] brydeld S.　1063. fare] fayr P.　1066. to] *om.* S.　1067. as] *om.* P. assent] ful-assent S.　1068. am] nam S. 1069. bij at G.　1070. bound] drowned Pr.　1071. to obey] to him S.

But for my part, so it be plesaunce   1072   But, for my
Vnto þe goddes, for trouþe in ȝour emprise,   part, I fully
I ȝow accepte fulli to my seruyse.   1074   accept you.

79.

For she myn hert haþ in subieccioun,   1075   My heart is
Which holi is ȝoures and neuer shal repent,   wholly yours
In þouȝt nor dede, in myn eleccioun :   and will ever
Witnes on Venus, þat knoweþ myn entent,   be;
Fulli to obei hir dome and Iugement,   1079   but yet, as
So as hir lust disposen and ordeyne,   Venus dis-
Riȝt as she knoweþ þe trouth of vs tweyne.   1081   poses, I must
                                                         obey.

80.

For vnto þe time þat Venus [list] prouyde   1082   For until she
To shape a wai for oure hertis ease,   deign to ap-
Boþe ȝe and I mekeli most abide,   pease our
To take a[t] gre, & not of oure disease   inward woe,
To grucch agein, til she list to appese   1086   we must
Oure hid[de] wo, so inli þat constreyneþ   meekly abide.
From dai to day & oure hert[es] peyneþ.   1088

81.

For in abiding, of wo & al affray—   1089   For in abiding
Whoso can suffre—is founden remedie,   is found
And for þe best ful oft is made delay,   remedy for
Er men be heled of hir maladie ;   woe;
Wherfore, as Venus list þis mater to guie,   1093   let us surren-
Late vs agreen & take al for þe best,   der ourselves
Til her list set oure hertes boþe at rest.   1095   to Venus'
                                                         will;

1072. pleaunce w.   1074. fulli] in P.   1076. holi] hol G.   hole S.—repete
w.   1077. 1st In] And in G.   nor] nen S.   1078. on] of G.   1079. to obei]
to beye W2. w. b.   to byde S.   1080. hir] she G. P.   1081. Riȝt] Lych G. S.
vs] bothe vs G. S.   1082. vnto] vn P.   þe] om. G. S.   list] om. T. P. F. B.
1084. mekeli most] most nedes þe tyme S.   1085. at gre] agre T.   in gree S.
L.   of] at G.   for S. b.   1086. agein] agrayne b.   til] til that Pr.   2d to] om.
B. S. b.   appese] hawe pece P.   1088. &] so S.   and of P.   hertes] hert T.
peyneþ] pleyneþe S.   peyryth G.   1089. al] om. L.   1090. Whoso] Who that
G. S. b.   Who P.   is founden] fyndeþe S. b.   1091. ful oft is] is ofte P. G.—
dely G.   1092. Er] Er that P.   men] man W2. w.   be heled] beheled W.   be-
helde W2. w.   1093. list þis mater] this mater lest G.   þis] the b.   to] om.
S. b.   1094. take] om. L.   al] al thing S.   al for] for al P.   1095. her] sche
G. S.   set—boþe] owre both hertes sett P.   oure—boþe] bothe our [w: out]
hertes Pr.   at] in Pr.

82.

for she can unite lovers.	For she it is þat bindeþ & can constreyne 1096

    Hertes in oon, þis fortunate planete,
    And can *relesen louers of her peyne,
    To turne fulli hir bitter into swete.

Now, blissful goddess, befriend us from thy starry seat.
    Nou blisful goddes, doun fro þi sterri sete,   1100
    Vs to fortune, caste ȝour stremes shene,
    Like as ȝe cnow þat we trouþe mene.'   1102

83.

And then I saw these lovers pass before the goddess,
    And perwithal, as I myn eyȝen cast   1103
    Forto perceiue þe maner of þese twein,
    Tofore þe goddes mekel[i] as þei past,

who linked their hearts together with a golden chain,
    Me þouȝt I saw, with a golden cheyne,
    Venus anoñ enbracen & constrein   1107
    Her boþ[e] hertes, in oon forto perseuer,
    Whiles þat þei liue and neuer to desseuer.   1109

84.

saying: 'My daughter,
    Saiyng riȝt þus with a benygne chere :   1110
    ' Siþ it is so ȝe ben vndir my myȝt,
    Mi wille is þis, þat ȝe, my douȝter dere,

of your grace, receive this man.
    Fulli accepte þis man, *as hit is riȝt,
    Vnto ȝour grace anoñ here in my siȝt,   1114
    That euer haþ ben so louli ȝou to serue :
    It is goode skil ȝour þank þat he desserue.   1116

85.

It is fitting that you should cherish him,
    Your honour saue, and eke ȝour womanhed,   1117
    Him to cherissen it sittiþ ȝov riȝt wele,
    Siþ he is bound, vnder hope & drede,
    Amyd my cheyne þat maked is of stele ;

1096. it] om. L. Pr. is] om. b. bindeþ] biddeth L. constreyne] destreyne S. 1098. relesen] recouer P. plesen T. F. B. 1099. To] And to P. into] vn to G. b. 1100. fro þi sterri] streght from þy S. 1101. Vs] Vn G. 1104. twein] sweyne W2. w. 1105. Tofore] Before S. b.—mekel T. þei] the P. F. 1106. a golden] of golde a S. *In the margin of* F, *opposite ll.* 1104—1106 : Corda amborum amancium cathenata per venerem. 1107. enbracen] enbrased P. enkrace b. 1108. bothis G. boþer S. boþe hertes] hertes both P. 1109. Whiles] Whyle b. liue] haue lyue L. to] for to S. desseuer] disserue F. 1110. *In the margin of* F : Verba veneris ad amantes. 1111. ȝe] that ye P. they G. S. 1112. þis] thus Pr. 1113. Fulli] Ful C. W. p. W2. w. as hit is] at his T. F. B. 1116. he] ye L. 1117. eke] also W. p. W2. w. b. 1118. riȝt] om. P. 1120. Amyd] And with S. maked] forged G. L. Pr. maked—stele] is golde yche dele S.

ȝe must of merci shape þat he fele   1121   and be gracious to him.
In ȝov som grace for his long seruise,
And þat in hast, like as I shal deuyse.   1123

86.

This is to sein : þat ȝe taken hede,   1124   Consider how, for all his faithfulness,
Hou he to ȝov most faiþful is & trwe
Of al ȝour seruauntis, & noþing for his mede
Of ȝov ne askiþ but þat ȝe on him rwe ;   he only asks your pity:
For he haþe *vowid to chaunge for no nwe,   1128   he has vowed never to change.
For life nor deþ, for ioy[e] ne for peyne—
Ay to ben ȝours, so as ȝe list ordeyne.   1130

87.

Wherfore ȝe must—or ellis it were wrong—   1131   Wherefore, admit him to your favour;
Vnto ȝour grace fulli hym receyue,
In my presence, bicause he haþ so long
Holli ben ȝoures, as ȝe may conceyue
That, from ȝoure merci nov if ȝe him weyue,   1135   else I must record cruelty against you.
I wil my self recorden cruelte
In ȝoure persone, & gret lak of pite.   1137

88.

Late him for trouth þen find[e trouth] agein ;   1138   Let grace be his guerdon;
For long seruice guerdone him with grace,
And lateþ pite wei[e] doun his pein ;
For tyme is nov daunger to arace   root 'Danger' out of your heart,
Out of ȝoure hert, and merci in to pace ;   1142   and let 'Mercy' enter.
And loue for loue would[e] wele biseme
To yeve agein, and þis I pleinli deme.   1144

1121. ȝe] She S. of merci shape] nedys of mercy P. he] ye W2. w. b. 1122. for] of Pr. 1123. like] om. P. 1125. Hou] How þat G. most] oft W. p. W2. w. is] it W. p. W2. om. w. hath ben b. 1127. ne] he b. þat] om. Pr. rwe] to rue b. 1128. haþe vowid] vowed hath L. Pr. vowid] woid T. 1129. nor] ne P. F. Pr. ne] nor G. ner L. no B. 1130. Ay] As W2. w. b. ȝe] yowe S. 1131. ȝe] yow S. 1132. fulli hym] him fully to S. 1133. he] that he L. 1135. ȝoure] om. w. b. nov] om. G. Pr. ȝe] I S. weyue] reve P. 1138. for] so S. for his L. Pr. þen] om. P. G. S. b. þen finde] fynde than C. W. p. W2. w. finde trouth] trouthe fynde G. 2d trouth] truwe S. om. T. F. B. L. C. W. p. W2. w. 1139. with] om. P. 1140. lateþ] late ye C. late your W. p. W2. w. b. weie doun] awey doon S. 1141. to arace] for tarace G. for to race S. vp to race P. 1142. Out] But S. pace] space W. p. W2. w. b. 1143. And] ffor P. woulde] It wel G. hit wolde S. world C. biseme] seeme S. 1144. þis] thus L. P. G. S. I] om. S.

89.

I will stand surety for his dutifulness.	And as for him, I wil bene his borow	1145
	Of lowlihed and bise attendaunce,	
	Hou he shal bene, boþ at eue & morov,	
	Ful diligent to don his obseruaunce,	
	And euer awayting ȝou to do plesaunce;	1149
And thou also, my son, list to my counsel.	Wherfore, my sone, list & take hede	
	Fulli to obey as I shal þe rede.	1151

90.

First, be faithful and humble;	And first of al, my wil is þat þou be	1152
	Feiþful in hert and constant as a walle,	
	Trwe, humble and meke, & þerwithal secre,	
	Withoute chaunge in parti or in al;	
In every trouble let thy heart be rooted in steadfastness.	And for no turment, þat þe fallen shal,	1156
	Tempest þe not, but euer in stidfastnes	
	Rote þin hert, and voide doublenes.	1158

91.

For thy lady's sake,	And forþermore, haue in reuerence	1159
	Thes women al for þi ladi sake,	
	And suffre neuer þat men *hem don offence,	
revere and defend all women.	For loue of oon; but euermore vndirtake	
	Hem to defend, wheþer þei slepe or wake,	1163
	And ay be redi to holden champartie	
	With al[le] þo, þat to hem haue enuie.	1165

92.

Be courteous, fresh and seemly;	Be curteis ay and lowli of þi spech	1166
	To riche and poure, ai fressh & welbesein,	
help all true lovers;	And euer bisie, weies forto sech	
	All trwe louers to relese of her peyne,	
disdain no one;	Siþ þou art oon; and of no wiȝt haue disdein—	1170
do not vaunt thyself of being cherished.	For loue haþ pouer hertis forto daunt—	
	And neuer for cherisshing þe to mych auaunte.	1172

1145. for] for for F. 1146. bise] lowly S. 1147. he] hit S. at] *om.* Pr. eue] even S. &] & at G. 1149. ȝou] *om.* S. to] for to F. B. L. G. S. do] *om.* P. 1150. list] listen P. L. F. B. Pr. hede] good hede G. 1151. to obey] obeye S. 1152. þat] at P. thys that F. B. þou] ye G. S. 1154. and] *om.* B. Pr. 1155. or] and b. 1156. fallen shal] may befall b. 1160. ladi] ladyis G. ladyes S. 1161. hem don] do þem T. L. b. do hem S. 1162. but] *om.* P. euermore] ever wher S. euer w. b. 1163. wheþer þei] wherso thow G. 1164. And] But G. S. to] for to P. champartie] truwe partye S. them party L. Pr. 1165. With] Ayenst Pr. þo] *om.* P. those b. 1166. ay] eke F. B. 1167. ai] *om.* S. Be b. 1168. euer] euery P. 1170. and] *om.* G. S. 1172. And] *om.* S. neuer for] for no G. S. þe] neuer G. S. to mych] to S.

93.

Be lusti eke, deuoid of al tristesse,	1173 Be devoid of melancholy,
And take no þouȝt, but euer be Iocond,	
And nouȝt to pensif for non heuynes ;	
And with þi gladnes let sadnes ay be found ;	yet earnest in thy gladness;
When wo approcheþ, lat myrþ most habound,	1177 be mirthful even in woe,
As manhod axeþ ; and þouȝ þou fele smert,	and do not wear thy
Lat not to manie knowen of þin hert.	1179 heart upon thy sleeve.

94.

And al vertues biseli þou sue,	1180 Seek virtue,
Vices eschew, for þe loue of oon ;	eschew vice;
And for no tales þin hert[e] not remue :	take no heed of tales;
Woorde is but winde, þat shal sone ouergoñ.	
What euer þou here, be dovmb as eny stoñ,	1184
And to answere to sone not þe delite ;	answer not hastily.
For here she standeþ þat al þis shal þe quite.	1186

95.

And where þou be absent or in presence,	1187
None oþirs beaute lat in þin *herte myne,	
Siþ I haue *ȝyue hir of beaute excellence,	Give place to no other's beauty in thy heart.
Aboue al oþir in vertue forto shine ;	
And þenk *in fire hou men ar wont to fyne	1191 Gold must be purified by
This purid gold, to put it in assay :	fire, and thou by delay.
So þe to preue, þou ert put in delay.	1193

96.

But tyme shal come þou shalt for þi sufferaunce	1194 In due time thy endur-
Be wele apaide, and take for þi mede	ance shall be paid with
Thi liues Ioy and al þi suffisaunce,	thy life's joy;

1173. deuoid] al voyde S. voyd Pr. al] om. S. 1174. euer] ay G. 1175. And nouȝt to] Ne be not S. 1177. approcheþ] approched C. myrþ] mercy G. 1178. axeþ] axid C. 1179. manie] fele S. 1180. biseli þou] besye the to G. S. þou sue] ensue b. 1181. eschew] eschuwe ay S. 1182. And] Ne S. not] ne S. þin—remue] let not thy hert renue P. remue] remeve G. renewe W. Wz. w. b. 1183. Woorde] Wordis L. þat] hit S. shal sone] sone shal G. ouergoñ] be gone w. begono S. 1185 reads in S : And soone to aunswere þat þou þe not delyte. not] do nat b. na P. þe] om. G. 1186. al þis shal] shall alle P. 1188. oþirs] other b. herte myne] hertes myuul T. 1189. ȝyue] om. S. ȝyue hir] hir ȝyue T. F. B. L. beaute] bountee S. 1190. in—shine] euer to be thyne b. vertue] beaute B. G. 1191. þenk] þenk þat T. P. F. B. L. in fire hou] hou in fyre Pr. ar] ben S. wont] wone G. 1192. in] at G. S. 1193. þe to preue] to the proue Pr. 1194. But] And S. 1195. take] thanked S. 1196. þi] this P.

TEMPLE OF GLAS. E

	So þat goode hope alway þi bridel lede.	
'Despair' and 'Dread' be far from thee.	Lat no dispeire hindir þe wíth drede,	1198
	But ay þi trust opon hir merci grovnd,	
	Siþ noon but she may þi sores sound.	1200

97.

	Eche houre and tyme, weke, dai and ȝere,	1201
Never vary;	Be iliche feithful, and varie not for lite;	
abide patiently, and endure delay; for in the end thou shalt win her.	Abide awhile, & þau of þi desire	
	The time neigheth, þat shal þe most delite;	
	And lete no sorov in þin hert[e] bite	1205
	For no differring, siþ þou shalt for þi mede	
	Reioise in pees þe floure of womanhede.	1207

98.

who is this world's light, the star of beauty, the empress of thy heart.	Thenk hou she is þis wor[l]dis sonne & liȝt,	1208
	The sterre of beaute, flour eke of fairnes—	
	Boþe crop and rote—and eke þe rubie briȝt	
	Hertes to glade Itroubled wíth derknes,	
	And hou I haue made hir þin hertes emperesse:	1212
Take him, daughter, by the hand,	Be glad þerfore to be vndir hir bonde.	
	Nou come nere, douȝter, & take him bi þe hond,	1214

99.

that he may be glad after his torment.	Vnto þis fyne þat, after al þe showres	1215
	Of his turment, he mai be glad and liȝt,	
	W[h]an, þuruȝ ȝoure grace, ȝe take him to be ȝoures	
	For euermore, anon here in my syȝt;	
	And eeke also I wil, as it is ryȝt	1219
Kiss him here in my presence;	Withoute more his langour forto lisse,	
	In my presence anon þat ȝe him kisse—	1221

100.

	That *þere mai be of al ȝoure old[e] smertis	1222
	A ful relese vndir ioy assured;	

1197. þat] shal S. alway] ay S. þi] the p. 1199. opon] on b. 1200. may] ne may G. sores] sorowes L. P. sorowe Pr. 1201. 1st and] om. b. weke] and euery S. dai] om. p. 1202. iliche] ay liche L. cylyche P. lyche G. S. liche C. lyke W. p. W2. w. b. 1204. þat shal] þow shalt S. 1206. no] om. G. S. differring] desyring S. shalt] shall P. om. Pr. 1207. Reioise] Shal [Shalt b.] reioyse Pr. 1208. þis] þe S. worldis] wordis T. G. &] om. B. 1209. flour] the flour Pr. eke] and eke L. 1210. eke] ete w. 1211. Itroubled] doubeld S. 1212. haue] om. G. S. 1215. fyne] syn C. þe] þy S. these Pr. showres] sorowes L. 1216. his] thys F. hire L. 1217. Whau] Wan T. þuruȝ] hy Pr. to be] to S. 1219. eeke also] firþermore S. also I wil] I wil also Pr. 1220. lisse] lesse P. 1222. þere] here T. P. B. F.

And þat oo lok be of ȝoure hoþe hertes   your hearts
Shet wit*h* my key of gold so wel depured,   shall be locked in one by my golden
Oonli in signe þ*a*t ȝe haue recured   1226 key.
ȝoure hole desire here in þis holi place,
W*i*t*h*in my temple, nou in þe ȝere of grace. 1228
101.
Eternalli, be *bonde of assuraunce,   1229 The knot is for ever knit:
The cnott *is knytt, which mai not beñ vnbovnd,
That al þe goddis of þis alliaunce,   all the gods bear record
Satu*r*ne, & Ioue, & Mars, as it is fovnde,
And eke Cupide, þ*a*t first ȝou did[e] wou*n*de, 1233
Shal bere record, & *euer*more be wreke   and will take vengeance on
On which of ȝou his trouþe first doþe breke: 1235 whichever is untrue.
102.
So þat bi aspectes of hir fers[e] lokes, 1236 The culprit shall be erased out of my books.
Wiþ-oute merci, shal fal[le] þe vengeaunce
Forto be raced clene out of my bokes,
On which of ȝow be found[e] variau*n*ce.
þerfore atones setteþ ȝo*ur* plesauns   1240 Therefore be ever of one accord;
Fulli to ben, while ȝe haue life and mynd,
Of oon accord vnto ȝoure lyues ende,   1242
103.
That, if þe spirit of nvfangilnes   1243 that, if new-fangledness and double-ness assail,
In any wise ȝoure hertis would assaile,
To meve or stir to bring in doubilnes
Vpon ȝo*ur* trouþe to giuen a bataile,
Late not ȝoure corage ne ȝoure force fail, 1247 your courage and force may not fail:
Ne non assautes ȝov flitteñ or remeve :   truth must
For vn-assaied men may no trouþe preue. 1249 be proved.

1224. of] on S.   1225. so wel] wel G.   depured] pured Pr.   1226. haue] ben S.   1227. hole] om. P.   in] right in L.   1228. in þe] þis S.   þe] this L.
1229. Eternalli be] Ye be eternally b.   be bonde of] ben bou*n*de & G.   bonde] bou*n*de T. P. L. Pr. S.   1230. is] ȝe T. F. B. L.   is knytt] om. P.   which] the wheche G.   that Pr.   1231. goddis] knottys G.   1232. 1st &] of F. om. Pr.   Ioue] Iuno L. w.   Iuue b.   2d &] as P.   1233. cke] þowe S.   ȝou dide] did you L. Pr.   ded yow P.   did him S.   1234. euer*more] our*more T. L. C.   be wreke] bewreke S. C.   1235. On] Of S.   his] þeyre S.   doþe] to S.   om. Pr.   1236. bi] om. S.   aspectes] the aspectes P. L.   þaspectes S. hir] his P. G.   ferse] first S. fair C.   fyry W. W2. w. b.   1237. Wiþ-oute] With S.   þe] to B.   te G.   þe foule S.   vengeau*n*ce] variance P.   1239. On] In G. S.   founde] found of Pr.
1243. nvfangilnes] reproued Ialousnesse S.   1244. ȝour*e* hertis would] wolde youre hertes S.   1245. or] and L.   1246. giuen] gy*u*ny*n* G.   1247. ne] ner L.   1248. Ne] Ner L.   Nor Pr.   assautes] assayis G.   or] nor G.   1249. men may no] may no man P.   no man may L. Pr.

E 2

104.

For white is whiter when set by black; swet is sweeter after bitterness:	For white is whitter, if it be set bi blak, And swete is swettir eftir bitternes, And falshode euer is drive & put a-bak, Where trouþe is rotid withoute donbilues;	1250
without proof is no security.	Wiþ-out[e] prefe may be no sikirnes Of loue or hate; and þerfor of ȝow t[w]oo Shal loue be more, þat it was bouȝt with wo.	1254 1256

105.

Everything is more prized when dearly bought; love is surer when won with woe.	As euere þing is had more [in] deinte, And more of pris, when it is dere bouȝt; And eke þat loue stond more in surete, When it tofore with peyne, wo & þouȝt Conquerid was, first when it was souȝt; And euere conquest haþ his excellens, In his pursuite as he fint resistence:	1257 1261 1263

106.

So love will be sweeter to you,	And so to ȝow more sote and agreable Shal loue be found—I do ȝou plein assure—	1264
because you suffered patiently;	Wiþ-oute grucching þat ȝe were suffrable So low, so meke, pacientli tendure, That al atones I shal nov do my cure	1268
I will bind your hearts together for ever.	For nov and euer ȝour hertis so to bynd, That nouȝt but deþ shal þe *knot vnbynd.	1270

107.

To make it short—be	Nou in þis mater what shuld I lengir dwel? Comeþ [off] at ones, and do as I haue seide.	1271

1250. bi] wyth P. 1252. falshode] falsenes P. S. euer] om. S. euer is] is neuer L. 1253. rotid] rote P. doubilnes] om. W₂. falsnes w. b. 1254. may] ther may Pr. be no] not be S. 1255. or] nor G. S. and P. 1256. loue] om. P. þat] sith S. for Pr. was] is S. 1257. As] And Pr. more in] in more L. P. G. in] om. T. F. B. deinte] dente W. W₂. w. dente b. 1258. bouȝt] I bought P. aboght F. B. G. S. 1259. þat] om. Pr. more in] in more L. 1260. When it] þat longe S. it] om. B. it is Pr. tofore] be fore P. b. peyne wo] wo peyne G. &] om. G. 1261. 1ˢᵗ was] is S. than b. first—was] whan hit is first S. souȝt] boght B. thought L. 1262. And] ffor S. 1263. he] it Pr. (it it W₂.) 1264. And] Right S. sote and] sett P. 1265. Shal loue be] Loue shalbe b. loue] om. P. do] om. b. do ȝou plein] playnly yon L. plein] pleynly S. (L.) Pr. assure] ensure L. sure S. 1266. þat] if b. þat ȝe] as he P. were] be b. 1267. So low so] Both lowe and b. pacientli] placently S. 1268. That] Than b. nov] om. P. nov do] do now Pr. 1269. ȝour] yon W₂. bynd] bende G. fynde S. 1270. but] saf P. shal þe knot] the knot shal G. S. þe] your P. knot] þnot with the þ scratched through T. 1271. In the margin of F: Conclusio verborum Veneris. 1272. Comeþ] Come ye Pr. off] om. T L. Pr. haue] yow P.

The Lady and Knight united. 53

And first, my douȝter, þat bene of bounte* well,   *gracious to him, my*
In hert and pouȝt be glad, and wele apaied   *daughter:*
To done him grace þat haþ, & shal, obeid   1275
ȝour lustes euer, and I wole for his sake   *I will stand*
Of troupe to ȝow be bounde and vndertake.'   1277 *surely for him.'*
108.
And *so forþewith, in presence as þei stonde   1278 *Then this*
Tofore þe goddes, þis ladi faire & wele   *lady took her servant by*
Hir humble seruaunt *toke goodli bi þe honde,   *the hand,*
As he toforne here mekeli did knele,
And kissed him after, fu[l]fillyng eueredele   1282 *and kissed him,*
Fro point to point in ful *þrifti *wise,
* As ȝe toforne haue Venus herd deuyse.   1284 *as Venus had deuised.*
109.
Thus is þis man to ioy and al plesaunce,   1285 *Thus has this man found*
From heuynes & from his peynes old,   *joy after pain:*
Ful reconsiled, and haþ ful suffisaunce
Of hir þat euer ment[e] wel, & would:
*That in goode faith, *and I tell[e] shuld   1289 *thus are their hearts filled*
The inward myrþe dide hir hertis brace,   *with inward mirth,*
*For al my life it were to lit a space.   1291
110.
For he haþe wonne hir þat he loueþ best,   1292
And she to grace haþe take him of *pite;
And þus her hertis beþe boþe set in rest,   *and set at rest;*
Wiþ-outen chaunge or mutabilite,
And Venus haþ, of hir benygnete,   1296 *for Venus has bound*
Confermed all—what [shal] I lenger tarie?—   *them in one for ever.*
This tweyñ in oon, and neuere forto varie: 1298

1273. bene] is S. ar Pr. bounte] bente G. well] wele T. the welle P.
1274. hert] hete G. wele] om. P. 1275. haþ & shal] shal and hath P. Pr. & shal] so longe S. 1277. be bounde and] by bounde I S. 1278. so forþewith in] soforþe within T. so forth within L. C. W. W2. w. so forth in b. stonde] dyd stande b. 1279. Tofore] He fore S. Before P. b. ladi] om. C. W. W2. w. 1280. toke] eke T. take F. 1281. toforne] before b. mekeli] om. P. knele] þer knede S. 1282. fufillyng T. eueredele] om. B. 1283. þrifti] tristi T. tristy L. P. wise] vise T. 1284. As] And T. toforne] before b. haue] hade L. had W. W2. w. haue Venus] Venus haue G. S. 1286. 2d from] om. S. 1287. haþ] om. S. 1289. That] And T. and] þow T. if b. 1290. myrþe] merthis G. mirthes C. myrthes L. W. W2. w. myrtes b. loye S. dide] that dede G. S. P. b. hertis] hert L. 1291. For] Forþe T. F. B. In P. life] lyf-to telle Pr. lit a] lytel F. B. P. Pr. 1292. loueþ] loned L. 1293. of] to T. 1294. beþe boþe] bothe ben G. in] at B. L. G. S. 1297. shal] om. T. shulde G. S. 1298. forto] to Pr.

111.

Therefore, laud and honour were given unto Venus and Cupid,	That for þe Ioy in þe temple aboute	1299
	Of þis accord, bi gret solempnyte,	
	Was laude and honoure with-in and with-oute	
	ȝeue vnto Venus, and to þe deite	
the Muses magnifying the goddess with their song.	Of god Cupide, so þat Caliope	1303
	And al hir sustren in hir armonye	
	*Gunne with her song þe goddes magnyfie.	1305

112.

All did her reverence:	And al at ones, with notes loude & sharpe,	1306
	Thei did her honour & her reuerence,	
Orpheus touched his harp,	And Orpheus among hem with his harp	
	Gan strengis touch with his diligence,	
and Amphion did his best to please her.	And Amphioun, þat haþe suche excellence	1310
	Of musike, ay dide his bisynes	
	To please and queme Venus þe goddes,	1312

113.

	Oonli for cause of þe affinite	1313
	Betwix þese twoo not likli to desseuere;	
The lovers all prayed Venus that the love of these two might ever endure and increase.	And euere louer of louȝ & heiȝ degre	
	Gan Venus pray, fro þens forþ & euer	
	That hool of hem þe loue may perseuere,	1317
	Wiþ-oute[n] ende, in suche plite as þei gonne,	
	And more encrese þat it of hard was wonne.	1319

114.

So the goddess made a solemn promise,	And so þe goddes, hering þis request,	1320
	As she þat knew þe clene entencioun	
	Of boþe hem tweyne, haþ made a ful bihest,	
	Perpetuelli, by confirmacioun,	

1299. for þe] for b. in] wyth in P. aboute] aboue w. 1301. honoure] om. P. preysing S. with oute] eke wyth out P. 1302. ȝene] loye S. vnto] to Pr. to] vnto L. 1305. Gunne] Can S. Sone T. L. F. P. Soon C. Swete W. W2. w. Gunne with her] With theyr swete b. her] om. L. C. song] songes Pr. magnyfie] to magnyfye S. W. W2. w. did magnifye C. 1307. 1st her] om. S. 2d her] om. w. b. 1308. Orpheus] or Phebus F.—amonges S. L. his] hir P. 1309. his] besy G. S. 1311. Of] In S. ay dide] dede ay ek G. 1312. and queme] and quene W2. the quene w. b. queme] quen P. þe] aud w. and b. 1313. for cause] bycause b. of] or P. þe] þis S. 1314. Betwix] Betwene b. Be twethe G. twoo] tweyne G. S. likli] lusty C. W. W2. w. 1315. louȝ & heiȝ] heigh and low P. b. 1316. Gan] Gunne G. pray] to pray L. 1317. hool—loue] ho the loue of hem G. loue] lyf S. 1318. in] wyt G. plite] wyse Pr. 1319. And] In S. 1320. so] om. Pr. þus S. 1322. haþ made a ful] made a Pr.

by the Lovers: 55

Whiles þat þei lyue, of oon affeccioun   1324   that their affection should last perpetually.
Thei shal endure—þer is no more to sein—
þat neiþer shal haue mater to compleyne.   1326

115.

' So ferforþ euer in oure eternal se   1327   'Thus haue the gods deuised and concluded
The goddes haue, in *her presscience,
Fulli deuysed þuruȝ hir deite,
And holi concludid bi hir influence,
That þuruȝ hir myȝt and iust[e] *providence   1331   that their loue shall continue for ever.'
The loue of hem, bi grace and eke fortune,
Wiþ-oute chaunge shal euer in oon *contune.'   1333

116.

Of which[e] graunt, þe tempil enuiroun,   1334   And then, in the temple,
þuruȝ heiȝ confort of hem þat were present,
Anone was gon[n]e with a melodius sowne,   a ballad with melodious sound
In name of þo þat trouþ in loue ment,
A ballade nwe in ful goode entent,   1338
Tofore þe goddes with notes loude & clere,   was sung before the goddess:
Singyng riȝt þus anon as ȝe shal here: 1340

117.

' Fairest of sterres, þat, wiþ ȝoure persaunt liȝt   1341   'Fairest of stars, whose radiant beams lighten hearts in love,
And with þe cherisshing of ȝoure stremes clere,
Causen in loue hertes to ben liȝt,
Oonli þuruȝ shynyng of ȝoure glade spere:
Nou laude and pris, o Venus, ladi dere,   1345   laud and praise be to you, O Venus.
*Be to ȝour name, þat haue withoute synne
þis man fortuned his ladi forto wynne.   1347

1324. Whiles] Whyle b. þat] *om.* P. Pr. lyue] loue B. of] by G.   1325. sein] fayne L.   1327. ferforþ] ferthermore L. euer] euermore Pr. oure] oon S.   1328. her presscience] oure presence T. P. F. B. L. Pr. hir heghe prescyence S.   1329. þuruȝ] in G.   1330 *and* 1331 *transposed in* P.   1330. holij] hol G. hoole S.—conclude b. hir] fynal G. S.   1331. þuruȝ] by Pr. myȝt] witt S. myth G. providence] prudence *all except* G. S.   1332. hem] hym p. eke] by S.   1333. euer in oon] euermore S. Pr. contune] tyme T. P. F (*corrected later to* tvne, *by Stowe?*). suvn B.   1336. gonne] gone T. p. goon W. W2. w. begun C. begon b. sowne] song P.   1337. In] An W2. w. In—þo] Namely of hem G. Namely of þoo S. þo] those b.   1338. in] with G. in—entent] with good avysement S.   1339. Tofore] Before S. b. with] of S. notes] note P.   1340. riȝt] *om.* F. þus] this C. W. p. W2. w. anon—shal] as ye shul affter S.   1341. þat] *om.* B. ȝoure] oour p.   1342. with] *om.* P. cherisshing] clerisshyng P. feyrnesse S. ȝoure] youres L. stremes] beames b.   1343. in] to L.   1344. þuruȝ] by Pr.   1345. pris] preyse P. L. B. G. b. Venus ladi] lady Venus S. w. b.   1346. Be] We T. P. ffor S.   1347. forto] made to F.

118.

<small>Bright Hesperus,</small> Willi planet, O Esperus so briʒt, 1348
þat woful hertes can appese and *stere,
<small>helper of all lovers,</small> And euer ar redi þuruʒ ʒour grace & myʒt
To help al þo, þat hie loue so dere,
And haue power hertis to set on fire : 1352
<small>honour be to you from all present,</small> Honor to ʒow of all þat bene here-inne,
That haue þis man his ladi made to wynne. 1354

119.

<small>Mighty goddess, day-star after night,</small> O myʒti goddes, daister after nyʒt, 1355
Glading þe morov whan ʒe done appere,
To voide derknes þuruʒ fresshnes of ʒour siʒt,
Oonli with twinkeling of ʒoure plesaunt chere :
<small>we lovers all thank you for your favour to these two.'</small> To ʒov we þank, loners þat ben here, 1359
That ʒe þis man—and neuer forto twyn—
Fortuned haue his ladi forto wynne.' 1361

<small>With this heavenly melody in the temple</small> And with þe noise and heuenli melodie
*Which þat þei made in her armonye
þuruʒ oute þe temple, for þis manes sake, 1364
<small>I awoke,</small> Oute of my slepe anone I did awake,
And for astonied knwe as þo no rede ;
For sodein chaunge oppressid so with drede
Me pouʒt I was cast as in a traunce : 1368
So clene away was þo my remembraunce
<small>sad at losing sight of this lady:</small> Of al my dreme, wher-of gret þouʒt & wo
I hade in hert, & nyst what was to do,
For heuynes þat I hade lost þe siʒt 1372

<small>1348. Willi] Worthy b. so] lady S. 1349. can] canst b. stere] sterre T. 1350. ar] be S. þuruʒ] by Pr. 1351. þo] those b. 1352. power—set] pore hertis so offt sette S. . hertis to set] to sette hertis L. on fire] affere G. a fere L. 1353. of] om. S. 1354 reads in S: þat þis man haue / fortuned his lady wynne. þis—to] made this man his lady P. 1355. O] And S. daister] day sterry P. 1356. ʒe done appere] the sunne apperyth G. S. 1357. þuruʒ] by Pr. siʒt] light G. S. w. b. 1358. with] of P.—twinkyng C. of—chere] as þat hit clerepe S. plesaunt] persaunt G. 1359 reads in S: Nowe we you thanken / þat yow seeþe or hereþe. To ʒov] Now alle G. 1361. Fortuned] Fortune C. Heading before 1362 in b: The author. 1362. And] Right S. melodie] maladye S. 1363. Which] With T. With L. C. W. p. W2. w. om. b. 1364. oute] om. L. 1365. Oute] Forthe b. 1366. And] As P. for] fer L. sore S. b. as þo] I than L. þo] than b. 1367. so] or S. om. L. Pr. 1368. Me þouʒt I] My thought W. p. W2. w. I] om. L. was cast as] lay liggynge G. was ay ligging S. cast as] casted P. as] om. Pr. 1369. þo] than b. 1370. gret] frete W2. w. frette b. 1371. hert] my hert L. was] om. G. S. 1372. þat] for that C. W. p. W2. om. S. lost] clost S.</small>

The Author's Awaking.—L'Envoy.

Of hir þat I, all þe long[e] ny3t,   *for never had I seen so fair a one before.*
Had dremed of in myn auisiou*n* :
Whereof I made gret lame*n*tacio*un*,
Bicause I had neuer in my life aforne   1376
Sei[n] none so faire, fro time þat I was borne ;
For loue of whome, so as I can endite,   *For love of her I purpose here to write*
I purpose here to make*n* & to write
A litil tretise, and a processe make   1380   *a little 'process' in praise of women,*
In pris of women, oonli for hir sake,
Hem to comende, as it is skil & ri3t,
For here goodnes, w*ith* al my ful[le] my3t—
Prayeng to hir þat is so bou*n*tcuo[u]s,   1384   *praying her to accept this trentise,*
So ful of vertue and so gracious,
Of womanhed & merciful pite
This simpil tretis forto take in gre,
Til I haue leiser, vnto hir hei3 renou*n*   1388   *until I can fully expound my vision.*
Forto expoune my forseid visiou*n*,
And tel in plein þe significau*n*ce,
So as it comeþ to my reme*m*brau*n*ce,
So þ*at* her-after my ladi may it loke.   1392
Nou go þi wai, þou litel rude boke,   *Now go thy way, thou little book,*
To hir presence, as I þe comaund,
And first of al þou me recomavnd   *and recommend me*
Vnto hir & to hir excellence,   1396   *unto my lady.*
And prai to hir þat it be noon offence,
If eny woorde in þe be myssaide,   *And if aught be missaid,*
Biseching hir she be not euel apaied ;
For as hir list, I wil þe efte correcte,   1400   *I will correct it.*
When þat hir likeþ againward þe directe :
I mene þat benygne & goodli of *face.   *Now put thee in her grace.*
Nou go þi way & put þe in hir grace.   1403

1373. þere *in the margin, marked by a caret to be put before* al S.   1375 *omitted in* F.   1376. in] *om.* S.   aforne] beforn Pr.   1377. fro] syn the G. sith S. fro time þat] sith that C. W. W2. w. b. syth p.   1378. as] *om.* p. 1379. to write] wryte P. W. W2. w. b. wyrte p.   1380—1403 *are missing in* G. S.   *In their stead there is a long addition, the* '*Compleynt*,' *in both these MSS.*   1380. 2ᵈ a] *om.* Pr.   1381. pris] preyse P.   praise b.   women] woman P. F.   1383. goodnes] goddes P.   fulle] *om.* Pr.   1385 *omitted in* F. B. 1386. Of] O L.   1389. Forto] ffor P.   1390. þe] *om.* F.   1391. So] *om.* Pr. to] vn to F. B. L.   1396. to] *om.* F.   1397. And] I F. þat] *om.* Pr.   1398. in þe be] be in the P. be] *om.* L.   1399. euel] wille P.   apaied] payd b. 1400. hir] she P.   efte] oft P.   1402. þat] the F.   face] hir face T. P. B. F. L. —*For the colophons in the MSS. and Prints, see the Introduction.*

APPENDIX I.

Compleynt.

[This ditty (595) or little book (622), given in MSS. G and S as a continuation of the Temple of Glass, was written by a lover to express his feelings, when he took leave of his mistress Margaret (the day's eye, 395), on the last day of March. In her presence, he cannot speak; she will not help him, or bid him do aught for her, tho' she sees his sorrow and love for her. On this March 31, the Sun rejoices because he'll spend the night with Diana; but the Poet has left his love. He reproaches March for its changes, and describes the charms of his Mistress. He appeals to Fortune to let his Margaret, the day's eye, whose beauty he praises, give him her grace and love in April, for he is hers only, till death; she is his joy, his heart's rest, but alas also the cause of his woe. For her, he is in a fever, first hot, then cold; he ever burns like the lamp of Albiston in Venus' shrine. Never had he felt such pain till this last of March, when he parted from his Love. So he writes her this Ditty to tell her his woe. He prays her to look at his little book; to tear it, if she will, with her soft hands: but rather look on it with her goodly face, and take heed of him, who is hers for ever.]

Allas for thought & inward *peyne, 1
That myn herte so constreyne,
With-oute reste day be day,
Euere sythe I wente a-way 4
Out of 3oure syght, myn lady dere,
That there is no thyng that may stere
Myne dolful harmys nor myn wo,
That ben so fer on me go, 8
With-oute remedy or bote,
Euyn onto myn herte rote,
That wel I fele by myn smert
That I from deth may not astert; 12
And trewely that is lytyl woundyr,
Sythe that we are so fer asundyr,
Myn lyuys lust, myn hertys quene,
So fayr, so good vp-on to sene, 16
That by myn trouthe, wher so I be,
I fare, whan I may 3ow nat se,
As doth the fysch vp-on the stronde,
Out of the watyr brought to londe, 20
That spraulynge deyeth for dystresse:
Ryght so fare I for heuynesse,
Whan I of 3ow haue lost the syght.
More drery than the derke nyght 24
For wantynge of the sterrys clere,
Ryght so forderkyd is myn cheere,

Lych as asshis dede, pale of hewe.
So myn constreynt doth renewe, 28
And cuere encresith more & more;
At myn herte it sit so sore,
Whan that I haue in remembraunce,
Myn owene souereyn suffysance, 32
How I of 3ow myn leue tok,
And in euery membre quok;
For verry wo & dystresse
Ne myghte [I] not a word expresse
Of al myn wo, allas the whyle! 37
For al myn olde peyntede style
Was clene a-gon & out of mynde:
For I ne coude a word not fynde 40
To speke to 3ow, I was so dul;
Fortune hath 3oue me swich a pul
In 3oure seruyse, that al is gon,
And mynne wittys, euery-chon, 44
Bothe tonge, speche & euery del,
Thow I recorde neuere so wel,
Whan I am come to 3oure presence,
Farwel, speche & eloquence; 48
A tunge I haue, but wordys none,
But stonde mut as *any stone.
I fele smert, & can not pleyne, 51
So *hoot myn feuere in euery *veyne,

Title: Compleynt S. La compleyn G. 1. peyne] pyne G. 6. 2ᵈ that] which S. 7. dolful] woful S. harmys] harome S. nor] and S. 11. smert] hert S. 12 reads in S: þat hit to depe wol me smert. 14. are] been S. 18. whan I may] if þat I S. 21. That] With S. deyeth] depe S. 27. as asshis] Ashen S. 30. At] To S. it sit] hit smyteþe S. 33. leue] love S. 36. I] om. G. 37. wo] sorowe S. 40. not] om. S. 44. mynne] my S. 48. Farwel] ffor wille S. &] or S. 50. any] a G. 52. hoot] halt G. hoot myn feuere] am I hoote S. veyne] weyne G.

60   *I am dumb in your presence.   You'll not bid me serve you.*

The wheche I haue so longe enduryd,
Wondyt but myn wou*n*de is curyd;
And ȝee, that myghte ben myn leche,
Ha*u* me for-nome tunge & speche,   56
Wit, & mynde, & al myn thought,
So that wi*th* me is left *ryght nou[g]ht,
But good wil only ȝow to serue,
Wi*th*-oute chaung, tyl that I sterue.
God wot, I haue no more rychesse,   61
Ioye, merthe, nor gladnesse,
But fully theron for to thynke,
Wher so that I *wake or wynke,   64
For to a-swage myn inward smert.
For wel ȝe wetyn that myn hert
Wi*th* ȝow onbit & nat remeuyt[h],
And aftyr mercy cu*er*remor seuyth   68
In ȝow to fynde pete or grace,
Sum reuthe ek in ȝou*r*e goodly face.
And *er I deye for treuthe & drede,
Ay thynkynge on ȝou*r*e womanhede,
On ȝoure beute & semelynesse,   73
Recordlynge ay in myn distresse
ȝoure schap, ȝoure forme, & ȝoure glad chere,
Thow ȝe ben there, & I am here,   76
Allas! tho*urgh* crewel auenture,
ȝoure schap, ȝoure forme, & ȝoure fygure
Amyd myn herte depeyntyd be:
By god, thow I may ȝou nat se,   80
The prent is there so depe I-graue;
And eue*r*emor schal so god me saue,
I ȝow ensure, by myn trouthe,
Thow that ȝe neuere haue on me routhe,
Ne neuere ne wele me do mercy,   85
ȝyt schal I scruyn, tyl I dey,
By god, on-to ȝoure womanhede,

How euere it falle, that I spede;   88
Of whyche ȝyf ȝe han dysdeyn,
It *wolde double al myn peyn,
And castyn me in swich seknesse,
That I ne schulde, in sothfastnesse,
To helthe neuere a-geyn recure,   93
But cu*er*e in malody endure
Vnto myn laste—thys is the trouthe—
For that ȝe leste to haue no routhe   96
Vp-on ȝoure scruau*n*t & ȝoure man,
In al that euere I may or can.
And of on thyng, soth for to seyne,
I haue gret mat*er* to compleyne,   100
That ȝe ne wolde, of al the tyme,
Nothyr at eue ne at pryme,
Comau*n*de me to do ryght nought,
Wherof I haue so meche thought,   104
And ay castynge in myn fantasye,
How ȝe, for ought I can espye,
Of myn seruise haue no deynte,   107
And seye: "allas what may this be?"
Astonyd so in al myn blod,
That I to symple—& ȝe to good—
For ȝoure worthy excellence,   111
That myn kendenesse yow doth offence,
Sythe ȝe [ne] wele In word ne thought
ȝowere serwa*n*t bidde do ryght nought.
What haue I gilt, allas, allas!
Othyr offendyt, in ony cas,   116
ȝou*r*e womanhed * or ȝou*r*e heyghnesse,
Ageyn ȝoure trouthe & gentillesse.
I-wis I se non othyr cause,
To telle shortly in a clause,   120
But only this that myn symplesse
Vnworthy is, to ȝou*r*e heighnesse
To do seruise agreable.
Allas, allas, I am vnable   124

53. wheche] whiche seeknesse S. so longe enduryd] longe dured S.   54. Wondyt] No wonder S. but] þat S. wou*n*de] hert S. 55. ben] best be S. 56. me for-nome] refft fro me boþe S. 57. 1ˢᵗ &] om. S. 58. ryght] ryth G. 62. nor] ne S. 64. Wher] Wheþer S. wake] slepe G. 67. abydeþe S.—remeweþe S. 68. suweþe S. 70. ek] ye haue S. goodly] om. S. 71. er] whan that G. treuthe &] thought er S. 73. beute] bountee S. 75. glad] om. S. 77. crewel] yuell S. 78. ȝoure—forme] Yit ay your shappe S. 80. ȝou nat] not you S. 81. depe] sore S. 82. eu*er*remor] euer S. 85. 2ᵈ ne] om. S. me do] do me S. 86. seruyn] serue you S. 87. on-to] and to S. 89. ȝyf] if þat S. 90. wolde] wele G. 93. To] Myn S. neuere a-geyn] ageyne neuer S. 96. ȝe] you S. 98. I] he S. 99. of] om. S. 102. even S. 103. do] om. S. 105. in] om. S. 110. I] om. S. 2ᵈ to] so S. 112. kendenesse yow doth] lewdenesse doþe yow S. 113. 1ˢᵗ ne] om. G. 116. Othyr] Or you S. 117. or] othyr G. 118. Ageyus S. &] or S.

Of cunnynge—& non-suffysau*n*ce—
To ʒow, myn lady, to don plesau*n*ce,
And ʒe ne wolde of crewelte
Onys [list] to comau*n*de me.   128
And ʒit this vow to god I make,
How eue*r*e it be, that ʒe it take,
To good or harm in ony wyse,
Herte, body, & myn servise,   132
Konnynge, wit, & dilygence,
Absent & In ʒou*r*e presence,
To ʒow I ʒeve & to no mo,
Myn. hertys quen, myn swete fo.   136
Pleynly it may non othyr be.
For lak of mercy thow that ʒe
Me slen & don non othyr grace,
Wherso I be, in ony place.   140
For I am bounde of olde & newe
To ʒow a-lone to ben trewe,
And to no mo in al myn lyve,   143
Ageyn the whiche I ma[y] nat stryve,
Thow that I wolde, ʒe *knowe it wel.
Wherfore doth awey the stel,
I mene the hardnesse of ʒou*r*e herte,
And letyth pete ʒow converte,   148
To clepe me ʒou*r*e owene man,
To serve forth, as I be-gan,
And ʒou*r*e servau*n*t me to calle,   151
And letyth nat swich vengeau*n*s falle,
Myn hertys lady, vp-on me—
Preyinge of ʒou*r*e benygnete,
ʒif that ʒe lyste myn lyf to save,
And me to kepyn fro*m* myn grave,   156
Me to comau*n*de hastely,
Of ʒou*r*e womanly mercy,
Of newe to don ʒow su*m* servise
By su*m* offys or su*m* empryse,   160
Wherwyth I myghte ʒow delyte.
The which[e] thyng but ʒif ʒe wryte,
As I have seyd, to biddyn me,
Myn herte shal neue*r*e in ese be,   164
I ʒow ensure by myn trouthe.

Wherfore on me havith su*m* routhe,
And thynkyth, sythe I am ʒou*r*e man,
To serve as lowly as I can,   168
I can not demyn how that ʒe
Of myn servise havyn deynte,
But ʒe lyste bidde me a-mong
Su*m* servise to vndyrfong,   172
That may ʒow turne to plesau*n*ce.
And ferthere hath in remembrau*n*ce,
Whanne I of ʒow tok last myn leve,
How sore that it dede me greve   176
That ʒe me ʒeve so meche large,
From ʒow to gon wit*h*-oute charge,
The wheche ʒaf my herte a wounde,
By myn cher as It was founde,   180
Of face bothe pale & dede,
Heviere than ony lede.
I trowe ʒe dede it wel espye
By the castynge of myn eye,   184
And also by myn pytous lok,
And how that I for sorwe quok,
For lak of blod that hym with-drow
Vn-to myn herte thus In a swow :   188
I hadde almost ful sodeynly
I-falle there, & cause why
Was that I depa*r*te shulde   191
From thens where myn herte wolde
Fayneste abyde, & euc*r*emor shal,
Wher it is set, not part but al ;
And I a word no myghte speke,
Myn hyde sorwe to vnreke,   196
Wherof I was su*m*del ashamyd ;
For tho of newe was a-tamyd
To me of sorwe the bittyr tonne,
That to myn herte hath I-ronne   200
The sharpe lyco*ur*, so fel & egre,
More than eysel or venegre,
Whiche dede myn herte sore enbrace,
Whan I be-held ʒou*r*e goodly face,
Ful pytously as I forth *yede,   205
[Thenking on youre godelyhed ;]

---

126. myn lady] dere hert S.   127. And ʒe ne] If ye S.   crewelte] youre curteysye S.
128. list] o*m*. G.   129. ʒit this vow] þat avowe S.   134. In] o*m*. S.   135. ʒeve] gaf S.
142. 2ᵈ to] for to S.   143. in] and S.   144. Ageyns S.   145. knewe G.   148. letyth] let S.
152. nat] o*m*. S.   155. ʒe] you S.   myn lyf] me S.   *Lines* 157–176 *wanting in* S.   177.
ʒeve] gaf S.   183. it] o*m*. S.   187. hym] hit S.   190. I-falle] Haue falle*n* S.   192. where]
when S.   193. eue*r*emor] euer S.   195. a] on S.   196. hyde] hertis S.   vnreke] buwrek
S.   205. yede] rod G.   206 *omitted in* G.

The body wente, the herte a-bod.*
So pytously wíth me it stod, 208
That, as me thoughte, thourw myn
  syde
A swerd of sorwe dede glyde,
That made me ful reufully
To loke thanne, so that I 212
Was lych a verry ded ymage.
It sene was in myn visage,
The sorwe that at myn herte sat,
Takynge non hed of this ne that, 216
Save by myn self, at good leyser,
A-syde that no man cam me ner,
To syghyn & to make mone,
And pytously *I gan to grone : 220
I felte so gret aduersite,
That it wolde non othyr be,
Wher-so me were lef or loth.
And wíth the sunne I was rygh[t]
  wroth 224
That he shon so bryghte & shene,
Whil that I felte so gret tene,
And that he shewede hym so bryght,
And of hyse bemys glad & lyght, 228
Whils I was in so gret trouble.
Myrthe made myn sorwe double ;
For Ioye & sorwe a-cordyn nought ;
No gladnesse to an hevy thought, 232
No laughtyr to hym that is in peyne.
For non acord may ben a-tweyne,
But they in herte & thought ben on
To parte, w[h]ere they ryde or gon,
Ioye & wo, euene a-lyche, 237
Whethyr they be pore or ryche.
Wherfore It sat me wondyr sore,
That Phebus alwey more & moore 240
So cler was shynynge In his spere,
Whils I so hevy was of chere,
Awaytynge, whan it wolde reyne,
With me to wepyn & compleyne 244
Myn hidde dol & drerynesse.

But cause, I trowe, of his gladnesse,
And that he was so frosch & gay,
In March vp-on the laste day, 248
Was for that he shulde mete
With Dy[a]ne in the arycte,
His owene lady & his quene,
And al the nyght to-gedere bene, 252
Ful merye as by commyxtyoun,
And make non departycyoun,*
þe nexst[e] day til hit be Eeve,
þat þe Moone takeþe hir leve, 256
And to þe whyte bulle hir dresse.
But I, allas, in hevynesse,
þe same day of Marche þe last,
But fro my lady sithe I past, 260
Of lyf, of dethe al cast in were,
Whas shyning of hir eyen clere
And comfort of þe bright[e] lemys,
Of þe sunne bright with his bemys, 265
Of hir looke so aungellyk,
þat in þis worlde is noon hir lyke,
Ne noon was, with-owten weene,
Heleyne neyþer Polixene, 268
To reken alle hir semlynesse,
To hir of beaute ner feyrnesse,
And hir trouthe boþe in feere,
þat with my lady may appere, 272
For to Alayene my distresse,
To recomforten and redresse
My woful lyff to myrthe ageyne ;
For þer is noon suche for to seyne 276
In al þis worlde, oonly but she,
That may til myn aduersite
Do remedy ne medecyne,
Saue she þat may my sorowes fyne,
To seken out est and west, 281
I mene you, myn hertis rest,
Of whame þis day in ful gret sorowe
I tooke my leve by þe morowe, 284
Ful trist and hevy in weping,
And wonder sore of compleynyng,

After 207 G *has the line :* And gan to louryn in myn hod.   209. thoughte] semed S.
210. A] þe S.   dede] did kerue and S.   212. thanne] vpoñ S.   213. a verry] verray a S.
214. It sene] A seen hit S.   in] by S.   218. cam me ner] might me here S.   219. syghyn]
sryen S.   220. And pytously] fful hevyly S.   I] me G.   223. Wher-so] Wher so þat S.
224. ryght] *om.* S.   229. Whils] Whyle S.   232. No] Ne S.   an] haue S.   234. may ben]
om. S.   a-tweyne] bytween tweyne S.   235. herte & thought] thought and hert S.   236.
To parte] No party S.   249. mete] þanne meete S.   253. commyxtyoun] conjuccyoun S.
255—330 *wanting in* G (*a leaf being cut out*).

þe which may neuer out of mynde.
þus Marche haþe made an hevy cende,
And take his leve ful bitturly,   289
That wot no man so wel as I,
Ne is expert, what þis may meene,
But I allone, þat al sustene,   292
With bone so hoote sette a fyre.
His crueltee, and woful Ire,
Allas þe whyle! hit wol me sloo,
Departing fro my swete foo.   296
O Marche, I may ful wel warye,
That art to me so contrarye,
Proving ay myn hevynesse,
As Iudith ful of doublenesse,   300
Wondurful, and ay vnstable,
Right dyuers and varyable:
Now canst þow Reyne, now shyne,
And so wrongely drawest þe lyne,   304
And al þy cours dost holde:
Nowe art þou hoot, now art þou colde,
Nowe canst þou loude and fully blowe,
Nowe smooþe and stilly bere þe lowe,
Now canst þou snewe, now canst þou
    heyle,   309
And vs with stormes sore assayle;
Ful sceld in oon þou doost abyde,
Gret cause haue I þe to chyde,   312
þat hast þis day so gret delyte,
As hit wer verray for despyte
Of me, to ben so gladd and feyre,
Whylest my lyf hongeþe in despeyre
Of parting, al in dole and dred,   317
Frome þe floure of wommanhed,
Whiche haþe my lyff and deeþe in
    honde,
Bope in water and in londe,   320
And is þe feyrest and þe best,
In whame yche vertue is at rest,
Bounte, youþe, and gentylesse,
Beaute, glad cheere, and semlynesse,

Wysdam, maner, and honestee,   325
Prudence and femynynytee,
Sykurnesse, and assuraunce,
Stylle porte, and gouvernaunce,   328
Lowlynesse, and al-so dred,
Sadnesse ymeynt with goodelyhed,
Trouthe, feyth, & stedefastnesse:
To alle exsaumple & maystresse   332
That lest in vertu for to lere;
To telle hire port & hire manere:
Large in refus & dangerous to take,
*Streytest of grant, ay redy to forsake,
Ferful euere to don a-mys,   337
Ful shamefast & sobre I-wys,
Merour of attemperaunce,
And rygh[t] demeur of dalyaunce;   340
Of worshepe, honour & mesure
She is the welle, I ʒow ensure;
Dotous of tungis, that ben large;
So hol in vertu is hire *charge,   344
In alle hire dedys vertuvous,
And [to] a coward *despitous,
As deth hatynge dyshoneste,
In here entent so clene is she.   348
How meche wit she can ek shewe,
Where as she lest, in wordys fewe!
There is no lak in no degre,
But of mercy & pete,   352
To sweche as ben in hyre scruyse.
Thus may I seyn in myn avise,
That d[i]eth thourgh hyre crewelte,
That leste not on-to me   356
Vnclose hyre lyppys for to speke.
Allas! she is to sore I-w[r]eke,
Sythe that she wele me nat comaunde,
Nor hyre centence countyrmaunde,
In here scruyse ne contune,   361
This day of March—allas, Fortune,
Thyn double whel that can so varye!
Thyn stormy cher may I wel warye,

64   *Fortune, turn my lovely lady Margaret, the day's eye, to me!*

That whylom is so glad & lyght,   365
Now derk as is the donne nyght;
Now fayr & frosch & pleyn of face,
Now frounynd & devoyd of grace;
Now lau[g]hynge, & rygh[t] merye of
    cheere,   369
Now dedly pale & nothyng cleere;
Now bryghtere than the clere sonne,
Now blak as ben the skyis donne;   372
Now as the rose, frosch & newe,
Now as the netyl row of hewe;
Now canst thow sette men aloft,
And now hem plonchyn ful vnsoft,
Doun from hegh felycyte,   377
Swich is thyn mutabylite.
Now canst thow smyle,& make a mowe,
Whan men arn wel from the I-throwe:
Thus may I seyn, allas, allas!   381
That causeles, for no trespas,
Hast mad myn lady most souereyn
Myn symple seruyse to dysdeyn.   384
Allas, therby I wot ryght wel,
But thow turne a-geyn thyn whel,
To make me a-ʒen purchace
Mercy of hyre & getyn grace,   388
Ther is non othyr remedye,
But shortly this that I mot deye.
Now mercy, Fortune, & haue pyte
On myn grete aduersyte,   392
And on myn woful maladye.
And graunt[e] that the day[e]sye,
The wheche is callyd margaret,
So fayr, so goodly & so meke   396
Of flour, of stalk, of crop & rote,
So frosch, so benygne & so sote,

That may a-lone to myn langour
Don remedye, to myn socour,   400
And lyssyn al myn langvissynge,
Of whyche I am so compleynynge,
From day to day, with-oute socour,
For lakkynge of this frosche flour, 404
That hath in curys so gret fame,
And 'petyt confort' beryth the name.
For it can sonde & hele a-geyn
Hertys woundit, that fele peyn,   408
Whos croune is bothe whit & red,
The stalke euere grene & neuere ded,
In medewe, valeyis, hillys & clyf,
The whiche flour pleynly ʒif   412
I myghte at leyser onys se,
And a-byde at lyberte,
Where as it doth so fayre sprede
A-geyn the sunne in euery mede,   416
On bankys hy a-mong the bromys,
Wher as these lytylle herdegromys
Floutyn al the longe day,
Bothe in aprylle & in may,   420
In here smale recorderys,
In floutys & in rede sperys,
Aboute this flour, til it be nyght;
It makyth hem so glad & lyght,   424
The grete bente to be-holde
Of this flour & sone onfolde
Hyre goodly fayre white levis,
Swettere than in ʒynge grevis   428
Is cheuyrfoyl or hawethorn,
Whan plente with hire fulle horn
Hyre sote baume doth out-shede
On hony-souklys in the mede,   432
Fletynge ful of sugre newe;

365. is] was S.   366. derk] in derknesse S.   is the donne nyght] at midnight S.   367. fayr & frosch &] ful of flesshe nowe S.   368. devoyd] al voyde S.   369. ryght] om. S.   of] om. S.   373. & newe] of huwe S.   374. of hewe] and nuwe S.   375. canst—men] sette in hope an hye S.   376. And] om. S.   hem plofichyn] plungen me depe S.   377. from hegh] for frome S.   378 *reads in* S : Curtesye þer wanteþe as semeþe me.   380 *reads in* S : And when I not me overthrowe S.   386. turne] tarye S.   390. this that I mot] þat I may now S.   392. On] Of S.   393. on] of S.   395. callyd] cleped S.   396. & so meke] I you byhete S.   397. flour of stalk of] folke þe floure þo S.   399. a-lone] anoon S.   400. to myn] and eke S.   401. al] also S.   langvissynge] langouryng S.   409. is] is ay S.   410. euere] ay S.   411. valeyis—clyf] in gardin in hil and dale S.   412 *reads in* S : Which is fresshe and neuer pale.   413 *in* S : If I might it at leyser se.   414. at] with S.   416. A-geyn] Ageyns S.   euery] þe S.   417. a-mong] amonges S.   418. as] on S.   these lytyll'e] pleyen þes S.   419. Floutyn] flloontyng S.   420. Bothe in] So fresshe S.   422 *reads in* S : In pypes made of erne spyres.   426. sone] sen S.   428. in ʒynge grevis] any rouhge grevys S.   429. Is] Or S.   431. sote] owen S.   432. On] To S.

Fortune, send me this April the love of my Lady, my joy, my heart! 65

Yit is ther non so frosch of hewe,
Nor half so fayr vn-to myn ye,
As is the lusty dayesye, 436
Whos frosche beute nygh me sleth.
For in hyre mercy [is] lyf & deth,
Ioye, helthe & euerydele,
That in short tyme, but I fel 440
Sum grace in this goodly flour,
I mot be ded of this langour.
*Yit god me sende this Aperylle
In syght therof to han myn fille, 444
More than I hadde in march now late,
Whan I tok leue now at the ʒate
Of this goodly day[e]sye,
With *sighing inward pryvylye, 448
I mene myn souereyn hertis rest,
For whom myn herte wele to-brest,
But she the rathere mercy shewe,
And Fortune ek, in wordys fewe, 452
Do here besynesse & cure,
To helpe to myn auenture.
Now help, Fortune, & have pete!
And help, myn owene lady fre, 456
For whom this pitous wo I make,
Sythe it is only for ʒoure sake,
And for non othyr, by myn trouthe!
Now mercy, swete, & hauyth sum
   routhe! 460
That I may only at the leste
To ʒow fulfyllyn myn beheste,
And myn *avow & oth also,
To servyn ʒow in wele & wo, 464
Whil that I leue, & not departe,
Tyl dethis darte myn herte parte—
That I to myn reconfortynge 467
May han this charg be ʒoure bedynge,
And by ʒoure comaundement,.
With al myn fulle beste entent

To ben ʒoure man in euery thyng,
With-oute chaung or departyng, 472
And ouer this, ay newe & newe
Vn-to ʒoure man, that is so trewe,
How dere of hym that it be bought,
Evene as it ly[e]th in *your thought,
With-oute feynynge or feyntyse, 477
To bidde & charge in ewery wise,
To don in loye, *or in disese
Euery thyng, that may ben ese 480
Vn-to ʒow, myn lady dere.
And letyth outwar[d] more appere
ʒoure inward hidde secrenesse,
So that ʒoure tunge more expresse 484
Youre hertys wil & pryuite
Pleynly, myn lady, onto me,
That am ʒoure owene man I-swore,
With herte & mouth & wil, wherfore
ʒe shulde nat so straunge be, 489
Sythe wel ʒe wete, how that ʒe
Of herte, body, good & al,
And euery thyng In specyal, 492
In verray trewe sothfastnesse
Ben souereyn lady & maystresse,
Myn wor[l]dely goddesse, & also 495
Myn Ioye, myn helthe & ek myn wo,
Myn fulle trust & myn grevaunce,
Myn seknesse, & myn hol plesaunce,
Myn myrthe & ek myn maledye,
Myn langour & ek myn remedye, 500
Myn hertys rest & perturbaunce,
Myn syghynge & myn suffysaunce,
Myn comfort & contrycyoun,
Myn dol, *myn consolacyoun, 504
Myn laughynge & myn wepynge ek,
And cause whi that I am sek,
Myn though[t] a day, myn wach a
   nyght, 507

435. Nor] Ne S. fayr vn-to] fresshe to S. 438. For—is] In hir is mercy S. is] *om.* G.
439. helthe] boope S. 442. mot] most S. 443. Yit] That G. this] in þis S. 444. fille]
will S. 446. now] *om.* S. 447. Of] Al of S. 448. sighing] seyinge G. 450. herte] lyve
S. to-brest] brek and brest S. 453. Do] Doþe S. 458. ʒoure] hir S. 460. hauyth] *om.*
S. 463. avow] awow G. oth] oþer S. 466 *reads in* S : Til deþe smyte me with his darte.
468. bedynge] bidding S. 473. ouer this ay] euery þus hoþe S. 474 *reads in* S : My
thought is sett hit nyl remuwe. 476. lyeth] is S. your] myn G. 477. fyntyse S. 478.
ewery] any S. 479. or] othyr G. disese] destresse S. 480. ben] hym S. 488. wherfore]
perfore S. 489. shulde] shul S. 490. wete] wot S. 493. sothfastnesse] stidfastnesse S.
494. Ben] My S. 496. helthe] welthe S. 498. seknesse] siknurnesse S. myn hol] hole S.
500. ek] *om.* S. 503. confort] desport S. 504. myn] & myn G.

TEMPLE OF GLAS. F

66 *I am in a fever; I burn like the Albiston in Venus' shrine.*

Myn dredful pes, myn glade fyght,
Myn quiete & myn busy werre,   509
Myn pensyfhed bothe nygh & ferre,
Myn softe salve, myn sharpe wounde,
Myn pley, myn penaunns most Iocounde,
Myn holsnm drem whan that I slepe,
But whanne I wake, thanne I wepe;
Myn hertys Ioye, where 3e gon,
And I in langeur ly alon,   516
Nothyr fully quik nor ded,
But al amasid in myn hed,
By-twixe hope & dred apeyrid,
Of myn lyf almost dispeyrid,   520
* By constreynt of myn greete penaunce,
And ofte I lay thus in a traunce;
Myn feuere is contynuel,
That me asayeth stoundemel,   524
Now hattere, than the verray glede,
And now as cold, with-oute drede,
As frost is in the wyntyr mone;
And thanne sodeynly & sone   528
For hete *and cold a-non I deye,
And thus forpossid *be-tween tweye,
Of hasty cold & sodeyn hete
Now I cheuere, & now I swete,   532
And now I am with cold I-shake,
And thanne a brennynge doth me take
Of fer, that may nat quenchid be
With al the watyr in the se.   536
Myn hete is so violent,
Wherwyth myn pitous herte is brent,
That may ben likkenyd to a ston,
Which is I-callyd albiston,   540
That onys whan it hath caught feer,
Ther may no man the flaumbe steer,
That it wel brenne aftyr euere,
And neuere from the fer disseuere,
So they acordyn of nature.   545
And for this ston may longe endure,
In fer to brenne fayr & bryght,

As sterrys in the wyntyr nyght,   548
I fynde, in Venus oratorye,
In hir worshepe & memorye,
Was mad a laumpe of this ston,
To brenne a-fore here euere in on,
For to queme the goddesse: 553
Ryght so myn lady & maystresse
Myn herte, as 3e shal vndyrstonde,
Iferede with Cupidis bronde,   556
That hath—& shal bothe day &
   nyght—
So hot, so clerly & so bryght
Enflaumbid me, in wondyr wyse,
And only brend in 3oure servise,   560
With-oute smoke of doubilnesse,
Chaung[e] or newfongylnesse.*
Qwyt of al, for wele or woo,
Saue of loue—þer ben no moo   564
þat may me lyf or dethe comaunde,
Pleynly þat is no demaunde;
And þer-fore, as ye willen hit be,
I mot obeye, at al degre.   568
And pleynely þus þe game haþe go,
Euer sith I parted yow fro,
Siþen, allas, I sayde amysse
Of oure departing last ywysse.   572
For sithen I had first a sight
Of youre peersand eyen bright,
þe sharp[e] poynt of Remembraunce
Mad[e] no disseueraunce,   576
þat hit naþe stiked in myn hert
Contynuelly, of Ioye or smert,
And not departed truwely.
But witteþe oon thing feythfully : 580
In al my lyf, sithe I was borne,
As felt I neuer suche peyne aforne,
Of no departing noon suche offence,
As whane I went from youre presence,
In Marche nowe þe last[e] day.   585
For euer sithe in suche affray

508. fyght] sight S.   510. pensyfnesse S.   512. penauns] prudence S.   516. ly] lyve S.
519. By-twixe] Between S. apeyrid] enpeyred S.   520. Of] þat S. almost] is neghe S.
521. By] Myn G.   522. ofte] as S.   lay] ley S.   523. is] is so S.   524. asayeth] assayllepe
S.   527. mone] morne S.   528. & sone] shyneþe þe sonne S.   529. and] of G. S.   530.
be-tween] a twethyn G.   533 *reads in* S : And þanne with colde ageine I shake.   534.
thanne a] alfter S.   539. to] til S.   540. Which] þat S.   I-callyd] clepid S.   albiston]
Alobastoun S.   541. That onys] þe whiche S.   556. bronde] honde S.   558. bryght]
light S.   562. Chaunge] Chaunging S.   583 *to end missing in* G.

Myn hert haþe been, in sothefastnesse,
In suche annoye and duresse, 588
þat hit haþe brought me right lowe.
And for by-cause ye shal hit knowe,
My sighing and my woful care,
And euer sith howe I haue fare, 592
Al be I can not tellen al,
To you I wryte in specyal
A certaine dytee, þat I made,
And offt[e] syþes a balade, 596
þe whiche I made þe selff[e] day,
From you when I went away,
With þis compleynt here byfore,
And syþen howe I haue me bore, 600
Day and night, in youre service,
Besechinge þat ye not despyse
þis litell quarell, but doþe grace
For to forgyve þis trespas, 604
If my worde amysse be spoke,
And or þat ye þer-on be wroke,
To casten fully in þe fyr,
I prey you first to maken cler 608
With a goode looke, and with no more.
And if hit shal be al to-tore,
With-outen mercy, and to-rent,
I prey yowe with my best entent, 612
þat with youre owen handes sofft
þat ye reende and brek it offt:
For youre touche, I dare wel seyne,
Wel þe lasse shal ben his peyne, 616
If ye may haue so myche grace,
þat you list with goodely face
þer-on for to loken oones,
And to rede hit efft sones, 620
þer-on wel to beholde,
And þe litel book vnfolde,
Of þe storye þat ye take heede;
I desyre noon oþer mede. 624
And euer of mercy I you prey,
Whedir þat I lyf or deye.
þis is al and some, my lady dere, 627
And I youre man frome yere to yere.

APPENDIX II.

¶ Duodecim abusiones.

Rex sine sapiencia.	Episcopus sine doctrina.	
Dominus sine consilio.	Mulier sine castitate.	
Miles sine probitate.	Iudex sine Iusticia.	3
Diues sine elemosina.	Populus sine lege.	
Senex sine religione.	Seruus sine timore.	
Pauper superbus.	Adolescens sine obediencia.	6

Goo forth, kyng, reule the by sapyence ;	7
Bysshop, be able to mynystre doctryne ;	
Lord, to treu counceyle yeue audyence,	
Womanhed, to chastyte euer enclyne ;	
Knyght, lete thy dedes worshyp determyne,	11
Be rightuous, Iuge, in sauyng thy name ;	
Ryche, doo almes, lest thou lese blys with shame.	13
People, obeye your kyng and the lawe ;	14
Age, be thou ruled by good religyon ;	
True seruaunt, be dredfull & kepe the vnder awe,	
And thou, poure, fye on presumpcyon :	
Inobedyence to youyth is vtter destruccyon.	18
Remembre you how god hath sette you, lo !	
And doo your parte, as ye ar ordeynd to.	20

1. ¶ Rex b.—sapientia w. b.—Episcopus b.   2. Dominus b.—consilio W2. b.   consilo w.—castistate W2.   3. probitate b.—iustitia b.   5. religiose W2. w.   6. Pauper b.—superbus b.—sine b.—obediencia W2.   obedientia w. b.   7. Go w.   ¶ Go b.—forthe b.—kynge w.—reull W2.   rule w. b.   8. Bysshoppe b.—mynyster w.   mynistre b.—doctrine w.   9. Lorde w. b.— trewe w.   true b.—counsell w.   counsayle b.—gyue w. b.—audience b.   10. Womanhede w.   Wowanheed b.—chastite b.   11. lette w.   let b.   12. ryghtwyse w.   rightous b.—sauynge w.   13. do w. b.—lose b.—blysse w. b. 14. kynge w.   15. relygyon w.   religion b.   16. Treu W2.   Trewe w.— sernant b.—dredful w.   dredefull b.   17. poore w. b.—fye on] defye b.— presumpcion b.   18. Inobedience b.—youth w. b.—distruction b.   19. you] om. b.—howe w. b.—set b.—lo] so b.   20. And] Than b.—do w. b.—part b.—are w. b.—ordeyned W2. w. b.

The Chaucer-Prints of 1561 and 1598 (fol. 336 d, in both), omit thou in l. 15, and have be for ar in l. 20. It would serve no purpose to give their orthographical variations.

NOTES.

LINES 1—3. The author seemingly wishes to represent himself in the light of a lover; at least his wofulness in going to bed and his wallowing to and fro is quite in accordance with Cupid's injunctions in the *Rom. of the R.* 2553—2564. See similar lines in *Parl. of F.* 88, 89, and cp. the 5th Statute in the *Court of Love* (l. 334). See also Ovid, *Amores* I, 2, 1—4; and note to l. 12 below.

1. thou3t.] This word is common in the love-poetry of Lydgate's time in the emphatic meaning "heavy thought," "sorrowful meditation," "trouble"; cp. for instance: "take no þou3t," *T. of Glas* 1174; "peyne, wo & þou3t," *ib.* 1260; "gret þou3t & wo." *ib.* 1370; "thought & inward peyne," *Compleynt* 1; "sorwe and thought," *Falls of Pr.* 207 c, *Rom. of the R.* 308, 2728, and *Court of L.* 990; "turment and thought," *Frank. Tale* 356; "care and thought," *Troy-Book* Cc₄ e; "thoght, pyne, and aduersitee," *Kingis Quair* 175, l. 2. Shakspere still frequently uses the word in this sense. Compare further:
"And thus to bedde I wente with thought my gest,"
Court of S. a₂ b;
"Devoyde of heuynesse and thoght," *Reason and S.* 271 b;
"For thought and woo pytcously wepynge," *Troy-Book* T₃ e;
"glad and mery . . . voyde of thought," *Falls of Pr.* 113 b.
constreint.] Occurs again in ll. 11 and 667; see also *Compleynt* 28 and 521. Very common in this context; see, for instance, *Falls of Pr.* 9 b: his [Jupiter's] constreint & his mortal distres; *Troil.* II, 776: joye, constreynte, and peyne; IV, 713: wo and constreynte. Cp. also note to l. 11. The reading *compleynt* in G and S is certainly wrong.

2. pensifhede.] The word occurs also in the *Black Knight* 102; *De duobus Mercatoribus*, MS. Hh. IV, 12, fol. 73 b; *Reason and S.* 237 b; *Compleynt* 510; print w replaces it by the modern *pensyfnes*.

3. To bed I went.] Similar beginnings of these "dreamers": *Rom. of the R.* 23; *Court of S.* a₂ b (see note to l. 1); *Parl. of F.* 88.

4—7. For the meaning of these lines see the Introduction, p. cxiv.
Titan (see l. 32) and *Phebus* are very common in Lydgate for the sun, *Lucina* for the moon. Cp. for instance, *Troy-Book* K₃ a:
"And Appollo is cal'ed eke Titan . . .
And he also ycalled is Phebus."
Life of our Lady, fol. a₆ a:
"she fayrer was to see (*the Virgin*)
Than outher Phebus platly, or Lucyne,
With hornes ful on (Caxton *of*) heuen whan they shyne."
See Koeppel, *Story of Thebes*, p. 73, l. 4.

4. "Lucyna . . . with hir pale lyght" comes also in the *Troy-Book* Dd₁ a; "Lucyna of colour pale and wan," *ib.* fol. A₁ d.

6. decembre.] Cp. *Hous of F.* 63, 111. Chaucer dreamt his wonderful dream of the House of Fame on the 10th of December.
Bradshaw's *Life of Saint Werburge* also begins "Amyddes Decembre," when "pale Lucyna" illuminates the earth.

8. derk Diane, ihorned.] Cp. "Þe mone pale wiþ hir derke hornes," Boethius, ed. Morris 508.

11. Cp. *Troy-Book* $S_6 b$ and $U_5 c$:
    "For the constreynt of his hydde (dedely $U_5 c$) wo";
    Ib. $U_2 d$: "Denoyde of slepe for constreynt of his wo."
    Ib. $S_6 a$: "Aye on his bedde walowynge to and fro,
                  For the constreynt of his hydde wo."
Falls of Pr. 201 a: "for constreint of her wo." Cp. note to l. 1.

12. waloing.] *i. e.* turning restlessly. The word occurs again, in the same meaning, in the *Leg. of Good W.* 1166:
    "She waketh, walweth, maketh many a brayd...";
Wife of Bath's Tale 229:
    "He walwith, and he tornith to and fro."
Rom. of the R. 2562: "And walowe in woo the longe nyght."
Compare also the quotation in the preceding line, from the *Troy-Book*, fol. $S_8 a$; further, the expressions: "walow and wepe," *Troil.* I, 699; "for-wakit and forwalowit," *Kingis Quair* 11, 1. Similar expressions referring to the restless state of lovers during the night are:
Rom. of the R. 4132: "Long wacche on nyghtis, and no slepinge...
                        With many a turnyng to and froo";
    Troil. II, 63: "And made ar it was day ful many a wente";
Dunbar, ed. Laing, I, 68, l. 213:
    "Than ly I walkand for wa, and walteris about."
Cp. the note to ll. 1—3.

13, 14. Cp. *Troy-Book* $Cc_2 b$:
    "And with theyr songe, or he take kepe,
    He shall be brought in a mortall slepe." (*Ulysses and Sirens*.)
"Take kepe" = take heed, a very common expression; cp. Chaucer's *Prol. to the Cant. Tales* 398, 503; *Knight's Tale* 531, etc.

Line 14 struck Hill, *De Guileville... compared with... Bunyan*, p. 35, as being similar to Canto I, 10, of the *Inferno;* see the Introduction, p. cxliv.

15, 16. Cp. *Hous of F.* 119, 120:
    "But as I sleep, me mette I was
    Within a temple y-mad of glas."
This seems to have suggested the title of our poem. See further Pope's *Temple of Fame*, ll. 132—134:
    "The wall in lustre and effect like glass,
    Which o'er each object casting various dies,
    Enlarges some, and others magnifies."
Cp. also *Falls of Pr.* 105 b:
    "Whose temple is made of glas & not of stele" (*Fortune's*),
and *The Isle of Ladies*, l. 72, 751.

17. I nyste how.] Cp. *Piers Pl.*, l. 12:
    "That I was in a wildernesse, wist I neuer where;"
further *Court of S.* $a_3 b$:
    "Thus brought on slepe my spyryte forth gan passe,
    And brought I was, me thought, in a place deserte,
    In wyldernes; but I nyst where I was."
The expression occurs also in the *Hous of F.*, l. 1049.

18. (as) bi liklynesse.] Cp. *Falls of Pr.* 9 d:
    "which, as by likelines,
    Was a place pleasant of larges."
The expression occurs also *Troy-Book* $H_5 a$; $M_5 c$; $P_6 a$; $Cc_6 c$; *Ascm. of Gods* $c_8 b$; *Edmund* I, 464; *Pilgrim.* 161 b; 173 a:
    "A womman as by lyklynesse."
Or may we read "likenesse," as the reading of MSS. T. F. B. L suggests?

Ll. 19—34. Stephen Hawes seems to have had these lines in his memory when he wrote the passage in the *Pastime of Pl.*, quoted on page cxxix.

19. *Hous of F.* 1130: "A roche of yse, and not of steel" (see Introduction, p. cxxiii).

A curious, indirect mode of expression. Cp. *Falls of Pr.* 93 c :
"This Erebus hath, of yron, not of stone,
For auarice built a foule great citie."
Ib. 105 b : "Whose temple is made of glas & not of stele" (*Fortune's*),
a symbolism which is explained by *Falls of Pr.* 127 b :
"Fortunes fauours be made—who loke welc—
Of brotill glasse, rather than of stele."
Cp. further, *Reason and S.* 278 b :
"And the poyntes of eche hede
Nat of Ireñ, but of lede."
St. of Thebes 356 b : "In a Cope of blacke, and not of grene."
roche.] Similarly *Hous of F.* 1115, 1116 :
"How I gan to this place aproche
That stood upon so high a roche."
The Castle of Sapience (*Court of S.* e₂ a) stands also on a "roche"; Nimrod's
tower, *Falls of Pr.* 5 b, is
"Like to a mountaine bilt on a craggy roche."
Many of Hawes's towers or castles stand "on a craggy roche," so the Tower
of Geometry, Chapter XXI ; the Tower of Correction, Chapter XXXII, etc.

21, 22. Cp. *Troy-Book* B₄ d :
"fresshe ryuers, of which the water clene
Lyke cristall shone agayne the sonne shene."
Douglas, ed. Small, I, 50, 14 : "Agane the sone like to the glas it schone."

29. *estres* = "inner parts" of a house. See Skeat, *Leg. of Good W.*, note to
l. 1715. The word occurs again in l. 549 ; *Falls of Pr.* 74 b ; *Reason and S.*
280 a, 282 a ; *Knightes Tale* 1113 ; *Reeues Tale* 375 ; *Rom. of the Rose* 1448,
3626, etc.

30—32. Similar expressions in *Life of our Lady* h₁ b :
"I fynde also that the skyes donne,
Whiche of custome curteyne so the nyght,
The same tyme with a sodayn sonne
Enchaced were that it wexid al light,
As at mydday whan phebus is most bright" (*at the birth of Christ*).
Falls of Pr. 160 d : "Though it so fall, sometime a cloudy skye
Be chased with wynd afore yᵉ sunne bright."
skyes donne] very frequent expression ; see, for instance, *Falls of Pr.* 193 b ;
Albon II, 1131 ; *Pilgrim*. 58 b ; *Compleynt* 372 ; *Flour of C.* 115 ; *Departing
of Th. Chaucer*, etc.

33. The *wihin* is somewhat anticipating, as Lydgate first tells us of his
entering into the temple in l. 39.

36. Of similar construction to our Temple of Glas is the Palace of Priam in
the *Troy-Book*, fol. F₃ a (repeated on fol. R₃ a, and alluded to in the *Court of S.*
e₆ b) :
"He made it bylde, hye vpon a roche . . .
The syght of whiche, iustly circuler
By compase cast, round as any sper."
In this case the monk gives us also the exact dimensions, and shows off his
knowledge of geometry :
"And who that wold the content of yᵉ grounde
Truely aconnte, of this place rounde,
In the theatre firste he muste entre,
Takynge yᵉ lyne yᵗ kerneth thorugh the centre,
By gemetrye, as longeth to that art,
And trebled it, with the seuenthe part. . ."
So our monk had an inkling of the Archimedean value of $\pi = 3\frac{1}{7}$.

37. In compaswise.] So again *Falls of Pr.* 154 d :
"In cumpas wise closed him withoute."
We have several times "In compas rounde" in Lydgate ; for instance : *Albon*
I, 358 : "in compas rounde and large" ; *Black Knight* 39 : "a parke, enclosed

with a wal In compas rounde." So also in the *Rom. of the R.* 4183 : "The tour was rounde maad in compas." Cp. also *Knightes Tale* 1031 : "Round was the schap, in maner of compaas."

bentaile.] *entaile* here seems simply to mean "forme," "shape"; in which meaning it is not uncommon in Lydgate, cp. *Reason and S.* 226 b:
"Of entayle and of fassoun
Lyche the blade of a fawchoun" (*a sword*);
a little lower down Lydgate says that Hercules, Hector, or Achilles
"had no swerd of swich entaylle;"
further, *Falls of Pr.* 63 a: "craggy roches most hidous of entaile;"
Ib. 174 d: (yron barres) "Brode of entayle, rounde and wonder long;"
Albon I, 256: "harnesse of plate and maile,
Curiously forged after moost fresshe entaile;"
Albon I, 242: "Ther was one of stature and entaile, (*Amphibalus*)
As ferre as kinde coulde her crafte preuaile;"
Edmund I, 659, speaks of God's "disposicioun most vnkouth off entayle;"
Pilgrim. 271 a: "And made hym ffyrst off swych entaylle" (*the carpenter his idol*);
Story of Thebes 357 b: (walles) "Passyng riche, and roiall of entaile."
Cp. also *Rom. of the R.* 3711: "This lady was of good entaile" (Venus).

39. wicket.] These "dreamers" usually find access to their Castles and Palaces and Temples through such "wickets"; cp. *Hous of F.* 477; *Rom. of the R.* 528—530:
"Tyl that I fonde a wiket smalle
So shett, that I ne myght in gon,
And other entre was ther noon."
Compare with this the version in *Reason and S.* 268 b:
"Til he fonde a smale wiket,
The which ageyn[e]s him was shet,
And fonde as thoo nooñ other weye."
Further, *Pilgrim.* 9 b:
"And ther I sawh a smal wyket
Ioynynge evene vp-on the gate."
See the Introduction, Ch. IX, § 3, p. cxxiii.

as fast.] This pleonastic prefix *as* is very common, especially before adverbs:
as faste *Troil.* II, 657, 898, 1358; *Chan. Yem. Tale* 94; *Troy-Book* G, d; *Reason and S.* 281 a; as swythe *Man of Lawes Tale* 539; *Chan. Yem. Prol.* 383; *Chan. Yem. Tale* 19, 183, 283, 298, 325, 415; *De duob. Mere.*, fol. 60 b; *Reason and S.* 282 b; as blive *Court of L.* 1441; *Fame* 1106; *Troil.* II, 1513; *Troy-Book* Y, c; as here *Doctoures Tale* 103; as now *Troil.* III, 584; *Shipm. Tale* 52; *Melibe*, p. 178, etc.

44. depeint] p.p. = depeinted. The line is of type C; the full form *depeinted* would make it of type A. The contracted form of the p.p. occurs again in ll. 89, 137, 275, in the last case rhyming with *meint*. Similarly, depeynt : seynt, *Pard. Tale* 488. Cp. also *Isle of Ladies* 712.

45. ful many a faire Image] Cp. *Court of Love* 230.

46, 47. The division of lovers according to their age is carried out at some length in the *Kingis Quair*, stanza 79, etc.; see also the *Court of L.*, and compare *Troy-Book* M₂ a: "Lyke theyr degrees, as they were of age."

50. billes.] These lovers' "billes," presented to the pitiless loved one or to the Queen of Love herself, when she holds her "high parliament," occur in many poems of Chaucer and his school; cp. again ll. 317, 333, 368 of the *Temple of G.*; further *March. Tale* 693, 708; *Kingis Quair* 82, 6, etc.; *Isle of Ladies*, l. 920, etc.; *Assem. of Ladies*, passim; *Court of Love* 577, 839, 916; *Parl. of Love* 83; *Lancelot of the Laik*, Prol. 142; *Hawes's Pastime of Pl.*, Chap. XXIX (ed. Wright, p. 142):
(lovers) "Whiche in the temple did walke to and fro,
And every one his byll did present
Before Venus in her hyghe parliament."

Cp. also Chaucer's *Compl. to Pite* 43:
>"A compleynt hadde I, writen, in my hond,
>For to have put to Pite as a bille."

53. Venus is often thus represented, see *Hous of F.* 130—133:
>'Hit was of Venus redely,
>This temple; for, in portreyture,
>I saw anoon-right hir figure
>Naked fletinge in a see."

Knightes Tale 1097, 1098:
>"The statu of Venus, glorious for to see,
>Was naked fletyng in the large see."

Troy-Book K₁ b:
>"And she stant naked in a wawy see."

In the *Troy-Book*, sign. G₃ b, this is symbolically interpreted (according to Fulgentius):
>"And therfore Venus fleteth in a see,
>To shewe the trouble, and aduersytee
>That is in loue, and in hir stormy lawe
>Whiche is byset with many sturdy wawe," etc.

Fulgentius (ed. Muncker), p. 72, says: "Hanc etiam in mari natantem pingunt, quod omnis libido rerum patiatur naufragia."

55—61. Dido was a favourite and often-quoted figure in mediæval times, owing, of course, to the pathetic treatment of her story by Virgil. Compare Chaucer's *Legend of Dido*, and the Prologue to the *Legend* 263; *Hous of F.* 140 —382; *Duchesse* 731—734; *Parl. of F.* 289; *Rom. de la R.*, ed. Méon, l. 13378, etc.; Gower, *Confessio*, Book IV (ed. Pauli, II, 4 etc.); *Court of L.* 231; *Intelligenza* 72, 3 and 4. Lydgate has treated Dido's story in the *Falls of Pr.* 11, 13; cp. further, for Dido and Aeneas, *Falls of Pr.* 139 d; *Reason and S.* 261 b; *Edmund* I, 275; *Black Knight* 375; *Troy-Book* U₃ b, Bb₃ a; *Life of our Lady* a₃ b, l₁ a; *Flour of C.* 211. There was another version of Dido's story current in the Middle Ages, according to which Dido put an end to herself, in order to escape another marriage and remain faithful to her dead husband. See *Falls of Pr.* 51 c and their original, Boccaccio *De Casibus* II, 10; see also Körting's *Petrarca*, p. 505 and 661; *Triumphes of Petrarch*, edited for the Roxburghe Club, by Lord Iddesleigh, Preface, p. vi; Koeppel, *Falls of Pr.*, p. 93, to whom I am indebted for most of the last-given dates. In our passage, as in *Reason and S.*, Lydgate follows the common version, according to Virgil. Aeneas, as arch-traitor to Troy, plays no very creditable part in the *Troy-Book*, see sign. Y₂ c, Y₃ c and d; Aa₄ b; he is also sharply rebuked for his faithlessness to Dido in the *Troy-Book*, Bb₃ a:
>"And how that he falsede (Pynson *falsehede*) the quene,
>I mene Dido, of womanhede floure,
>That gaue to hym hir rychesse and treasoure . . . .
>But for all that how he was vnkynde—
>Rede Eneydos, and there ye shall it fynde;
>And how that he falsely stale away,
>By nyght tyme, whyle she a bedde lay."

57. "And tak thyn aventure or cas." *Hous of F.* 1052.

59. *Troy-Book* D₃ a:
>"And how that he was false and eke vnkynde
>For all his othes . . ." (*Jason*).

60. The words "alas, þat euer she was borne" agree with *Leg. of Dido* 385:
>"That I was born! allas! what shal I do?"

and with *Hous of Fame* 345:
>"O, welawey that I was born!"

But, at the same time, the exclamation: "alas, that (ever) I was borne," is in poems of that time so commonly put into the mouth of those in extreme distress that Lydgate need not here have copied from either of these two poems; see *Knight's Tale* 215, 365, 684; *Manne. Tale* 169; *Reeves T.* 189; *Doctors T.*

215: *Shipm. T.* 118, 119; *Frankel. Tale* 725, 814; *Duchesse* 566, 686, 1301; *Troilus* III, 255, 1024, 1374; V, 690, 700, 1276; *Cleopatra* 79; *Thisbe* 128; *Cuckoo and Night*, 208; *Isle of Ladies* 1611, 1643; *Black Knight* 484; Halliwell, *M. P.*, p. 115. In *Duchesse* 90, *Monk's Tale* 439, and *Legend of Adriane* 302, with slight variation: "Alas ... that (ever) I was wrought!" Compare also the *Pastime of Pleasure*, Chapter XXXII, where Godfrey Gobelive gives vent to this exclamation, when whipt by Correcciouu (ed. Wright, p. 156).

62. The story of Medea and Jason is given at great length in the *Troy-Book*, Book I, Chapter V, VI, VII (the description of Medea, etc., *Troy-Book* B, b, is by no means the least of Lydgate's poetical achievements); again, in the *Falls of Pr.* I, 8, and in the *Confessio Amantis*, Book V (ed. Pauli II, 236 etc.). Jason is sharply lectured by the monk for his inconstancy in the *Troy-Book* D₁ b—D₁ c.—See further mention of Jason or Medea *Black Knight* 372, 373; *Story of Thebes* 371 b; *Flour of C.* 214; *Reason and S.* 261 b; *Æsop* 4, 100; *Legend of Hypsipyle and Medea*, beginning; Prologue to the *Legend* 266; *Squieres Tale* II, 202; *Man of Law's Prologue* 74; *Hous of F.* 400, 1271; *Duchesse* 330, 726; *Rom. de la R.* 13432, etc.; *Intelligenza* 73, 3. Medea is mentioned, with Circe, as an enchantress in the *Knightes Tale* 1086.

63. falsed = deceived; see *Troilus* III, 735, 757; *Anelida* 147; *Duchesse* 1234, etc.

64—66. Adoun.] Compare *Falls of Pr.* 32 a; *Black Knight* 386—388; *Knightes Tale* 1366; *Troilus* III, 671. Lydgate has also the form Adonés, rhyming with peerelés (*Falls of Pr.* 32 a), and Adonydes, *Reason and S.* 252 b. The prints corrupt the name into Atheon, which could only mean Actæon; see *Knightes Tale* 1445. The Italian form Ateone occurs in Frezzi's *Quadriregio* I, 4, 137, and Taccone wrote a drama *Attrone* (see *Gaspary* II, 216). The story of Actæon is given by Gower I, 53 and alluded to in the *Black Knight*, ll. 94—98.

67—69. Penelope.] See Gower, Book IV (Pauli II, 6 etc.), and list at the end of the *Confessio* (Pauli III, 363); *Rom. de la R.* 8693. High praise is bestowed on Penelope's faithfulness in *Troy Book* Cc₂ c and d; see, further, *Trionfo d'Amore* III, 23; *Duchesse* 1081; *Legend*, Prologue, 252; *Anelida* 82; *Man of Lawes Prol.* 75; *Frankel. Tale* 707; *Troilus* V, 1792; *Intelligenza* 74, s. See also, further on, l. 407; *Flour of C.* 203.

69. pale and grene.] Frequent *formula*; see *Duchesse* 497, 498; *Anelida* 353; *Troy-Book* H₆ b: "Now pale and grene she wexyth of hir chere."

70. aldernext.] Similarly alderlast 247. Alder, of course, is O.E ealra, *of all*; Lydgate has even "for our alder ease," *Troy-Book* Y₃ a; "of theyr alder sorowe," *ib.* Y₆ d; in theyr alder syght, *Albon* II, 888.

70—74. Alceste.] On Alcestis, her transformation into a daisy, and the poetical worship of that flower, see Skeat, *Leg. of Good W.*, p. xxii, etc.; *Minor P.*, p. xxv; ten Brink, *Geschichte der engl. Litter.*, II, 115; Morris, *Prologue*, XVIII; H. Morley, *English Writers*, 2d. ed., V, 133. Compare particularly the Prologue to the *Leg. of Good W.*; *Confessio Amantis*, book VII (ed. Pauli III, 149), and list at the end (III, 364); *Court of L.* 105, etc.; Lydgate's *Minor P.*, p. 161 (Halliwell); *Falls of Pr.* 37 b; *Secreta Secretorum* (Ashmole 46), fol. 127 a:

"Whan the Crowne of Alceste whyte and Red,
Aurora passyd, fful ffresshly doth appere,
For loye of which with hevenly nootys Clere
The bryddes syngen in ther Armonye,
Salwe that sesofi with sugryd mellodye."

See further, *Troilus* V, 1540, 1792; *Frankel. Tale* 706; *Lancelot of the Laik*, Prol. 57; *Flour of C.* 198; Add. MS. 29729, fol. 157 a; *Compleynt* 394—437; Occleve, *Letter of Cup* d, stanza 6 from end; *Flower and Leaf* 348. Compare further, note to l. 510. As is well known, the story of Alcestis has often been treated in poetry and music; in modern times by Hans Sachs, Hardy, Quinault, Wieland, Herder, Handel, Gluck, etc.; see G. Ellinger, *Alceste in d'r modernen Litteratur.* For the mention of Alcestis, and poetical treatments of her story, in ancient times, see Sandras, *Étude sur Chaucer*, p. 58. In the following words "Ce sujet que la science moderne croit retrouver dans la vieille littérature de l'Inde," Sandras alludes, I suppose, to the beautiful *Savitryupakhyana* in the *Mahabharata*.

75, 76. Grisildis.] This is, of course, from the *Clerkes Tale*. The story comes, as is well known, from Boccaccio and Petrarch. has been painted by Pinturicchio, and again treated by Radcliff, Dekker, Chettle and Haughton, Hans Sachs, Lope de Vega, Halm, etc. Compare F. v. Westenholz, *Die Griseldissage*. Griseldis is also mentioned in Lydgate's *Bycorne* 87; *Flour of C.* 199; Add. MS. 29729, fol. 157 a; *Falls of Pr.* A₃ a; 60 b; 99 a (where Lydgate mentions Petrarch's treatment), and again in our *Temple of G.* 405. Also in MS. Ashmole 59, fol. 53 a:

"Gresylde whylome sheo hade gret pacyence,
As it was proeved far vp in Ytayle."

Further, in Feylde's *Controversy* (twice), etc.

77—79. Isolde.] *Confessio*, Book VI (Pauli III, 17). Tristram and La Bele Isolde head Gower's list in Book VIII. See also *Trionfo d'Amore* III, 80, 82; *Parl. of F.* 290; *Hous of F.* 1796; *Leg. of Good W.*, Prologue, 254; *Black Knight* 366; *L. Lady* l₁ a; *Le Dit du bleu chevalier* 299; *Intelligenza*, 72, 7.

80, 81. Pyramus and Thisbe.] Mentioned again, l. 780. Compare particularly *Reason and S.* 256 b, where the story is told; further, *Leg. of Thisbe*, and Prologue 261; *Parl. of F.* 289; *March. Tale* 884; *Confessio*, Book III (Pauli I, 324, etc.), and list in Book VIII; *Trionfo d'Amore* III, 20; *Troy-Book* X₃ d; *Black Knight* 365: "yonge Piramus," see *Temple of G.*, l. 780; *Le Dit du bleu Chevalier* 242, 243.—Of course I might mention Ovid, Shakspere, etc.

81. him Piramus.] With respect to this combination of pronoun and proper name, see l. 123: hir Almen; 130 him Mercurie; *Black Knight* 368: of him Palemoune; *Troilus* III, 834: she Cryseyde; *Non. Prestes Tale* 574: he Iakke Straw; *ib.* 321: Lo hire Andromacha; *Knightes Tale* 352: him Arcite; *Duchesse* 286: he mette, king Scipion; *March T.* 124: him Oliphernus; *ib.* 129: him Mardoche; *Boethius* 293: hym Trigwille, etc.

82—85. Theseus.] See *Leg. of Ariadne*, and Gower's *Confessio*, Book V (ed. Pauli II, 302, etc.); *Hous of F.* 405, etc.; *Knightes Tale*, 122; *Falls of Pr.* 3 c; 14 b; 23 c.

84. Dedalus.] *Hous of F.* 919, 1920 (see Skeat's note); *Duchesse* 570; *Rom. de la R.* 5241; *Falls of Pr.* 86 c. The Story of Daedalus and Icarus is given in *Reason and S.* fol. 259 a and b.

for-wrynkked.] *Leg. of Ariadne* 127:
"for the hous is crinkled to and fro,
And hath so queinte weyes for to go."
Falls of Pr. 14 a: "Labirinthus, diuers and vncouth,
Ful of wrincles and of straungenesse."
Reason and Sens., fol. 251 b:
"For this the house of Dedalus ....
It is so wrynkled to and fro."
Chaucer's *Boethius*, ed. Morris, 2981: "þat hast so wouen me wiþ þi resouns. þe house of didalus so entrelaced. þat it is vnable to ben vnlaced."

86—90. Phyllis and Demophoon.] Their story was very popular in the Middle Ages; see Chaucer's *Leg. of Phyllis*, and Prologue, 264; *Man of Law's Head-Link* 65, and Skeat's note; *Hous of F.* 388—396; *Duchesse* 728; *Rom. de la R.* 13414—13417; Dante, *Paradiso* IX, 100; *Trionfo d'Amore* I, 127; *Falls of Pr.* 37 a; *Reason and S.* 261 b; *Flour of C.* 204; Gottfried von Strassburg, *Tristan* 17193; Dirk Potter's *Minnen loep* 1, 325, etc.; Al. Chartier, "L'Hospital d'Amours." Lydgate represents here, and *Black Knight* 68—70, Phyllis as hanging herself on a filbert-tree. This seems to originate in Gower's *Confessio*, Book IV (ed. Pauli, II, 30):

"That Phillis in the same throwe
Was shape into a nutte-tre,
That a'le men it mighte se;

And after Phillis philliberd
This tre was cleped in the yerd."

See Skeat's *Etymological Dictionary*, under *filbert*, and Webster. This version
is not, as far as I know, borne out by the classics. Ovid, *Heroides* II, gives no
particular tree (nor does Chaucer); see further the short account in *Hyginus* (59
and 243, not quite consistent with each other). According to a tradition
given by Servius (ad Virg. Ecl. V, 10) Phyllis was changed into an almond
tree, which tree seems to be meant in *Pliny* 16, 45; Palladius, *De insitionibus*
61, and 97; and *Culex*, ll. 130, 131; cp. *Spenser's* translation:
"And that same tree in which Demophoon,
By his disloyalty lamented sore,
Eternal hurt left unto many one."
We read further in Rolland's *Court of Venus*, book III, 30:
"The Quene Phillis, and luif to Demophoon,
And in ane tre scho was transfigurat,
[Q]uhen he on sey be storme was tribulat."
Our version with the filbert tree, however, seems to have sprung from one of
Virgil's Eclogues (VII, 63):
"Phyllis amat corylos; illas dum Phyllis amabit,
Nec myrtus vincet corylos, nec laurea Phoebi."

92, 93. Paris & Eleyne.] See particularly *Troy-Book* II, Chapter XIII,
where the rape of Helen is narrated in detail. See also *Duchesse* 331; *Parl. of
F.* 290, 291; *Legend*, Prologue 254; *Hous of Fame* 399; *Squieres T.* II, 202;
Man of Law's Prologue 70; *March. Tale* 510; *Troil.* I, 62, 455; V, 890; *L.
Lady* a,b; l,a; *Flour of C.* 191; *Albon* I, 475; *Intelligenza* 71, l. 8.
Line 93 occurs nearly word for word in the *Troy-Book* II, b:
"This fayre Eleyne, this fresshe lusty quene."

94, 95. Achilles and Polyxena.] *Troy-Book* IV, Chapter XXXII, tells how
Achilles was treacherously slain in Troy; see also *Falls of Pr.* I, 21. Cp. further
Duchesse 1067 (and Skeat's note); *Parl. of F.* 290; *Legend*, Prologue 258; *Troil.*
I, 455; *Black Knight* 367; *Flour of C.* 190; *T. of Glas* 785 and 786; *Intelligenza*
72, 1.₂ and 273, 1.₂.

97—99. Philomene.] See Chaucer's *Leg. of Philomela; Gower*, book V (ed.
Pauli, II, 313, etc.); also *Troil.* II, 64—70; *Falls of Pr.* 9 a; *Black Knight*
374; *Kingis Quair*, stanza 55. The above form of the name, instead of Philomele, is common in the Middle Ages, not only in England. There was, for
instance, a *Hist. of Felix and Philomena*, acted 1584 (interesting with respect to
The Two Gent. of Ver.); the name of the maid in Ayrer's *Pelimperia* is Philomena; Lope de Vega wrote a *Philomena*, and Gascoigne a *Complaint of Philomene*. In the *Kingis Quair* 62, 1, Philomene rhymes with *quene* (see Skeat's
note); *ib.*, 110, 3 with *schene;* in Lydgate, *Falls of Pr.* 9 a, with *eleane;* Gower
rhymes the name with *tene, betwene, sene, grene, mene;* Andrew of Wyntoun
(*Cronykil* II, 1913) with *kene;* Pulci, *Morgante maggior.* I, 3, 1 with *pena*.

100, 101. Lucrece.] See *Livy* I, 57—59; Ovid, *Fasti* II, 721—852 (and, of
course, Shakspere, Thomas Heywood, etc.). Chaucer has also treated the story
in the *Leg. of Luc.;* cp. also the Prologue 257, and Skeat, *Legend*, p. xxxi; St.
Augustine, *De civ. Dei. caput* XIX; *Gesta Rom.*, Tale 135; Gower, *Confessio*,
book VII (ed. Pauli, III, 251 etc.), and, again, the list in the eighth book.
Lydgate has treated the same story in the *Falls of Pr.* II, 5; and, again, III, 5
(see Koeppel, *Falls of Pr.* p. 66, 93). See further *Life of our Lady* a,b; *Flour
of C.* 201; *Edmund* I, 277; and Lydgate's *Poem on the Mar. of Humphrey and
Jacqueline* (MS. Add. 29729, fol. 158 b); further, *Duchesse* 1082 (and Skeat's
note); *Frank. Tale* 669—672; *Man of L. Prol.* 63; *Anelida* 82; *Rom. de la
Rose* 8649; Boccaccio, *De claris Mul.* 46.

100. The expression: to *halowe a feast* occurs often; for instance, *Troy-Book*
H,a; S,d; T,a; *Falls of Pr.* 14 b; 174 c, etc.

102—110. Palamon and Arcite.] This, of course, is from the *Knightes Tale*.
Lydgate alludes to the same story again in the *Black Knight* 368, and *Story of
Thebes*, fol. 372 d. Many of the expressions in our passage agree word for word

with the *Knightes Tale*; cp. *Kn. T.* 219 : He caste his eyen upon Emelya (see also 238); 13 : eek hire yonge suster Emelye ; 114 : Emelye hire yonge suster scheue ; 177—179 :
"Emelie, that fairer was to seene
Than is the lilie on hir stalke grene,
And fresscher than the May with floures newe ; "
190 : I-clothed was sche fressh for to devyse ; 210 : the fresshe Emely the scheene. Line 976 speaks of the "stryf and jelousye," l. 1926 of the "stryf and rancour" between the two brothers. If Shirley, in l. 82, speaks of *Duc* Theseus, it is quite in accordance with the *Knightes Tale*, where Theseus is often called "Duke," see l. 2, 15, 35, etc. We have a "Duke Theseus" also in the *Falls of Pr.* 15 a, 23 b, etc. ; a "Duke Hannibal" in the *Falls of Pr.*, a "Duke Moyses" in the *Secreta Secretorum*, etc.

105. These "castings of an eye" were very dangerous at that time ; cf. *Troy-Book* Aa₂ b :
"Whan that he was wounded to the herte,
With the castynge oonly of an Eye" (*Achilles*).
De duobus Merc. (MS. Hh. IV. 12, fol. 62 a) :
"Cupides dart on me hath made arest,
The clere stremys of castyng of an eye :
Thys is the arow that causyth me (for) to deye."
See again ll. 231, 232, and compare *Merciless Beaute*, l. 1 etc., *Troilus* II, 534, etc.

110. Chaucer.] Lydgate is fond of introducing the name of his great "master" into his writings. Koeppel, *St. Thebes*, p. 78, has pointed out the instances in the *Story of Th.*, and in the *Falls of Pr.*, namely *St. Th.*, Prologue, fol. 356 a and b ; fol. 377 e (Chaucer-edition of 1561) ; *Falls of Pr.*, Prologue, fol. A₂ b, I, 6 (fol. 8 d), VI, 16 (fol. 164 e, *Leg. of Antony and Cleopatra*) :
"Thyng once sayd by labour of Chaucer,
Wer presumpcion me to make agayn " ;
VIII, 6 (fol. 180 a) ; IX, 38 (fol. 217 c), to which II, 4 (fol. 46 a) and III, 18 (fol. 9Q c) may be added. I have made note of the following occurrences in other works : *Troy-Book* N₃ a :
"And Chauncer now, alas ! is nat alyue,
Me to refourme, or to be my rede ;
For lacke of whom slower is my spede ;
The noble Rethor, that all dyde excelle :
For in makynge he dranke of the welle
Under Pernaso, that the muses kepe,
On whiche hylle I myght neuer slepe
Unneth slombre, for whiche, alas, I playne."
See further *ib.*, l₄ c and d (*Story of Cryseyde*); Q₄ d (*Troilus*) ; Dd₃ c ; *Court of S.* a₂ a (see Introduction, p. cxxvii, note 1, together with Gower) ; *Horse, goose, and sheep*, 76 and 77 (see note to ll. 141, 142) ; *Life of our Lady* c₁ b :
"And eke my master chauceris now is graue . . ."—
(a well-known passage, see Morris's *Chaucer* I, 81) ; *Flour of C.* 236 ; *Minor P.* (Halliwell), p. 28 and 128 ; the *Serpent of Division* (see Miss Toulmin Smith's *Gorboduc*, p. xxi) ; Translation of *Deguileville's First Pil.*, MS. Cott. Vit. C. XIII, fol. 256 b and 257 a (see Skeat, *M. P.*, p. xlviii ; Dr. Furnivall's *Trial Forewords*, pp. 13—15 and 100 ; *Hill*, pp. 8, 9).

Does "my maister" in *Chorl and Bird*, 380, also refer to Chaucer ? The *Court of S.*, fol. f₁ b, speaks of "Galfryde the poete laureate " ; but this, I believe, refers to Geoffrey de Vinsauf, the highly-celebrated author of the *Nova Poetria*, not to Chaucer. Galfridus de Vinosalvo, also called "Galfridus Anglicus." wrote a didactic poem "*De nova Poetria*" (dedicated to Pope Innocent III.), a monody on the death of Richard I., and treatises on Rhetoric and Ethics (see Morley, *English Writers* I, 603 and 604). He is very frequently quoted by poets of that time, and celebrated for his "purpurat colours of rhetorike." Chaucer's humorous allusion to him in the *Nonne Prestes Tale* (l. 527, etc.) is well known. He is further unmistakab'y quoted by Bokenam, *Prol.* 83, etc. (Horstmann, *Introduction*, p. xi, is on the wrong track in believing that Chaucer is meant in this passage):

"Aftyr the scole of the crafty clerk
Galfryd of Ynglond, in his newe werk,
Entytlyd thus, as I can aspye:
'Galfridus anglicus,' in his newe poetrye," etc.

Cp. also "Galfryd of Ynglond" in I, 171, Chaucer being mentioned in addition, together with Gower and Lydgate, further on, l. 177.

The poem by the "Dull Ass" (cp. *Introduction*, p. cxlii) in MS. Fairfax mentions both, Chaucer and Geoffrey de Vinsauf, side by side (fol. 309 a):

"Cum oñ, Tulius, with sum of thy flouris;
Englesshe geffrey with al thy colourys,
That wrote so wel to pope Innocent;
And mayster Chauser, sours and fundement
On englysshe tunge swetely to endyte—
Thy soule god haue with virgynes white!—
Moral gower, lydgate, Rether and pocte;
Ouide, stase, lucan of batylls grete" . . .

Chaucer and his older namesake are similarly put together in *Little John* (Speght's *Chaucer*, 1598, fol. c. ii):

"O cursed death, why hast thou those poets slain,
I meane Gower, Chaucer, and Gaufride."

It is thus extremely doubtful to me that the "Galfride" in the *Court of Love* (l. 11) is intended for Chaucer, as Skeat, *Chaucer's Minor Poems*, p. xxxii, maintains.

112—116. Phoebus and Daphne.] The story is alluded to in *Reason and S.* 236 a and 247 a, and told at length in the *Confessio*, book III (ed. Pauli I, 336), where Cupid "casts a dart throughout Phebus' heart"—

"Which was of golde and all a fire,
That made him many fold desire
Of love more than he dede.
To Daphne eke in the same stede
A dart of led he caste and smote,
Which was all colde and no thing hote."

In a similar way we have in the *Kingis Quair*, stanza 95, a reference to Cupid's different species of arrows, viz., of gold and steel, with the addition of silver ones, which, it seems, King James introduced on his own account. This fiction comes from the *Rom. de la R.*, where (English Translation 918, etc.) Swete-lokyng, in attendance on Cupid, carries two bows, made of different kinds of wood, and two sets of five arrows, the first of which is of gold. Lydgate has introduced this into *Reason and S.* (MS. Fairfax 16, fol. 277 a, etc.); his first bow is made of ivory, the second black, full of "knottys" and "skarrys." The names of all ten arrows are given as in the *Rom. de la R.*, and it is stated that the first set had heads of gold, the second of lead. Cf. also *St. Thebes*, fol. 363 b:

"That his [*Cupid's*] arowes of golde, and not of stele
Yperced han the knightes hertes tweine."

Spenser also speaks of Cupid's "bow and shafts of gold and lead" (*Colin Clout*, l. 807), and we read in the *Court of L.* 1315 and 1316:

"The Golden Love, and Leden Love thay hight:
The tone was sad, the toder glad and light."

"The arrow of gold" occurs again in *T. of Glas* 445, and in *Reason and S.*, fol. 236 a, where the story of Daphne is told. Cp. also Watson's sonnet 63, where the first book of Conrad Celtis's *Odes* is quoted. Barnfield, in his *Tears of an affectionate Shepherd* (Arber, p. 6), speaks of

"Death's black shaft of steel, Love's yellow one of gold."

Line 114, with its allusion to Cupid's envy, is explained by the following passage from *Troy-Book* K₃ a, which speaks of Apollo's victory over the dragon Python:

"For of Pheton he had the victorye,
Whan he hym slewe, to his encrease of glorye,
The great serpent, here in erthe lowe,
With his arowes and his myghty bowe,
Of whiche conqueste the great[e] god Cupyde
Hadde enuye, and euen thorugh the syde
He wounded hym, depe to the herte,
With ye arowe of gold, y^t made hym sore smerte."

This goes back to Ovid, *Metam.* I, 452 etc.

The amours of Phœbus are also alluded to in *Black Knight* 358—364, and *Troilus* I, 659—665; the whole story of Phœbus and Coronis is given in Gower's *Confessio* I, 305 etc., and in Chaucer's *Manciples T.* (according to Ritson, a Fable of Lydgate, No. 46 of his list).

115. Daphne.] *Diane*, the reading of MSS. T. P. F. B, is of course wrong, as Daphne is meant; but perhaps I might have left the *Dane* of MS. G in the text; see *Knightes T.* 1204—1206:
"Ther sawgh I Dane yturned til a tree,
I mene nought the goddesse Dyane,
But Peneus doughter, which that highte Dane."

To discriminate between three names as similar as Diana, Danae, and Daphne was too much for the Middle Ages; so Dafne occurs for Danae in Edition B of Calderon's *La Vida es Sueño* III, 560. See further *Troilus* III, 677—679 (with the form *Dane*); *Black Knight* 64; *Reason and S.* 236 a (Fairfax MS. 16 has rightly *Daphne*); *Court of L.* 824: Dane = Danae; both names, Daphne and Danae, occur close together in *Reason and S.*, with curious spellings in MS. Fairfax 16, fol. 247 a.

117—120. Jupiter and Europa.] See *Leg. of Good W.*, Prologue 113; *Troilus* III, 673; *Falls of Pr.* I, 7; *Reason and S.* 247 a; *Troy-Book* A₆ d; *Court of L.* 823; *Court of S.* g₂ a:
"He come an oxe, and toke Europa, they sayd,
Wherfore the bole they worshyp of theyr grace."

117. For *Jores cope*, see the Introduction, Chapter X, p. cxl.

121—123. Amphitryon and Alcmene.] See also Gower's *Confessio*, Book II, ed. Pauli 1, 242 (where Amphitryon supplants his friend Geta in the love of Alcmene). "Alcmenia" is also mentioned *Court of Love* 821.

124. for al his deite.] Similarly *Troy-Book*, A₈ d:
"for all his deyte (*Jupiter and Alcmene*)
He was rauysshed thurgh luste of hir beautie."

Falls of Pr. 9 b: "As he that was, for al his deitie, (*Jupiter and Europa*)
Supprised in hert with her great beautie."

Troy-Book D₆ b: "Iubiter, for all his deyte,
Upon Dyane (!) begat them all[e] thre."
(*Helen, Castor and Pollux.*)

Falls of Pr., fol. 8 h: (Isis) "enclined her heart vnto his deitie."

Cp. also Petrarch, *Trionfo d'Amore* I, 159, 160:
"E di lacciuoli innumerabil carco
Vien catenato Giove innanzi al coro."

126—128. Mars & Venus.] Alluded to again in stanza 3 d. See further, Chaucer's *Compl. of Mars*, and *Compl. of Venus*, and Skeat's note, *M. P.*, p. 274 (to the classical names given there, Lucian might be added); Gower's *Confessio*, Book V (ed. Pauli II, 148); *Knightes Tale* 1525; *Troil.* III, Proem 22; III, 675 ("Cyphes" in Morris must surely mean *Cypris*). Compare *Reason and S.* 254 a:
"the bed of Vulcanus,
Al with cheynes rounde enbracyd,
In the which he hath ylacyd
Hys wyf Venus and Mars yfere,
Whañ Phebus with hys bemys clere
Discurede and be-wreyed al,

And al the goddys celestial
Of scorne and of derisioun
Made a congregacioun." . . .
In the *Troy-Book*, A₁ a the monk invokes Mars thus:
"Nowe for the loue of Vulcanus wyfe,
With whom whylom yᵘ were at myschef take,
So helpe me now, onely for hir sake."
Lines 127 and 128 are similar to ll. 621—623 of the *Black Knight:*
"For that joy thou haddest when thou leye
With Mars thi knyght, when Vulcanus yow founde,
And with a cheyne unvisible yow bounde."
Curiously enough, the monk is quite on the side of the guilty couple; see *Reason and S.* 254 a; *Black Knight* 389—392:
"But Vulcanus with her no mercy made,
The foule chorle had many nyghtis glade,
Wher Mars, her *worthy* knyght, her *trewe* man,
To fynde mercy comfort noon he can."
In the *Troy-Book*, K₄d, he vents his spite on Phoebus, who awoke them, thus:
"And for that he so falsely them awoke,
I haue hym sette laste of all my boke."

129—136. Mercury and Philology.] This alludes to Martianus Capella's work, *De Nuptiis Philologiæ et Mercurii*, which was much read in the Middle Ages (see *Warton-Hazlitt* III, 77; ten Brink, *Chaucer-Studien*, p. 99; Koeppel, *St. Thebes*, p. 25 and 74; Skeat, *M. P.*, p. 344). Chaucer mentions him, *March. Tale* 488; *Fame* 985; so does Bennet Burgh in an Epistle to Lydgate, MS. Add. 29729, fol. 6 a. See further, *Story of Thebes*, fol. 360 a and b, and *Falls of Pr.* 67 d:
"Mercury absent and Philologie."
Edmund I, 99: "For Mercurie nothir Philologie,
To-gidre knet and ioyned in mariage,
Withoute grace may haue noon auauntage."
A similar passage to that in our text occurs in Lydgate's poem on the marriage of Duke Humphrey and Jacqueline of Holland, Stowe's MS. Addit. 29729, fol. 160 a:
(and Hymenæus, thou) "Make a knott, feythfull and entiere,
As whylome was betwene phylogonye (!)
And Mercury eke, so hyghe aboue yᵉ skye,
Wher yᵗ Clye, and eke Calyope,
Sange wᵗ hir sustren in nombre thryes thre."

132. god of eloquence.] The article, as supplied by the Prints, is not necessary; see again, l. 572: "To god of loue"; so also *Troil*. I, 967; *Black Knight* 304; *Rom. of the Rose* 3289. Mercury is very commonly called the "god of eloquence" by Lydgate; cp. for instance, *Assembly of Gods* b₁ b:
"In eloquence of langage he passed all the pake."
Troy-Bk. G₃ a: "The sugred dytees, by great excellence,
Of rethoryke, and of eloquence,
Of whiche this god is soueraygne & patrowne."
Ib. G₃ b: "This god of eloquence kynge."
Ib. K₃ d (Mercurius):
"That in speche hath moste excellence,
Of rethoryke, and sugred eloquence,
Of musyke, songe and Armonye
He hath lordshyp, and hole the regalye."
St. Thebes 357 a: "Marcurie, God of eloquence."
Secreta Secr. 124 b: "In Rethoryk helpith Mercuryvs."
Falls of Pr. 67 a: "Wynged Mercury, chief lord and patron
Of eloquence, and of fayre speakyng."
Ib. 168 b: "Mercury, God of eloquence."
See particularly the description of Mercury in *Reason and S.* 225 a, etc.

Compare also the *Interpretation of the names of the gods and goddesses*, prefixed
to the *Assembly of Gods*, where "Marcuryus" is called the "God of langage."
Cf. further Dunbar, *Golden Targe* 116, and Lyndsay's *Dream*, 393 :
"Than we ascendit to Mercurious,
Quhilk Poetis callis god of Eloquence,
Rycht Doctourlyke, with termes delicious,
In arte exparte, and full of sapience."

136. Istellified.] Occurs frequently; see *Hous. of F.* 1002; *Legend*, Prologue
525; *Troy-Book* B₁ c (referring to Callisto); *ib.* I₃ b (Castor and Pollux); *Falls of
Pr.* 65 a (Romulus); *ib.* 107 b (Alexander), etc. In our passage the word scarcely
means "placed as a star in the firmament," but "received into heaven and
there glorified"; cp. *Pilgrimage*, MS. Cott. Tib. A. VII, fol. 48 a :
[Cyprian] "is in heuene stelleffyed,
And with seyntis gloreffyed."
The French original here has only : "Et est ou ciel glorifie."
Cp. also Skelton, *Garland of Laurel* 961 :
"I wyll my selfe applye . . . .
Yow for to stellyfye."

137—142. The story of Canace is the subject of the unfinished *Squieres T.*
Waldron, as quoted by Park in *Warton-Hazlitt* III, 63, note 3, seems to think
that our passage proves that Chaucer wrote more of this Tale than is now exist-
ing; but the passage hardly bears out this supposition: ll. 138—140 are
sufficiently illustrated in Chaucer's Tale; with ll. 141 and 142 compare *Squieres
T.*, II, 317—320 :
"And after wol I speke of Algarsif,
How that he wan Theodora to his wif,
For whom ful oft in great peril he was,
Nad he ben holpen by the hors of bras."
MS. Ashmole 53 gives John Lane's continuation of the Story; on the back
of the last leaf 81, Ashmole has written ll. 137—142 of the *T. of Glas* (see Dr.
Furnivall's edition, p. 237). Spenser's version of part of the Story in the *Faerie
Queene*, Book IV, is well-known; cf. also Milton's *Penseroso :*
"Or call up him that left half told
The story of Cambuscan bold,
Of Camball, and of Algarsife,
And who had Canace to wife,
That own'd the virtuous ring and glass;
And of the wondrous horse of brass,
On which the Tartar King did ride."
This Canace is mentioned again by Lydgate in *Flour of Curtesie*, l. 206.
The magic mirror of Canace occurs also in Douglas's *Palice of Honour* I, 57, 11
(ed. Small) :
"Or ʒit the mirrour send to Canace,
Quhairin men micht mony wonders se."
Not to be confused with this Canace is the other Canace, whose story is told
in Ovid's *Heroides*, ep. XI. Gower introduced it at the beginning of Book III
of the *Confessio*, and Chaucer's allusion to it in the *Man of L.'s* Prologue, l. 77, etc.,
is well known. It has been advanced that Chaucer meant, in this passage, rather
to humour his "moral" friend than to censure him; a further argument in favour
of this opinion would be that our monk also did not take exception to this story,
but introduced it at great length into the *Falls of Pr.* I, 22 and 23), evidently,
moreover, making use of this very narrative of Gower's (see Koeppel, *Falls of Pr.*,
p. 98). This story from the *Falls of Pr.* is very highly praised by Gray in his
article on Lydgate (*Works*, ed. Matthias II, 66, 67), and is also the very one
selected in Thomas Campbell's *Specimens of the British Poets*, p. 15. See also
Legend, Prologue 265, and Thomas Feylde's *Controversy.* Gottfried von Strassburg mentions this Canace also (*Tristan* 17194); so does Petrarch in the *Trionfo
d'Amore* II, 181—183, and Skelton, *Garland of Laurel* 934; Sperone Speroni
wrote a drama *Canace.*
There is a third person with the very similar name Caudace, connected with

TEMPLE OF GLAS.   G

the Alexander-Saga ; she is mentioned, *Parl. of F.* 288 ; *Ballade on Newfangelnesse*, l. 16 ; Gower, *Confessio*, Book V (ed. Pauli, II, 180). Cp. further Thomas Feylde's *Controversy*, fol. B₄b, where "Candacys" is mentioned ; MS. Ashmole 59, folio 52 b :

"And ryche was eeke þe faire qwene Candace."
Life of our Lady, l₁a : "Riche candace of ethyope quene."

The last line reminds one at once of Candace, queen of the Ethiopians, whose eunuch Philip baptized (Acts viii, 27). According to Pliny (VI, 35), "Candace" was a transmitted title of the Ethiopian queens ; cp. also Strabo XVII, 820, Dio Cassius 54, 5, and Suidas. For the story of Alexander, Candace, and her son Candaules, see especially, *Wars of Alexander*, l. 5090, etc. (ed. Skeat, p. 257) ; *Kyng Alisaunder*, ed. Weber, p. 305, etc. ; *Intelligenza* 229, etc. : *Li Romans d'Alixandre*, by Lambert li Tors and Alexandre de Bernay, ed. Michelant 371, etc. ; 380, etc. This story goes back to the *Pseudo-Callisthenes* III, 18, etc.— Calderon, in *La Sibila del Oriente*, has a King Candaces of Egypt, reigning at the time of Solomon.

138. For the magic power of Canace's ring, see *Squieres Tale* I, 138, etc. ; for that of the "stede of bras," *ib.*, I, 107, etc.

139. ledne] = language ; comp. *Squieres T.* II, 89, 90, 132 ; *Albon* II, 873 ; *Warton-Hazlitt* II, 58, note 2 ; *Harl.* 2251, fol. 229 a (A saying of the nightingale) ; *Pilgrim.* 22 b :

"A foul that was of colour blak,
And in hys lydene thus he spak."
Spenser, *Colin Clout*, l. 744 ; *Intelligenza* 3, 6 :
"Udia cantar li angelli in lor latino."

141, 142. hir broþir.] Algarsif ; see *Squieres T.* II, 317, etc. Lydgate has another allusion to the *Squieres T.* in *Horse, goose, and sheep*, l. 76, 77 :
"Chawcer remembrith the swerd rynge & glasse
Presented were vpon a stede of brasse."

144. mani a þousand.] Shirley, not content with this, makes it many an hundred thousand. But he is beaten by King James (*Kingis Quair* 78, 4), who has "mony a mylioun" of lovers, and King James, in his turn, is outdone by the *Court of Love*, l. 589, where we find "a thousand milion" lovers.

145. complein.] Very similar to the following list of complaints is the one in the *Kingis Quair* and also in the *Court of L.* ; see the Introduction, Ch. ix, § 4.

147. Envie.] Personification from the *Rom. de la R.* (*Rom. of the R.* 248, etc.) ; *Reason and S.* 270 b ; *Pilgrim.*, fol. 223 b, etc. Sins of Envy fill the second Book of Gower's *Confessio*. See also *Black Knight*, l. 257, and 336 :
"The more he was hindred by envye," and *Flour of C.* 84.

In the *Assembly of Gods*, b₇ b, Envy is introduced as one of the seven deadly sins, sitting on a wolf. Cp. further the description of Envy in the *Court of Love*, l. 1254, etc.

148. Ielousie.] *Parl. of F.* 252 ; *Kingis Quair* 87, 7 ; *Reason and S.* 280 b ; *Black Knight* 663, and see the *Rom. de la R.*, English Translation, l. 3820, etc. "Serpent Ialousie" occurs again, stanza 3 b and 25 a ; in *Troil.* III, 788 ; in the *Falls of Pr.*, fol. 124 a :
"Stiered by the serpent of false gelousye."

Similarly "a fals serpent, callyd Ignorance" occurs, *Edmund* III, 147 ; "serpent of doublenes," *Falls of Pr.* 21 c ; "serpent of discorde," *Troy-Book* Y₂b ; "serpent of foryetfulnesse," *Troy-Book* A₂a ; "serpent of newfanglenes," *Falls of Pr.* 53 b ; "the false serpent of discencion," *Falls of Pr.* 79 b ; "serpent of high presumpcion," *Falls of Pr.* 82 a ; "serpent of enuy," *Falls of Pr.* 141 a. The "Serpent of Division" is the title of a work by Lydgate.

149. yput abaek.] So again l. 1252, *Secreta Secret*, fol. 111 a, etc.

151. In the *Falls of Pr.*, fol. 99 a, Lydgate says that Ovid wrote :
"Ful many a pistle compleynyng for absence."

He means, of course, the *Heroides*. In the *Kingis Quair* 93, the lovers also complain of "dissencrance."

153. Wicked Tongues.] Personification from the *Rom. de la R.* (English translation, ll. 3027, 3257, 3799, etc.); the French name Malebouche appears in stanza 25 *b*; in *Flour of C.* 84; *Black Knight* 260; *Reason and S.* 280 *b*; *Flower and Leaf* 580; in the *Pilgrim.*, fol. 202 *a* and *b*. Compare l. 1182 of the *T. of Glas*, and stanza 3 *a*, 3. In the *Black Knight*, l. 207, we have
"false tonges, that with pestilence
Sle trewe men that never did offence."
Flour of C. 157: "Dredful also of tonges that ben large."
Falls of Pr. 91 *a*:
"But there is no poyson so wel expert nor preued,
As is of tonges the hateful violence,
Namely whan princes list yeue them audience."
Pilgrim. 121 *b*: "For ther ys addere nor serpent
So dredful nor malycyous,
As ys a Tonge venymous."
Troil. I, 38 speaks of them
"that falsly ben apeyred
Thorwgh wikked tonges, be it he or sche."
Ib. II, 785: "Also thise wikkede tonges ben so preste
To speke us harme"...
See also *ib.* II, 804, and V, 755 and 756, and cp. *Maunciples Tale* 215—258. fals suspecioun.] Cp. *Black Knight* 505, and *Flour of Curtesie* 86.

154. This is a stock-line of Lydgate's; it occurs again in *Troy-Book* I₂ *a*, and Y₁ *d*; *Falls of Pr.* 57 *c*, and 147 *d*; cf. also *Pilgrim.* 206 *b*:
"For mercy nor remyssyoun."
Similarly, *Falls of Pr.* 39 *a*:
"Voyde of al mercy and remission."
Albon III, 873: "Without mercy of any remyssyoun";
ib. II, 418: "Without fauour or remyssyon."

156. Daunger.] He and Malebouche are (together with Shame) the guardians of the Rose-tree in the *Rom. de la R.*, and frighten away those who intend to pluck the rose; *Rom. of the R.* 3015, etc.; 3130, etc. Cp. also *Legd. of Good W.* 160, and Skeat's note (to which, towards the end, the *Court of S.* might be added). This cruel "Daunger," the lover's principal opponent in the heart of his mistress, is very frequently introduced, as a more or less distinct personification, often together with his associates Disdeyn, Pride, Drede, as opposed to Pity and Grace. See, again, *T. of Glas*, l. 631, 646, 652, 739, 776, 1141; further, *Parl. of F.* 136; *Troil.* II, 384, 399, 1376;—*Black Knight* 13, 250; *Falls of Pr.* 31 *b*; *Reason and S.* 236 *a*; 238 *b*; 280 *a* (following closely the *Rom. de la R.*); 294 *b*; *Flour of C.* 81; *Isle of Ladies*, 472; *Merciless Beaute* 16; *Court of Love* 831, 973; *Rt. of the Rose* 1524. In Al. Chartier, *Le Parlement d'Amour* (ed. Tourangeau, 1617, p. 696), we read:
"Et sur icelle estoit montez (*la porte*)
Dangier, pour y faire le guet."
Dangier occurs also frequently in the same poet's *Hospital d'Amours*. In Skelton's *Bowge of Court* (l. 69), Daunger is "chyef gentylwoman" to Dame Saunce-pere.

Disdain.] A similar personification to Daunger. He is "chambreleyne" to the lady of the *Black Knight* (see that poem, l. 504); in the *Court of Love*, ll. 129 and 130, Daunger and Disdeyne are the chief councillors of King Admetus and Queen Alceste. In the *Parlement of Foules* also, l. 136, Disdayn and Daunger are mentioned together. Cp. also *Bowge of Court*, l. 140.

159—161. poverte.] Cp. the *Rom. of the R.* 450 etc., and *Reason and S.*, fol. 270 *b*. "Poverty" is also a personification in the *Falls of Pr.*, disputing with Fortune (Book III, beginning). Cp. further *Court of L.* 1137—1139:
"And as I yede, full naked and full bare
Some I beholde, lokyng dispiteously
On poverte, that dedely caste here ye."
Kingis Quair. 87, 4: "Sum for desyre, surmounting thaire degree."

161. Perhaps *in open* (reading of G and S) is right; cp. *Falls of Pr.* 47 c:
"To you in open my gylt I wil confesse."
Æsop 2, 124 "shewid in opyn."

162. wanting.] Wanting in what? In means? or good looks? Cp. *Court of Love* 1161—1163. In the *Kingis Quair*, stanza 87, l. 7, there are also some who complain "for to moch."

165. *Kingis Quair* 87, 5: "Sum for dispite and othir Inmytee."

166—168. *Kingis Quair* 136, 1, 6, 7:
"Fy on all suich! fy on thaire doubilnesse! ...
That feynen outward all to hir honour,
And in thaire hert hir worschip wold denoure."

Kingis Quair 137, 4—7: "for quhich the remanant,
That menen wele, and ar noght variant,
For otheris gilt ar suspect of vntreuth,
And hyndrit oft, and treuely that is reuth."

169—174. The same sentiment is expressed in the *Legend of Hypsipyle* 17—21, and in the *Black Knight*, ll. 412, 413. Cp. further *Duchesse* 1024, etc., and Skeat's note, who quotes Gower, Book IV (*Pauli* II, 56), the *Rom. de la R.* 18499—18526, and Machault's *Dit du Lion*.—See also *Kingis Quair* 86, 7.

175—178. Richesse is again a personification in the *Rom. de la R.*; see the English translation, l. 1033; she is "porter" of Venus in *Parl. of F.* 261. Cp. also *Rom. of the R.* 5360, etc.

179 etc., and the similar complaints in 209 etc., may be compared to *Kingis Quair* 91 and 92, which speaks of people whose bodyes were
"bestowit so,
Quhare bothe thair hertes gruch[en] ther-ageyne,"
for which "Thaire lyf was noght bot care and repentance."
See *ib.*, 92, 5—7:
"Off ȝong[e] ladies faire, and mony lord,
That thus by maistry were fro thair chose dryve,
Full redy were thaire playntis there to gyve."

180. peping.] "An imitative word, allied to *pipe*, to express the chirping of a bird." So says Professor Skeat in his note to the following line from the *Kingis Quair* 57, 6: "Now, suete bird, say ones to me 'pepe.'"
Cp. also *Dunbar*, ed. Laing I, 85, l. 64: "Quhen of the Tod wes hard no peip," and Lyndsay's *Peder Coffeis* 23: "Peipand peurly with peteouss granis."

182. croked Elde.] One of the pictures in the *Rom. de la R.*; see *Rom. of the R.* 349, and *Reason and S.*, fol. 270 b. The expression "croked elde" occurs again *Falls of Pr.* 3 a; *Rom. of the R.* 4889; "croked age," *Troy-Book* T₁ a; *Falls of Pr.* 176 c; *Reason and S.* 289 a; *S. of Thebes* 360 b; *Testament*, Halliwell, p. 241, 246; *Edmund* III, 422; "age croked and lame" *Falls of Pr.* 18 b; "stale croked age" *Falls of Pr.* 67 d.

184, 185. May and January.] This is an allusion to the *Marchauntes Tale*, with the story of the ill-coupled old, gray January and fresh May. Lydgate himself has imitated this story in a poem printed by Halliwell (page 27—46), containing the story of Decembre and Iuly. Lydgate quotes Chaucer in this story (*Halliwell*, p. 28):
"Remembre wele on olde January,
Whiche maister Chauncers ful seriously deseryvethe,
And on fresshe May" ...
King James has also an allusion to Chaucer's tale (*Kingis Quair* 110, 2):
"Eke Ianuarye is [vn] like vnto may."

186. Cp. *Story of Thebes*, fol. 370 b:
"Thus selde is sen, the trouthe to termine,
That age and youth drawe by O line."
Miller's Tale 43: "Men schulde wedde aftir here astaat,
For celde and youthe ben often at debaat."

189. *Rom. of the R.* 82:
"Than younge folk entenden ay
For to ben gay and amorous."
Ib. 1288. "For yonge folk wole, witen ye,
Have lytel thought but on her play."
Reason and S. 279 *a*: (these lusty folkes all—youth among them):
"nentende nyght nor day
But vn-to merthe and vn-to play."
The same is said of Cupid and Deduit in *Reason and S.* 268 *a*:
"The which entende never a day
But vnto myrthe and vn-to play."

189. *Myrthe* is "lord of the garden" in the *Rom. de la R.*; see *Rom. of the R.* 601, etc., and 817, etc.; and "Dame Gladnesse" is "his leef," *ib.* 818; but in the present passage we have hardly a prosopopœia. "Gladnesse" is personified in *Reason and S.* 274 *b*.

190. *Rom. of the R.* 3893, 3894:
"For he loveth noon hevynesse, (*Bialacoil*)
But mirthe and pley, and alle gladnesse."

191. Cp. Chaucer's *Compleynt unto Pite* 23:
"Allas! that day! that ever hit shulde falle!"
The repetition of þat is peculiar; but the best MSS. have it, and, without it, the metre is incomplete.

192. sugre and gal.] A frequent simile; compare, for instance, *Falls of Pr.* 24 *d*:
"Their pompous suger is meint with bitter gal" (*of princes*).
Reason and S. 248 *b*: "The sugre of hir drynkes all (*Venus*)
At the eude ys meynt with gall."
Pilgrim., fol. 2 *a*: "hyr sugre vnder-spreynt wyth galle" (*Fortune's*).

195. shape remedie.] See again l. 721; *Story of Thebes*, fol. 364 *b*; *Albon* II, 1289. The expression occurs frequently elsewhere in Lydgate; also in the *Kingis Quair* 102, 5:
"and shapith remedye
To sauen me, of ȝour benigne grace."

196—208. This passage seems to have served as a model to *Kingis Quair* 88—90, and *Court of L.* 1095, etc. (see also *ib.* 253). Compare particularly *Kingis Quair* 90, 3—7, with ll. 207 and 208 of our poem:
"Sum bene of thaim that haldin were full lawe,
And take by frendis, nothing thay to wyte,
In ȝouth from lufe Into the cloistere quite;
And for that cause are cummyn recounsilit.
On thame to pleyne that so thaim had begilit."
See further *Kingis Quair* 88:
"ȝone were quhilum folk of religioun," etc.
Very similar is also the passage in the *Court of L.*, 1095—1136; particularly 1104—1106:
"Alas! . . . we fayne perfeccion,
In clothes wide, and lake oure libertie;
But all the synne mote on oure frendes be"
(see *T. of Glas.*, ll. 204 and 208);
the "copes wide" (l. 204) are also found in *Court of L.* 1116, and the "tender youþe" (l. 199) in *Court of L.* 1111. Cp. further ll. 196 and 197 with *Court of L.* 1100:
"So howe thei crye and wryng here handes white,
For thei so sone went to religion!"
and with *Court of L.* 1135:
"Thus leve I hem, with voice of pleint and care,
In ragyng woo crying full petiously."
The passage is quite in accordance with Lydgate's views on monastic life as

expressed elsewhere; see his *Testament.* In the *Troy-Book* Dd₂ b he represents himself as
"Usynge an habyte of perfeccyon,
Albe my lyfe accorde nat therto."

209—214. See above, under 179.

215—222. Cp. *Kingis Quair* 134:
"Bot there be mony of so brukill sort,
That feynis trenth In lufe for a quhile,
And setten all thaire wittis and disport
The sely Innocent woman to begyle,
And so to wynne thaire lustis with a wile."

Troilus II, 786: "ek men ben so untrewe,
That right anon, as cessed is hire leste,
So ceseth love, and forth to love a newe."

See also *Fame* 341, etc.

219. *Anelida* 251: "Upon me, that ye calden your maistresse."

220. entere] = entirely devoted; cp. *Troy-Book* C₂ d:
"Whiche is to me moste plesaunt and enteer."

The word is common in this sense; we have also a noun formed from it, with similar meaning, in *Edmund* II, 938:
"How gret enternesse they hadde vnto ther kyng."

The synonym *hool* is also used in the same way: trew and hool *Troilus* III, 952.

223. Similarly *Troy-Book* Q₃ c: "And into terys he began to rayne."

Falls of Pr. 16 d: "Like a woman that would in teres reyne."

Ib. 39 b: "I pray the not disdayne,
Upon my graue some teares for to rayne."

Cp. also *Troilus* IV, 818 and 845, and further on, l. 961 and note.

228. *Falls of Pr.* 13 b: "But she al turned to his confusion."

229. *Black Knight* 479:
"Mot axe grace, mercy, and pite,
And namely ther wher noon may be founde."

230. forth-bi pace.] So again *Falls of Pr.* 18 a; *Rom. of the Rose* 4096; *Pard. Tale* 206; *Prior. Tale* 117. To "passe (or come) forby," is also not unfrequent; see, for instance, *Doct. Tale* 125; *Troilus* II, 658, and cp. Skeat's note to l. 175 of Chaucer's *Prologue* to the *Cant. Tales.*

231, 232. See note to l. 105.

233. peraeunture.] To be read as a trisyllable *peraunter*; so also, for instance, *Troil.* II, 921, 1373; III, 442. Cp., further on, l. 241.

234. The same sentiment occurs in the *Compl. of Mars*, l. 231:
"And that is wonder that so lust a king
Doth such hardnesse to his creature."

See also *Duchesse* 467—469.

242. This lover evidently endeavours to carry out the 20th Statute of the Court of Love (namely, to seek his absent lady, see *Court of L.* 498—504); but his bump of locality would not seem to be sufficiently developed for the task.

244. *Coretise* is again to be found in the *Rom. de la R.*, English translation, 181, etc.; and in the *Assembly of Gods*, c₂ b (riding on an "Olyfaunt"). It is the vice against which the Pardoner preaches with particular zeal; see the *Pard. Prol.* 138, 147. It is akin to "Avarice," treated by Gower in the 5th book of the *Confessio.* See further, *Melibe*, p. 152, and Lydgate's *Serpent of Division*, fol. A₃ a, which speaks of "that contagious sinne Couetousnes, intermedled with Enuie."

Sloth is the subject of Gower's 4th Book. This vice often occurs personified; we have, for instance, a description of Sloth in the *Pilgrimage*, fol. 210 a:
"My name ys yeallyd slouthe;
For I am slowh & encombrows,
Haltynge also and Gotows

>   Off my lymes crampysshynge,
>   Maymed ek in my goynge,
>   Coorbyd lyk ffolkys that ben Old,
>   And afowndryd ay with cold."

In the *Assembly of Gods*, $c_2 b$, Sloth rides on a "dull asse." See again, l. 379, 1010.—A subdivision of Sloth is "Idelnesse" (see the *Confessio*, book IV), very frequently personified and held up as a thing to be avoided. In the *Roman de la Rose*, "Idelnesse" is "porter" of the garden (see the Engl. Translation 531 etc., 593, 1273 etc.). She has the same function in the *Knightes Tale*, l. 1082, and frequently comes in Lydgate and Hawes. See also *Melibe*, p. 181; *Sec. Nun's Tale* 2; *Faerie Queene* I, 4, 18 etc.

245. hastines.] See note to l. 863.

248. crystal shield.] This attribute of Pallas is often spoken of; cp. *Troy-Book* $G_3 b$:

>   "And next venus, Pallas I behelde
>   With hir spere, and hir cristall shelde."

After these lines follows the interpretation of this symbol, according to Fulgentius, as given in the *Introduction*, p. cxxvii. Again, *ib.* $K_4 a$:

>   "And Pallas eke with hir cristall shelde."

ib., $Z_4 a$: "Whiche on hir brest haueth of cristall
>   Hir shelde Egys, this goddesse inmortall."

ib., $Z_4 a$: "To fayre Pallas with hir Cristall shelde."

Lydgate again has the "shelde of Crystall clere" and its interpretation as:

>   "The shelde of fortytude and of pacyence,"

in the *Court of S.* $e_7 a$, and there also refers to Fulgentius, who says (ed. Muncker, p. 68): "Gorgoneam etiam huic addunt in pectore, quasi terroris imaginem, ut vir sapiens terrorem contra adversarios gestet in pectore." See further, *Reason and S.* 218 b:

>   "In hir lyfte hande she had also
>   A myghty shelde of pacience,
>   Ther-with to make resistence
>   Ageyñ al vices out of drede" . . . .

Again, *L. Lady* $i_8 a$:

>   "It [*the name of Jesus*] is also the myghty pauyce fayre
>   Ageyn wanhope and dysperacion,
>   Cristal shelde of pallas for dispayre."

Assembly of Gods, $b_2 a$:

>   "She [*Minerva*] wered two bokelers, one by her syde,
>   That other ye wote w[h]ere; this was all her pryde" [*namely, on her breast*].

Compare also the following passage from Frezzi's *Quadriregio* II, 1, 40—42:

>   "Scolpita avea l'orribile Gorgone (*Minerva*)
>   Nel bello scudo, ch' ella ha cristallino,
>   Il quale porta, e contro i mostri oppone."

The virtue of this shield is thus expressed (*ib.*, II, xix. 40):

>   "O figlio mio, se adocchi
>   Per mezzo del cristallo del mio scudo . . .
>   Tu vederai il vero aperto, e nudo;
>   E non ti curerai dell' apparenza,
>   Alla qual mira l'ignorante, e rudo."

Cf. also *Quadriregio* II, XVI, 19, etc. See further, Peele's *Arraignment of Paris* IV, 1:

>   "because he knew no more
>   Fair Venus' ceston than Dame Juno's mace,
>   Nor never saw wise Pallas' crystal shield."

251 and 252. *Parl. of F.* 298:

>   "ther sat a queue
>   That, as of light the somer-sonne shene
>   Passeth the sterre, right so ouer mesure
>   She fairer was than any creature."

Flour of C. 113 -116:
>"Ryght by example, as the somer sonne
>Passeth the sterre with his beames shene,
>And Lucifer amonge the skyes donne
>A morowe sheweth, to voide nightes tene" ...

Machault, *Fontaine Amoureuse* (see Skeat, *M. P.*, p. 259):
>"Qui, tout aussi com li solaus la lune
>Veint de clarté,
>Avait-elle les autres sormonté
>De pris, d'onneur, de grace, de biauté."

253, etc. Compare *Story of Thebes*, fol. 363 a:
>"And like, in soth, as Lucifer the sterre (l. 253)
>Gladeth the morowe at his vprising :
>So the ladies, at her in coming, (ll. 282 and 283)
>With the stremes of her eyen clere .....
>To al the Courte broughten in gladnesse."

Cp. also, further on, ll. 328—331 and 1348.

255. *Testament*, Halliwell, p. 244:
>"May among moneths sitte lyk a queene."

257—261. Cp. *Flour of C.* 120—123:
>"Aud as the Ruby hath the sonerainte
>Of riche stones, and the regalie ;
>And the rose, of swetnesse and beaute,
>Of freshe floures, without any lye" ...

For eloquent praise of the rose as the queen of flowers, see Dunbar's *Thrissill and Rois*, l. 141 etc.

259. *L. Lady* a, b:
>"And as the Rubye hath the renoun
>Of stones al and domynacion,
>Right so this mayde, to speke of holynesse,
>Of wymmen alle is lady and maistresse" (cf. l. 296).

Falls of Pr. 88 a:
>"so clere his renoune shone ....,
>As doth a Rubye aboue eche other stone."

Edmund I, 977 :
>"And as the Ruby, kyng of stonys alle,
>Reioiseth ther presence with his naturel liht."

Albon I, 298: "As amonge stones the Ruby is moost shene."

Reason & S. 294 a:
>"For this Royal stoon famous
>Was a Ruby vertuous,
>Which hath by kynde the dignite
>Of stonys and the sonereynte."

ib. 295 a:
>"the Rubye vertuous,
>Which is a stoon Most plentenous,
>Of vertu, yif I shal nat tarye,
>Preferred in the lapydarye,
>With grace and hap a man to avaunce."

Ll. 265, 266 occur almost word for word in the *Troy-Book* H, a:
>"So he meruayleth hir great semelynesse, (*Helen*)
>Hir womanhede, hir porte and hir fayrenesse."

267—270. *Troy-Book* H, a:
>"For neuer afore ne wende he that nature
>Coude haue made so fayre a creature :
>So aungellyke she was of hir beaute,
>So femynyne, so goodly on to se."

ib. S, d: (*Achilles*) "gan meruayle greatly in his thought,
>How god or kynde euer myght haue wrought,
>In theyr werkes, so fayre a creature."

Cp. also the description of Cryseyde, *Troilus* I, 100—105.

271. This line contains one of Lydgate's favourite phrases, "hair bright like gold-wire" (golden thread). Compare the following passages :

Notes to p. 11, l. 271.

Troy-B. C₂ c : " His sonnysshe heer, crisped lyke golde were " (*Jason*).
  ib. I₁ d : " Hir sonnysshe heer, lyke Phebus in his spere
    Bounde in a tresse, bryghter than golde were " (*Cryseyde*).
  ib. I₆ a : " With lockes yelowe, lyke gold wyre of colour " (*Paris*).
  ib. S₃ d : " Hyr heer also resemblynge to golde wyere " (*Polyxena*).
  ib. Q₃ c : " And eke vntrussed hir heer abrode gan sprede,
    Lyke to golde wyre, for-rent and all to-torne " (*Cryseyde*).
  ib. Z₆ a : " With heer to-rent, as any golde wyer shene " (*Polyxena*).
  ib. C₂ d : " With berde yspronge, shynynge lyke gold weer " (*Jason*).
Assembly of Gods b₂ b :
  " Whoos long here shone as wyre of golde bryght " (*Venus*).
Chorl and Bird 59 :
  (a bird) " With sonnyssh feders brighter then gold were."
Reason and S. 223 b :
  " Whos here as eny gold wyre shoñ " (*Venus*).
It seems that this expression was started by Lydgate ; at least I cannot point to
an earlier instance. We have the phrase again in the *Kingis Quair* 1, 4 :
  " tressis like the goldin wyre ; "
it occurs in one of the *Roxburghe Ballads* (62, stanza 5) :
  " First is her haire like threds of golden wyre ; "
cp. further, Henryson, *Testament of Cresseide* 177 :
  " As golden wier so glittring was his heare" (*Jupiter*) ;
Lyndsay, *Ane Satyre*, 342 :
  " Hir hair is like the goldin wyre."
These two examples are also quoted by Henry Wood, *Chaucer's influence upon
King James I.*, p. 5, note.
Hawes, *Past. of Pleasure*, p. 79 :
  " Her heer was downe so clerely shynynge,
    Lyke to the golde, late purifyed with fyre ;
    Her heer was bryght as the drawne wyre."
It is found in Speuser's " Hymn in honour of Beauty," stanza 14 :
  " That golden wire, those sparkling stars so bright,
    Shall turn to dust, and lose their goodly light ; "
further in his *Ruins of Time*, stanza 2 :
  " A woman . . . Rending her yellow locks, like wiry gold,
    About her shoulders carelessly down trailing ; "
more than once in the *Fairy Queen* ; for instance, II, 3, 30, 1 :
  " Her yellow lockes, crisped like golden wyre " (*Belphœbe*) ;
cp. also *ib.* II, 4, 15, and II, 9, 19 ; in Gascoigne's *Dan Bartholomew*, stanza 9 ;
and several times in Peele ; see *David and Bethsabe* II, 2 :
  " Thou fair young man, whose hairs shine in mine eye
    Like golden wires of David's ivory lute " (*Absalon*),
and, again, II, 3 :
  " His hair is like the wire of David's harp,
    That twines about his bright and ivory neck."
Even Shakspere seems to allude to the phrase, in the *Sonnets* 130, 4 :
  " If hairs be wires, black wires grow on her head ; "
cp. further *King John* III, 4, 64.
A passage in the *Celestina* has also this idea ; Calisto praises his beloved Melibea
thus : " Comienzo por los cabellos : ¿ vés tú las madejas del oro delgado que
hilan en Arabia ? Mas lindos son, y no resplandescen menos " (see the English
translation in Dodsley-Hazlitt, I, 61). The notion of "golden," "sunnish"
hair, as being ideal in colour, was common at the time ; Chaucer also has it
frequently ; see *Duchesse* 858 ; *Hous of F.* 1387 ; *Doctor's Tale*, l. 37 etc.
(Virginia) ; *Knightes Tale* 191, 1308, 1431 ; *Wife of Bath's Prol.* 304 ; *Troilus*
IV, 708 :
  " Hire ownded here, that sonnyssh was of hewe."
ib. IV. 788 : " Hire myghty tresses of hire sonnysshe heres."
See further, *Kingis Quair* 46, 2 (Lady Joan is described as having "goldin
hair "), and *Rom. of the R.* 539 (Idelnesse) ; *Court of Love* 138, 654, 780 ;

Douglas's *Palice of Honour* I, 10. 22 (ed. Small); Dunbar, *Golden Targe* 61 and 62 (similar to *Parl. of Foules* 267, 268) and I, 61, l. 19 (ed. Laing):
"So glitterit as the gold wer thair glorius gilt tressis."
Troy-Book I₄ b: "Lyke golde hir tresses" (*Andromache*);
Story of Thebes 371 c:
"And gan to rende her gilte tresses clere."
Court of S. a₁ b: "She gan vnlace her tressed sonnysshe here" (*Mercy*).
Pur le Roy, Halliwell, p. 8:
"Lyke Phebus bemys shone her goldyn tresses" (and cp. p. 6, l. 18).
Falls of Pr. 13 b:
"Her father had a fatal heere that shone (*Scylla and Nisus*)
Brighter then gold" (occurs again in *Reason and S.* 261 b);
Ib. 60 b: "Her here vntressed like Phebus in his sphere."
Ib. 119 b: "Her golden heere was al to-torne and rent."
Cp. also *Ballad of the fair Rosamund* (in Percy):
"Her crisped lockes like threads of golde
Appeard to each man's sight."
I hope these passages will sufficiently prove that Shakspere had not to go to Italy for this idea. Some of the Italian paintings present to us, it is true, an exact illustration of this "hair like gold-wire;" especially those of the Venetian school, and many of Botticelli's.

272—277. Compare the description of Helen in the *Troy-Book*, II₃ a, which bears a striking likeness to our passage:
"Hir golden heer, lyke the sonne stremes
Of fresshe Phebus with his bryght[e] bemes,
The goodlyhede of hir fresshely face, (l. 273)
So replenysshed of beaute and grace, (l. 274)
Euen ennewed with quycknesse of colour,
Of the rose, and the lylye flour,
So egally that nouther was to wyte,
Thorugh none excesse, of moche nor of lyte."

275. ennuyd.] See the passage quoted in the last note; also *Life of our Lady* a₆ a, where the Virgin is described as "ennewyd" with the "rose of womanly sufferaunce and the lily of chastity"; further *Troy-Book* C₄ b:
"But euer amonge, to ennewe hir coloure, (*Medea's*)
The rose was meynt with the lylye floure."
Reason and S. 217 a:
"And hir colour and hir hiwe
Was euere ylych[e] fresh and nywe" (*Pallas*).
Duchesse 906: "And every day her beaute newed."
Cp. also *Calisto and Melibœa* (Dodsley-Hazlitt, I, p. 62):
"Her skin of whiteness endarketh the snow,
With rose-colour ennewed;"
further, Skelton, *Philip Sparrow* 1003, 1032; *Garl. of Laurel* 985; also *Garl. of Laurel* 389, *Phil. Spar.* 775, and Dyce's quotations in the note to the last-named passage. See also the quotation from Skelton in note to next line.

276. *L. Lady* a₃ b:
"Whos chekes weren, her beaute for to eke,
With lilyes meynte & fressh[e] roses reed."
Skelton, *Garland of Laurel* 883:
"The enbuddid blossoms of roses rede of hew
With lillis whyte your bewte doth renewe."
Cp. also *Doct. Tale* 32—34.

279, etc. Compare ll. 267, etc.; and 578, etc. Similarly, *Chartier*, p. 695 (ed. 1617):
"Tant bien l'ont voulu apprester
Dieu & nature à leur vouloir."

283. enlumynd.] It is a poetical idea that the Lady's beauty should "illu-

mine" the whole temple round about her. We have it again in *Life of our Lady* f₁ b:
"And as she entrid, a newe sodeyn light
All the place enlumyned enuyron"
(*The Virgin in the stable at Bethlehem*).
Similarly, *King Horn*, l. 391, 392:
"Of his faire siȝte
Al þe bur gan liȝte";
Dunbar, *Thrissill and Rois* 155—157:
"A coistly croun, with clarefeid stonis brycht,
This cumly Quene did on hir heid inclois,
Quhyll all the land illumynit of the licht."
Edmund III, 224: "a child . . . Which sholde enlumyne al this regioun."
Troy-Book C₁ c:
"That hir comynge gladeth all the halle" (*Medea*).
Intelligenza 15, 1:
"La sua sovramirabile bieltate
Fa tutto 'l mondo più lucente e chiaro."
Cp. also *Reason and S.* 204 b, etc.:
"the beaute of hir face, (*Dame Nature*)
The whiche abouten al the place
Caste so mervelous a lyght,
So clere, so percynge and so bryght . . .
That I ne myght[e] nat sustene
In hir presence to abyde,
But went[e] bak and stood asyde."

284, etc. Compare with these lines the very similar description of a lady in the *Parliament of Love*, 60 etc.

291. dalliaunce.] Very much the same as "beauparlaunce" in the *Court of S.* f₁ b, and "parladura" in the *Intelligenza* 7, 9. In Lydgate the word *dalliaunce* seems always to refer to speech; cp. *Falls of Pr.*, fol. 53 b and 145 d: "(faire) speche and daliaunce," and 1, 18, fol. 34 c:
"He axed was among great audience, (*Xenocrates*)
Why he was solayne of his daliaunce:
His aunswere was that neuer for scilence
Through little speaking he felt[e] no greuaunce."
Ib. 69 b: "Men with thee wyl haue no daliaunce" (*Poverty*).
Ib. 119 d: "Under a curtayn of double daliaunce."
Ib. 144 c: "Iohn Bochas sate & heard al her daliaunce."
Ib. 163 d: "Of Rethoriciens whilom that wer old,
The sugred language & vertuous daliaunce."
Ib. 197 a: "Through his subtill false daliaunce,
By craft he fyll into her acquaintaunce."
Albon II, 730, 731:
"Of Christis fayth and (of) his religion
Was theyr [talkynge] and theyr dalyance";
Ib. II, 1612: "theyr langage and theyr dalyance" . . .
In the *Pilgrimage of Man*, MS. Cott. Tib. A. VII, fol. 43 b, we have the lines:
"Though sche and I bothe two
Hadde I-ffere longe dalyaunce,"
which are a translation of the French:
"Combien qua moy long parlement
Ait tenu" . . . (Barthole et Petit, fol. 63 b).
Ib. MS. Cott. Vit. C. XIII, fol. 10 a:
(Doctors and prelates) "By speche and by dallyavnce
Techyng pylgrymes."

292. The beste tauȝt.] See p. lxix of the Introduction, and ten Brink § 246, end of note. L. 558 is doubtful (The moste passing?).

292, 293. well of plesaunce.] *well* is very common in this usage; cp. *Wife*

of Bath's Prol. 107 ; *Sec. Nun's Tale* 37, etc. ; so is *mirrour* (l. 294) ; see again,
T. of Glas, ll. 754 and 974 ; *Man of Law's Tale* 68, etc.
   295. secrenes.] This is the 2nd Statute in the *Court of Love* (l. 309) and
always much commended in lovers; see again l. 900 ; 757, 1005, 1154 ; *Troil.*
III, 93, 429.—*Ib.* l. 245:
            "That firste vertu is to kepe tonge."
The same maxim occurs also in a poem of Lydgate's in the Harl. MS. 2255,
fol. 150 a :
            "And Catoñ wrytt in pleyn language,
             The first vertu, whoo-so lyst it rede,
             Keep your tonge froom al Outrage."
In the *Kingis Quair*, stanza 97, l. 3, "Secretee" is "chamberere" of Venus.
   296. *Troy-Book* $Y_1 c$:
            "Of women all lady and maystresse" (*Penthesilcia*).
See again l. 972, and note to line 259. The expression "lady and maystresse"
occurs also in the *Pilgrimage* 59 a ; *Isle of Ladies* 2003 ; *Rom. of the Rose* 5881 ;
Douglas's *Palice of Honour*, ed. Small, I, 3, 17, and frequently elsewhere.
   297. *Life of our Lady* $a_1 a$:
       "If that hem lyst, of hyr they myght[e] lere" (*the Virgin Mary*).
Lere (O.E. lèran) meant originally "to teach," as in l. 656 ; here and in l.
1021, it means "to learn." *Vice-versâ*, "leine" (O.E. leornjan) means also "to
teach," for instance, *Falls of Pr.* 213 c. Similar to our passage is further *Doct.
Tale* 107—110. In the *Sec. Nun's Tale* 92, Chaucer explains the name of St.
Cecilia as meaning
            "the way of blynde,
       For sche ensample was by way of techyng."
   299. grene and white]. This, the redactor of group **A** changed into *in blak
In red*, as the green colour was considered the token of inconstancy, whilst blue
signified faithfulness ; cf. Chaucer's *Ballade on Newe-fangelnesse*, of which the
burden is :
            "In stede of blew, thus may ye were al grene."
This is taken from Machault (ed. Tarbé, p. 56). See also *Squieres T.* II, 298,
299, and Skeat's note ; further, *Court of Love* 246, etc. ; *Anelida* 146, 330, and
Skeat's note, where he quotes from Lydgate :
            "Watchet-blewe of feyned stedfastnes, . . .
             Meint with light grene, for change & doublenes."
                                   (*Falls of Pr.*, fol. 143 c.)
In the *Rom. of the Rose* 573, Ydelnesse is represented as wearing a coat of green
colour ; in *The Flower and the Leaf*, the worshippers of the quickly fading flower
are clad in green (l. 329, etc.).
   But there was nevertheless no occasion to make the alteration in Group **A**.
Thus, Alceste in Chaucer is "clad in real habit grene" (*Legend*, Prologue, 214) ;
similarly Emelye in the *Knightes T.*, l. 828, corresponding to Boccaccio's *Teseide ;*
cp. canto XII, stanza 65 of that poem :
            "ella fosse . . . riccamente
             D'un drappo verde di valor supremo Vestita."
Diana's statue is "clothed in gaude greene," *Knightes T.* 1221, and Rosiall in
the *Court of L.* 816, has a green gown on. In *Edmund* III, 115, we read :
            "The wattry greene shewed in the Reynbowe
             Off chastite disclosed his clennesse."
   Pilgrim. 12 b :
       (*Grace Dieu*) "In a surcote al off whyt,
                       With a Tyssu gyrt off grene,
                       And Endlong ful bryht & shene" ;
the French original reads :
       (sembloit) "Vestement avoir dor batu
                   Et cincte estoit dun verd tissu."
   Ib., fol. 100 a :   "thys skryppe . . . mot be grene,
                       Wych colour—who so looke a-ryht—

Doth gret comfort to the syht,
Sharpeth the Eye, yt ys no dred."
Compare also Barclay, as quoted in Dyce's *Skelton*, p. xiv:
"Mine habite blacke accordeth not with grene,
Blacke betokeneth death as it is dayly sene;
The grene is pleasour, freshe lust and iolite;
These two in nature hath great diuersitie."
In the *Castle of Perseverance*, Truth is represented as wearing "a sad-coloured green"; see Skeat's note to *Piers Plowman*, C-text XXI, 120 (p. 406).
Kindermann's *Teutscher Wolredner* (Appendix, p. 19) has: "Grün gibt Freude / Ehre / Liebe und Hoffnung zuerkennen." (Green was, according to the astrology of that time, Venus's colour; see Morley, *Eng. Writers*, 2nd ed., V, 139; and cp. *Love's Labour's Lost* I, 2, 90: "Green, indeed, is the colour of lovers."

301. stones and perre.] Occurs again in l. 310. Lydgate has it often, for instance, *Falls of Pr.* 109 b; 128 c; 159 a; 170 d; 191 c; 198 c; "perre and stones" occurs in *Falls of Pr.* 183 c.

301, etc. Cp. *Assembly of Ladies* 257 c:
"Her gowne wel was embroudred certainly
With stones after her owne denise,
In her purfil her worde by and by
Bien & loyalement, as I coude denise."

311. This is to sein.] Very frequent in Lydgate; it occurs again in ll. 426, 512, 715, 1124. Also in Chaucer, *Squ. T.* II, 186, 293; *Prior. T.* 48; *Melibe*, p. 146, 158, 159, 161, 163, 168; *Pers. T.*, p. 266, 286, 289, etc.
þis benigne.] Occurs again, without a noun, in l. 1402. Cp. also *Kingis Quair* 42, 3: "that verray womanly."

312. For the motto see *Flower and Leaf* 548—550:
"For knightes ever should be persevering,
To seeke honour without feintise or slouth,
Fro wele to better in all manner thing."
Edmund I, 361: "Fro good in vertu to bettre he dide encresse."
Pilgrim. 291 b: "Fro good to bet alway profyte."
Lydgate seems to have some difficulty in explaining the motto; at any rate, he does so very awkwardly, which might point to its being the actual family-motto of some fair lady. Similar mottoes with comparatives are not rare; for instance: "Altiora peto," or "Excelsior." Numerous French mottoes are found in the *Assembly of Ladies*, but none like ours. Perhaps a negative counterpart to our present expression may serve to illustrate it further, *Falls of Pr.* 138 a:
"Fro better to worse she can so wel transmue [*Fortune*]
The state of them that wyll no vertue sue."

320. This line occurs word for word in the *Troy-Book* B, e. See also *Compl. unto Pite* 56:
"Theffect of which seith thus, in wordes fewe."

321. Similar in tone to this prayer is the one in ll. 701, etc.; 1341, etc.; *Knightes T.* 1363, etc.; the proem to Book III in *Troilus*; *Kingis Quair*, stanza 52, 99 etc.; Chapter XXX of the *Pastime of Pleasure*.

322, 323. With respect to this all-dominating power of Venus, Lydgate proposes the following etymology (*Reason and S.*, fol. 265 a):
"Venus ys sayde of venquysshing,
For she venquyssheth euery thing."
If this etymology should not be acceptable, there is another one, deriving *Venus* from *rener* (to hunt), *Pilgrim*. 128 a, and yet another, deriving Venus from venom (*Reason and S.* 248 b)!—See also note to l. 619.

322. Similar expressions, *Leg. of Dido* 121:
"Fortune that hath the world in governaunce;"
Doct. Tale 73: "That lordes doughtres hun in governaunce."

Court of L. 1371 : "The God of Love hath erth in governaunce."
Generydes (ed. Wright), 2049, 2050 :
  "The formest ward . . . . The kyng of Turkey had in gouernaunce."
Compl. of Mars 110 : "she that hath thyn herte in governaunce."
Reason and S. 229 b : "Which hath loue in gouernaunce" (*Venus*).
There was, therefore, no need of Caxton's alteration.

323. Cp. *Reason and S.*, fol. 222 b :
  "And thorgh hir myght, which ys dyvyne,
  She the proude kan enclyne
  To lownesse and humilyte" (*Venus*).

hauteyn.] The word is curiously corrupted in our best MSS., although it is not of rare occurrence ; for instance, *Parl. Prol.* 44 ; *Legend of good W.* 1120 ; *Rom. of the Rose* 6104 ; Wyntoun, *Cronykil* V, 12, 271 ; *De duob. Merc.* (MS. Hh. IV. 12, fol. 69 b) :
  "That whilom was in rychesse so hauteyn" (*rhyming with* paine).
Magnus Cato: "Refreyne thy self, be nat hawteyne ne to hye"
(Caxton reads *haute*, which we have also *Falls of Pr.* 138 b).
Reason and S. 275 a :
  "For ther is nouther halt nor lame
  So hawteyn nor so surquedous . . .
  But they must of diwe ryght . . .
  Stonde vnder his obeyssaunce" (*Cupid's*).

325. Causer.] MS. G reads, in opposition to all other texts, *Cause*, which no doubt is wrong. We read also in the *Compleynt of Mars*, l. 46 :
  "The faire Venus, causer of plesaunce."

328. blissful.] Common epithet for Venus ; see further on l. 1100 ; *Knightes Tale* 1357 ; *Parl. of F.* 113 ; *Troilus* II, 234, 680 ; III, Proem 1 ; III, 656, 663 ; IV, 1633 ; *Kingis Quair* 76, 6 ; 101, 6 ; *Court of L.* 580.

persant.] This does not seem to be a Chaucerian word ; see Skeat, *Why "The Romaunt of the Rose" is not Chaucer's*, p. 446. It is common in Lydgate : in the *T. of Glas* it occurs again in ll. 756, 1341 ; we have it several times in the *Black Knight* (ll. 28, 358, 591, 613), and elsewhere ; also in the *Compleynt* 574 (-*and*, I believe, does not here denote the northern participle, but is written for *ant*, *aunt*). The word occurs further in the *Rom. of the Rose*, ll. 2809 and 4179 ; *Court of Love* 849 ; *Fairy Queen* I, 10, 47, 5 etc. Cp. also *Kingis Quair* 103, l. 1.

328—331. With these lines compare ll. 253, 254, and 1355—1358.

331. woful.] MS. L and Prints read *woful hertes*, which is too much for the metre. Nor does grammar require it ; cp. *Man of Law's Tale* 752 :
  "to whom alle woful cryen,"
and *Chorl and Bird* 249 :
  "Comfortith sorowful, and makith heny hertis light."—
"voide" is similarly construed in *L. Lady* l, a :
  "To voyde hem out of al derknesse."
Stanza 3 a, 3. Wekkede tongis.] See note to l. 153.
  „   3 b. See note to l. 148.
  „   3 c. fried in his owne grease.] Occurs in the *Wife of Bath's* Prologue, l. 487 ; see Hazlitt, *English Proverbs*, p. 258.
  3 d. For Mars, Venus, and Vulcan, see ll. 126—128, and note ; for Adonis, l. 64, and *Black Knight* 644.

341. The meaning of some of the lines in the Lady's complaint is not clear ; the author makes her express her wishes in a very vague way.

342. Mi worship sauf.] Similarly *Kingis Quair* 143, 5 : "Hir worschip sauf" = her honour being kept safe ; and see *ib.* 142, 7, and *Duchesse* 1271. Cp. also *Anelida* 267 : "My honour save" ; the same expression occurs in *Troil.* II, 480 ; III, 110 ; and see *T. of Glas* 1117. In the *Falls of Pr.* 73 d we read :
  "Iniury done or any maner wrong,
  Agayn my worship or mine honestie" (*Lucrece*).

In *Magnus Cato* the expression "salvo tamen ante pudore" is paraphrased by:
"Ay sauyng thy worship and honeste."
346. Compare *Rom. of the Rose* 2424:
"And I abyde al sole in wo,
Departed from myn owne thought,
And with myne eyen se ryght nought."
348. *Story of Thebes* 363 b: "Atwene two hanging in a balance."
Edmund III, 477: "Thus atween tweyne hangyng in ballaunce."
Cp. also further on *T. of Glas*, l. 641.
350, 351. Compare *Parl. of F.* 90, 91:
"For bothe I hadde thing which that I nolde,
And eek I ne hadde that thing that I wolde."
Court of L. 988: "But that I like, that may I not come by;
Of that I playn, that have I habondaunce."
See also *Compl. unto Pite* 99, etc., and poem XXI in Skeat, Chaucer's *Minor Poems*, l. 47:
"For al that thing which I desyre I mis,
And al that ever I wolde nat, I-wis,
That fynde I redy to me evermore;"
further Boethius, 3 d prose of book III: "Nonne quia vel aberat, quod abesse non velles; vel aderat, quod adesse noluisses?"
356 and 357. heat and cold.] These lovers are constantly in extremes of temperature; see *Troil.* I, 420; II, 698; *Compleynt* 523, etc.
358. access = an attack of fever; cp. *Troy-Book* Aa₆ d; *Falls of Pr.* 172 d; 217 a; *L. Lady* g₁a. Exceedingly common with these lovers; see *Troil.* II, 1315, 1543, 1578; *King's Quair* 67, 5; 144, 5; Skelton, *Garland of Laurel* 315; *Cuckoo and Night*, 39; *Black Knight* 136; *De duobus Merc.* fol. 62 b; *Falls of Pr.* 124 a;
"With loues axcesse now wer thei whote now cold."
In the *Play of the Sacrament*, l. 611, we have the word as a monosyllable axs, rhyming with laxe (see the *Transactions of the Phil. Soc.* 1860/61, Appendix):
"Who hat[h] yᵉ canker yᵉ collyke or yᵉ laxe,
The tercyan yᵉ quartane or yᵉ brynny[n]g axs."
sweltre and swete.] *Rom. of the Ro.* 2480:
"Though thou for love swelte and swete."
Similarly *Miller's Tale* 517.
362. Cp. *Troil.* II, 538, 539:
"And wel the hootter ben the gledis rede
That men hem wren with asshen pale and dede."
De duobus Merc. (MS. Hh. IV. 12, fol. 62 a):
"I am I-hurt, but closed is my wond;
My dethes spere stykkyth in my brest;
My hollyng festryth that it may nat sond,
And yit no cicatrice shewith at the lest."
Flour of C. 26: "And though your lyfe be medled wᵗ grenaunce,
And at your herte closet be your wounde."
Soliman and Perseda (Dodsley-Hazlitt V, 296):
"And I must die by closure of my wound."
385. This line occurs again word for word further on in our *T. of Glas*, as l. 1295. Similar to it is line 639 of the *Court of Love*:
"Withoute offence of mutabilite."

388. According to Chaucer and Lydgate, Saturn is Aphrodite's father; see the *Knightes Tale* 1595, where Saturn addresses Venus " my deere doughter Venus "; further on, l. 1619, Saturn calls himself Venus's *ayel*. Lydgate's *Reason and Sensuality* (fol. 219 b etc., and 221 b etc.) tells the same story concerning Venus's birth, as Hesiod's *Theogony*, with the difference that the part of Uranus is given to Saturn, and that of Saturn to Jupiter. Comp. especially fol. 222 a:
"For writyng of poetis halt

> That she roos of the foom most salt,
> Which ryseth in the wawes felle,
> That fynaly, as clerkes telle,
> The See was moder to Venus,
> And hir fader Saturnus."

Lydgate may have taken this from his favourite Fulgentius (ed. Muncker, p. 70). Cp. also *Rom. of the Rose* 5956—5959. Chaucer, however, calls Venus also "doughter to Dyon" (*Troilus* III, 1758), a version well-known from the *Iliad*. —The astrological influence of Saturn is the most baneful of all planets; see *Troil.* III, 667; *Knightes T.* 229, 470, and particularly 1595 etc.; Dunbar, *Golden Targe* 114; *Kingis Quair* 122:

> "Or I sall, with my fader old Saturne,
> And with al hale oure hevinly alliance (see *T. of Glas*, l. 1231)
> Oure glad aspectis from thame writh and turne."

Lyndsay's *Dream*, 474:

> "Tyll Sáturnús, quhilk trublis all the hewin
> With heuy cheir, and cullour paill as leid"...

394. I suppose "a dropping mone" means a wet or misty moon, as portending rainy weather. Cp. *Falls of Pr.* 67 b:

> "Of Diana the transmutacion,
> Now bright, now pale, now clere, now dreping."

Some texts of the *Temple of Glas* also read *dreppyng*, which, of course, is O.E. strong *dréopan*, whilst *dropping* comes from O.E. weak *dropian*.

395, 396. Cp. *Troilus* III, 1011—1015; further *Guy of Warwick* 11:

> "The sonne is hatter affter sharpe schours . . . .
> And affter mystys Phebus schyneth bright."

Troy-Book I, b: "For after stormes Phebus bryghter is."
Albon II, 1918: "as passed is the daungere
> Of stormy weders, Phebus is most clere."

Piers Plowman, C-text XXI, 456, 457:

> "After sharpest shoures . . . most sheene is þe sonne;
> Ys no weder warmer þan after watery cloudes."

Spenser, *A Hymn in honour of Love*, ll. 277, 278:

> "As after stormes, when clouds begin to clear,
> The sun more bright and glorious doth appear."

Cp. also Boethius, *De cons. phil.*, 2nd metre of book III.

397. "Joy cometh after whan the sorow is past."
Hawes, *Pastime of Pl.* (ed. Wright, p. 148).

398, 399. *Rom. of the R.* 2119:

> "To worshipe no wight by aventure
> May come, but if he peyne endure."

400 and 401. Similar sentiments in stanzas 104, 105.

401. That.] The same construction in l. 362, and *Falls of Pr.* 71 d:

> "For more contrarye was their falling lowe
> That they tofore had of no mischief knowe."

401. (a)*waped and amate*], frequent expression; see *Black Knight* 168; *S. of Thebes*, fol. 359 d; *Troy-Book* A₂ c, O₁ b, O₃ a, U₃ a, X₃ d; *Pilgrim.* 22 a, 298 b. *awhaped* alone occurs *Troy-Book* O₂ a; *Falls of Pr.* 39 b; *Anelida* 215; *Legend*, Prol. 132; *Thisbe* 109; *Philomele* 94; Gower and Spenser also have it. L and b read *wrapped;* cp. Miss Toulmin Smith, *Gorboduc*, p. 68.

403, 404. Very much the same is expressed in l. 1251. Cp. also *Troil.* I, 638:

> "For how myght evere swetenesse han ben knowe
> To hym that nevere tasted bitternesse?"

Court of S. a₂ a: "as tasted bytternesse
> All swete thynge maketh be more precyous."

De duobus Merc. (Hh. IV. 12, fol. 60 a):

> "But as to hem that hath I-tasted galle,
> More agreable is the hony soote."

Court of S. a, b: "And ryght as swete hath his apryce by soure."
Surrey (Aldine Poets, p. 30): "by sour how sweet is felt the more."
Dunbar, ed. Laing, I, 89, 1. 81:
"And how nane deservis to haif sweitness,
That nevir taistit bitterness."
The sentiment is reversed in the *Rom. of the Rose* 4138.
405. Grisilde.] See l. 75.
407. Penelope.] See l. 67.
dulle as an intransitive verb occurs *Troy-Book* I, b, M, b; *Falls of Pr.* 35 d, 105 b, 136 b, 159 d; *Troilus* IV, 1461; *Rom. of the R.* 4795. MSS. G and S read *dwelle;* similarly we have in MS. Cott. Tib. A. VII, fol. 88 b (*Pilgrimage of Man*):
"And affter that sche lyste not dwelle,
But gan hir hanker vp to pulle."
409. Dorigene.] This is taken from the *Frankeleynes Tale.* Compare particularly Dorigene's Complaint, ll. 619—718. She is also mentioned in *Flour of C.* 192:
"Stedfast of herte, as was Dorigene."
411. *Troil.* I, 952: "And also joye is next the fyn of sorwe."
414. *Pilgrim.*, fol. 101 a:
"For seyntys wych that suffrede so,
I wot ryht wel that they be go
To paradys, & Entryd iu."
Isle of Ladies 941, 942:
"And saied he trowed her compleint
Should after cause her be corseint."
419. þe maner and þe guyse.] Common formula; see, for instance, *Troil.* II, 916; *Reason and S.* 273 a, 281 a, etc.
421. The word *emprise* usually means "undertaking"; but it seems also to have the meaning "lore, teaching (cp. *apprise*), governance"; for instance:
"To folwe themprises of my professioun."
Testament, Halliwell, p. 257.
"For whilom he learned his emprise
Of his Maister, Amphiorax the wise." *S. of Thebes* 376 a.
Cupid's *emprise* comes often in the *Rom. of the R.*, see ll. 1972, 2147, 2286, 4908; cp. further, *Edmund* II, 124, and *Reason and S.* 286 b:
"Who that ys kaught in his scruise,
And y-bounde to his emprise" (*Love's*).
424. Again a stock-line of our monk's, repeated in l. 879. It occurs also in the *Black Knight,* l. 554; *Troy-Book* Bb, d; *L. Lady* f, a. Similarly, *Pilgrim.* 183 b:
"Gruchchyng nor rebellioun,
Nor no contradiccioun."
431. in parti and in al], *Formula,* occurring again l. 1155; also in the *Troy-Book* H, a, N, c, X, c; *L. Lady* c, b; *Falls of Pr.* 184 a; *Albon* I, 228.
436. See l. 838. Cp. also *Reason and S.*, fol. 223 b:
(Venus) "hild also in hir ryght honde
Rede as a kole A firy bronde,
Castyng sparklys fer a-broode,"
where, in the rubric, the following wise remark stands: "hoc fingunt poete propter ardorem libidinis." This passage is immediately followed by an interesting allusion to the Greek fire.
445. þe arow of gold.] See l. 112.
450. to eschew vice.] See l. 1181. The sentiment that true love is able to make the lover "eschew every sin and vice," is frequently met with in poems of this period; cp. *Troilus* I, 252; III, 1751—1757, and III, proem 24:
"Alȝates hem that ye wol sette a fyre,
Thei dreden shame, and vices thei resigne."

See further *Cuckoo and Nightingale* 14, 151 etc., 191 etc.; *Court of Love* 598 etc., 1066—1078; Al. Chartier, *Le Parlement d'Amour*, ed. Tourangeau, p. 697:

"Car luy, qui n'a comparaison,
Ne peut souffrir en son serf vice."

451. spice.] Cp. *Falls of Pr.* 115 b:
"And spoyled he was, shortly to specifye,
With al the spises of pride and lecherye."

Reason and S. 299 a:
(Idelnesse) "bryngeth in al maner spices
Of vnthryfte and al vyces." ...

Cp. also *Henry VIII.*, II, 3, 26:
"For all this spice of your hypocrisy,"
where Al. Schmidt rightly explains *spice* by *taste, tincture*. We have similar'y "spice of heresy" in *Calisto and Melibœa*, Dodsley-Hazlitt I, 58. Cp. also "a spyced conscience," in Chauc.'s Prol. to the *Cant. Tales*, l. 526, and Skeat's note.

455. crop and root.] Common *formula* of Lydgate's. See, further on, l. 1210; and *Troy-Book* A₂ b, A₄ d, G₂ c, G₄ c, H₄ d, I₃ c, L₄ d, O₃ a, Z₆ a, An₁ c, Dd₁ c; *L. Lady* b₆ a; *Assem. of Gods* b₁ b; *S. of Thebes*, fol. 360 d; *Falls of Pr.*, fol. 8a, 30a, 75a, 116d, 199a (ground, chief, crop & roote); *Leg. of Margaret* 322; *Reason and S.*, fol. 203 b, 205 b (where we hear that the "mevyng of the speres nyne" is

"both crop and roote
Of musyk and of songis soote"), 239 b, 289 b.

Cp. further, *Compleynt* 397; *Troil.* II, 348; V, 1245; *Generydes*, ed. Wright, l. 4940; *Letter of Cupid*, stanza 3 etc.

We have almost certainly to read *trouthë*.

460. orisoun.] Such addresses to heathen gods are often called *orisouns* in the style of this period (see also l. 696). The word occurs, for instance, in the same usage, in the *Knightes T.* 1403; *Kingis Quair* 53, 1 (in both cases addressed to Venus). In the *Troy-Book* S₂ b, "deuoute orysons" are offered by the priests for Hector, etc.

462. of goode ȝit þe best.] Cp. the line
"For of al goode she is the beste lyvynge,"
which forms the burden of the ballad at the end of *Cuckoo and Nightingale*.

463, etc. The story is told in the *Troy-Book*, Chapter XII (Book II), and again in *Reason and S.*; see particularly fol. 228a—230a. Similar to our passage are the words of Mercury to Paris (*Troy-Book* G₃ d), where he tells him that the three goddesses

"Were at a feste, as I the tell[e] shall,
With all the goddes aboue celestyall, (cp. l. 466)
That Iubyter helde at his owne borde."

The story is again alluded to in the *Assem. of Gods* b₂ a.
Line 466 occurs also nearly word for word in *Troy-Book* N₄ c:
"To the goddes aboue celestyall."

Cp. also *Reason and S.*, fol. 209 b:
"Lych to the goddys immortall,
That be aboue celestiall."

In *Reason and S.* 224 a, Venus holds the apple in her hand, as an attribute, and emblem of her victory.

472. See the similar vow of Anelida, at the end of Chaucer's poem, and that of Alcyone, *Duchesse* 114. In the *Life of our Lady* h₂ a we read:
"And with encence cast in the sencere
He dyd worshyp vnto the aultere" (*Octavian*).

Knightes T. 1393:
"Thy temple wol I worschipe evermo,
And on thin auter, wher I ryde or go,
I wol do sacrifice, and fyres beete."

See also *ib.* 1417, etc.; *Court of Love* 324, and *T. of Glas* 537, etc.

486. To bring to rest, to set in (at) rest, are common expressions; see, for instance, further on ll. 1095, 1294; *Troil.* II, 760; III, 917, etc.
490. Compare Lydgate's poem *Wulfric*, l. 8 (*Halliwell*, p. 72).
494, 495. *Troil.* III, 1224:
"laude and reverence
Be to thy bounte and thyn excellence!"
Stanza 25 a, 7. serpent Ielosye.] See l. 148.
Stanza 25 b, 7. Cp. *Court of L.* 582:
"And ponysshe, Lady, grevously, we praye,
The false untrew, with counterfete plesaunce."
For Malebouche, see note to l. 153.
Stanza 25 c, 6, 7. Cp. *Squierres Tale* II, 301—303; further *Parl. of F.* 346: "the scorning Iay"; *ib.* 345: "the Iangling pye"; 347: "The false lapwing"; 343: "The oule eek, that of dethe the bode bringeth"; cp. Skeat's notes. "As the howle malicious" occurs in *Secreta Secretorum*, fol. 150 b (Burgh's part); see further, *Troilus* V, 319, 382. We also recall poems like *The Owle and Nightingale*, and Holland's *Howlat*. For the jay, see *Man of Law's Tale* 676: "thou janglest as a jay"; *Chau. Yem. Tale* 386: "chiteren, as doon these jayes"; *Garland of Laurel* 1262: "iangelyng iays." See further a poem in MS. Gg. 4. 27, fol. 9 a:
"ʒit in þe wode þere was discord
þourgh rusti chateryng of þe Iay;
Of musik he coude non acord.
Ek pyis vnplesaunt to myn pay,
þey iangeledyn & made gret disray."
Cp. further *Pilgrim.* 218 b:
"And Iangleth euere lyk a Iay,
A bryd that callyd ys Agaas."
For the pie, cp. further *Reeves Tale* 30: "proud and pert as is a pye"; *March. Tale* 604: "ful of jargoun, as a flekked pye." The pie is also enumerated among the disagreeable birds by Lyndsay, *Papyngo* 647.
496. This = This' = This is; occurs again l. 1037, where *is* is written in full in the MS. See *Parl. of F.* 411 (and Skeat's note) and 650; the contraction occurs also in *Frank. Tale* 161, 862; *Sec. Nun's Tale* 366; *Troilus* II, 363; IV, 1165, 1246.

505. hawethorn.] Venus is usually represented with a chaplet of roses; see *Knightes T.* 1102:
"And on hire heed, ful semely for to see,
A rose garland fresch and wel smellyng."
Again, *Fame* 134:
"And also on hir heed, parde,
Hir rose-garlond whyte and reed."
Reason and S. 223 b:
"But she had of roses rede
In stede therof a chapelet,
As compas rounde ful freshly set."
So also *Troy-Book* K₁ b:
"And on hir hede she hath a chapelet
Of roses rede, full pleasauntly yset."
Troy-Book G₃ b we are told that the red roses mean:
"hertely thoughtes glade
Of yonge folkes, that be amerous."
Kingis Quair 97, 6 and 7:
"And on hir hede, of rede rosis full suete,
A chapellet sche had, faire, fresch, and mete."
Peele also, *Arraignment of Paris* I, 1, speaks of Venus's "wreath of roses."
In explanation of the monk here choosing hawthorn for Venus's garland, rather than roses, I may mention that the May-queen used to be crowned with hawthorn; it was also used in Greek wedding-processions, and the altar of

Hymen was strewn with it.—Hawthorn is mentioned in the *Knightes Tale* 650 ; *Black Knight* 71 ; *Court of L.* 1354, 1433 ; *Rom. of the Rose* 4002 ; *Flower and Leaf* 272 ; *Kingis Quair* 31, 5 ("hawthorn hegis knet"), and, similarly, *Dunbar*, ed. Laing, 1, 61, l. 4 ; these passages form, however, no illustration to our line.

506. Cp. *Troy-Book* B₆ *d* :
  "That to beholde a Ioye it was to sene."

510. MSS. G and S introduce here "Margarete" as the name of the Lady ; their reading is certainly not the original one, as the two other MSS. of their group, F and B, preserve the old reading. The name Margarete was, no doubt, introduced in connection with the glorification of the daisy by Chaucer. See above, l. 70.

514 etc.] Cp. *Flower and Leaf*, ll. 551 etc.

524. *Knightes Tale* 1407 : "But atte laste the statue of Venus schook."

525. was in peas = was silent. Similarly *Troy-Book* B₁ *b* :
  "And than anone as Iason was in pes."
Pilgrimage, 83 *b* : "She stynte a whyle & was in pes."
Isle of Ladies 1008 :   "every wight there should be stille,
  And in pees."

526. "femynyne of drede" occurs also in *L. Lady* a₇ *a*.

533, 534. *Troy-Book* Aa₁ *c* :
  "Great was the prease that in the weye
  Gan Croude and shoue to beholde and sene."

536. shortli in a clause.] Frequent stop-gap ; see *Troy-Book* Y₂ *b* ; *Pilgrimage* 149 *a* ; *Rom. of the Rose* 3725 etc.

536, etc. In the *Troy-Book* also, fol. II₄ *a*, Venus is honoured
  "With gyftes bryngynge, and with pylgrymage,
  With great offrynge, and with sacryfyse,
  As vsed was in theyr paynem wyse."
Helen, *Troy-Book* H₂ *a*, makes
  "hir oblacion ....
  With many iewell, and many ryche stone."

537. Cp. *Troy-Book* X₁ *b* :
  "To telle[n] all the rytes and the gyse."
Court of Love 244 :
  "They .... did here sacrifice
  Unto the god and goddesse in here guyse."

539. *Story of Thebes*, fol. 377 *d* :
  "Nor how the women rounde aboute stood,
  Some with milke, and some also with blood ...
  When the asshes fully were made cold."

540. floures.] Fulgentius, ed. Muncker, p. 71 : "Huic [*Veneri*] etiam rosas in tutelam adjiciunt. Rosæ enim & rubent & pungunt, ut etiam libido."

soft as silk.] Occurs also in Lyndsay's *Anc Satyre*, l. 341.

541. sparrows and doves.] *Troy-Book* K₁ *b* :
  "And enuyron, as Poetes telle,
  By downes whyte flyeuge and eke sparowes."
Parl. of F. 351 : "The sparow, Venus sone ;" see Skeat's note, who quotes Lyly's well-known song on Cupid in *Alexander and Campaspe*. See also Peele, *Arr. of Paris* 1, 1 :
  "Fair Venus she hath let her sparrows fly,
  To tend on her and make her melody ;
  Her turtles and her swans unyoked be,
  And flicker near her side for company."
Further, see *Tempest* IV, 100, and Sappho's famous song on the " ποικιλόθρονος 'Αφροδίτη." See further, *Troy-Book* G₂ *b* :
  "Aboute hir hede hadde doues whyte (*Venus*)
  With loke benyngne, and eyen debonayre ;"

we are also told that these doves mean
"very Innocence
Of them in loue that but trouthe mene."
Fulgentius is again given as the source; he, however, explains this symbol very differently, see Muncker's edition, p. 71: "In hujus etiam tutelam columbas ponunt, illa videlicet causa, quod hujus generis aves sint in coitu fervidæ."
Knightes Tale 1104:
"Above hire heed hire dowves flikeryng."
Parl. of F. 237: "And on the temple, of doves whyte and faire
Saw I sittinge many a hundred paire."
Past. of Pleasure, Chapter XXXI (ed. Wright, p. 155):
"A turtle I offred, for to magnefy
Dame Venus hye estate, to glorify."
Venus's doves are also mentioned in *Hous of F.* 137.
Cp. further *Reason and S.* 224 a:
"Ther was gret novmbre of dowes white,
Rounde about hyr hede fleyng" . . . .
Assembly of Gods e, b says of "Doctrine:"
"Ouer her hede houyd [Wynken *honyd*] a culuer fayre & whyte."

544. desire, viz., desire to be released from.

545. *shortli to conclude*, another stop-gap; see *Knightes Tale* 1037; *Story of Thebes*, fol. 356 a; 366 d, etc.

552. This solitary walk is in accordance with the 6th Statute of the Court of Love (see that poem, l. 338). Cp. also *Black Knight*, l. 587.

554, etc. Compare with this the description of the "Black Knight" (l. 155, etc.); with line 554 in particular, cp. also *Troy-Book* Dd₃ c:
"And if I shall shortly hym descryue" (*Chaucer*).

558. Have we to read: The mostë passing? See line 292.

559. "Man is here used emphatically," says Prof. Skeat, in his Note to a similar passage in the *Leg. of Dido* (l. 251):
"For that me thinketh he is so wel y-wroght,
And eek so lykly for to be a man" (*Æneas*).
Cp. also *Falls of Pr.* 180 c:
"Them to chastise toke on hym like a man."
Halliwell, *M. P.*, p. 4:
"How lyke a man he to the Kyng is gone" (*the Lord-Mayor of London*);
cp. *ib.* p. 207, l. 2: "But lyk a man upon that tour to abyde";
and *Generydes*, ed. Wright, ll. 2243, 2244:
"Generides ayenward lik a mañ
With-stode his stroke, and smote hym so ageyñ."

582. Ewrous.] Exactly corresponding to French *heureux*. The word occurs also in *Troy-Book* P₃ b:
"For no wyght may be aye victoryous
In peas or werre, nor ylyche Eurous;"
Reason and S., fol. 216 b, and 275 b, "ewrous and fortunat;" "ewrous and happy," fol. 272 b; "ewrous," fol. 274 a; *Edmund* I, 1057 and II, 177; *Falls of Pr.* 5 a: "Most ewrous, most mightie of renoume."
Ib. 121 d: "The same day not happy, nor Eurous."
Pilgrimage 62 a: "Happy also & ryht Ewrous;" similarly "happy And Ewrous," *ib.* 260 b.
Magnus Cato: "As to be eurous, mighty, stronge, and rude"
(*eurous* stands in Caxton's print; MS. IIh. IV. 12 has *virous* instead). We have the word also twice in the English translation of Alain Chartier's *Curial*, ed. Furnivall, 5/15, and 15/21 (again the same phrase "ewrous and happy"). The corresponding noun (e)ure (= augurium) is in common use; so is another ure = Lat. opera, O.F. uevre (still in Mod.-Engl. inure); an adjective *urous* is also derived from this second *ure: Story of Thebes* 363 b (or rather, 362 b):
"Urous in armes, and manly in werking."

567. The poet's complaint in the *Flour of Curtesie*, l. 53, begins similarly: "alas what may this be."

568. *Chorl and B.* 89: "Now am I thral and sume tyme I was free." *Clerkes Tale* l, 91: "Ther I was fre, I mot ben in servage."

572. For the omission of the article, see l. 132.

574. of nwe.] Occurs again in l. 615; see note to l. 1319.

575. enbraced.] The word may here also have the meaning of French *embraser*, as it no doubt has in l. 846. Cp. *Pilgrimage*, fol. 281 *a*:
"And *with* the flawme he kan enbrace [Satan]
Folkys hertys,"
a translation of the French line:
"Fait tous fumer et embraser" (Barthole and Petit, fol. 76 *c*).
Pilgr. of the Soul, fol. 50 *b*: [they shall ben . . .] "al enbracyd with brennyng brondes;" French original:
"Et de feu tous les embrasez" (*ib.* fol. 115 *d*).

578, etc. See l. 279, etc.; 267, etc.

591 etc. Cp. *Rom. of the Rose* 3529 etc.

596. yold.] Reminds one of expressions like "serf rendu" in the French love-poetry.

604. pantire.] See for this word, Skeat's note to the *Leg. of Good W.*, Prologue 130, and his *Etym. Dict.* (under painter). The word occurs also in *Rom. of the Rose* 1621; *Remedie of Love* (1561), fol. 323 *c*; *Chorl and Bird*, ll. 77, 174, 268; *Troy-Book* G₂ *a*; *Falls of Pr.* 66 *c*; *Reason and S.* 291 *b*; *Pilgrimage*, fol. 227 *a*; *ib.* fol. 208 *a*: (Lyk a byrd . . . wych . . . .)
"for dred begynneth quake,
Whan she ys in the panter take,
Or engluyd with bryd lym."
[French original: "Tant com loisel va costoyant,
Et ca et la le col tournant,
Sounant aduient quan las est pris," etc.]

606, etc. *Troilus* I, 415: "thus possed to and fro,
Al stereles withinne a boot am I
Amyd the see, betwexen windes two,
That in contrarie standen ever mo."
Leg. of Phyllis 27: "and posseth him now up now doun."
Falls of Pr. 69 *d*: "They be so possed with windes in thy barge."
"Forpossyd" occurs in *Compleynt* 530; *Troy-Book* Q₁ *a*; *Falls of Pr.* 3 *b*; *L. Lady* e₁ *b*: "As in balaunce for-possyd vp and doun."
Troy-Book I₃ *b*: "Now vp now downe, forcast and ouer throwe
Theyr shyppes were with tempest to and fro."
Edmund II, 100: "With sondry tempestis forpossid to and fro."

609. Perhaps the reading *sturdy* in F. B. G. S, for *a soudri*, is right; cf. *Troy-Book* I₃ *b*: "The see gan swelle with many sturdy wawe;"
Pilgr., fol. 297 *a*: "Boyllyng with many sturdy wawe."
Ib., Cott. Tib. A. VII, fol. 54 *a*: "Amonge the sturdy wawys alle."
And see the 2nd quotation from the *Troy-Book* in note to l. 53.

614. ouershake.] *Troy-Book* H₆ *d*:
"Wherfore I rede to let ouershake
All heuynesse."

614, etc. This is a difficult passage to construe. The anacoluthon seems to begin with "for who," in l. 615, unless we may be allowed to assume that the expression "for who is hurt of newe" may mean "being one who is newly hurt," parallel to "for astoneid," etc. (see note to l. 632). *your*, in l. 620, is very peculiar. Can it mean "*Venus's* war" = love? It is more likely that the monk thought that he—or his knight—had apostrophized Cupid, so that *your* refers to Cupid: "no one, warring with you (Cupid), may vaunt himself to win a prize, except by meekness." For the comparison of love to war, cp. the "Militat omnis amans" of Ovid, *Amores* I, 9.

615. of nwe.] See the notes to ll. 574 and 1319.

618. kouþe.] We should expect the reverse construction of *couth:* the harms of Cupid are known to him, not he to them. Thus *couth* comes to have the meaning of "acquainted with." An instructive instance of this transition is *Liflade of St. Iuliana,* ed. Cockayne, p. 22: "ȝef þu cucowe aut were cuð wið þe king."

619, etc. For the might of Cupid, which neither gods nor men can withstand, see especially *Reason and S.* 235 b, etc., where the instance of Phœbus and Daphne is quoted at length (see *Temple of Glas,* ll. 111—116); and again, folio 275 b, etc. Cp. further, *Troilus* III, 1695 etc.; *Cuckoo and Night.* 1—20; *Court of Love* 92 etc.; *Rom. of the Rose* 878 etc., 4761 etc. See also note to l. 322. With l. 620 cp. *Isle of Ladies* 2112:
    "Against which prince may be no wer."

622. *Troilus* III, proem, l. 38:
    "That who-so stryveth with yow (*Venus*) hath the worse."
Ib. I, 603:   "Love, ayeins the which who-so defendeth
        Him-selven most, him alderlest availleth."
Cp. also *ib.* III, 940; V, 166.

631. Drede and Daunger, Personifications from the *Rom. de la R.*, see note to l. 156. For "Drede" see *Rom. of the Rose* 3958, etc.; *Court of Love* 1034; *Troilus* II, 810. In the *Bowge of Court,* l. 77, Skelton introduces himself as "Drede."

632. for vnknowe.] This construction of *for* with the p.p. occurs also in l. 934 and 1366, and is in general of frequent occurrence. We even have "for pure ashamed," *Troil.* II, 656; for pure wood, *Rom. of the R.*, 276; for verry wery, *Black Knight* 647; for very glad, *Generydes* 1255.

634. These exaggerations are as common as they are absurd; see *Introduction,* Chapter XI, p. cxxxix. Cp. further on, l. 724; *Black Knight* 512:
    "And thus I am for my trouthe, alas!
    Mordred and slayn with wordis sharp and kene."
Menelaus, *Troy-Book* I₂ c, falls into "a swowne....
    Almoste murdred with his owne thought."
In the *Court of S.* a₃ a, man is also represented as being doomed to "dye at the lest." For similar exaggerations see *Troilus* II. 1736; *Anelida* 291; *Squieres Tale* II, 128; *Frankeleynes Tale* 97, 112, 352, 613; *Knightes Tale* 260, 474, 709; *Merciless Beaute,* 1; *Isle of Ladies,* 520; *Compleynt* 437. The least thing that these unlucky lovers do, is to swoon constantly; once, twice, three times, according to the intensity of their feeling; in *Generydes,* ed. Wright 4099, Clarionas swoons fifteen times running.

637. wisse.] To teach, = O.E. wissian. Common in Lydgate. See *Troy-Book* N₃ c (to guye and to wysse); S₄ b (wysshe me or teche); *Assembly of Gods* d₁ a: "axed yf ony wyght
        Coude wysshe hym the wey to the lord of lyght."
Reason and S. 250 a; *L. Lady* K₁ a (wysse : blysse : mysse); *ib.* K₁ b:
    "And like a prophete to wisshen vs and rede";
similar expression in *Falls of Pr.* 9 c; 42 d. See also *Troil.* I, 622; *Freres Tale* 117; *Morte Arthure,* ed. Brock, 9, 671, 813.

641. Cp. *Black Knight* 563: "That lye now here betwexe hope and drede;" *Troilus* V, 1207: "Betwixen hope and drede his herte lay."

643, 644. A similar allegorical battle between Hope and Drede (or Daunger and Dispeyr) is found in the *Court of Love* 1036—1057; see also *Black Knight* 12, 13. Compare further the conflict in Medea's breast, between "Love and Shame," in the *Troy-Book;* particularly folio C₁ c:
    "For whan that loue of manhode wolde speke...
    Cometh shame anon, and vtterly sayth nay."
Very similar to our passage is also *Falls of Pr.* 217 a.

648. *Falls of Pr.* 178 d: "Nowe liest thou bound, fettred in prison."

650. Cf. *Knightes T.* 368, 379.

651. were.] = doubt; occurs several times in Chaucer, very frequently in Lydgate, and in the northern poets. See *Duchesse* 1295; *Hous of F.* 979; *Legend* 2686. The word occurs again in the *T. of Glas*, l. 906, and in the *Compleynt* 261; cp. further *Troy-Book* U₂d:
"And thus he stode in a double weer."
Similarly *Falls of Pr.* 67 c; *Legd. of St. Giles* 367; *Guy of Warwick* 27, 5; *Reason and S.*, 232 b, 242 a, 244 a; *Lancelot of the Laik* 84. A very common phrase is "withoute were," so in *Reason and S.* 202 b, 206 b; *Floure of Curt.* 223; *Pilgrim.* 147 b, 252 a, 252 b, etc.; *Rom. of the Rose* 1776, 2568, 3351, 3152, 5488, 5660, 5695; Lyndsay's *Dream* 613, 642; also "but weir," *ib.* 485, 496; *Dunbar*, ed. Laing, I, 89, l. 70. In Skelton's *Bowge of Courte*, l. 31, we find a p.p. *enwered*, evidently derived from *were*.

656. Despair, frequently personified: see ll. 895, 1198; *Black Knight* 13; *Troil.* II, 530; *Court of L.* 1036, and especially the *Assembly of Gods*. Cp. also *Troy-Book* T₁c (love-complaints of Achilles similar to those of our knight):
"Anone dispeyre in a rage vp sterte,
And cruelly caught hym by the herte."
666. *Troil.* II, 385: "That of his deth ye be nought for to wyte."
673. *Wanhope*, similarly repeated in l. 895.
678. *De duob. Merc.*, fol. 65 a: "My lyfe, my deth, is purtred in ʒowre face."
678, 679. Common sentiment in poems of the time; cf. again l. 749, 763. Simiarly *Isle of Ladies* 815:
"He said it was nothing sitting
To voide pity his owne leggyug."
684. Similar idea in Skeat, *M. P.*, p. 216, l. 93:
"I am so litel worthy, and ye so good."
689. dumb (still) as (any) stone, is a very common expression in Chaucer and Lydgate: still as any stone, *Milleres Tale* 286; *Temple of Glas* 689; *Troy-Book* H₁c; *L. Lady* k₂b; *Kingis Quair* 72, 6; as stille as eny stoon, *Squieres Tale* I, 163; *Troilus* II, 1494. still as stone, *Life of Edmund* III, 1212; *Story of Thebes* 372 b; *Isle of Ladies* 583. as still as stone, *Clerkes Tale* I, 65; *March. T.*, 574; *Troil.* III, 650; V, 1743. doumb as any stone, *T. of Glas* 1184. dome as a stoon, *Rom. of the R.* 2409. dome and styll as any stone, *De duobus Merc.*, fol. 72 b. as dowmb as stok or ston, *Pilgrim.* 271 a. muet as a stone, *Troy-Book* Dd₁d; *Story of Thebes* 369 d; *Compleint* 50; *Reason and S.* 244 b, 289 b. as hard as is a stone, *March.* 746. trewe as stone, *Rom. of the R.* 5251. stable as any (a) stone, *Falls of Pr.* 190 c; *St. Ursula* 6; *Albon* II, 1009. dffe as stok or ston, *Reason and S.* 291 b; (as) blynd (ys) a ston, *Pilgrim.* 149 a, 152 b; *March. Tale* 912; similarly *Rom. of the Ro.* 3703; deed as (eny) stoon, *Squ. T.*, II, 128; *Pite* 16; *Court of L.* 995.

691. withoute more sermon.] So also *Troy-Book*, H₃c.

696. oratorie.] See the Introduction, Chapter X, p. cxxxvii, and cp. note to l. 460. Mention is made of an oratory of Venus, *Troy-Book* D₁c, H₃d; *Knightes Tale* 1047; *Compleynt* 549; of Apollo at Delos, *Troy-Book*, K₃c; of Diana, L₁a; *Knightes Tale* 1053, 1059. We have the expression "oratory" often, of course, in the *Life of our Lady*, namely on folios b₄a, c₁a, c₂a, g₅b. *Troy-Book* H₃d speaks of "the chapell called Citheron"; *Reason and S.* 252 b of the chapel of Venus, in which the Sirens do their service day and night!

700. (anon) as ʒe shul here.] So again l. 1340; also *Black Knight* 217; *Albon* II, 176; *March. T.* 623; *Doct. T.* 177; *Parl. Prol.* 40; *Isle of Ladies* 70, 948, 1287; *Generydes* 2002, 3899, etc.

701, etc. This is the passage quoted in Skeat's *M. P.*, p. xlv, and in Wood-Bliss, *Athenæ Oxonienses*, I, 11, note.

701. *Citheria*, common for Venus; for instance, *Parl. of F.* 113; *Knightes Tale* 1357; *Troy-Book* P₁d; *L. Lady* d₂a; *Court of Love* 50, 556, etc. The name comes, of course, from Cythere; the author of the *Court of Love*, however, evidently confuses the island of Cythere and the mountain Cithæron; see ll. 49, 50, 69 of that poem.

Redresse.] In the *Court of Love*, l. 591, Venus is similarly addressed :
"Venus, redresse of al divysion."
703. Compare with this line *Knightes Tale*, 1365 :
"Thou gladere of the mount of Citheroun."
Cirrea.] See *Anelida* 17 : "By Elicon, not fer from Cirrea."
Ten Brink, *Chaucer-Studien*, p. 181, note 35, and Skeat, in the note to this line of *Anelida*, point out the occurrence of *Cirra* in *Paradiso* I, 36, whence Chaucer may have taken the name. Lydgate mentions Cirrea often; twice in the beginning of the *Troy-Book*, fol. A₁ a :
"And for the lone of thy Bellona, [Pynson *belloua*]
That with the dwellyth, beyonde Cirrea,
In Libye londe vpon the sondes rede"; and again, fol. A₁ b :
(the Muses) "that on pernaso [Pynson *pernasa*] dwelle
In Cirrea, by Elycon the welle."
Troy-Book L₄ b, speaks of the rape of Helen as perpetrated
"In the temple of Cytheia,
That buylde is besyde Cirrea."
Ib. Aa₂ d: "Nor the Muses that so synge can
Atwene the Coppys of Nysus and Cyrra,
Upon the hylle, besyde Cyrrea."
Falls of Pr. 17 d : (Apollo) "Which in Cirrha worshipped was yᵉ tyme."
We meet again with our Cirrea in a complete muddle of geographical names, in Lydgate's *Letter to Lord-Mayor Estfeld*, MS. Addit. 29729, fol. 132 b :
"towardes Ierusaleme,
Downe costynge, as bokes makyn mynde,
By Lubyes londes, thrughe Ethiope & Ynde,
Conveyed downe, wher Mars in Cyrria
Hathe bylt his palays,vpon yᵉ sondes rede,
And she Venus, callid Cithera,
On Parnaso, with Pallas full of drede . . .
Where Bacus dwellethe, besydes yᵉ Ryver
Of ryche Thagus, yᵉ gravylles all of gold," etc.
The further context tends to make it probable that Lydgate has here confused Syria with Cirrea. Who is "Cyrrha yᵉ goddesse," *Falls of Pr.* 147 a ?
705. Perhaps we have to scan : "wásshen and ófte wéte."
706. Here, for once, our MS. T alone has made a glaring mistake, in writing *eleccion* instead of *Elicon*. Or did the scribe object to the "riuer of Elicon"? Lydgate has "Elicon the welle" again in the beginning of the *Troy-Book*, fol. A₁ b (see above, note to l. 703), and speaks of it as
"Rennynge full clere with stremys cristallyn,
And callyd is the welle Caballyn,
That sprynge (!) by touche of the pegase,"
having, of course, Hippocrene in his mind. See further *Troy-Book* B₆ e : Medea had drunk, the monk tells us, "at Elycon of the welle"; so did Chaucer, as *Troy-Book* N₅ a tells us.
The note to line 703 will have sufficiently shown that Lydgate's geography is, in general, rather shaky; but here he may have been misled by Chaucer, *Hous of F.* 521 :
"that on Parnaso dwelle
By Elicon the clere welle."
See Skeat's note to *Anelida* 15. As an excuse for Chaucer we must add that Helicon is frequently called a well or fountain about this period. Skelton, *Garland of Laurel*, l. 74, speaks of "Elyconis well"; in the *Court of Love*, l. 22, we read of the
"suger dropes swete of Elicon;"
Lyndsay, in the Prologue to the *Monarche*, l. 229, says :
"Nor drank I neuer, with Hysiodus,
Off Hylicon, the sors of Eloquence,
Off that mellifluus, famous, fresche fontane."
In the notes to Spenser's *Shepherd's Calendar*, we even find it expressly stated

that "*Helicon* is both the name of a fountain at the foot of Parnassus, and also of a mountain in Bœotia, out of which floweth the famous spring Castalius," etc. The mediæval poets evidently applied the name Helicon, which properly belongs to the mountain, also to the famous springs on it, Aganippe and particularly Hippocrene, having also in their mind the Castalian fount on Mount Parnassus.

743. *March. Tale* 934:
"Ye ben so deep emprinted in my thought."

749. Cp. above, ll. 678, 679. Similarly we have in a small poem by Lydgate (MS. Add. 29729, fol. 157 *b*):
"I see no lacke but only y^t daunger
Hath in you voyded mercy and pyte;"
further, *Court of Love* 831:
"There was not lak, sauf daunger had a lite
This godely fresch in rule and governaunce."

750. sad demening.] *Secreta Secretorum*, fol. 121 *b*, we are told that a king must be:
"Sad of his Cheer, in his demenyng stable."
Sad, of course, meant "serious, grave." Cp. also *March. Tale* 360.
"Hir wommanly beryng, and hir sadnesse."

754. Mirrour, see l. 294.
governaunce] = discreet, well-controlled behaviour; the poets of this period often make mention of, and commend, this quality in woman. See *Duchesse* 1008; *March. Tale* 359; further, Henryson's *Garment of good Ladies*, l. 31; *Troy-Book* N$_4$d (Hector's *gouernaunce* praised). In a characteristic passage in the *Court of S.* sign. e$_4$a, "good Socrates" is called the "fyrst founder of gouernaunce" (= ethics). "Governance" is one of the two allegorical greyhounds at the beginning of Hawes's *Pastime of P.* The verb "governe" is used similarly; cp. *Secreta Secretorum*, fol. 99 *b*: (Aristotle wrote "Epistelys" to Alexander)
"By cleer Exaumple by which he myght[e] knowe
To governe hym, bothe to hih and lowe."

755. This is not the worst line in our *T. of Glas.* We have similarly in the *Troy-Book* H$_3$a:
"Within the cerclynge of hir eyen bryght (*of Helen*)
Was paradys compassed in hir syght."

761. pride.] *Rom. of the Ro.* 2239: "Loke fro pride thou kepe thee wele," etc. Similarly in l. 2352. Comp. further *Man of Law's Tale* 64:
"In hire is hye bewte, withoute pryde."
See. *Nun's Tale* 476:
"We haten deedly thilke vice of pryde."
Pride is the first sin in Gower's *Confessio*, and in the *Persones Tale*, p. 294: Lydgate also often warns against it. Pride characterizes herself in a very amusing way in the *Pilgrim.*, fol. 217 *b*:
"And offte tyme I boste also
Off thyng wher neu*er* I hadde a do,
My sylff avaunte off thys and that,
Off thynges wych I neu*er* kam at . . .
Vp w*ith* my tayl my ffethrys shake,
As whan an henne hath layd an Ay,
Kakleth affter al the day;
Whan I do wel any thyng,
I cesse neuere off kakelyng,
But telle yt forth in euery cost;
I blowe myn horn, & make host,
I sey *Tru tru*, & blowe my ffame,
As hontys whan they fynde game," etc.

In the *Assem. of Gods*, fol. b$_7$ *b*, Pride is introduced among the seven deadly sins, sitting on a lion.

778. I believe we must read the line:
"To ben as trwe as euer was Antonyús,"
and l. 781 with trisyllabic first measure, "Thăt wăs hĕlp-." The readings of G and S, which present no metrical difficulty, are not borne out by F and B. See the Introduction, pp. LII and LIX.

Antony and Cleopatra.] Their history is told in the *Falls of Pr.* VI 16, and in Chaucer's *Leg. of Cleopatra*. See also *Black Knight* 367; *Flour of C.* 195; *Troy-Book* $X_2 d$; *Parl. of Foules* 291; *Court of Love* 873, and Gower's list at the end of the *Confessio* (ed. Pauli, III, 361). Cp. also MS. Ashm. 59, fol. 53 a:
"And Cleopatre, of wilful mocyoun,
Lyst for to dye with hir Anthonius."

780. Pyramus and Thisbe.] See l. 80.

782. Antropos.] This is a common form of the name at that time. It occurs often in the *Assembly of Gods* and in the *Troy-Book*; for instance, $U_2 a$:
(Antropos) "That is maystresse & guyder of the rother
Of clothes shyp, tyll all goth vnto wrake."
See *ib.* $Y_1 a$, $Cc_6 c$; and *L. Lady* $g_5 b$, where all the three Fates are mentioned; *Reason and S.* 219 a, etc.; *Story of Thebes* 359 d; *Albon* II, 764.

785. Achilles and Polyxena, see above l. 94.

787. Hercules and Dejanira.] This is not a well-chosen example; Chaucer, more in accordance with classical mythology, has (*Hous. of F.* 397, 402):
"Eek lo! how fals and recchelees
Was . . . Ercules to Dyanira;"
and see again, *Wife of Bath's Prol.* 724.

The Story how Hercules won Dejanira, is told in the *Confessio Amantis*, Book IV (ed. Pauli, II, 70 etc.); how he deserted her for Iole, in the same work, Book II (*ib.*, I, 232 etc.). See also *Heroides*, epistle IX; *Metam.*, Book IX. Lydgate, however, seems to have believed that Hercules was faithful to Dejanira throughout, see the *Falls of Pr.* I, 14, and *Black Knight* 357. Hercules' exploits are narrated in detail in the *Troy-Book* $A_6 d$, etc., and $E_3 b$ etc.; in the *Falls of Pr.* I, 14; in the *Monk's Tale* 105—152; the *Garland of Laurel* 1284—1314, and they are also mentioned in the *Black Knight* 344—357; his name occurs further in *Parl. of F.* 288. In the *Falls of Pr.*, fol. 28 d, Lydgate calls Hercules a philosopher! "The great[e] Hercules" he is also called, *Troy-Book* $A_6 d$; "the worthy conquerour," *ib.* $D_6 b$. Cp. also *Reason and S.*, fol. 240 a:
(Hercules) "That was of strengthe pereles,
Rounde and square and of gret height."

788. shottes kene.] We have the same expression in *Troil.* II, 58.

792, 793. *Troil.* III, proem 31, 32:
"Ye (*Venus*) know al thilke covered qualite
Of thynges, which that folk on wondren so."

799, 800. Similar sentiment in l. 979. Cf. also *Troy-Book* $Dd_1 a$:
"More of mercy requerynge, than of ryght,
To rewe on me whiche am your owne knyght."

Frankel. Tale 588, 589:
"Nat that I chalenge eny thing of right
Of yow, my soverayn lady, but youre grace."
It is the 10th Statute in the *Court of Love*, ll. 368, 369. Compare also *Flour of Curt.* 106, 107:
"What euer I saye, it is of du[c]te,
In sothfastenesse, and no presumpcioun."

806. þe guerdon & þe mede.] Occurs elsewhere in Lydgate; for instance *L. Lady* $i_1 b$.

808. I think we had better leave out *your*, and let the line pass as acephalous; *your* stands only in G and S, not in the two other MSS. F and B of group **A**.

823. A mouth I haue.] This graceful expression occurs again *Troy-Book* $Q_3 d$:
"He had a mouthe, but wordes had he none" (*Troilus*).

Falls of Pr. 38 *d*: "A mouth he hath, but wordes hath he none."
See also *Compleynt* 49: "A tunge I haue, but wordys none."
In the *Falls of Pr.*, fol. 26 *a*, our roguish monk says of women:
"Thei mai haue mouthes, but langage haue thei none,"
and similarly *Reason and S.* 289 *b*:
"A mouthe they hañ, her tonge ys goñ."

829. Almost word for word in *Troil.* V, 1319:
"With herte, body, lyf, lust, thought, and alle."

838, 839. Cp. *Troy-Book* C₂ *c*:
"Lone hathe hir caught so newly in a traunce,
And I-marked with his fury bronde."
Ib. H₅ *a*: "Cupides darte . . . hath hym marked so."
Ib. H₅ *b*: "And venus hath marked them of newe
With hir brondes fyred by feruence."
Ib. X₁ *b*: "He was so hote marked in his herte."
Reason and S. 258 *b*:
"And even lyke shaltow be shent,
Yif Venus Marke the with hir bronde."
Cp. also *March. Tale* 483 and 533.

863. hasti.] Often censured as a fault, whereas the contrary is commended as a virtue. See above, l. 245; cp. also *Falls of Pr.* 24 *d*, and the whole chapter I, 13; the same idea expressed negatively, *Leg. of Margaret* 148:
"She, not to rekel for noon hastynesse,
But ful demure and sobre of contenaunce;"
Edmund I, 1001: "Koude weel abide, nat hasty in werkyng."
Ib. II, 514: "nat rakel . . . Lyst for noon haste lese his patience."
Cp. further l. 1203, and note. See also *Troy-Book* B₂ *c* (*Jason*); *Melibe*, p. 152, and *Troilus* IV, 1539, 1540. Compare further a beautiful passage in the *Pilgrim.*, fol. 54 *a*:
"Al thyng that men se me do, (*Nature*)
I do by leyser by & by,
I am nat Rakel, nor hasty;
I hate in myn oppynyouns
Al sodeyn mutacyouns;
My werkys be the bettre wrouht
Be cause that I haste nouht."
The passage reminds one strangely of the creator of the "*Erdgeist*," and his dearly-cherished belief in the tranquil, grand, silent working of Nature, as she weaves the "living garment of the godhead."

866. true as (any) steel.] Very frequent formula: *Hypermnestra* 21; *Squire's Prol.* 8; *Reason and S.* 297 *a*; *Rom. of the R.* 5149; *S. of Thebes* 363 *a*; *Troy-Book* I₂ *a*, I₃ *d*, R₄ *a*; several times in Shakspere, etc.

869, etc. Compare Minerva's admonitions to the poet in the *Kingis Quair*, stanza 129.

877. dilacioun.] Cp. ll. 1091, 1193, 1206. Both meaning and metre require this reading.

878. Resoun.] Personification from the *Rom. de li R.*; see *Rom. of the R.* 3034, 3193, etc.; cp. also *Reason and S.*; and *Assem. of Gods* c₁ *a*; *Pilgrim.* 25 *a*, etc.; Dunbar, *Golden Targe* 151. Similar to our line is *Troil.* IV, 1650:
"And that youre reson brideled youre delite," etc.;
further Halliwell, *M. P.*, p. 219:
"Lat reson brydle thy sensualite."
Cp. also *Troil.* IV, 1555: "And forthi, sle with reson al this hete."

879. This line is exactly the same as l. 424.

881, 882. Cp. again, l. 1090; further *Troil.* IV, 1556:
"Men seyn, the suffraunt overcomth, parde!"
See further, *Frank. Tale* 43—50; *Rom. of the Rose* 3463-5.

892. hope.] See ll. 641 etc., and further on l. 1197. "Good Hope" is King James's guide to Minerva; see the *Kingis Quair*, stanza 106, 5: "and lat gude hope the gye." Cp. also *Rom. of the R.* 2754, 2760, 2768 etc., 2941; further *Pilgrim.*, fol. 108 a:
"Good hope alway thow shalt yt calle:
Thys the name off thy bordoun."

897, etc. All these personifications are quite in the style of the *Rom. de la R.*

904. ri3t of goode chere.] The text-criticism is for this position of the words; "of right good chere," as F. B. L. b have it, occurs again *Falls of Pr.* 183 b, *Edmund* III, 493; with right good cheere, *Sec. Nun's Tale* 304; *Rom. of the Rose* 3617.

913—917. Cp. *Troil.* I, 857, 858:
"For who-so liste have helynge of his leche,
To hym behoveth first unwre his wounde."
Pilgrim. of the Soul, Caxton, fol. 21 a (chapter 23):
"What helpyth it thus for to telle and preche,
But shewe thy sore to me that am thy leche."
See further *Lancelot of the Laik*, ed. Skeat, l. 103:
"And It is weil accordinge It be so
He suffir harme, that to redress his wo
Previdith not; for long ore he be sonde,
Holl of his leich, that schewith not his vound."
Fairy Queen I, 7, 40:
"Found never help who never would his hurts impart."
Fletcher, *The Faithful Shepherdess* II, 2:
"that man yet never knew
The way to health that durst not show his sore."
Boethius, *De consol. philosophiæ* I, prose 4: "Si operam medicantis exspectas, oportet vulnus detegas."

915. oute of his hertis graue.] Curious expression. I suppose it means "out of his heart's grave" = out of his innermost heart. We constantly hear that these love-wounds are most dangerous when near the heart, and especially if they close up. See note to l. 362.

937. pale and wan.] Exceedingly common formula; cp. *Miller's Tale* 640; *Generydes*, ed. Wright, 752, 1297, 4703, 6760; *Black Knight* 131; *Troy-Book* A₁ d, A₃ c, D₂ a, Cc₄ c, Dd₁ d; *De duobus Merc.*, fol. 65 a; *Troil.* II, 551; IV, 207. "deadly pale and wan" occurs in *Falls of Pr.*, fol. 196 a. "Dead, pale & wan," ib. 123 b. The formula was still very common in Elizabethan times; see, for instance, *Shepherd's Calendar*, January, l. 8; *Fairy Queen* I, 8, 42; *Com. of Errors* IV, 4, 111; *Tit. And.* II, 3, 90; *Tamburlaine* 985, 2235, 3555, 4458. Perhaps we must consider "deedli" as an adjective, and then put a comma after it; cp. *Knightes T.* 224:
"That art so pale and deedly on to see;"
Black Knight 132: "And wonder dedely also of his hiwe;"
Kingis Quair 169, 2: "thy dedely coloure pale;"
S. of Thebes 371 c: "Dedly of looke, pale of face and chere;"
Albon III, 684: "Theyr dcedly faces."

939, 940. Cp. *Troy-Book* S₆ c:
"Of lyfe nor deth that he ronght[e] nought."
Falls of Pr. 95 d: "By manly prowesse of deth he rought[e] nought."
Troil. IV, 920:
"As he that of his lif no lenger roughte."
Cp. also the 6th Statute in the *Court of Love*, l. 340.

941. Most likely we have to read: "So mychë fere"; mychë corresponding to O.E. mycel.

947. Mi penne I fele quaken.] A favourite expression of Lydgate's. Cp. *Troy-Book* E₃ a:
"I wante connynge, and I fele also
My penne quake, and tremble in my honde."

Ib. Bb₄ *a* :   "For whiche, alas, my penne I fele quake.
                   That doth myn ynke blotte[n] on my boke."
L. Lady c₄ *a* :   "And though my penne be quakyng ay for drede."
Similarly *Troy-Book* R₄ *c* :   "that for wo and drede
                   Fele my hande both[e] tremble and quake";
and *Black Knight* 181.
Secreta Secretorum (MS. Ashmole 46, fol. 103 *b*) :
                   "With quakyng penne my consceyt to expresse."
Falls of Pr. 30 *c* :   "O Hercules ! my penne I fele quake,
                   Mine ynke fulfilled of bitter teres salt,
                   This piteous tragedy to write for thy sake."
Ib. 39 *b* :   "In her right hand her penne gan to quake" (*Canace*).
Ib. 46 *b* :   "Whose deadly sorow in English for to make
                   Of piteous ruth my penne I fele quake" (*Lucrece*).
Ib. 67 *d* :   "Mine hand gan tremble, my penne I felt[e] quake."
Ib. 89 *c* :   "My penne quaketh of ruth and of pitie."
Ib. 119 *d* :   "With quaking hand whan he his pen[ne] toke" (*Boccaccio*).
Ib. 136 *c* :   "My penne quoke, my heart I felt[e] blede"
                   (*in rehearsing the tragedy of Hannibal*).
Ib. 161 *a* :   "Myne hand I fele quakyng whyle I write."
Ib. 217 *a* :   "In which labour mine hand full oft[e] quooke,
                   My penne also, troubled with ignoraunce" . . .
Edmund III, 89 :   "That hand and penne quake for verray dreed."
Leg. of Margaret 57 :   "my penne, quakyng of verray drede."
Albon I, 928 :   "But now, forsothe, my penne I fele quake."
Cp. *ib.* I, 27, 28.
Application for Moncy 4 (Halliwell, p. 49) :
                   "this litel bille,
                   Whiche whan I wrote, my hand felt I quake."
Other affections of, and manipulations with, his pen are mentioned, *Troy-Book*
Z₄ *d* : (to describe their woe)
                   "My penne shulde of very routhe ryue."
Ib. Cc₄ *c* :   "For I shall now, lyke as I am wonte,
                   Sharpe my penne, bothe rude and blont."
Chaucer has the expression in *Troil.* III, 1784, 1785 :
                   "And now my penne allas, with which I wryte,
                   Quaketh for drede of that I most endite."
It occurs also in *Mother of norture*, l. 50 (*Morris's Chaucer* VI, 277).
Similarly, Gawain Douglas has (*Small* I, 48, 7) :
                   "Now mair to write for feir trimblis my pen."
   The following amusing lines from Bokenam's *Leg. of Margarete* (ed. Horstmann, I, 659—669) should also be compared with our present passage, and ll. 962, 963 of the *T. of Glas:*
                   "My penne also gynnyth make obstacle
                   And lyst no lengere on paper to renne,
                   For I so ofte haue maad to grenne
                   Hys snowte vp-on my thombys ende
                   That he ful ny is waxyñ vnthende (!)—
                   For euere as he goth, he doth blot
                   And in my book makyth many a spot,
                   Menyng therby that for the beste
                   Were for vs bothe a whyle to reste,
                   Til that my wyt and also he
                   Myht be sum craft reparyd be."

950. Cp. *De duobus Merc.*, MS. Hh. IV. 12, fol. 65 *a* :
                   "For with my self thowh I euermore strive."
wel unneþe = not at all easily ; scarcely ; with great effort ; *Monkes Tale* 431 ; *Frank. T.* 8 ; *Clerkes Tale* V, 108 ; Chaucer's *Boethius*, ed. Morris, 1515 ; *Troilus* V, 31, 399 ; *Flower and Leaf* 46 :
                   "That well unneth a wight ne might it se."

952—956. Cp. *Black Knight* 176 :
"But who shal now helpe me for to compleyne?
Or who shal now my stile guy or lede?"
Falls of Pr. A₂ b :
"But O alas, who shal be my muse,
Or vnto whom shall I for helpe call?
Calliope my calling will refuse,
And on Pernaso her worthy sustern all,
They will their suger temper with no gall;
For their swetenes and lusty freshe singing
Ful ferre discordeth from maters complaining."
De duobus Merc. (MS. Hh. IV. 12, fol. 66 b) :
"But now, alas! who shall my stile guye,
Or hen[ne]s-forth who shall be my muse?" ...

954, 955. Cp. *Falls of Pr.*, fol. A₃ d :
"Dities of mourning and of complayning
Doe not pertayn vnto Calliope . . . . .
And vnto maters of aduersitee,
With theyr sugred aureat licour,
They been not willye for to don fauour" (*the Muses*).

955. þei delite.] I think we must omit þei, following MSS. F. B. G. S. The construction of *delite*, which we should get by adopting the reading of the other texts, would be very unusual.

958. This invocation of the Furies is very common in Lydgate, whenever he has woe or horrors to relate. Chaucer started it in *Troil.* 1, 6 and 7 :
"Thesiphone, thou help me for tendite
This woful vers, that wepen as I write."
Ib. III, 1793 etc. :
"O ye Herynes! nyghtes doughtren thre,
That endeles compleynen evere in pyne,
Megera, Alecto, and ek Thesiphone! . . .
This ilke ferthe book me helpeth fyne."
Lydgate has it often; for example in the *Troy-Book* R₄ c :
"O who shall now helpe me to endyte,
Or vnto whom shall I clepe or calle? (1. 952)
Certys to none of the Musys alle, (1. 953)
That by accorde synge[n] euer in oon
Upon Pernaso besyde Elycon . . . .
It sytte them noughte for to helpe in wo,
Nor with maters that be with mournyng shent. (1. 954)
To them, alas! I clepe dare nor crye,
My troublyd penne of grace for to guye, (1. 956)
Nouther to Clyo, nor Callyope,
But to Allecto and Thesyphone, (11. 958 and 959)
And Megera that euer doth complayne."
De duobus Merc. (MS. Hh. IV, 12, fol. 67 a) :
"Alas, Meggera! I most now vnto the
Of hert[e] call, to help me to complayn;
And to thi sustur eke, the Siphone, (*sic*)
That aftyr iny goddessys ben of payñ."

Similar to these passages are stanzas 2 and 3 of Spenser's *Daphnaida*; Lyndsay's Prologue to the *Monarche*, ll. 216, etc., 237, etc.; *Remedie of Love* (1561), fol. 322 b :
"Aspire my beginnyng, O thou woode furie
Alecto with thy sustern" . . ., and fol. 322 d.
Somewhat different is *Falls of Pr.*, fol. 67 d :
"Me to further I fond none other muse,
But hard as stone Pierides and Meduse."
See on this passage Koeppel, *Falls of Pr.*, p. 72. Further *L. Lady* e₈ a :

"Nether to clyo ne to calyope
Me list not calle for to helpe me,
Ne to no muse, my poyntel for to gye ;
But leue al this and say vnto marie."

He says, however, elsewhere that Alecto hinders him (*Troy-Book* N₃ a):
"Cruell Allector (*sic*) is besy me to lette,
The nyghtes doughter, blynded by derkenesse."

By these constant invocations of the Furies, King James (*Kingis Quair* 19, 3) was misled into believing that Tisiphone was a Muse.

The Furies appear also in a different function in the *S. of Thebes*, fol. 360 b, and similarly, *Falls of Pr.* 198 b (cp. also *Æsop* 7, 27). These passages may be imitated from Chaucer's *Leg. of Philomela*, ll. 22—25, itself an imitation of Ovid's *Met.* VI, 428—432.

961. Compare *Black Knight* 178 :
"O Nyobe, let now thi teres reyne
Into my penne, and eke helpe in this nede,
Thou woful Mirre!"...

Similarly, *Troy-Book* R₄ d :
"Wherfore helpe now, thou wofull nyobe,
Some drery tere in all thy peteous payne,
Into my penne dolefully to rayne."

De duobus Mercatoribus (MS. Hh. IV. 12, fol. 67 a) :
"O wepyng mirre, now lett thy terys reyñ
In to myñ ynk, so clobbyd in my penne,
That rowght [*rowthe*, Harl. 2255] in swagyng a-brod make it renne."

Falls of Pr. 38 c (Canace writes a letter) :
"The salt[e] teares from her iyen clere
With piteous sobbing fet from her hert[e]s brinke
Distilling downe to tempre with her ynke."

962. blot.]   See *Falls of Pr.* 115 b :
"But to declare the vicious liuyng . . . (*of Agathocles*)
It would through perse & blot[te] my papere."

Ib. 120 b :   "O cursed Ceraunus, I leue thy story here,
Thy name no more shal blot[te] my papere."

Troy-Book Aa₃ b :
"And though my style be blotted with rudenesse."

Ib. Bb₂ a : (my penne) "That doth myn ynke blotte[n] on my boke."

Douglas, *Palice of Honour* (Small I, 54. 7) :
"It transcendis far aboue my micht
That I with ink may do bot paper blek."

Cp. also the quotation from Bokenam, in the note to l. 947.

963. To paint with fresh colours, with gold and azure, etc., is a phrase of common occurrence ; Lydgate often modestly says that he can only paint in black and white—"aureat colours," etc., being denied to him — ; here the turn for black has come (as also in ll. 551, etc.), and he must "blot" and "spot" his paper, instead of "illumining" it.

967. evil fare.]   Also in *Troy-Book* Cc₄ a ; *Falls of Pr.* 2 b ; *Story of Thebes* 360 c, etc.

970. Princess of youth, etc.]   We have similar addresses in *Garland of Laurel* 897, 904 :
"Princes of yowth, and flowre of goodly porte."

See also *Bowge of Court* 253, and *Court of Love* 843.

978. The natural position of the words would be : with hert quakyng of drede. Similar constructions in *Gorboduc*, see Miss Toulmin Smith's edition, note to l. 433, where we are referred to Abbott's *Shakspearian Grammar*, § 419 a. Compare also *Court of Love*, l. 1 :
"With tymeros hert and tremlyng hand of drede ; "

further, *Melibe*, p. 193 :
"these trespasours and repentynge folk of here folies" ; etc.

979. See l. 800, and note.

996. *feyne* seems here to mean "to be slack, idle;" like O.F. feindre (and its Participle feignant, in modern French made into fainéant). Cf. *Troilus* II, 997; *Duchesse* 317; *Rom. of the Rose* 1797, 2996; *Pilgrimage* 189 a:
"To don thy labour & nat ffeyne,
And myghtyly thy sylff to peyne."

999. chaunge for no newe.] See again further on, l. 1128; *Leg. of Dido* 312; *Leg. of Lucrece* 196; *Anelida* 219, etc.

1011. bi god and be my troupe.] Not unfrequent formula; see, for instance, *Troilus* III, 1464; *Court of L.* 648, etc.

1025. There is hardly a doubt that we must scan "hennës."

1026. inouȝ suffise.] This expression, which now appears pleonastic, was very common; see *Falls of Pr.* 13 c, 77 a; *Æsop* 7, 50; *Albon* II, 695; *Pilgrimage* 52 b, 64 a, 77 b, 78 a; *March. T.* 296; *Pard. Prol.* 148; *Shipm. T.* 100; *Monk's Prol.* 94; *Monk's Tale* 468; *Manne. T.* 232 etc.

1029. Are we to leave the second *as* in the line, and read the line with a trisyllabic first measure?
Comp. with this line, *Story of Thebes* 367 b:
"And as forforthe as it lith in me;"
further, *Troil.* IV, 863: "As ferforth as my wit kan comprehende."
Man of Lawes T. 1001: "As ferforth as his connyng may suffise."
Chan. Yem. Tale 76: "Als ferforth as my connyng wol strecche."
Frankel. Prol. 31: "As fer as that my wittes may suffice."
Parl. of F. 460: "As wel as that my wit can me suffyse."
Both, "as ferforth as," and "as fer as" are frequent constructions.

1036. Comp. *Black Knight* 517:
"And to youre grace of mercie yet I preye,
In youre servise that your man may deye."

103*. This is.] Read *This*; see l. 496.

1042, 1043. *Parl. of F.* 442—445:
"Right as the fresshe, rede rose newe
Ayen the somer-sonne coloured is,
Right so for shame al wexen gan the hewe
Of this formel"...

Troilus II, 1198: "Therwith al rosy hewed tho wex she."
Ib. 1256: "Nay, nay," quod she, "and wex as rede as rose."
Court of L. 1016:
"And softly thanne her coloure gan appere
As rose so rede, throughoute her visage alle."

1045. femynynite.] The proper form of the word in Chaucer and Lydgate seems to be *femininite*; cp. *Man of Lawes Tale* 262:
"O serpent under femininite."
The MSS. of Chaucer and Lydgate, however, frequently have the shorter form *feminite*, which we find in Spenser; cp. *Colin Clout*:
"And only mirror of feminity."
F. Queen III, 6, 51: "And trained up in trew feminitee."
Our line is indecisive; the full form makes it of the regular type A, the shorter form of type C.

1049. *Troy-Book* C₂ d:
"Ne lette no worde by hir lyppes pace" (*Medea*).

1052. Cp. *Troy-Book* X₁ d: [in Hector was]
"gouernaunce medlyd with prudence,
That nought asterte hym; he was so wyse & ware;"
and again S₄ b: "Unauysed / for no thynge hym asterte."
Ib. X₄ d: 'Of womanhede, and of gentyllesse,
She kepte hir so that no thynge hir asterte." (*Penthesileia*.)

1060. Cp. *Court of Love* 890:

"Truly gramercy, frende, of your gode wille,
And of youre profer in youre humble wise!"
1061, 1062. Cf. *Kingis Quair* 144, 1 and 2:
"Now wele," quod sche, "and sen that It is so,
That in vertew thy lufe is set with treuth" (... I will help thee).
1074. *Troilus* III, 112:
"Receyven hym fully to my servyse."
1078. Witnes on Venus.] *Nonne Prestes Tale* 416:
"Witnesse on him, that eny perfit clerk is."
Troy-Book A a₁ d : "Wytnesse on you that be iumortall."
The construction with *on* occurs further in *March. T.* 1038 ; *Pard. T.* 172 ; *Monkes Tale* 735 ; *Pers. T.*, p. 289 ; also in the poem by the "Dull Ass" (see the Introduction, p. cxlii, and note to l. 110), MS. Fairfax 16, fol. 308 b:
"Wytnes oñ Ambros vppoñ the bible."
We find also the construction with *of*, and *at;* cp. *Flower and Leaf* 530:
"Witnesse of Rome," and *Falls of Pr.* 16 a:
"I take witnes at (*off* Digby 263) Ieroboall."
A similar frequent expression is : Record on, vpon, or of.
1081. Perhaps we ought to read : "þe trouthë" in spite of the hiatus.
1082. unto þe time.] The omission of þe, as in MSS. G and S, makes the metre smooth. The article is often omitted before *time;* cp. further on, l. 1377; also *Falls of Pr.* 114 a:
"For vnto time that she gaue vp the breath."
See further *Generydes*, ed. Wright, ll. 4228, 6012, 6755.
1083. To shape a way.] Frequent expression ; cp. *Secreta Secretorum,* fol. 108 a ; *Story of Thebes,* fol. 358 a, 361 b, etc.
1085. To take at gre, to accept (receive) in gre, are frequent phrases.
1089. See l. 1203.
1090. Whoso can suffre.] This parenthetic, brachylogic construction is very frequent in Lydgate ; Chaucer has it also ; for instance, *Cant. Tales,* Prol. 741:
"Eek Plato seith, whoso that can him rede"...
Cp. further, for the maxim expressed in ll. 1089, 1090, above, ll. 881, 882, and note.
1094. *Troy-Book* C₄ b:
"And what I saye, to take it for the beste."
1106—1108. *Troy-Book* N₃ b:
"That theyr hertes were locked in a chayne" (*Achilles and Patroclus*).
Albon II, 756 : "So were theyr hertes ioyned in one cheyne."
1110. blisful.] Common epithet of Venus; see l. 328, and note.
1117. Your honour saue.] See note to l. 342.
1136. recorde.] See the Introduction, Chapter X, p. cxxxix, and again, l. 1234. Cp. also Gower, in the passage on Chaucer towards the end of the *Confessio :*
"So that my court it may recorde" (*Pauli* III, 374).
Scogan 22 : "Thou drowe in scorn Cupyde eek to record
Of thilke rebel word that thou hast spoken."
1138, 1143. Cp. *Troil.* II, 391, 392 :
"That ye hym love ayeyn for his lovynge,
As love for love is skylful guerdonynge."
Edmund I, 479 : "Bounte for bounte, for loue shewe loue ageyn."
1146. "Lowliness" to his mistress is the 7th Statute for the lover ; *Court of Love* 349.
1152, etc. With these admonitions of Venus to the Knight, compare the Statutes in the *Court of Love ;* see the Introduction, p. cxxxi.
1153. constant as a wall.] So also *Clerkes Tale* 109 ; *L. Lady* e₃ b. Similar expressions are common :

stable as a wal, *Edmund* I, 211; III, 390.
sturdy as a wall, *Troy-Book* U₄ d.
close as any wall, *Troy-Book* U₂ c.
stedfaste as a wall, *Troy-Book* Cc₃ a; *Falls of Pr.* 75 b, 128 a; *Reason and S.* 288 a; *Rom. of the R.* 5253; *Albon* II, 91.
stylle as a walle, *Troy-Book* Cc₁ a.
vpright as a wall, *Falls of Pr.* 142 c.

1154. Cp. *Court of L.* 315; *Troil.* III, 92: "humble, trewe, Secret." *Kingis Quair* 132, 1: "Be trewe, and meke, and stedfast in thy thoght." secre.] See note to l. 295.

1157. Tempest.] Rare verb; compare Chaucer, *Truth* 8:
"Tempest thee noght al croked to redresse."
Chaucer's *Boethius*, ed. Morris 1060: "so þat þou tempest nat þe þus wiþ al þi fortune" (te tuae sortis piget).—See further the *Century Dictionary*.

1159, 1160. *Rom. of the Ro.* 2229, 2230:
"And alle wymmen serve and preise,
And to thy power her honour reise."

1161—1165. *Rom. of the Ro.* 2231, etc.:
"And if that ony myssaiere
Dispise wymmen, that thou maist here,
Blame hym, and bidde hym holde hym stille."

1163. slepe or wake.] Absurd use of a common formula, which occurs in the *Sec. Nun's Tale* 153; *Rom. of the Rose* 2730; *Flour of Curtesie* 95, etc.

1164. champartie.] Lydgate seems to have got this word from *Knightes T.* 1090, 1091:
"Beaute ne sleight, strengthe, ne hardynesse,
Ne may with Venus holde champartye."
Champartie means "a share of land," and, generalized, "a share, or partnership, in power." But Lydgate was reminded, by the "champ parti," of the tilting ground, and "to holde champartie *with*" (or *against*) means with him "to fight against," "to hold the field against." This is rightly pointed out in the N. E. Dictionary. The word is very common in Lydgate, and may even serve as an evidence for the genuineness of doubtful writings. See *Reason and S.* 229 a, 246 b; *L. Lady* g₇ b; *Troy-Book* K₂ b, K₄ a, P₃ b, Y₆ a; *Story of Thebes* 366 d; *Bycorne* 41; *Pilg. of man*, fol. 59 a, 91 a, 128 b, 148 a, 299 a; *Falls of Pr.* 6 a, 16 b, 26 d, 34 (or rather 35) b, 69 c, 70 d, 148 d, 159 b, 195 b, 204 c.

1166, 1167. *Rom. of the Ro.* 2351, etc.:
"Who-so with Love wole goon or ride,
He mote be curteis, and voide of pride,
Mery and fulle of jolite."
Troil. III, Proem 26: "Ye (*Venus*) don hem curteis be, fresshe and benigne."
The 18th Statute of the *Court of Love* commands the lover to eschew "sluttishnesse," to be "jolif, fressh, and fete, with thinges newe, Courtly with maner ... and loving clenlynesse."

1167. fressh & welbesein.] So also *Troy-Book* l₁ c, Cc₁ c; *Macabre* (Tottel, fol. 223 d); *Pilgrim.* 176 a; similar expressions occur in *Story of Thebes*, fol. 363 c: "riche and wel besein" (so also *Generydes* 1978); "richely biseye," *Clerkes Tale* VI, 46; *Troy-Book* C₁ c: (Medea) "was bothe fayre and well besayne"; *ib.* C₃ b: "Full royally arayed and besayne" (chambers); "fresshely besene," *Troy-Book* Cc₃ b; "ryally beseen," *Court of Love* 121; "ffül ryally and wel beseyn," *Pilgrim.* 14 a; "goodely byseyn," *Troil.* II, 1262; "ille byseye," *Clerkes Tale*, VI, 27.

1168—1170. Similar expressions are not unfrequent in the love-poetry of the time, and betray a very brotherly feeling among these fellow-sufferers. Cp., for instance, *Kingis Quair* 184, 1:
"Beseching vnto fair Venus abufe
For all my brethir that bene In this place,
This Is to sevne that servandis ar to lufe,

And of his lady can no thank purchase,
His paine relesch, and sone to stand In grace." ...

Troil. III, 1741—1743 :
". . . esen hem that weren in distresse,
And glad was he if any wight wel feerde
That lover was, when he it wiste or herde."

Comp. also *Court of L.* 468, 469, which gives it a jocose turn.

1172. auaunte.] Compare for "avauntours" particularly, *Troil.* III, 240, 259, 269 ; further, *Pastime of Pl.*, Chapter XXXII :
"make none aduaunt
When you of loue haue a perfite graunte."

And see the amusing description of the "Avaunter" in the *Court of Love* 1219, etc.; also *Compl. of Mars* 37.

1173—1175. Compare with this sentiment the *Provençal Poem on Boethius*, l. 221, where "tristicia," together with "avaricia," "perjuri," etc., is enumerated as a sin :
"contr' avaricia sun fait de largetat,
contra tristicia sun fait d'alegretat" (*the rungs of the ladder*).

Dante puts the "tristi" into Hell ; comp. *Inferno* VII, 121 :
"Fitti nel limo dicon : tristi fummo
Nell' aer dolce che dal sol s' allegra,
Portando dentro accidioso fummo :
Or ci attristiam nella belletta negra."

So does Deguileville, *Pèlerinage de la vie humaine*, fol. 119 c (Barthole and Petit):
"Ce sont dist les filz de tristesse,
Gens endormiz en leur paresce " ;

in the English translation (*Caxton*, fol. 55 b): "these ben . . . the children of tristesse that slepyn in slouthe and lachesse." In consideration of the promises of the Faith, "tristesse" was accounted a great sin. Compare also the quotation from *Matthew* VI, 16 : "Nolite fieri sicut ypocrite, tristes," in *Piers Plowman* B XV, 213, and Dante's "collegio degl' ipocriti tristi" (*Inferno* XXIII, 91). Similar to our passage is *Secreta Secretorum* 126 b :
"Be nat to pensyff, of thought take no keep."

Pastime of Pl., p. 96 : "And let no thought in your herte engendre."

See further the passage from the *Rom. of the Ro.*, quoted above in the note to l. 1166 ; and *ib.*, ll. 2289, etc.:
"Alwey in herte I rede thee,
Glad and mery for to be,
And be as joyfulle as thou can ;
Love hath no joye of sorowful man."

Compare also *Kingis Quair*, stanza 121; further the picture of "Sorrow," *Rom. of the Ro.* 301—348, and the figure of Sansjoy in the *Faerie Queene*.

1176. sadness = earnestness. See *Magnus Cato* :
"Nat alway sad ne light of contenaunce,"

and again : "It is a good lesson . . .
to be glad and mery eft sones" (quoted in *Jack Juggler*,
Edmund I, 693—695 : beginning).
"Sadnesse in tyme, in tyme also gladnesse,
With entirchangyngis off merthe and sobirnesse
Affter the sesouns requered off euery thyng."

Duchesse 880 : "She nas to sobre ne to glad."

1177—1179. We must not fail to put it down to our monk's credit that, amongst so many commonplaces, he gives us at least one moral which has a manly ring. The same sentiment also forms the kernel of Agamemnon's discourse to Menelaus in *Troy-Book* l₂ c and d. Cp. also *Wanderer*, ll. 11—18 :
"Ic tô sôðe wât,
þæt bið on eorle indryhten þêaw,
þæt hê his ferðlocan fæste binde,
healde his hordcofan, hycge swâ hê wille ;

ne mæg wêrig môd wyrde wiðstondan,
nê se hrêo hyge helpe gefremman:
forþon dômgeorne drêorigne oft
in hyra brêostcofan bindað fæste."

1177. It is best for the metre to read *myrþē*.
1180, 1181. Cp. l. 450, and note.
1182. tales.] See note to l. 153; the whole Chapter I, 13 of the *Falls of Pr.* inveighs against such indiscreet "tales." In the *Secreta Secretorum*, fol. 98 b, the monk tells us that Aristotle hated "ſforgid talys"; *ib.* 121 a we hear that a king must not be

"lyghtly credible
To talys that make disceneioun."

The 14th Statute in the *Court of Love* is to believe no "tales newe" (l. 412).

1183. Word is but wind.] This simile occurs also *Troy-Book* l₁ d; Aa₁ c: (he is) "but worde and wynde."

Ib. U₁ b : "For lyke a wynde that no man may areste,
Fareth a worde discordaunt fro the dede."

Falls of Pr. 216 a : "Worde is but wind brought in by envye."
Pilgrim. 218 a : "Wynd and wordys, rud and dul,
Yssen out fful gret plente."

Secreta Secretorum (Ashm. 46, fol. 125 a):
"Trust On the dede, and nat in gay[e] spechys;
Woord is but wynd ; leve the woord & take the dede."

In *Magnus Cato* the Latin hexameter, "Contra verbosos noli contendere verbis" is paraphrased by:

"Agayns tho folkes that ay ben full of wynd,
Stryue not at all, it may the nat profite."

In the same poem we have the lines:

"Of thy good dede clamour nat ne crye ;
Be nat to wyndy ne of word[es] breme."

"Word is but wind" occurs also in Kyd's translation of Garnier's *Cornelie*, Dodsley-Hazlitt V, 216 ; in *Calisto and Melibœa*, ib. I, 69 ; Ingelend's *Disobedient Child*, ib. II, 301 ; Skelton's *Magnificence* 584 ; Wyatt, Aldine edition, p. 138 ; *Comedy of Errors* III, 1, 75 ; *Much Ado* V, 2, 52.

1184. dovmb as eny ston, see l. 689.

1185. This childish maxim reminds one of the philistine rules drawn up by the monk for children. Cp. also Burgh's part of the *Secreta Secretorum*, fol. 159 a :

"Whoo spekith soone Or ony man hym Calle,
Is vnresonñable, as philisophres expresse."

1188. myne.] Cp. *Falls of Pr.* 41 c:
"The vnkynd worme of foryetfulues,
In his heart had myned through the wall."

Ib. 67 b : "Let this conceit aye in your heartes mine."
Ib. 79 b : "That grace none myght in his heart[e] myne" (*Coriolanus*).
Ib. 150 d : "Under al this there did his heart[e] mine
A worme of auarice, his worship to declyne" (*Marius*).
Ib. 183 b : "Royal compassion did in hys heart[e] mine."
Testament 33 : "In amerous hertys brennyng of kyndenesse
This name of Jhesu moost profoundly doth myne."
Edmund II, 447 : "And heer-upon a werm most serpentyne
Of fals ennye gan in his herte myne."
S. of Thebes 372 b : "The rage gan mine on him so depe."
Pilgr. 65 a : "Thys mortal werm [*of conscience*] wyl neuere fyne
Vp-on hys mayster for to myne,
And gnawe vp-on hym day & nyht."

1191, 1192. L. *Lady* e₃ a :

"As golde in fyre fyned by assaye,
And as the tryed sylner is depured."

1197. See above l. 892. Cp. also *Falls of Pr.* 3 b:
"And thus false lust doth your bridell lede."
Ib. 6 c: "Pride of Nembroth did the bridell lede."
Rom. of the Ro. 4935:
"Delite so doth his bridil leede" (*of youth*).
Ib. 3299: "Take with thy teeth the bridel faste,
To daunte thyne herte."
Cp. also l. 878, and note.

1203. Abide a while.] *Rom. of the Ro.* 2121:
"Abide and suffre thy distresse,
That hurtith now; it shal be lesse" . . .
Kingis Quair 133:
"All thing has tyme, thus sais Ecclesiaste;
And wele is him that his tyme wel abit:
Abyde thy time; for he that can bot haste,
Can noght of hap, the wise man It writ."
March. Tale 728: "For alle thing hath tyme, as seyn these clerkis."
Melibe, p. 146: "He hastith wel that wisly can abyde."
In the *Secreta Secretorum*, fol. 104 b, "tretable abydyng" is enumerated as a virtue.

1208. Similarly *Troy-Book* T₆ b:
"That was this worldes very sonne and lyght" (*Hector*).

1210. crop and rote, see l. 455.

1220. his langour forto lisse.] The same expression occurs in *Albon* II, 658.

1221, 1225. Cp. *Rom. of the Ro.* 2087, etc.; 3320; *Anelida* 131:
"Her herte was wedded to him with a ring;
So ferforth upon trouthe is her entente,
That wher he goth, her herte with him wente."
Falls of Pr. 38 c: "Under one key our hertes to be enclosed."
Troy-Book N₃ b:
"That theyr hertes were locked in a chayne" (*Achilles and Patroclus*).
Ib. R₃ c: "She locked hym vnder suche a keye" (*Cressida and Diomed*).

1229. *L. Lady* g₄ a: "Eternally be bonde that may not fayle."
Reason and S. 230 a: "To han hir knyt to him by bonde,"
and again similarly 233 b.

1230. *Troy-Book* I₁ d:
"For euer more to laste atwene them tweyne,
The knotte is knyt of this sacrament" (*Marriage of Paris and Helen*).
De duob. Merc., Hh. IV. 12, fol. 65 b:
"and hath a day I-sett
Of hyr spousage to se the knott I-knett."

1231. alliaunce.] Cp. the quotation from the *Kingis Quair* in note to l. 388.

1234. record.] See note to l. 1136.

1234, 1235. Cp. Chaucer's *Legd. of Ariadne*, ll. 6 and 7:
"For which the goddes of the heven above
Ben wrothe, and wreche han take for thy sinne."
"To be wreke" (on) is a common construction in Lydgate: *Black Knight* 663;
Troy-Book Q₃ d, T₂ c, U₅ c; *Falls of Pr.* 59 a. 101 c; *Macabre* (Tottel 224 d);
Pilgrim. 62 a, 63 b, 65 a (in that place we have the form *wroke* rhyming with *spoke*; cp. *Compleynt* 605, 606). Shirley and Caxton read *bewreke*; but "to be wreke" is not to be mixed up with "to bewreak"; the latter word occurs, for instance, *Troy-Book* K₂ a:
"On Troyans our harmes to bewreke."
Chaucer has not unfrequently "to ben awreke," see *Frank. Tale* 56; *Maunc. Tale* 194; *Mill T.*, 564.

1238. Cp. *Falls of Pr.* 169 d:
"If that I might, I wolde race his name
Out of this boke that no man should it rede" (*Nero*).

1250. Cp. *Troil.* I, 642 :
"Ek whit by blak, ek schame by worthynes,
Ech sett by other, more for other semeth."
Falls of Pr. 160 d :
"Two colours seen that be contrarius,
As white and blacke—it may bee none other—
Eche in his kynd sheweth more for other."
Skelton, *Garl. of L.* 1237 : "The whyte apperyth the better for the black."
Pastime of Pl., p. 56 :
"As whyte by blacke doth shyne more clerely."
1251. See ll. 403, 404.
1252, 1253. Similarly, *Edmund* II, 592 :
"For alwey trouthe al falsheed shal oppresse."
S. of Thebes, fol. 366 d :
"Ayens trouthe, falshode hath no might."
Albon II, 1915 : "Trouthe wyll out, magre fals enuie."
The reverse is found in *Black Knight* 325 :
"He shal ay fynde that the trewe man
Was put abake, whereas the falshede
Yfurthered was."

1257. deinte = value, estimation, liking ; see *Anelida* 143 ; *Troil.* II, 164 ; *Frank. T.* 275 ; *Frank. Prol.* 9. "To have (hold) in deinte" is a frequent expression ; so, *Falls of Pr.* 9 a, 127 b ; *Rom. of the Rose* 2677 ; *Dunbar*, ed. Laing, I, 75, l. 376, etc.

1266. suffrable.] The suffix -*able* in an active sense (*i. e.* inclined to do or undergo something) is very common in Lydgate, in cases where in Modern-English it would have a passive sense ; Lydgate has deceivable, partable, defensible, credible (see quotation in note to l. 1182), etc. ; *suffrable* occurs again *Reason and S.* 289 b (also in *Wife of Bath's Prol.* 442) ; and cp. *Pilgrim.* 154 a :
"Thy body . . . . insensyble,
Wych muste witℎ the be penyble.—
Sustene also & be suffrable ;
For he wyl also be partable
Off thy merytes & guerdouns."
In Shakspere we find still "a contemptible spirit" = a contemptuous, scornful spirit (*Much Ado* II, 3, 187), and "an unquestionable spirit" = an unquestioning spirit (*As You Like It* III, 2, 393).

1271. *Troy-Book* B₈ a :
"What shulde I lenger in this mater dwell?"
1272. Comeþ off.] MSS. T. L, and the Prints omit *off ;* that the majority of MSS. are right, is made probable by the following passages : *Troil.* II, 310 : "com of, and tel me what it is" ; similarly, *ib.* 1738, 1742, 1750 ; *Miller's Tale* 540 ; *Freres Tale* 304 ; *Court of Love* 906 ; *Assembly of Ladies*, fol. 258 c. *Troy-Book* L₁ b : "Wherfore come of, and fully condescende."
Ib. Q₃ a : "Come of therfore, and let nat be prolongued."
De duobus Merc. (MS. Hh. IV. 12, fol. 64 a) :
"Tel on for shame ; cum of & lat me see."
Pilgrim. of the Soul, Caxton, fol. 66 a :
"Come of, come of, and slee me here as blyue."
1275. haþ, and shal, obeid], *i. e.* hath obeyed and shall obey. For this shortened form of construction see *Troil.* II, 888, 998 ; III, 1558 ; IV, 1652 ; V, 833 ; *Clerkes Tale* IV, 36 ; *Frank. Prol.* 16 ; *Hous of Fame* 82 ; *Rom. of the R.* 387 ; *Generydes*, ed. Wright, 4906 ; *Court of Love* 922 ; *Æsop* 8, 1 :
"An olde proverbe haþe beo scyde and shal."
1279. *wele* is here used as an adjective ; its opposite *woo* often occurs so also ; see *Knightes Tale* 68 ; Prol. to the *Canterbury T.*, 351, and Skeat's note ; further Abbott, *A Shakespearian Grammar*, § 230 ; Zupitza's notes to *Guy of Warwick*, ll. 1251 and 3474 ; Einenkel, *Streifzüge*, p. 112.

1283.]rifti] = well-ordered, becoming, seemly ; cp. *Troil.* III, 162 :
"She toke hire leve at hem ful thriftily,
As she wel koude," . . .
Frank. Tal; 444 : (a clerk) " Which that in Latyn thriftily hem grette."
Cp. also the use of "thrifty" in Prol. to the *Cant. T.*, 105 ; *Chan. Yem. Prol.* 50 ; *Shipm. Prol.* 3 ; *Chan. Yem. Prol.* 340 : unthriftily = slovenly.

1290. For the omission of the relative, cp. *Kingis Quair* 61, 3 :
"To here the mirth was thaiū amang."
Nonne Prestes Tale 355 : " he had found a corn lay in the yard."
Duchesse 365 ; " I asked oon, ladde a lymere."
Peele, *David and Beths.* III, 2 :
"And muster all the men will serve the king."
See Abbott, § 244 ; Mätzner, Engl. Transl. by Grece, p. 524 etc.

1295. The same as l. 385.

1297. *Troil.* II, 1622 : "What sholde I longer in this tale taryen ?"
Man of Law's Tale 276 : " What schuld I in this tale lenger tary ?"
Chan. Yem. Tale 210 : " What schuld I tary al the longe day ?"
Troy-Book S, d : "what shulde I lenger tarye."

1303. Calliope.] See *Hous of F.* 1400 ; *Troil.* III, Proem 45 ; *Court of Love* 19 ; *L. Lady* e, a, quoted in the note to l. 958, etc. Lydgate is particularly fond of saying that Calliope never took him under her patronage. Calliope plays a very prominent part in Douglas's *Palice of Honour.*

1307. The same expression occurs *Pilgrim.* 270 b :
"Doth hym honour and reuerence."

1308. Orpheus.] Son of Calliope and Apollo ; see the beginning of the *Troy-Book* (fol. A, b) :
"And helpe also, o thou Callyope,
That were moder vnto Orpheus,
Whose dytees were so melodyous
That the werbles of his resownynge harpe
Appese dyde the bytter wordes sharpe
Bothe of parchas, and furyes infernall." . . .
Again, in the *Falls of Pr.* 32 a, he is called
"Sonne of Apollo and of Caliope" ; further
"Orpheus, father of armonye," *ib.* 32 b ;
so also *Duchesse* 569 : "Orpheus, god of melodye."
Orpheus is also mentioned *Assem. of Gods* b, a, as a "poete musykall" ; further in the *Hous of Fame* 1203 ; in Douglas's *Palice of Honour*, ed. Small, I, 21, 15 ; in MS. Ashmole 59, fol. 64 a :
"And Orpheus with heos stringes sharpe
Syngepe a roundell with his temperd herte"
(*herte*, in the MS., is evidently a mistake for *harpe*).
Reason and S. 279 b :
"the verray heuenly soun
Passed in comparisoun
The harpis most melodious
Of Danid and of Orpheous."
Orpheus and Eurydice are mentioned together in Lydgate's *Testament*, Halliwell, p. 238 ; in *Albon*, ed. Horstmann, p. 37, note, stanza 4 ; and Henryson wrote a poem *Orpheus and Eurydice.* Orpheus is not unfrequently mentioned together with Amphion, as in our passage ; see note to l. 1310.

1309. strengis touch.] We find "touchen cords" in the *Isle of Ladies* 2153.

1310. Amphion.] How he built the walls of Thebes, is related in the *S. of Thebes* 357 a ; see also *Falls of Pr.*, fol. 8 a, 145 b, 163 d ; *Maunciples Tale* 12 ; *Knightes Tale* 688 ; Douglas's *Palice of Honour*, ed. Small, I, 21, 2 and 3. Orpheus and Amphion are mentioned together in *March. Tale* 472, and Skelton's *Garland of Laurel* 272 and 273.

1312. queme and pleaso], frequent phrase ; see *Troy-Book* T, b ; *De duobus*

Merc., fol. 60 *b* ; *Falls of Pr.* 72 *b* ; *Reason and S.* 242 *b* ; queme or plese, *Troy-Book* II, *b*.

1319. of hard.] This way of forming an adverbial expression occurs also in l. 574 and 615: "of newe"; in *Troil.* II, 1236:
"That ye to hym of harde now ben ywonne."
Falls of Pr. 72 *a*: "of olde, and not of newe"; *Compleint* 159, 198; *Reason and S.* 283 *a*. *Troy-Book* M₃ *a* presents even a comparative:
"Ne came none hoost of more harde to londe."

1325. þer is nomore to sein.] Exceedingly common formula in Chaucer and Lydgate; cp., for instance, *Squieres Tale* 1, 306; *Frank. Tale* 862; *Maunc. Tale* 162; *Pite* 21, 77.

1328. *Troy-Book* U₁ *a*:
"That fynally, as goddes haue be-hyght,
Thorugh prescyence of theyr eternall myght
To victorye that ye shall attayne."
"Prescience" is a personification in the *Assem. of Gods*.

1331. "by iuste purveiaunce" occurs also *Troil.* II, 527. "providence" is, of course, only the learned doublet of "purveiaunce."

1334. *enviroun* is used as a post-position; the sentence is thus to be construed: In consequence of this grant, a new ballad was straightway begun throughout the temple, by reason of the great satisfaction of all present.

1348. Willy planet.] The same as "welwilly" in *Troilus* III, 1208:
"Venus mene I, the welwilly planete!" and
Black Knight 627: "O feire lady, wel-willy founde at al!"

1348, 1349: *Black Knight* 612, etc.:
"Esperus, the goodly bryghte sterre,
So glad, so feire, so persaunt eke of chere,
I mene Venus with her bemys clere,
That hevy hertis oonly to releve
Is wont of custom for to shewe at eve."
See also *ib.*, ll. 5, 6 and *Temple of Glas*, ll. 253, 254, and 328—331; further *Kingis Quair* 72, 5 and Skeat's note.

1355. daister.] Cp. *Albon* II, 1749: "Venus, called the daysterre."

1362. There is always some contrivance or other to wake these dreamers. Here—and it is a good idea, I think--it is the heavenly melody of the lovers' song; Chaucer, *Duchesse* 1322, is waked by the castle-bell; in the *Parl. of F.*, by the song of the birds; so also Dunbar, in the *Thrissill and the Rois*, and the poet of *Cuckoo and Nightingale*; Deguileville, by the sound of the matin-bell; King James, by Fortune taking him by the ear to place him on the top of her wheel; Alanus (*De Planctu Naturæ*), by the light of the candles going out; Octavien de St. Gelais, at the end of the *Vergier d'Honneur*, by the noise the people make in uttering their opinions; the writer of the *Assembly of Ladies*, because water "sprang in her visage"; Skelton, in the *Bowge of Court*, by imagining he was leaping into the water; Douglas, at the end of the *Palice of Honour*, by falling into a pool; Lyndsay (*Dream*), by the sound of cannon, etc.
noise.] Cf. *Albon* II, 1943:
"Heuenly angels, that made noyse and sowne";
further *Edmund* II, 911:
"This heuenly noise gan ther hertis lyhte."
Of course, we need not substitute *noise*, as Horstmann thinks. We have again a "heavenly noise" in the *Fairy Queen* 1, 12, 39, and in Painter's *Palace of Pleasure* (ed. Haslewood II, 272); a "sweete noyse" occurs *Maunc. Tale* 196.

1366. Cf. *Rom. of the R.* 3859:
"I was a-stoned, and knewe no rede."

1372. With similar regret Deguileville awakes from his vision:
"Bien dolent que si tost auoye
Perdu mon solas et ma ioye ;
Iesu le me doint recouurer" (*Barthole and Petit*, fol. 148 *a*).

1374. auisioun.] See *Hous of F.* 7; *Duchesse* 285; *Sompnoures Tale* 150; *Persones Tale*, p. 268, etc. The word occurs often in the *Troy-Book*, in *Albon* II, 521, 561, 589. Compare also *Falls of Pr.* 59 d:
(consider...) "Howe dremes shewed by influence deuine
Be not lyke sweuenes, but like auisions."
1380. The "treatises" mentioned in the following lines are not clearly defined; I suppose ll. 1378—1383, and again ll. 1388—1392, allude to a "treatise," with which the world has not been favoured; the "simpil tretis" in l. 1387 must mean the *Temple of Glas*. Similar to our passage is the conclusion of the *Flour of C.*, to which, consequently, a "ballad" of three stanzas is appended.

1380. processe.] = progress; progress of a story, or narrative; the story or treatise itself. Very common in the latter meaning. Cp. *Leg. of Ariadne* 29; *Troilus* II, 268, 292, 424; III, 421; *Leg. of Austin*, Halliwell, p. 149:
"Doth your deveer this processe to corecte."
Falls of Pr. 112 c: "In this processe briefly to procede."
 Ib. 218 d: "And pray al tho that shal thys processe see."
Story of Thebes, fol. 360 d:
"and gan a processe make,
First how he was in the forest take."
Troy-Book Aa$_6$ c: "And shortly here Guydo doth forth pace,
And lyst of them no lenger processe make."
 Ib. Cc$_3$ c: "Of them can I none other processe make."
 Ib. Cc$_6$ b: "Fro hensforth I can no processe rede."
De duob. Merc., fol. 66 a:
"I will entrete thys processe forth in playn."
Secreta Secretorum (MS. Ashmole 46, fol. 97 a):
"Excellent prynce, this processe to compyle
Takith at gree the Rudnesse of my style."

1392. Who is "my ladi?" Does the monk represent himself as a lover, in the conventional style of the period, or does *my lady* mean the lady of the "amoreux," at whose request, according to Shirley, the monk composed the poem? The first assumption is made more probable by the Envoy of the *Black Knight*.

1393, etc. Similar Envoys occur in *Black Knight* 674: "Go litel quayre" (so also Skelton, *Garl. of Laurel* 1533); *Chorl and Bird* 379: "Go, gentille quayer;" *Troy-Book* Dd$_1$ d: "Go lytell boke," etc.; *L. Lady* m$_1$ b: "Goo lityl book" (this however seems to be added by Caxton); *Edmund:* "Go, litel book!" *Falls of Pr.*, fol. 218 c: "With letters and leaues goe litle booke tremblyng;" *Kingis Quair* 194, 1: "Go litill tretise;" *Pastime of Pl.:* "Go, little boke;" *Belle Dame*, the last stanza but three: "Go litile booke;" *Troilus* V, 1800: "Go, litel boke, go, litel myn tragedie."

1400. correcte.] See the Introduction, p. cxli. Cp. Boccaccio, *De casibus*, at the end: "nt suppleatur quod omissum sit, & superfluum resecetur;" further *Troilus* V, 1872; *Persones Prol.* 55, etc.; *See. Nun's Tale* 84: "And pray yow that ye wol my werk amende." The *Falls of Pr.* ask the readers "to correct where as they se nede" (fol. 217 b), and, again (fol. 217 c):
"I pray them y^t they would
Fauour the Miter and doe correccion."
At the beginning of the *Falls of Pr.* (fol. A$_1$ c), Lydgate commends Laurent for his
"entencion to amende, correcten and declare,
Not to condemne of no presumpcion."
Dance of Macabre, fol. 224 c:
"Lowely I pray with all myne heart entere
To correct where as ye se nede."
Reason and S. 202 b: "Besechinge him for to directe
Al that y^s mys, and to correcte."
 L. Lady b$_4$ a: "I put hit mekely to hir correccion."
 Esop, Prol. 46: "I me submyt to theyr correccioun."

Flour of C. 109 :   "it is al vnder correction,
                        What I reherse in commendacion."
Guy of Warwick 74, 1 : "Meekly compiled vnder correccyoun."
Chorl and Bird 385 : " Alle thing is saide vndre correccioun."
Similarly *Secreta Seeretorum*, fol. 97 b.
Pilgrimage of the Soul, end (Caxton 1483) :
                        "and goodly correcten
            where that it nedeth oughte to adden or withdrawen ;"
in the original French : . . . . "doulcement corrigeront,
                        Se riens y a a corriger,
                        A amender ou retracter."
Troy-Book E₃ a : " Prayeng the reder where my worde myssyt,
                    Causynge the metre to be halte or lame,
                    For to correcte, to saue me fro blame " . . . .
    Ib. E₃ b : "And where I erre, I praye you to correcte."
    Ib. D₄₃ b : "To correcte rather than disdayne."
    Ib. D₄₁ d : "And the submytte to theyr correccyon."
See also *ib*. E₄ b.
    Edmund : "Meekly requeryng, voyde off presumpcioun,
                Wher thow faylest, to do correccioun."
The word *correccioun* forms here the burden of five stanzas.
Albon II, 1993 :   "I wyll procede vnder correction."
    Pur le Roy 63 : " For to correcte where as thei see nede."
    Pilgrimage 4 a : "For my wrytyng, in conclusioun,
                        Ys al yseyd vnder correccioun."
Leg. of Austin (Halliwell, p. 149) :
                        " By cause I am of wittis dul and old,
                        Doth your deveer this processe to corecte."
    Belle Dame : "Where thou art wrong . . .
                    Thee to correcte in any parte or all."
Cf. also *Lancelot of the Laik*, Prol. 184, 185 ; fur'her Skelton's *Phil. Sparrow* 1246, and his Envoy to the *Garland of Laurel*, l. 1533, etc.

1402. Perhaps we ought to adopt the reading of MSS. T. P. F. B. L, and scan the line :
            "I méne þat bénygne ‖ & góodli óf hir fáce."

COMPLEYNT.

19—21. The same simile occurs in the Prologue to the *Canterbury Tales*, ll. 179—181 ; further *Troil*. IV, 737 :
            " How shold a fissh withouten water dure ? "
Departing of Th. Chaucier (MS. Ashm. 59, fol. 46 b) :
            "What is a fisshe oute of þe see,
            For alle heos scales (MS. *selcs*) silver sheene,
            Bot dede anoone as man may see."

42. ȝoue me swich a pul.] The same expression occurs in the *Falls of Pr.*, fol. 140 b.

125. "noun-suffysaunce" occurs also in the *Pilgrim.*, fol. 197 a. Chaucer translates *impotentia* by nounpower, *Boethius* 2074.

136. myn swete fo.] Very frequent expression ; it occurs *Troilus* I, 874 ; V, 228 ; *Anelida* 272 ; poem XXI in Skeat's edition of Chaucer's *M. P.*, p. 214, l. 41 ; *De duob. Merc.* (MS. Hh. IV. 12, fol. 62 a) : "My swete foo is hard as any stele." See again l. 296 of the *Compleynt*.

196. Read *vnwreke*. Shirley's reading is *vnwrek*, not *buwrek*, as given, on p. 61, in the various readings.

198. Many allusions to the two casks containing sweet and bitter liquor (represented as attributes of Fortune or Jupiter) are to be found in contemporary

poetry. See particularly Gower, *Confessio Amantis*, book VI (*Pauli* III, 12, etc.); similar to this passage is *Reason and S.*, fol. 202 b :
  (Fortune) " Had throgh hir subtil gyn be-gonne
      To yive me drynke of her tonne,
      Of which she hath, with-oute where,
      Couched tweyñ in hir celler :
      That ooñ ful of prosperite,
      The tother of aduersyte,
      Myd hir wonderful taverne . . . . .
      And of this ilke drynkes tweyne
      Serveth fortune in certeyne
      To alle foolkys eve and morowe,
      Some with ioye and some with sorowe."
Cp. further *Pilgrim.*, fol. 4 b :
      "Nor I drank newer of the sugryd tonne
      Off Jubiter, couchyd in hys celer ;
      So strange I fonde to me hys boteler,
      Off poetys callyd Ganymede."
De duob. Merc. (MS. Hh. IV. 12, fol. 70 b) :
      "As Iupiter hath cowchid tunnys too
      With-in hys celar, platly, and no moo :
      That ooñ is full of ioy and gladnes,
      That other full of sorow and bitternes.
      Who that will entyr to tamen on the swete,
      He must as well takyn hys auenture
      To taste the bytter, or he the vesell lete."
Comp. also *ib.*, fol. 65 b ; further *Legend of Good W.*, Prol. 195 ; *Wife of Bath's Prol.* 170. We have the fiction further *in extenso* in the *Roman de la Rose*, ed. Méon 6836, etc., and read also in Boethius, *De consol. philos.*, book II, prose 2 : "Nonne adolescentulus δύο τοῖς πίθοις, τὸν μὲν ἕνα κακῶν, τὸν δὲ ἕτερον καλῶν, in Jovis limine jacere didicisti ?" The whole fiction goes back to *Iliad* xxiv, 527, etc.:

      " Δοιοὶ γάρ τε πίθοι κατακείαται ἐν Διὸς οὔδει
      δώρων, οἷα δίδωσι, κακῶν, ἕτερος δὲ ἑάων," etc.

  202. eysel or venegre.] Cp. *Troy-Book* E₁ c :
      "Of bytter eysell, and of egre wyne."
  203. enbrace.] See note to *Temple of Glas*, l. 575.
  300. We find Judith often mentioned ; see, for instance, *Man of Law's Tale* 841 ; *March. Tale* 122 ; *Melibe*, p. 150 ; *Albon*, ed. Horstmann, p. 37, note, stanza 5, and particularly, the *Monk's Tale* 561—584. Nowhere, however, is any emphasis laid on her "doublenesse" to Holofernes, as in our passage.
  304, etc. Cp. *Falls of Pr.*, Book VI, beginning.
  335. dangerous.] Cp. the note to l. 156 of the *T. of Glas*; see also Chaucer's Prologue 517. "Dangerous" is a woman, in whom "Daunger" has his abode ; it means thus "unapproachable, inaccessible." The word occurs thus in the *Wife of Bath's Prol.* 151, 514, *Tale* 234 ; further *Court of Love* 901 ; *Rom. of the Rose* 490, 591, 1492, 2312, 3727, etc.—Has "Large in refuse," in the main, the same meaning as "dangerous to take," or have we to adopt Shirley's "Large yiving"? "Large in yenyng" occurs also *Edmund* I, 1006.
  336. Does *streyt* mean here "straightforward," "ready"? *Falls of Pr.* 170 a has the word in the opposite meaning :
      "Streyt in keping, gein liberalite " (*Galba*).
Similarly *Pilgrm.* (MS. Cott. Tib. A. VII, fol. 94 b) :
      '' They seyne eke they be lyberal,
      Though they be streyte and ravynous."
  379. Similarly *Falls of Pr.* 146 c : "laugh & make a mowe."
Pilgrm. 169 b :   "gruchche & mowhes make " ;
      Ib. 225 b :   "Scornyng off the Iewes alle, (*of Christ*)
      Ther mowyng & derysioun" (similarly *Pers. Tale*, p. 279) ;

further *Troilus* III, 1778:
"Than laugheth she, and maketh hym the mowe" (*Fortune*).
Rom. of the Ro. 4355:
(Love and Fortune) "Which whilom wole on folke smyle,
    And glowmbe on hem another while."
395, etc. This is a distinct allusion to the worship of the daisy-flower; cp. note to l. 70 of the *T. of Glas*.
476. We have *lyeth* as a dissyllable in the *Pilgrim*, 174 a:
"Shal lete the way that ly[e]th wrong."
477. This line occurs word for word in *Rom. of the Ro.* 1971.
494—515. The writer was evidently highly pleased with this interminable litany of antitheses and oxymora. His model may have been *Rom. of the Ro.* 4706, etc.
529. Both MSS. read "hete of cold." Being perfectly sure that this must be nonsense, I changed *of* into *and*. Nevertheless *of* seems to be right; cp. *Black Knight*, 237, 238:
    "So that my *hete*, pleynly as I fele,
    Of grevouse colde ys cause every dele;"
further *Troil.* I, 419 and 420:
    "Allas, what is this wonder maladye?
    For hete of cold, for cold of hete I dye."
This example shows what even "obvious" emendations may be worth. Nevertheless, to die for heat of cold, and for cold of heat, is indeed a "wonder maladye."

539, etc. Our author probably derived his information with respect to this wonderful lamp from Bartholomaeus, *De Proprietatibus Rerum* XVI, 11 (MS. Harl. 4789), who says of the stone "Albeston": "For in a temple of Venus was made a candyll sticke: on whyche was a lantern so brennynge that it myght not be quenched wyth tempeste nother with reyne: as Ysider sayth . li⁰. XV⁰., Capitulo de Gemmis." In Isidore's *Etymologiæ*, Book XVI, Chapter IV, No. 4, we find: "Denique in templo quodam fuisse Veneris fanum (dicunt), ibique candelabrum, et in eo lucernam sub dio sic ardentem, ut eam nulla tempestas, nullus imber exstingueret" (Migne, *Patrologia*, vol. 82, col. 565). The earliest mention, however, of this lamp, seems to be in Ampelius, *Liber memorialis*, cap. 8 (shortly after the passage on the Pergamenian sculptures): "Argyro est fanum Veneris super mare; ibi est lucerna super candelabrum posita, lucens ad mare sub divo cælo, quam neque ventus aspergit, nec pluvia exstinguit" (Thomas Munckerus, *Mythographi Latini* 1681, 17, 283, note *b*, conjectures *dispergyit* for *aspergit*). For the stone asbestos, see Pliny 37, 54; Solinus 7, 13; Augustine *De civ. Dei* 21, 7, 1, and a note to Krasinski's *Irydion*; further *Court of S. C₆b*; *Falls of Pr.* 183 c, stanza 4; *Reason and S.* 297 b; *Intelligenza* 43, 2. Cp. with our present passage also the following lines from the *Pilgrim.*, fol. 134 b:
    "And the name off thys dredful ston
    Ys ycallyd Albeston,
    Wych, whan yt receyveth ffyr,
    To hete yt hath so gret desyr
    That [MS. *Than*] when *with* ffyr yt ys ymeynt,
    Affter neuere yt wyl be queynt."
The lamp is again mentioned, in 1567, by John Maplet, *A greene Forest*, fol. 2: "*Isidore* sayth in his .XVI. booke, that in a certaine temple of *Venus* there was made and hoong vp such a Candlesticke, wherein was a light burning on that wise, that no tempest nor storme could put it out, & he beleueth that this Candlesticke had somewhat of *Albeston* beset within." The name *Albeston* instead of "asbestos" is due to a perverse etymology from *lapis albus*.—For many particulars in this note I am indebted to Dr. von Fleischhacker. See also the N. E. Dictionary under "Albeston."

575. Cp. *Anelida* 211:
    "So thirleth with the poynt of remembraunce
    The swerde of sorowe . . . Myn herte."

The quotations in the Notes are, as a rule, taken from the following texts:

Falls of Princes, from Tottel's print, 1554.
Troy-Book, from Pynson's print, 1513.
Story of Thebes, from Stowe's *Chaucer*, 1561.
Court of Sapience, from Wyuken de Worde's print, 1510.
Pilgrimage of Man, from MS. Cotton Vit. C. XIII and Tib. A. VII.
Pilgrimage of the Soul, from Caxton's print.
Life of our Lady, from Caxton's print.
Reason and Sensuality, from MS. Fairfax 16.
Assembly of Gods, from Wynken de Worde's print (British Museum, press-mark C. 13. a. 21).
Secreta Secretorum, from MS. Ashmole 46.
De duobus Mercatoribus, from MS. Hh. IV. 12 (Cambridge).
Guy of Warwick, from Znpitza's edition.
Aesop, from Sauerstein's edition (*Anglia* IX).
Horse, goose, and sheep, from Sykes's reprint for the Roxburghe Club (1822).
Chorl and Bird, from Halliwell (*Minor Poems*), and MS. Longleat 258.
Edmund and Fremund, from Horstmann's edition.
Albon and Amphabel, ,, ,, ,,
Legend of St. Margaret, ,, ,, ,,
Dance of Macabre, from Tottel's *Falls of Princes*.
Flour of Curtesie, from Stowe's *Chaucer*, 1561.
Chaucer, from Skeat's annotated texts, and the Aldine edition.
Kingis Quair, from Skeat's edition.

The abbreviations used in the Notes will be easily understood by means of the above list.

GLOSSARY.

[*For the more interesting or rare words, the Notes should also be compared.*]

TEMPLE OF GLAS.

abaisshed, abashed, dumb with confusion 1046.
abraide, to start, break forth abruptly 1054.
accesse, see *axcesse*.
accoye, see *akoye*.
acordid, reconciled 110.
agaīnward, again, back, in return 644, 1401.
akoye, to calm, quiet, appease 409.
al, although 365.
alderlast, last of all 247.
aldernext, nearest of all, next 70.
amate, dismayed, daunted, cast down 401.
and, if 1002, 1289.
apaid, satisfied, contented; *wele apaide* 1195, 1274; *euel apaied* 1399.
aquarie, Aquarius 5.
arace, to eradicate, tear away 894, 1141.
as, expletive, before adverbs: *as fast* 39; *as þo* 525, 1366; *as now* 956.
assay, test, proof 1192.
astert, p. t., escaped 1052.
astonied, astonyed, astounded, benumbed, dismaid 24, 1044, 1366; *astoneid* 876, 934.
atones, at once 458.
atte, at the 13, 30, 405.
atwixen, between 348.
auaunce, to advance, further, help 660.
auaunte, to vaunt oneself, boast 1172.
auisioun, vision, dream 1374.
auters, altars 473.
avowe, avowal, solemn promise 771.

axcesse, access, attack of fever 358.
axen, to ask 672, 725, 765, 800, 1178.
bataile, battle 592, 1246.
baume, balm 258.
behest, bihest, promise 1036, 1057, 1322.
bemys, beams, rays 272, 329, 718.
bentaile, = be entaile 37.
bet, bette, adv., better (312), 1063.
bie, buy 719, 1351.
bihest, see *behest*.
bihote, vb., promise 383, 418.
bise, busy 535, 1146; *bisie* 1168.
biseme, to beseem, become 1143.
bole, bull 119.
borow, surety, pledge, bail 1145.
bote, relief, remedy 457.
bowȝis, boughs 510.
brace, to brace, strengthen 1290.
brenne, burn 356, 362, 842; p. t. *brente* 840.
brid, bird 603.
buxumnes, obedience 878.

can, know 688.
cercled, circled, made circular 716.
champartie, see note to l. 1164.
chere, cheer, countenance, face 52, 290, 298, 315, etc.
chese, to choose 214, 336.
clepe, call 804.
compas, circle; *in compasiwise* 37.
compassid, encompassed, enclosed 755; *compast* 1053.
compassing, designing, plotting 871.
connyng, knowledge, skill 951.
contune, to continue 1333; p.p. *contuned* 390, *contynued* 374.
coupe, known 200. See also *koupe*.

crop, protuberance; top, fruit 455, 1210.
croude, to push 534.
curen, to cover, hide 205.
curteis, courteous 1166.

daister, day-star 1355.
daliaunce, speech, conversation 291. See note to this line.
daunte, to subdue 482, 619, 1171.
debate, strife 399.
dedeli, deadly 14, 937, 945.
deinte, value, worth, esteem 1257.
demening, demeanour 750.
demeyned, behaved 1051.
departid, separated, divided, parted; p.p. 354; p.t. 781.
depured, purified 1225.
denyse, to devise 471, 927, etc.; to tell 538, 698.
deroider, dispeller 329.
differring, deferring, delay 1206.
dilacioun, delay 877.
discure, to discover 161, 629, 916.
dispitous, spiteful 761.
dole, dolefulness 551.
dome, sb. doom 1079.
donne, adj., dun, dark 30; vb., to darken 252.
doublenes, duplicity 441, 1158, 1245, 1253; stanza 25 c, l. 5.
dul, vb., to become dull, feel dull 407.
dures, roughness 515.

eft, efte, again 41, 1400.
efter, eftir, after 233, 1251.
egalli, equally 277.
eke, also 77, 97, 108, etc.
elde, eld, old age 182, 187.
emprise, undertaking; teaching, lore? 421, 1073. See note to l. 421.
enbrace, to set on fire, inflame 846. See note to l. 575.
enbracen, to embrace 1107, 575.
enbrouded, embroidered 301, 309.
endite, tell, describe 946, 1378.
ennuyd, renewed, made fresh and new 275.
entaile, shape, form 37.
entendep, is given to, inclined to 189.
ententif, attentive 470.
entere, (entirely) devoted 220.

enviroun, adv., round about 283, 505; postposition 1334.
er, ere, before 13, 572, etc.
estres, apartments, inner parts of a house 29, 549.
euer in one, at all times, continually 25, 1333.
eueredel, adv., every deal, throughout 1058.
euerich, every 535.
ewrous, happy 562.
examplaire, exemplarie, pattern, model 294, 752.
expoune, to expound 304, 1389.
eysel, vinegar, stanza 3 b, l. 5.

fadur, father 389.
falsed, deceived 63.
fantasie, phantasy, mind 513.
fasoun, fashion, shape 35.
feine, to feign 204, 522, 762, 911; to be slack 996 (see note to this line).
femynynite, womanliness 1045.
fer, ferre, far 345; *ful fer* 17.
ferforp, far forth, far 1327; *as ferforpe (as)* 1029.
ferse, fierce 1256.
fest, feast 464; festival 101, 473.
fine, fin, sb., end 411, 692, etc.
(*fine), fyne,* vb., to end (intrans.) 372; (trans.) 910.
(*fine), fyne,* vb., to refine 1191.
fire, adj., fiery 574.
flammed, inflamed 843.
fleting, floating 53.
flitten, to remove 1248.
for, on account of, because of, out of 1, 2, 10, 11, 29, etc.; in spite of 59, 124, 823; with the participle 632, 934, 1366: conj., because 68; *for þat* 408, *for cause þat* 953.
forcasten, fordriven, to drive out of the right way, to toss about; *forcasteþ* 606; *fordriue* (p.p.) 609.
forseid, afore-said 1389.
forth bi pace, to pass by 230.
fortune, vb., to favour, make fortunate 903, 1101; p.p. *fortuned* 1347, 1361.
for-wrynkked, crooked 84.
foule, bird 139.
fresshli, adj., fresh 273.
fyne, see *fine.*

gan, began 10, 13, 23, 26, etc. (often merely paraphrastical).
garnement, garment 303.
gentilles, *gentilesse*, gentleness 287, 970.
gie, *guie*, to lead, guide 973, 1093.
gif, to give 597.
ginneþ, begins 656.
glade, to gladden 1211; *gladest* 703; *glading* 1356.
graue, p.p., buried 239, 1039.
gre, to *take at (in) gre*, to accept in good part, graciously 1085, 1387.
gru(c)ch, to grudge, murmur 592, 1086.
guerdon, sb., reward 806.
guerdone, vb., reward 1139.
guie, see *gie*.

halowe, hallow, celebrate 100.
hatter, hotter 362.
hauteyn, haughty 323.
hest, promise 498; plural *hestis* 59 (promises); 853 (commands).
het, p.p., heated, inflamed 842.
hole, *hool*, whole, entire 97, 364, 488, 497, 857, 1227, 1317.
holi, wholly, entirely 1076, 1330; *hoolly* 630; *hoolli* 722; *holli* 1134.
homagere, one who pays homage 571.
hool, see *hole*.
hwe, hue 48, 454, 616, 937.

Iblent, blent, mingled 32.
ich, *Iche*, each 748, 1007.
Iewise, judgment, pain, torment 238.
Ifrore, frozen 20.
iliche, equally, equably 1202.
I-mevid, moved 669.
inli, inwardly, deeply 765, 1087.
inspeccioun, examination 278.
I persid, pierced 987.
Istellified, changed into a star, glorified 136.
I voide, void, devoid 413.
Iȝolde, yielded, surrendered 586.

kepe, sb., heed 13.
kiþe, to make known, show 194.
kouþe, acquainted with 618. See note.
kunnyng, knowledge, skill 538.

TEMPLE OF GLAS.

kynd, nature 177, 224, 279, 343.

laiser, leisure 393.
lak, lack, defect 150, 564, 749, 791, 820, 1137.
lase, snare, net 423.
laurer, laurel 115.
lech, leech, physician 916.
ledne, language, speech 139.
lenger, longer 390, 1297.
lere, to teach 656; to learn 297, 1021.
leuyr, liefer, rather 1012.
lich, like 46, 272, 603, 628, 784, 798, 813, 1030; *liche* 850.
liklynesse, likeness, semblance 18.
lisse, to ease, relieve 1220.
loft, *on l.*, aloft 645.
longiþ, belongs 875.
loureþ, looks sullen 218.

male bouche, wicked tongue, stanza 25 b, l. 7.
maseþ, amazes, bewilders 682.
mede, meed, recompense 353, 415, etc.
meint, mingled 276.
meruaile, sb., marvel 267.
meruaile, *mervaile*, vb., to marvel, wonder 279, 585.
meve, to move 1245.
modir, mother 321.
mot, must 357.

ne, not 27, 68, 184, 240, 399, etc.
ne, nor 161, 178, 403, 508, 594, etc.
neueradele, in no way, by no means 426.
noise, sound 1362.
nrfangilnes, newfangledness 1243.
nyl, will not 956.
nys, is not 794.
nyst, knew not 17, 1371.

obeissaunce, obedience 324, 864.
of, *of grace*, in grace 490; *of right*, by right 954, 1063. See also note to l. 1319.
offencioun, offence 429, 801, 884.
ones, *onys*, once 675, 725, 925, etc.
oþer, *oþir*, or 943, 1038.
oþer next, next following 209.
ouerdrawe, to pass over 610.
ouershake, to pass away, abate, stop 614.

K

Glossary.

overslake, to abate, slacken 614 (reading of L. S. Pr.).

pantire, snare 604.
pensifhede, pensiveness 2.
peping, crying, screaming 180.
peraueuture, peradventure, perhaps 233, 241.
percaas, perhaps 237.
perre, jewelry 301, 310.
persant, piercing 328, 756, 1341.
ple, plea 681.
plein, plainly 1265; *in plein* 1390.
plete, to plead 686.
port, bearing 266, 291, 745, 901, 975.
possid, pushed 608.
prefe, sb., prove 1254.
prese. pres, sb., press, crowd 533, 545, 547.
pris, esteem, highest reputation 259, 621; value 1258; praise 1345, 1381.
purid, purified 1192.
purueaunce, purveyance 862.

qu me, to please 1312; stanza 3 *b*, 1. 7.
quite, to quit, requite 1186.

race, to run, rush 756.
raced, erased, cancelled 1238.
recch, care, mind 982.
recounford, comfort 330.
recured, recovered 1226.
rede, sb., counsel, advice 642, 688, 1366.
rede, vb., to advise 1151.
regalie, supremacy, first rank 261.
reherse, to relate 560, 949.
remue, change, remove 1182.
rouȝt, cared 850, 939.

secrenes, secrecy 295.
seld, seldom 212.
semlyhed, seemliness 290.
shene, shining, bright 1101.
sikirnes, security, certainty 1254.
siþ, since 369, 423, 478, etc.; *siþin* 482; *siþen* 735.
siþe, *ofte s.*, ofttimes, often 193.
skil, reason 1116, 1382.
skyes, *skies*, clouds 30, 611.
somwhile, sometimes 655.
sonnyssh, sunny 271.

sote, *soote*, sweet 458, 540, 1264.
sopefast, true 974.
sound, to cure, heal 602, 1200.
soune, *sowne*, sb., sound 197, 1336.
spere, sphere, globe 272, 396, 716, 1344.
spill, to destroy, kill 439.
stere, to steer, guide, direct 1349.
stert, to escape 584.
sterue, *sterve*, to die 435, 791.
stile, writing instrument, pen 956.
stoneiþ, astounds 683.
stremes, rays 32, 252, 263, 326, 582, 702, 815, 1101, 1342.
strengis, strings 1309.
suffrable, suffering, enduring 1266.
supprised, overpowered, overcome 765, 938.
swelt, feel sultry 844.
sweltre, feel sultry 358.

tast, takest 602.
tempest, vb., to worry, disquiet 1157.
thouȝt, heaviness 1, 1174, 1260, 1370.
tofore, before 32, 198, 249, 251, etc.; *toforn* 883; *toforne* 994, 1281, 1284.
togedir, together 276.
transmwe, to transform 120.
trete, treaty 214.
twyn, to part, separate 1360.
þilke, the same, that 81; stanza 25 *a*, l. 7.
þo, adv., then 370, 525, 1366, 1369.
þo, dem. pr., those 1165, 1337, 1351.
þrifti, see note to l. 1283.

vaileþ, avails 622.
verre, *verrai*, *verrey*, very, true 571, 980, 1001.
riage, voyage, journey 900.
vnfortuned, unfortunate, luckless 389.
vnwarli, unawares 95, 105, 617.
voide, to chase away 253, 1158, 1357; *to voide oute of*, to empty of, free from 331.
vppermore, higher up 137.

walk, walked 34, 247, 552, 565. See *welk*.
waloing, turning restlessly 12.
wanhope, despair 673, 895.

Glossary. 131

waped, dismayed, dejected 401.
wawe, wave 609.
weddir, weather 395.
weke, week 1201.
welbesein, seemly, comely, of good appearance 1167.
welk, walked 140; *welke* 550.
were, wire 271.
weymentacioun, lamentation 949.

wizt, person, creature 360, 398, 403, 553, etc.
willi, willing, ready, propitious 1348.
wirship, *worship*, dignity 342, 399.
wisse, teach 637.
wite, sb., blame 166, 208.
wite, vb., to blame 666.

COMPLEYNT.

acordyn, agree 231, 545.
aforne, before 582.
alayene, to allay 273.
albiston, 540. See note to l. 539.
amasid, amazed, bewildered 518.
a-mong, sometimes 171.
apeyrid, impaired, injured 519.
aryete, Aries, the Ram 250.
astert, to escape 12.
astonyd, stunned 109.
a-tamyd, broached 198.
attemperaunce, temperance 339 (Shirley reads *attemporaltee*).
a-tweyne, between two people 234.
avise, opinion 354.

bawme, balm 431.
bedynge, bidding 468.
brend, burnt 560.
brenne, to burn 543, 547, 552.
bromys, broom 417.

chere, countenance 26, 75, 180, etc.
cheuere, shiver 532.
cheuyrfoyl, honey-suckle 429.
clepe, to call 149.
commyxtyoun, union, uniting 253.
continue, to continue 361.
crop, top, fruit 397.

dalyaunce, conversation 340.
del, part 45.
demyn, doom 169.
departycyoun, separation 254.
depeyntyd, portrayed 79.
despitous, spiteful, contemptuous 346.
deynte, liking 107, 170.
dol, *dole*, grief 245, 317.
donne, dun, dark 366, 372.
dotous, doubting, mistrustful 343.
duresse, hardship 588.

efft, again; *efft sones*, soon again 620.
egre, sharp, acid 201.
ek, also, likewise 70, 349, 452, etc.
empryse, undertaking 160.
enbrace, to burn 203. See note to T. of Glas, l. 575.
euery-chon, every one 44.
eysel, vinegar 202.

feer, *fer*, *fyr*, fire 541, 544, 607.
feere, *in f.*, together 271.
fel, strong, biting, sharp 201.
femynynytee, womanliness 326.
feyntyse, feigning 477.
flaumbe, sb., flame 542.
forderkyd, darkened 26.
for-nome, taken from, deprived 56.
forpossid, pushed about, tossed 530.
frounynd, frowning 368.
fyne, to end 280.

ȝaf, gave 179.
ȝan, began 220.
ȝate, gate 446.
ȝeve, give 135; gave (=O.E. geáfon) 177.
gilt, committed 115.
glede, burning coal 525.
ȝone, given 42.
gouernaunce, discreet behaviour 328.
grevis, groves 428.

herdegromys, herd-grooms, herds-men 418.
heyle, to hail 309.

Ifrerde, fired, inflamed 556.
I-wis, *I-wys*, certainly 119, 338.

K 2

Glossary

I-wreke, revenged 358.

large, sb., liberty 177.
lasse, loss 616.
leche, leech, physician 55.
lemys, rays 263.
lere, to learn 333.
lyssyn, to ease, relieve 401.

mede, reward 624.
mo, moo, more 135, 143, 564.
mot, must 390, 442, 568.
mowe, grimace 379
mut, mute 50.

nape, has not 577.
ne, not 40, 85, 92, 101, 127, etc.
ne, nor 85, 113, 216, 279, 291.
newfongylnesse, newfangledness 562.
non-suffysaunce, insufficiency 125.

onbit, abideth 67.
othyr, or 116.
out-shede, to pour out 431.

parte, to divide, share 236.
peersand, piercing 574.
pensyfhed, pensiveness 510.
pes, peace 508.
pete, pity 69, etc.
pleyne, to complain 51.
plonchyn, to plunge 376.
porte, bearing, demeanour 328, 334.

queme, to please 553.

recorderys, flutes, flageolets 421.
recure, to recover 93.
row, rough 374.

sceld, seldom 311.
seyne, to, to say 99, etc.
shene, bright 225.

sithe, sithen, sythe, etc., since 4, 14, etc.
skyis, clouds 372.
slen, sloo, to slay 139, 295.
sonde, to make sound, heal 407.
sote, sweet 398, 431.
sothefastnesse, truth 92, 493, 587.
spere, sphere 241.
sperys, rede sp., reed-spears 422.
spraulynge, sprawling 21.
steer, to stir 542 (or, to manage, control? see *Leg. of G. W.*, 935).
stere, to steer, guide, restrain 6.
stilly, quietly 308.
stoundemel, hourly 524.
streytest, most straightforward (?) 336.
sumdel, somewhat 197.
swow, swoon 188.
sykurnesse, security, reliableness 327.
sypes, ofte s., ofttimes, often 596.

tene, grief 226.
tho, then 198.
thought, trouble, heaviness 1.
to-brest, to burst 450.
to-rent, rent asunder 611.
to-tore, torn 610.
trist, sad 285.
tweye, two (things) 530.

vndyrfong, to undertake 172.
vn[w]reke (?), to unfold 196.

weene, doubt 267.
were, doubt 261.
worshepe, dignity 341, 550.
wroke, revenged 606.
wynke, close the eyes, sleep 64.

yede, went 205.

LIST OF PROPER NAMES.

TEMPLE OF GLAS.

Achilles 94, 785.
Addoun (*Adonis*) 64.
Admete 72.
Alceste 71.
Almen 123.
Amphioun 1310.
Amphitrioun 122.
Antonyus 778.
Antropos 782.
Britayne 410.
Caliope 1303.
Canace 138.
Cartage 55.
Chaucer 110.
Cirrea 703.
Citheria 701.
Cleopatre 779.
Crete 85.
Cupide 114, 321, 444, etc.
Daphne 115.
Dedalus 84.
Demophon 87.
Diane 8.
Dianyre 788.
Dido 56.
Dorigene 410.
Elicon 706.
Emelie 106.
Eneas 58.
Esperus 1348.
Europe 118.
Grisildis 75, Grisilde 405.
Heleyne 93.
Hercules 787.
Ianuari 185.
Iason 63.

Ioue 117, 1232.
Isaude 77.
Iubiter 136, 465.
Lucifer 253.
Lucina 4.
Lucresse 101.
Mars 126, 1232.
May 184.
Medee 62.
Mercurie 130.
Minatawre 83.
Musis 133, 953.
Orpheus 1508.
Palamoun 102.
Pallas 248.
Paris 92.
Penalope 67, 407.
Phebus 5, 112, 272.
Phillis 86.
Philologye 130.
Philomene 98.
Piramus 81, 780.
Policene 94, Polixene 786.
Progne 99.
Rome 101.
Sabyns 100.
Saturne 389, 1232.
Tesbie 80, Tesbe 780.
Theseus 82, 109.
Thesiphone 958.
Titan 32.
Tristram 79.
Troie 95.
Venus 52, 64, 127, 194, etc.
Vulcanus 127.

COMPLEYNT.

Cupidis (gen.) 556.
Dyane 250.
Fortune 42, 362, 391, 452.
Heleyne 268.

Iudith 300.
Phebus 240.
Polixene 268.
Venus 549.

ADDENDA.

Page XIII. To Prof. Zupitza's contributions to Lydgate-literature, add his paper *Zu Lydgates Isopus*, in his *Archiv für das Studium der neueren Sprachen*, vol. 85, pp. 1—28. We find in it the version of the Trinity College MS. R. 3. 19, and the fragment in MS. Ashmole 59, besides valuable notes, and important additions to Sauerstein's edition.

Page XXIX. Thanks to the kindness of Mr. Gordon Duff, I am in a position to give a more accurate date for the fragments of Pynson's print. Mr. Gordon Duff believes its date to be about 1502—6, for the following reason. The border of the device used in Pynson's print was cut in metal, and was first used about 1500. It very soon began to get damaged, owing to the bending of the metal, and about the year 1510, the lower part broke away altogether. In the *Temple of Glas* the lower margin is slightly bent, and thus Mr. Gordon Duff is inclined to put it nearer 1502 than 1506.

Page LXXIII, note. I am sorry that I was not sooner acquainted with Wischmann's Dissertation *Untersuchungen über das Kingis Quair*. It would have been interesting to compare Lydgate's treatment of the final *e* with that of King James.

Page XCVI. In the last volume of the *Dictionary of National Biography*, the article on John Hoveden notices the poem in MS. Calig. A. II, entitled "The Nightyngale," and says that it is an imitation of Hoveden's shorter version of the *Philomela*. Through Prof. Napier I have become acquainted with another copy of the Caligula version, contained in MS. No. 203 of Corpus Christi College. From it, my supposition that the British Museum copy must be deficient at the beginning, has been confirmed. Two stanzas, addressed to Anne, Duchess of Buckingham, are missing at the beginning in the London MS., so that this poem has altogether 59 stanzas (see p. xcv, note 3). The stanza on the death of Henry of Warwick occurs in this MS. on page 17. An entry at the beginning of the MS. rightly points out that this poem must thus have been written between 1444 and about 1446, as the title "Duchess of Buckingham" was not conferred upon Lady Anne till 1444. Both MSS. are mentioned by Tanner, p. 491, l. 11 from top.

Page XCVII. We find further information concerning John Baret in a publication of the Camden Society: *Wills and Inventories from the registers of the Commissary of Bury St. Edmund's and the Archdeacon of Sudbury*, ed. by Samuel Tymms, 1850. The will of John Baret is given in that work on pp. 15—44. It was drawn up in 1463, and proved May 2nd, 1467. Thus John Baret doubtless outlived Lydgate, whose share in the pension granted to them jointly must thus have fallen to Baret. Some account of Baret and his tomb in St. Mary's Church, Bury St. Edmunds, is given on pp. 233—238 of Tymms's book.

Page XCIX. Through Mr. Peskett's renewed kindness I have been able to identify the "War between Cæsar and Pompey" which Skeat (*Academy*, Oct. 3, p. 286) inclines to believe is identical with the "Tragedye of Rome" in MS.

Ashmole 59. Mr. Peskett has very kindly sent me a transcript of the beginning and end which, as he rightly points out, leaves no doubt that the piece is identical with Lydgate's *Serpent of Division* (issued together with the 1590 edition of Gorboduc). The Ashmole MS. is not available to me at present, but judging from the Catalogue of the Ashmole MSS., the "Tragedye o: Rome" seems to be nothing else than the Envoy to the *Falls of Princes* II, 31 (Tottel's print, fol. 66 d—67 b), followed by that to *Falls of Princes* III, 5 (Tottel, fol. 77 a and b).

Page CIX. From the new (printed) Catalogue of the British Museum I see that Lydgate's *Assemble de Dyeus* had already been printed in 1498 by Wynken de Worde, at the end of an edition of the *Canterbury Tales*. See also Hazlitt's *Handbook*, p. 97, col. 2. This print is particularly interesting as assigning the authorship of the poem to Lydgate.—If I can trust an old note taken some time ago at Cambridge, the poem is also found in the Trinity College MS. R. 3. 19, fol. 68 a—97 b.

Page CXVII, note. Add, as two other important treatments of the Pleading between Mercy, Truth, Right and Peace, the Salutation in the "*Coventry Plays*, and the *Castle of Perseverance*. Cp. also Rothschild, *Mystère du viel Testament* I, p. LXI.

Page CXLIII. I forgot to add that in E. K.'s introduction to the *Shepherd's Calendar*, Lydgate's name is mentioned in a very laudatory manner, and that he is introduced with Gower and Chaucer in G. Harvey's *Letterbook* (ed. Scott, p. 57). Ben Jonson quotes him frequently in his *English Grammar*. Lydgate is further mentioned in the translation of Terence's *Andria* (see Collier II, 364); again, in a Latin poem before *Alcida Greene's Metamorphosis* (Grosart's *Greene* IX, p. 13), and by Whetstone, in a poem on Sir James Dier (see Köppel, *Studien zur Geschichte der italienischen Novelle*, p. 31, note 1); further by T. Nashe in his *Letter to the Gentlemen Students*, before Greene's *Menaphon* (ed. Grosart, VI, 24); also in John Lane's *Continuation of Chaucer's Squire's Tale*, ed. Furnivall, III, 330:

"Don Chaucer, Lidgate, Sidney, Spencer dead!"

No bad company for our monk!

Note to ll. 86—90. Phyllis is also represented as having hanged herself on a filbert-tree in Lodge's *Rosalind*, signat. K₁ a.

Note to l. 271 (see also p. cxxxii). I am sincerely sorry that I have after all come across an earlier instance of the expression, "hair like gold wire," namely, in Layamon's *Brut*, ll. 7047, 7048, which read (Cotton Calig. A. ix):

"Seoððen com a king þe hæhte Pir:
his hæð (read hær) wes swulc swa beoð gold wir;"

the reading of Cotton Otho C.xiii is:

"Suþþe com Caper. and Pir:
Þat [hadde] heer so gold wir."

Note to l. 510. The *Merry ballad of the hawthorn-tree*, attributed to Peele, illustrates well why this tree was chosen as a symbol of constant love. See Dyce's edition of Greene and Peele, 1874, p. 604 sq.

Note to l. 1272. Come off.] This phrase occurs further in the Salutation in the *Coventry Plays*, ed. Halliwell, p. 113; in *Mary Magdalene*, ed. Furnivall, ll. 379 and 739; in Skelton's *Magnificence* 103 and 977 (cp. Dyce's notes); in Heywood's *Four P's*, Dodsley-Hazlitt I, 352, l. 7; in *Thersites*, ib. I, 421; in Ingelend's *Disobedient Child*, ib. II, 272, 283, 305; in *Marriage of Wit and Science*, ib. II, 376; in Bale's *Kyng Johan*, ed. Collier, p. 66; in *Marriage of Wit and Wisdom*, ed. Halliwell, p. 17, l. 7. There remains thus little doubt that, by the insertion of *off*, we get the correct reading.

www.ingramcontent.com/pod-product-compliance
Lightning Source LLC
Chambersburg PA
CBHW031330230426
43670CB00006B/294